Graham,

Over the past eleven years you have been far more than a mentor and teacher, you have become a [friend]. It's surreal working side by [side ... will] not be [the same]? I will dearly miss your teachings and leadership but most of all I will miss our conversations and your company. I can't even begin to tell you the impact that you have had on my life, and I'm a better person and a far better leader having known you.

I'm sad knowing you're going across the pond, but I know that you will be back and that we will one day again be working together. I'm so excited for you in your new venture.

Safe sailing my good friend!

Sincerely,
Jim Moore

THE LIFE

OF

BENEDICT ARNOLD;

HIS

PATRIOTISM AND HIS TREASON.

BY

ISAAC NEWTON ARNOLD,

AUTHOR OF
"LIFE OF ABRAHAM LINCOLN."

"I have done the state some service, and they know it.
No more of that.—I pray you, in your letters,
When you shall these unlucky deeds relate,
Speak of me as I am; nothing extenuate,
Nor set down aught in malice."

"He will give the devil his due."

FOURTH EDITION

CHICAGO
A. C. McCLURG & COMPANY
1905

COPYRIGHT
JANSEN, McCLURG & CO.
1879.

COPYRIGHT
A. C. McCLURG & CO.
1905

INTRODUCTION.

STANDING, not very long ago, on the battle-field of Saratoga, near where Benedict Arnold was grievously wounded, as he led as gallant a charge as was ever made, I realized that if he had died on that bloody field how brilliant would have been his record as a soldier and patriot. His name, associated with those of Montgomery and Warren, would have been canonized in American history, and his faults and foibles would have been lost in the blaze of glory which would have encircled it.

Standing there, I was impressed with the injustice which has been done him; not in condemning his treason, but in ignoring his virtues, and in refusing to recognize his great services; and I resolved to tell the story of his life truthfully and fairly. Yet conscious of the deep and merited and universal prejudice existing against him, I fear the American people will listen with some impatience to such a story of his life. He was not so black as he has been painted. I have no desire to change the indignation and resentment felt towards him for his treason. I can neither excuse nor extenuate his guilt. But I wish to make known his patriotic services, his sufferings, heroism, and the wrongs which drove him to desperation, and converted one of the most heroic men of a heroic age to the perpetration of an unpardonable crime. I wish to introduce one drop of pity into the bitter cup of indignant denunciation which has been so constantly poured upon his head.

The time may come—I think there are indications of its approach—when there will mingle with his condemnation that "infinite pity," which George William Curtis, standing on Bemis' Heights, so eloquently expressed in his oration on the Surrender of Burgoyne—"infinite pity," that a nature so heroic, and with a record so brilliant, should have been driven, by a sense of bitter wrong and the violence of his passions, to a crime so inexcusable.

On the exposure of his treason, it became the passionate desire of a whole nation to blacken his character. Instantly he became an outcast and an outlaw. Every pen denounced, and every tongue cursed him. If this had been confined to his treason, none would have questioned its justice, but in their just hatred, the people wished to make him wholly odious. He who had been the trusted friend of Washington and Warren and Schuyler, was now declared guilty of every crime, and denied a single virtue. Even his undeniable bravery, exhibited on so many battle-fields, was declared to be only "Dutch courage." He who in Philadelphia and elsewhere had been the courteous and honored host, at whose table the highest and most intelligent officers of the army and of civil life were glad to meet, was now declared a "low, vulgar, illiterate horse-jockey and skipper." These were the natural results of his odious crime. But Arnold was not the first character in history who has shown that great crimes are not incompatible with great virtues.

The great duke of Marlborough was, according to Macaulay, doubly a traitor: false and treacherous to James and the Prince of Orange in turn—both a spy and a traitor.[1] And yet, go to

---

[1] "Not till the archives of the House of Stewart were exposed, was it known "to the world that Talmash had perished by the basest of the hundred villainies "of Marlborough."—*Macaulay's England*, V. 7, p. 328.

the palace of Blenheim, and behold how England forgave his crimes and rewarded his virtues.

It is difficult to conceive of darker and more execrable crimes than those of David, the great king of Israel—murder and perfidy from the vilest motives! And yet the heart that conceived and executed the treacherous murder of Uriah, indicted the Psalms, and was so tender and affectionate that David would have gladly died for the unnatural Absalom!

The king repented and God and man forgave him. If we cannot forgive Arnold, we can and ought to be just to him.

To him "sharper than a serpent's tooth" was the ingratitude of his country, and crazed and maddened by his wrongs, real and imaginary, when the tempter came, he fell. His punishment was, and will be, forever terrible; poor André's was comparatively light—"a momentary pang," as he expressed it, when he mounted the scaffold. General Arnold's after life must have been a long agony of remorse, chagrin and disappointment. The ever consciousness of a great crime and a still greater blunder, must have given him a lifelong heartache; and to his name, which down to that fatal event had been among the most brilliant of American soldiers, he brought the punishment of everlasting infamy.

But before his treason he had been a self-sacrificing, zealous patriot, shedding his blood like water for his country. I wish to portray him as such patriot—to tell the story of his life up to the time of his fall, as it would have been told had he died on the bloody field of Saratoga.

This part of his life I shall demonstrate, has not been fairly,

"He (Marlborough) had while commanding William's troops, while sitting at William's council, while waiting in William's bed-chamber, formed the most artful and dangerous plot for the subversion of William's throne."—*Macaulay's England*, V. 7, p. 394.

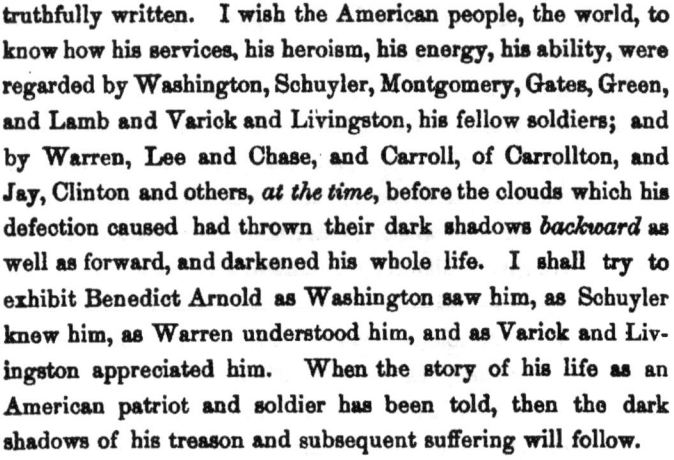

truthfully written. I wish the American people, the world, to know how his services, his heroism, his energy, his ability, were regarded by Washington, Schuyler, Montgomery, Gates, Green, and Lamb and Varick and Livingston, his fellow soldiers; and by Warren, Lee and Chase, and Carroll, of Carrollton, and Jay, Clinton and others, *at the time*, before the clouds which his defection caused had thrown their dark shadows *backward* as well as forward, and darkened his whole life. I shall try to exhibit Benedict Arnold as Washington saw him, as Schuyler knew him, as Warren understood him, and as Varick and Livingston appreciated him. When the story of his life as an American patriot and soldier has been told, then the dark shadows of his treason and subsequent suffering will follow.

His capacities for good and for evil were very great; ever the generous and liberal friend, he was a proud, bitter and unyielding enemy. During one period of his life he was the brilliant, dashing soldier, possessed of a hopeful and sanguine temperament, which no difficulty nor danger could overcome, and his wonderful successes prove, that with all his reckless daring, he united great skill, forethought, and readiness of invention. His life is full of dramatic interest, and while true to his flag, the career of no soldier of the Revolution is more full of thrilling incidents, heroic deeds, and examples of fortitude and energy. When driven to desperation, wounded by injustice, disappointed and chagrined, he became bitter and revengeful, and seemed willing to sacrifice the cause for which he had so often bled, so that his enemies should be crushed in the ruins. The story of this strange life, Arnold as *patriot* and traitor, I shall endeavor truthfully to tell, and in such a spirit as to merit, and I trust, to obtain, the sympathy of all lovers of fair play.

The identity in the name of the author and the subject, and

possibly the treatment, may suggest a relationship which does not exist. Had General Arnold died on Lake Champlain, when desperately fighting with his single vessel the whole British fleet, that the remainder of his own might escape; or had the bullet that shattered his leg while leading his troops in the assault on Quebec pierced his heart, there would have been found among those who now bear the name, many who would have proudly claimed a blood relationship. As it is, I have met very few indeed who admit such kinship. I did, indeed, once hear a beautiful and spirited young lady, of very great taste, culture and talent, audaciously and ironically say she had the best blood of any family in the republic, for she was related to Benedict Arnold by one of her parents, and Aaron Burr by the other!

Two hundred and fifty or three hundred years ago there was a common ancestor of General Arnold and the author, and under these circumstances I shall be pardoned the egotism of saying that my grandfather, Thomas Arnold, was an humble soldier in the war of the Revolution, and was *faithful;* and that such was his admiration of the commander-in-chief, that he gave to my father the name of George Washington.

I have endeavored to make an exhaustive investigation of facts in relation to General Arnold. I have consulted his manuscript letters in the Force collection in the library of Congress; manuscript letters of Arnold and his wife and sister, in the Department of State at Washington; the very large and valuable Schuyler manuscripts in the possession of the family of General Schuyler; and the Gates and Lamb papers, in the possession of the New York Historical Society.

Also the Shippen papers and Shippen manuscripts, which contain letters from General Arnold and his wife, from the time of Arnold's courtship and marriage to the day of his death, in 1801.

Also the correspondence of his children in England, with Chief-Justice Shippen; letters from his wife and children to and from his sister, Hannah Arnold, and his sons by his first wife—Richard and Henry—in Canada. I am especially indebted to Edward Shippen, of Philadelphia, and to the family of a granddaughter of Arnold, in Canada, for very valuable and new material; also to a grandson of General Arnold—the Rev. Edward Gladwin Arnold, of Great Massingham Rectory, Norfolk, England, for many valuable letters and manuscript documents of great historic interest, and many incidents relating to the life of his grandfather and family in England.

From these papers and persons, from the writings of Washington, and Force's American Archives, and other sources, I have drawn the material for the following work. I think I have been able to contribute something new and valuable, and considerable that is not generally known to this part of American history.

For General Arnold, the patriot and soldier, I ask a fair hearing and justice; for Benedict Arnold, the traitor, I have no plea, but "guilty."

SEPTEMBER, 1879.

CONTENTS.

CHAPTER I.
HIS EARLY LIFE.

The Ancestors of Benedict Arnold—His own Immediate Family, and Early life—His Feats of Daring—Education—Marriage—His First Duel, ... 15-32

CHAPTER II.
TICONDEROGA AND CROWN POINT.

The Boston Massacre—Arnold's Fiery Patriotism—His Letter—Battle of Lexington—Capt. Arnold Volunteers and Leads his Company to Cambridge—Expedition to Ticonderoga—Captures St. Johns—Warren his Friend—Injustice to Arnold—Death of his Wife—Touching Letter of his Sister, Hannah Arnold, ... 33-48

CHAPTER III.
EXPEDITION TO QUEBEC.

Expedition to Quebec, and March Through the Wilderness—Arnold proposes the Expedition to Washington—Washington Approves, and Selects for it "Picked Men" of his Army, and Gives the Command to Arnold—Their Difficulties, Sufferings and Dangers—Enos gets frightened and Abandons his Comrades—Arnold, with Morgan, Pushes on—Provisions Exhausted—Arnold with Six Men Makes a Forced March to the Canadian Settlements, Obtains Food, and Saves the Detachment, ... 49-72

CHAPTER IV.

ASSAULT UPON QUEBEC.

Arnold Holds an Indian Council—His Speech to the Indians—Crosses the St. Lawrence, Climbs to the Plains of Abraham, and Menaces Quebec—Receives thanks of Washington and Schuyler—Montgomery and Arnold Assault Quebec—Montgomery Killed—Arnold Shot while Leading the "Forlorn Hope"—Made a Brigadier-General—Blockades Quebec, ... 73–88

CHAPTER V.

RETREAT FROM CANADA.

The Affair at the Cedars—Visit of Franklin, Chase and Carroll to Arnold's Quarters—The Seizure of Goods in Montreal—Trial of Colonel Hazen by Court-Martial—Controversy Between Arnold and the Court—Charges against Arnold by Lieut. Col. John Brown—Action thereon by Wooster, Schuyler and Gates—Charges Declared by Congress to be Cruel and Groundless—Arnold's Retreat from Canada, . 89–104

CHAPTER VI.

NAVAL BATTLE OF VALCOUR ISLAND.

The British, Greatly Superior in Numbers and in Guns, Attack the American Fleet under Arnold, on Lake Champlain—The Fight Continues from Noon until Night, when the British Retire—The Americans Escape Through the British Line—Are Overtaken, and Arnold, in the Congress, Fights and Retards the Enemy until his other Vessels Escape—He Runs the Congress Ashore, Burns her, and with his Men, Reaches Ticonderoga, ... 105–120

CHAPTER VII.

ARNOLD SUPERSEDED—HIS FIGHT AT RIDGEFIELD, ETC.

Arnold in Washington's Camp—Sent to Rhode Island—Advances £1,000 to aid Lamb in Raising his Regiment—Offers Himself to the Beautiful Miss Deblois—Five Junior Brigadiers Promoted over Him—Withholds his Resignation, at Washington's request—Desperate Battle, and Escape at Ridgefield—Congress Vote him a Horse, and Commission him a Major-General—Declare the Charges of Brown to be Cruel Aspersions upon his Character—Washington begs Congress to send him North to aid in Repelling Burgoyne, . . 121–139

CONTENTS. 11

CHAPTER VIII.
CAMPAIGN ON THE MOHAWK, AND RELIEF OF FORT STANWIX.

St. Leger Invests Fort Stanwix—Herkimer going to its relief, falls into an Ambuscade, and at the Battle of Oriskany is Mortally Wounded—Arnold Volunteers to go to the relief of Gansevoort—Reaches German Flats, and although a Council of War resolve that they must wait for Reinforcements, he determines to "Push forward and hazard a Battle," rather than see the Garrison fall—He resorts to a Ruse—He Frightens the Indians, who abandon the Siege, and Fort Stanwix is relieved, ... 140-162

CHAPTER IX.
FIRST BATTLE NEAR SARATOGA.

Battle of 19th of September—Arnold leads the Troops to Victory—Error of Bancroft—Testimony of Cols. Varick and Livingston, Generals Schuyler, Burgoyne, and others—Verdict of Irving, Lossing, and others, ... 163-190

CHAPTER X.
SECOND BATTLE OF SARATOGA.

Quarrel between Gates and Arnold—Action of October 7th—Heroism of Arnold—Gates tries in vain to recall him from the Field—Morgan, by direction of Arnold, orders his Riflemen to Fire at Fraser—Fraser Shot—Senator Foster's Account of Arnold's Charge, as witnessed by his Father—Arnold Shot—Saves the Life of the Soldier who Shot him—Congress votes him Thanks and the Rank hitherto Refused—Washington Sends him his New, Ante-dated Commission, and Declares he is Restored "to a Violated Right," 191-211

CHAPTER XI.
WASHINGTON'S FRIENDSHIP—ARNOLD'S GENEROSITY.

Arnold's Wound—He is carried to Albany, thence to Connecticut—Reception at New Haven—Receives Pistols, Epaulettes and Sword-Knots from Washington—He supplies Money for the Education and Maintenance of the Orphans of General Warren—Goes to Valley Forge—Washington Assigns him to Command of Philadelphia, . 212-221

CHAPTER XII.
ARNOLD'S COURTSHIP AND MARRIAGE.

Philadelphia during the Revolution—Arnold Assumes Command, and Succeeds Sir William Howe in Occupying the Penn House—The Shippen Family—Major John Andre—The "Mischienza"—Peggy Shippen, the Belle of Philadelphia—Arnold her Suitor—His Courtship—Settles upon her Mt. Pleasant—Marriage and Domestic Life—Letter of Hannah Arnold to Mrs. Arnold at West Point, . . 222-236

CHAPTER XIII.
ARNOLD'S CONTROVERSY WITH THE AUTHORITIES OF PENNSYLVANIA.

Arnold's Conduct in Command of Philadelphia—His Controversy with President Reed and the Authorities of Pennsylvania—The Action of Congress—Reports of Committees Exonerating Him—A Court-Martial Ordered for his Trial, ... 237-249

CHAPTER XIV.
ARNOLD'S TRIAL—WASHINGTON'S REPRIMAND.

Arnold's Trial Continued—His Defense—Judgment of the Court—Washington's Reprimand and Eulogy, ... 250-264

CHAPTER XV.
ARNOLD'S TREASON.

The Motives which Led to Arnold's Treason—His Wrongs—Inducements Held Out to Him by British Emissaries—They try to Convince Him the Contest Hopeless, and that England offers All for Which he Drew his Sword—Supposed Meeting between Him and Beverly Robinson—Letter to Arnold Attributed to Robinson by Marbois—Arnold yields to the Temptations Offered, and Seeks the Command of West Point—Meets Washington at King's Ferry, who Offers Him the Command of the Left Wing of his Army—Tradition that Arnold said his Defection was to Prevent more Bloodshed—Meeting of Arnold and Andre—Supposed Conversation between Them—Andre's Capture—His Letter to Washington, ... 265-293

CHAPTER XVI.

ARNOLD'S ESCAPE—ANDRE'S EXECUTION.

Arnold Hears of Andre's Capture—Flies to the Vulture—Washington Arrives at West Point—Mrs. Arnold's Distress—Arnold's Letter to Washington, Declaring Her Innocence, and Begging Washington to Protect Her—Declares His Military Family Innocent—Hannah Arnold's Letter Begging the Pity of all Her Friends, and Praying Them not to Forsake Her—Andre's Trial as a Spy—Efforts to Save His Life—Arnold's alleged offer to Surrender Himself in Exchange—Andre's Execution, ... 294-315

CHAPTER XVII.

MRS. ARNOLD'S INNOCENCE—WAS ANDRE A SPY?

Was Mrs. Arnold Guilty of Complicity with her Husband's Treason?—Was Andre a Spy, and Executed in Accordance with the Laws of War? 316-328

CHAPTER XVIII.

ARNOLD VAINLY ATTEMPTS TO JUSTIFY HIS TREASON.

Arnold in New York City—His Address to the American People—His Proclamation to the Officers and Soldiers of the American Army—Attempt to Kidnap Him—His Wife Joins Him in New York, . 329-341

CHAPTER XIX.

ARNOLD LEADS BRITISH SOLDIERS AGAINST HIS NATIVE COUNTRY.

Arnold Leads an Expedition Against Virginia and Connecticut—Massacre at Fort Griswold—Arnold's Narrow Escape from Death by the Hands of a Woman at New London, ... 342-354

CHAPTER XX.

ARNOLD AT THE COURT OF GEORGE THE III.

Arnold's Departure with Lord Cornwallis for England—His Reception by the King and Cabinet—His Paper on a Reunion Between the Colonies and the Crown—General and Mrs. Arnold at Andre's Monument in Westminster Abbey, ... 355-366

CHAPTER XXI.

GENERAL ARNOLD ENGAGES IN BUSINESS.

Arnold Settles in Portman Square, London—He Lives Beyond his Means—Engages in Trade—Removes to St. John's, New Brunswick—His Family Correspondence—Mrs. Arnold Visits her Family at Philadelphia, ... 367–374

CHAPTER XXII.

ARNOLD'S DUEL WITH THE EARL OF LAUDERDALE.

Arnold and Talleyrand—Arnold's Duel with the Earl of Lauderdale—Statement of Lord Hawke—Mrs. Arnold's Letters to her Father and to Richard Arnold, Giving an Account of the Duel, . 375–384

CHAPTER XXIII.

ARNOLD'S SERVICES IN THE WEST INDIES—HIS DEATH.

General Arnold in 1794 Fits out a Ship for the West Indies—Ship Lost—At Gaudaloupe—His Danger—Escapes to the English Fleet—His Services to the Government in the West Indies—Receives the Thanks of the Planters—The King Grants to Him 13,500 Acres of Canada Lands for his "Gallantry," &c.—He Begs the Duke of York for Military Service Against the French—His Death. . . . 385–398

CHAPTER XXIV.

THE FAMILY OF GENERAL ARNOLD.

Mrs. Arnold's Executive Ability—She Settles General Arnold's Estate and Pays his Debts—Educates her Children, and Procures for her Sons Commissions in the Army—Her Death—The Arnold Family in Canada—"Poor Ben's" Death from a Wound Received in Battle—The Family in England—All the Sons in the Public Service—James Appointed Military Aid to the King—Attains the Rank of Lieut. General—A Grandson Killed at Sebastopol, . . . 399–417

APPENDIX, ... 419

INDEX, ... 429

LIFE OF BENEDICT ARNOLD.

CHAPTER I.

HIS EARLY LIFE.

"For I was wayward, bold and wild,
A self-willed imp."
—MARMION.

"A great, a gifted, but a turbid soul
"Struggled and chafed within that stripling's breast.
"Passion which none might conquer or control."

THE ANCESTORS OF BENEDICT ARNOLD—HIS OWN IMMEDIATE FAMILY, AND EARLY LIFE—HIS FEATS OF DARING—EDUCATION—MARRIAGE—HIS FIRST DUEL.

TIME, by bringing to light new manuscripts, is constantly increasing the accuracy and completeness of our knowledge of the Revolution. As events recede into the past, this period of American history is becoming more and more attractive and picturesque.

The name of Benedict Arnold is doomed to live in that history forever as the only conspicuous instance of treason: "Sadly conspicuous," as Washington Irving says, "to the end of time." His punishment has been terrible but just. In the sense in which Satan has been called the hero of Paradise Lost, he was one of the heroes of the revolutionary war. One great crime obliterated the memory of years of hard and patriotic service. A century has gone since his abortive conspiracy, and there is, I think, a disposition to be less relentless—I may say more just to his memory.

There is a willingness to look behind the black shadow of his treason; to recognize behind the traitor of West Point the hero of Saratoga. In proportion as history is severe, it should be scrupulously just. With the conviction that General Arnold has not had fair treatment; that his life as a patriot and soldier should be truthfully told, I ask a hearing.

William Arnold, born in Leamington, England, in 1587, settled in Providence in 1636, was the ancestor of the Arnolds of Rhode Island and Connecticut. He was a contemporary of Roger Williams, and associated with him as one of the fifty-four proprietors in the first settlement of the first named little commonwealth. His ancestors in England, and still earlier in Wales, were highly respectable, and their lineage has been traced back for several centuries. There is a genealogy of the family of apparent accuracy, going back to the year 1100, and naming Monmouthshire, Wales, as the place where the family originated. William,[1] the founder of the family in Rhode Island, had three sons, Benedict, Thomas and Stephen. Benedict, the eldest, removed to Newport about the year 1653.[2]

[1] He was the son of Thomas Arnold, of Melcome Hersey, of Cheselbourne, County of Dorset, England. who was son of Richard Arnold, Lord of the manor of Bagbere, Parish of Middleton, Co. of Dorset.
See Arnold Genealogy in N. Y. His. Society.

[2] I have received from a grand daughter of General Arnold, residing in Canada, a curious, antique paper, apparently of ante-revolutionary origin, containing a genealogy of some of the Arnold family, from 1571 to 1776. Some parts of it seem to have been prepared by Governor Benedict Arnold, the successor of Roger Williams, as President and Governor of the Colony. He says:

"We came from Providence with our family to dwell in Newport, in Rhode Island, the 19th of November, Thursday in afternoon, and arrived ye same night, anno Domini 1651. Memorandum: my father and his family sett sayle from Dartmouth, in old England, the first of May, Friday, and arrived at New England June 24th. anno Domini 1635. Mem'n: We came to Providence to dwell the 20th of April, 1636. *Memorandum.*

"Benedict and Demaris Arnold were married the 17th of December, anno Domini 1640. Our sonne Benedict was born February 10, 1641—being our first-born, and bearest therefore his father's name—about two hours before day.

"Our second sonne we named Caleb. He was born the 19th of December, anno

HIS PATRIOTISM AND HIS TREASON.

He succeeded Roger Williams as President of the Colony, under the first charter, and was several times elected Governor under the second charter; serving as Governor from 1663 to 1666, and from May, 1669, to 1672; also from 1677 to 1678, when he died.[1]

The son of Governor Benedict Arnold, named Benedict, was a member of the Assembly in 1695, and the grandson, also named Benedict, moved to Norwich, Connecticut, in 1730, and was the father of the subject of this memoir. He was by trade a cooper, carrying on the business quite largely, and in addition he engaged in general traffic, owning several vessels, and sometimes commanding them, and making voyages along the coast, and to the West Indies. As the commander of his own vessels he acquired the title of captain, by which he was generally designated. He was respected by his townsmen, and by their selection held various town offices, such as surveyor, collector, lister (assessor) and selectman. He married Nov. 8, 1733, Hannah, the young and "beautiful" widow of Absalom King, her maiden name being Waterman. Her family was respected, and she herself was distinguished for her piety, good sense and rigid Puritan character. She was a strict Presbyterian, of the type of that day and colony, but in her this form of Christianity was softened and made gentle and sweet by a most affectionate, and kind disposition.[2]

1646, about 8 o'clock in the evening. We called him Caleb, in memory of that worthy Caleb, which only accompanied Josiah into ye land of promise of all yt came out of Egypt, &c.

"Our third sonne was born December 22nd, 1647, about midnight. He was our third child, and we named him Josiah, in memory of that good Josiah which purged the house of Israel from idolatry, &c.

"Our fourth sonne was born ye 21st of October, 1651, and we named him *William*, intending he should have the name of his grandfather, but God pleased in his wisdom to take him away."

1. Arnold's History of Rhode Island, 565.
It is mentioned in the genealogy above quoted, that a daughter "lyeth interred under a tomb in my land, between my dwelling house and a *stone wind-mill*."
This is the old stone wind mill still standing in Newport.

2. I have received the following memorandum from a descendant of the mother

The children of this marriage were six, three sons and three daughters.

Benedict (a family name running through several generations), the eldest, died in infancy, and to the second son, the subject of this memoir, the same family name was given. He was born at Norwich, on the 14th of January, 1741.[1]

Of all the six children of Captain Benedict Arnold, this son and a sister, Hannah, only survived the period of childhood.

It has been quite the fashion for our historians and annalists to stigmatize Benedict Arnold as of low birth and vulgar habits, but in this, as in many other particulars, the passionate desire to throw discredit upon the traitor, has

of Benedict Arnold, claiming for her, as will be seen, very distinguished ancestry. I have no means of determining the truth of its statements, but insert it for the curious in such matters:

GENEALOGY—MRS. WATERMAN—ARNOLD—MOTHER OF B. ARNOLD.—Lieut. Thomas Tracy, one of the original proprietors of Norwich, Conn., born in England in 1611, was a lineal descendant of the 29th generation from Egbert, the first Saxon king of all England. He had seven children, viz.: *John, Jonathan, Thomas, Miriam,* Solomon, David, and Samuel.

John Tracy was an ancestor of Hon. Reuben Hyde Walworth, Chancellor of the State of New York, and also of Mrs. Gideon M. Davidson, the mother of C. M. Davidson.

Jonathan Tracy, born in 1644, married Mary Griswold and had nine children, the second of whom was

Hannah Tracy, who was married in 1695 to Thomas Davison, 1st, the great, great grandfather of Gideon M. Davison, the father of Clement M. Davison.

Mirriam Tracy, born in 1648, the only daughter of Lieut. Thomas Tracy, was married in 1668, to Thomas Waterman, one of the original proprietors of Norwich, son of Robert Waterman, of Elizabeth Brown, an ancestress of Mrs. G. M. Davison. They had eight children, viz.: Thomas, Elizabeth, *John,* Miriam, Martha, Lydia, Joseph and Anne.

John Waterman, born in 1672, married in 1701 Elizabeth Lathrop, second daughter of Samuel Lathrop and Hannah Adgate, of Norwich; they had four children, one of whom was the mother of Gen. Benedict Arnold, who was the third cousin of Thos. Davison, 2nd, the great grand father of C. M. Davison. The grand children of Gen. Arnold, and the father of C. M. Davison are consequently 5th cousins, and are of the 33d generation, in a lineal descent from King Egbert.

WINDSOR, Canada, Sept. 6th, 1862.

1. Genealogy of Arnold family—also manuscript letter of his grandson, Rev. Edward Gladwin Arnold. See, also, Miss Caulkins' History of Norwich, p. 409.

rendered them inaccurate and unjust. His ancestors in England, and his forefathers in Rhode Island, were, as has been stated, men of character, education and position, and certainly no family in Rhode Island, up to the time of the Revolution, had been more honored in official positions, and it is but simple justice to place them among the most prominent of the founders of that small, but admirable State. Whether of great or little importance, it is a fact that there were few colonial families whose lineage, by both father and mother, was more entirely respectable.

Captain Benedict Arnold died in 1761. The house occupied by him, and in which the subject of this memoir was born, stood in the old part of the town of Norwich, and was not demolished until 1853. There were in and around it many memorials of young Benedict. After his removal to New Haven, the house and house-lot were sold by him to one Hugh Ledlie, for seven hundred pounds sterling. In consequence of the insanity of the wife of Ledlie, and exaggerated tales growing out of this circumstance, the house was believed to be haunted, and many wild stories of supernatural appearances were told of it, and credited by the superstitious.

In the year 1775, Deacon William Phillips, of Boston, father of Lieutenant Governor Phillips, moved to Norwich and occupied the old Arnold mansion until the British left Boston.[1]

The famous Malbones, of Newport, were the next occupants, and the misfortunes of that family added to its weird reputation.

Next, Col. Moore, of Norfolk, Virginia, father of Richard Channing Moore, Bishop of Virginia, occupied it, and died there in 1784. It was afterwards purchased by Uriah

[1]. See Miss Caulkins' History of Norwich, page 411, manuscript letter of O. C. P. Waterman.

Tracy, who lived in it for many years undisturbed. The strange noises and sights for which it had been so long noted now ceased. The garden and groves were no longer infested with strange visitants, and the chambers were now quiet and peaceful.

The mother of Benedict Arnold has been described by her contemporaries, and by tradition, as a woman of extraordinary strength of character, and entirely devoted to her family. "Benedict Arnold's mother," said one who knew her well, "was a saint on earth, and is now an angel in heaven."[1]

Several letters of hers still extant, prove that all which was said in her praise was true. She died Aug. 15th, 1758. The inscription on her tomb-stone confirms what has been said.

"In memory of *Hannah*, the well-beloved wife of Captain Benedict Arnold, and daughter of Mr. John and Mrs. Elizabeth Waterman. She was a pattern of piety, patience and virtue: who died Aug. 15th, 1758. Ætatis 52."[1]

Captain Oliver Arnold, the uncle of Benedict, died in New Haven, in 1781. He had long been an invalid, and left very little for the support and maintenance of his family. After the death of his uncle, Benedict was always liberal and kind to them; and even after his exile in England, did not forget his cousins, and his remittances to them are said to have been generous. He assisted the eldest son to a liberal education; but the young man, grieved and indignant at the conduct of his cousin, joined the naval service of the United States, and attaching himself to the celebrated Paul Jones, hoped by deeds of desperate daring to efface the disgrace which his cousin's treason had attached to the name. He returned to New Haven with his health broken, and soon died.

1. Miss Caulkins' History of Norwich, page 409, and manuscript letter of C. C. P. Waterman.

Another son, named Oliver, was a bright lad, and as he grew up developed a talent for making impromptu rhymes; happening in at a book store in New Haven one day, he met there the poet Joel Barlow, and was presented to him. Barlow had lately published an altered, some thought, an improved, edition of Watts' Psalms and Hymns. Young Oliver being pressed by Barlow to give a specimen of his improvisations, finally complied by addressing Barlow as follows:

"You've proved yourself a sinful cretur,
You've murdered Watts and spoilt the metre;
You've tried the word of God to alter;
And for your pains deserve—a halter." [1]

He, like his elder brother, was a devoted patriot, condemning with the utmost severity the conduct of his cousin Benedict.

This lad, mischievous, wild and reckless, very early became distinguished for personal courage, a love of adventure, and a passionate love of approbation. The excitement of danger had for him an irresistible charm; but he had a quickness, a readiness of invention and skill, which made the most daring feats to him comparatively safe. The restraints of New England puritanic life were very irksome to him, and he became known among the deacons and selectmen as a young "dare-devil." He was the fearless leader of the wildest boys in every bold exploit, and sometimes reckless and unscrupulous. Anecdotes of his boyhood have been published, indicating cruelty. It has been said that he would scatter pieces of broken glass in the paths frequented by his schoolmates, that they might cut their feet in returning from school; and that one of his amusements was the robbing of bird's nests, and torturing the young birds.

[1] See manuscript letter of C. C. P. Waterman.

Perhaps the intense indignation created by his treason has caused these early anecdotes to be exaggerated, and possibly too great a significance has been attached to them. Certainly if the mischievous robbing of birds' nests is to be regarded as conclusive proof of total depravity, and if among the critics of Arnold, only those who had in thoughtless boyhood been guiltless of this cruelty, should throw the first stone, there would probably be fewer harsh judges of his boyish freaks than have appeared. But of his bold, rash feats of daring, all who knew him bear witness; and many anecdotes exhibiting these traits, have come down to us. For instance, when a lad he was often sent to the mill with Indian corn, to be ground. While waiting for his grist, he would astonish his playmates and alarm the lookers-on, by clinging to the arms of the great water-wheel, and holding on as it made its revolutions, he would be carried high in the air, and then rapidly descending, pass beneath the water of the stream by which the great wheel was turned.[1]

He "was active as lightning, and with a ready wit always at command."[2] He early developed the qualities of a natural leader.

In every kind of sport, especially if it had a dash of mischief about it, he was a "dauntless captain, and as despotic among the boys as an absolute monarch." On a day of public rejoicing over some success of the British over the French, he brought a field-piece out upon the common and placing it on end, the muzzle pointing to the sky, he emptied into it a powder-horn full of powder, and then with his own hand dropped into it a blazing fire-brand! Only his activity saved him; he started back barely in time as the blaze followed within an inch of his face. And yet undaunted, his huzza was the loudest of the crowd.

1. Spark's Life of Arnold, page 6.
2. C. C. P. Waterman.

A story is told of his fighting, at the age of fourteen, a constable who sought to reclaim from him and his comrades some tar barrels, which they had appropriated for a "Thanksgiving bonfire."[1]

As is usual with the brave, he was generous, and his sympathies were always with the weak; he was the champion of the smaller lads and those of his own age, and no bully was ever permitted, in his presence, to practice any injustice upon the younger boys. He was kind to his friends, but would never submit to force.

He received the advantages of what would be regarded now as a fair common school and academic education, including some knowledge of Latin and mathematics. His father at one time was a man of considerable means, as we have seen, and Benedict was sent abroad to school. A letter from his mother has been published, dated Aug. 12th, 1753, addressed to him at Canterbury, some twelve miles from Norwich, in which this good Puritan lady says: "Pray, my dear son, whatever you neglect, don't neglect your precious soul, which once lost can never be regained."[2]

She begs him, for her, to "give service to Mr. Cogswell and lady." He was then twelve years old.

Another very interesting letter of hers is as follows:

"NORWICH, April 12th, 1754.

DEAR CHILDE:—I received yours of the 1st instant, and was glad to hear that you were well. Pray, my dear, let your first concern be to make your peace with God, as it is of all concerns of the greatest importance. Keep a steady watch over your thoughts, words and actions. Be dutyful to superiors, obliging to equals, and affable to inferiors, if any such there be. Always choose that your companions be your betters, that by their good examples you may learn.

"From your affectionate mother,
"HANNAH ARNOLD.

"P. S.—I have sent you 50s. Use it prudently, as you are accountable

1. Miss Caulkins' History of Norwich, page 412.
2. New Haven Journal, Sept. 8, 1859.

to God and your Father. Your Father and Aunt join with me in love and service to Mr. Cogswell and Lady, and yourself. Your sister is from home.[1] Your Father puts in twenty more."[2]

This sum sent to a boy of thirteen, as pocket-money, would indicate that the family were in a condition to give him whatever advantages of education the country then afforded. There is also evidence to show that he was sent to school to a Dr. Jewett, of Montville.[3]

His letters, his writings, his speeches, particularly his defense on his trial before the Court-martial, near Philadelphia, show him to have been a man of respectable education for the days in which he lived.

I have seen in the hands of a connection, a copy of a latin school book, "Cornelius Nepos," (published in 1748,) and in his own hand-writing, "Benedict Arnold, Ejus Liber."

Those writers who have spoken of him as illiterate and vulgar, have been neither accurate nor just. Although not a man of what to-day is called a "liberal education," his would compare favorably with that of many officers of rank in the army of the Revolution.

In 1755, the war between France and Great Britain, known in American Annals as the "Old French War," broke out. In the following year Arnold, then less than fifteen years of age, was carried away with the romantic idea of being a soldier. His love of adventure and a romantic wish to perform daring exploits, led him to run away from home to Hartford, from where the Connecticut troops were to start for Lake George and the Northern frontier, and enlist as a soldier. His mother sought and obtained the kind offices of the Rev. Dr. Lord, and through him, her darling son was restored to her. But the Connecticut boy, destined to a life of strange adventure on land and sea, grew

1. Lossing's Field-Book of the Revolution, note; Vol. 2, page 605.
2. Hill's Life of Arnold, page 12.
3. Hill's Life of Arnold, page 20.

moody and restless, and yearned for the wild life of the frontier; so excited was his imagination with his dreams of a soldier's life, that he left his home a second time, and joined the provincial troops. The incidents of the journey to Albany and the Lakes by the school-boy volunteer are not recorded. If this soldier-lad had kept a journal, and told us what he saw as he passed through the old Dutch town of Albany, and the incidents of his march through the forests, it would have possessed peculiar interest; but we only know that the wilderness was then unbroken and wild, frequented only by the scout and the Indian, and that Lake George lay beneath its over-hanging Highlands, with none to admire its beauty, except when some hunter or soldier, some Leatherstocking, Uncas, or Heyward, paused a moment on its shores, to be led from "Nature up to Nature's God." Philip Schuyler, then lately married, commanded a provincial company. George Washington was preparing himself by severe service under the British flag to lead his country to Independence.

With what anxiety the fond mother waited the return of this her only surviving son, may be imagined. The fancied charm of a soldier's life was soon dispelled by experience; he soon wearied of military discipline, deserted, and returned through the wilderness alone to his home. Although an infant in law, and too young to execute a valid contract of enlistment into military service, yet some apprehensions seem to have been felt by his mother and friends that he might be arrested as a deserter, and he was hidden away while a recruiting officer was in the town.

He had already become familiar with fire-arms, and with the pistol and the rifle had few if any superiors as a marksman. To his great skill he was on one occasion, at least, as will be seen hereafter, indebted for his life.

He was strong, hardy, active, and excelled in all athletic

sports and gymnastic exercises. In fencing, boxing, in skating, in running and leaping, he had no superiors. It is said that even after he recovered from his wound received at Quebec, when making the campaign to relieve Fort Stanwix, he could readily vault over a loaded ammunition wagon without touching hand or foot.[1]

Previous to his adventure as a soldier, he had entered the employ of Doctors Daniel and Joshua Lathrop, who were relatives of his mother. They kept a large drug store in Norwich, and were gentlemen of education—both were graduates of Yale College; and Daniel had finished his medical studies in London. They seem to have been especially kind towards this boy, and being related to his mother, they manifested more than usual interest in his fortunes. They gave him a home in the family of Dr. Lathrop, the head of the house. They had a large business, importing their own medicines, and had furnished medical stores to the English army in the French War.[2]

Benedict remained with them until he reached the age of twenty-one, and then removed to New Haven, where aided by his former employers, he established himself as a druggist and bookseller.[3] His business rapidly increased. He engaged in general trade and exchange, and his energy and enterprise enabled him rapidly to acquire considerable property. He embarked in the West India trade, and purchased and shipped to those Islands, horses, mules, beef cattle, and other provisions. He sometimes sailed his own ships. He had quite a large business connection in Quebec,

---

1. Manuscript letter of Rev. J. S. Leake.
2. Miss Caulkins' History of Norwich, pages 326-7.
3. His sign is still preserved in Connecticut Hist'l Society.
" B. Arnold,
Druggist, Bookseller, &c.,
Sibi Totique."
" Sibi Totique."—For himself and for all."
Miss Caulkins' His. of Norwich, page 413.

which he visited frequently, buying horses in Canada and shipping them from there to the West Indies.

From his extensive trade in horses, some writers have called him a "horse-jocky." He knew and loved a good horse, and none knew better how to ride,

"To turn and wind a fiery Pegasus,
And witch the world with noble horsemanship,"

and during the revolution he was noted for always being particularly well mounted.

This business of bookseller and druggist, and general trader, he carried on for several years. His residence in New Haven was near the ship-yard. "It was a handsome frame building, embosomed in shrubbery." Young, finelooking, prosperous and popular, a contemporary says of him, "he had been a general favorite with the ladies, fond of their society, and floating in the gayest circles of the day."[1]

On the 22nd of February, 1767, he married Margaret, daughter of Samuel Mansfield, High Sheriff of the county. She was a lady of good family, young, interesting and accomplished, "and as far as is known, his first love."[2]

All concur in representing her as attractive in person, gentle and graceful in manner, amiable and affectionate in disposition, and of devoted piety. They had three sons, Benedict, born February 14, 1768, Richard, born August 22, 1769, and Henry, born September 19, 1772.[3]

His only sister, Hannah, never married. A story of her brother's interference and opposition to the attentions of a French adventurer has been often told; and it is said a duel grew out of the affair; but not being able to verify it, I am inclined to believe the circumstances have been exaggerated, and that some of the alleged facts are untrue. It is per-

1. Miss Caulkin's History of Norwich, p. 413.
2. Miss Caulkin's History of Norwich, p. 413.
3. Arnold's Genealogy.

fectly clear, that whatever may have occurred, nothing was done on the part of the brother which disturbed, to any extent, the tender devotion and affection which she always manifested towards him. She adhered to him through evil, as well as good repute, and was ever his useful friend and adviser, and the watchful guardian of his interests.

Mr. Sparks, speaking of this sister, says several of her letters which he had seen justify the tribute to her good name, "as a woman of rare endowments of mind, refinement and delicacy, and other qualities of female excellence."[1] "Her ardent and unceasing attachment to her brother, at the same time that it proves the depth of her own feelings, may argue the existence of better traits in his domestic character than would be inferred from his public conduct. His sister was his devoted friend and adviser, and a watchful guardian over his family and interests."[2] As evidence of this, in January, 1776, she procured, through Silas Deane, the settlement of a claim of some $800.19, the balance found due to her brother "for his expenses and disbursements in the taking of Crown Point and Ticonderoga."[3]

Mr. Deane says, in a letter to her, "I shall ever consider the opportunity I have had of serving your gallant brother among the most happy incidents of my life, and his friendship and confidence as a particular honor."[4] She, in reply, Feb. 1st, 1776, "thanks him for his kind services, and desires him to obtain for her liberty to ship a cargo of lumber to the West Indies; the long absence of her brother in Canada, on the expedition against Quebec, rendered it necessary for her to attend to his affairs. She expresses her fears of the loss by her brother of a vessel and cargo at Quebec."[5]

1. Spark's Life of Arnold, p. 11.
2. Spark's Life of Arnold, p. 11.
3. Collections of Conn. Historical Society, Vol. 2, p. 354.
4. Collections of Conn. Historical Society, Vol. 2, p. 355.
5. Collections of Conn. Historical Society, pages 357-8.

Her letters all indicate a gentlewoman of refinement, dignity, intelligence, and much more than ordinary good sense and judgment.

Whatever may have been the faults and misfortunes of Benedict Arnold, he had the great good fortune to have a mother, a sister and a wife, each an ornament to her sex; women, all of them of the purest character, and each attached to him with a devotion which nothing could change. With all his faults, there must have been, as Mr. Sparks suggests, a bright side to his character.

He was a man of commanding figure; athletic, strong and active. An old soldier[1] who fought with him at Bemis' Heights, says (I quote his own quaint language): "He was dark-skinned, with black hair, and middling height; there was n't any waste timber in him; he was our fighting general, and a bloody fellow he was. He did n't care for nothing; he'd ride right in. It was 'Come on, boys'— 't wasn't 'Go, boys.' He was as brave a man as ever lived."

Another soldier, a comrade with him in his expedition to Quebec,[2] says: "Arnold was brave, even to temerity; he was beloved by his soldiers. He was well formed, very stoutly built, with a florid complexion." Still another describes him as having "light eyes, black hair and dark complexion."[3]

An anecdote is told of him, occurring at this period of his life, which sounds more like the adventures of a rough knight of Medieval times, or the legends of Greek or Ro-

---

1. Samuel Downing.
2. Henry's Journal, page 12.
3. Mr. Leake, in the letter already quoted from, says: "My father, some fifteen years his (Arnold's) junior, and a near neighbor to his residence and business establishments, has often described him to me, as about his own size, which was something below the middle height, well formed, muscular, and capable of great endurance. He described him as a finished adept in all athletic exercises, and as the most accomplished and graceful skater" (himself no mean performer) " that he had ever seen."

man mythology, than the exploit of a captain of a New England militia company; but its truth has never been questioned. Once, while driving beef-cattle on to a vessel, a refractory steer refused to go aboard; mad and wild with rage and fright, the animal broke loose, and dashing through the crowd of men engaged in loading the vessel, defied pursuit. Arnold mounted his horse, and riding rapidly, overtook the animal, seized the enraged brute by the horns and nose, and held him fast until he was subdued and secured.

Another anecdote, illustrating the violence of his unrestrained passions, is told. Previous to 1766 British Revenue Acts had been enacted which were generally felt to be most unjust and oppressive by the Colonies, and the custom-house officers were often regarded as instruments of oppression. It is said that Arnold was not particularly scrupulous in paying the duties on imported goods; nor was his evasion of custom exactions thought by his neighbors in those days, to be a very serious offense. A sailor who had sailed on one of Arnold's vessels to the West Indies, in revenge for some real or supposed injury, accused him of smuggling. Arnold gave him what he called "a little chastisement," but which others called a flogging, and obtained from him a promise in writing to leave New Haven and never return. The sailor did not go, and Arnold finding him still in the place, headed a party who took him to a public whipping post, where he received forty lashes and was conducted out of the town. Arnold was tried for the offense, and fined fifty shillings.[1]

On one of his voyages to the West Indies, the ship of which Arnold was master, lying in the bay of Honduras, was nearly ready to sail for home. Some circumstances induced him to send the ship back in charge of the mate.

---

1. Arnold's own account of this transaction may be found in *Hill's Life of Arnold*, pages 22 to 25.

While very busy preparing the papers and arranging for the departure of the vessel, a card of invitation was brought to him from a Captain Croskie, commanding a British merchant ship in the bay, inviting him to attend a social party that evening. Being very much occupied, he did not attend, and neglected to send his regret. The next morning he called on the British officer to pay his respects and apologize for the neglect. He was received very rudely, and called " a d—d Yankee, destitute of good manners or those of a gentleman."

The young American made no reply, except quietly to draw off his glove, and handing it to the Englishman, retired. A hostile meeting was arranged for the next morning on an island near by, and each was to be accompanied by a surgeon and his seconds only. Arnold, with his surgeon and seconds, was promptly on the ground, and after waiting some time beyond the hour named, and supposing Croskie was not coming, was about to leave, when the English Captain was seen approaching, accompanied by six or eight swarthy natives. Suspecting treachery, Arnold consulted with his seconds and surgeon, and they agreeing to stand by him, he resolved that none but the Englishman and his authorized friends should be permitted to land. When Croskie and his party came within hailing distance, Arnold commanded a halt and demanded why the natives were brought, in violation of the agreement.

Croskie made some excuse, but Arnold standing on the beach with his pistol cocked, forbade their approach on peril of their lives, but permitted his antagonist and his seconds to come ashore, compelling the boat and natives to keep off. The ground being then measured, the Englishman as the challenged party, had the first fire. This Arnold received without injury. Arnold then fired, wounding but not disabling his adversary. The wound having been dressed, Arnold called upon him to resume his position, and announced that he was ready to receive another shot, adding, "I give you notice, if you miss this time I shall kill you." The Englishman thereupon apologized for his insults and extended his hand, which "the Yankee" received, and they then returned together in the same barge.[1]

[1]. The above particulars were furnished me by Thomas Waterman, of the same family of Waterman to which the mother of Arnold belonged.

CHAPTER II.

TICONDEROGA AND CROWN POINT.

"Our worthy friend, Col. Arnold, not having the sole honor of reducing Ticonderoga and Crown Point, determined upon an expedition to St. Johns, in which he happily succeeded."
"GENERAL JOSEPH WARREN."

THE BOSTON MASSACRE—ARNOLD'S FIERY PATRIOTISM—HIS LETTER—BATTLE OF LEXINGTON—CAPT. ARNOLD VOLUNTEERS AND LEADS HIS COMPANY TO CAMBRIDGE—EXPEDITION TO TICONDEROGA—CAPTURES ST. JOHNS—WARREN HIS FRIEND—INJUSTICE TO ARNOLD—DEATH OF HIS WIFE—TOUCHING LETTER OF HIS SISTER, HANNAH ARNOLD.

DURING the years of 1765, and on to 1770, Arnold was actively engaged in a large and increasing business, and apparently contented and happy with his family. His active and adventurous spirit found employment in visits to Canada and voyages to the West Indies, and an occasional trip to London.

Meanwhile, the discontent of the colonies with the mother country was constantly increasing. The home government was arbitrary, oppressive and arrogant. The colonies were beginning to realize their power, and the seeds of the revolution were beginning to germinate.

In March, 1770, a collision occurred in the streets of Boston, between the people and the British soldiers, in which several citizens were killed.

The incident known in contemporary American history as "the Boston massacre," caused an intense feeling of indignation throughout the thirteen colonies.

Arnold was at the time absent on a voyage to the West Indies, but when news of the event reached him, all the fiery zeal and impetuosity of his character were roused, and he wrote home, saying, "I was very much shocked the other day on hearing the accounts of the most wanton, cruel and inhuman murders committed in Boston by the soldiers. Good God! are the Americans all asleep, and tamely yielding up their liberties, or are they all turned *philosophers*, that they do not take immediate vengeance on such miscreants?"[1]

This was among the first utterances of this then fervid patriot. He was at that time personally very popular in New Haven, and was at about that period elected captain of the Governor's guards, an independent military company, composed of the most spirited and active young men of the city.

When after near five years of hard and active service—a service which involved as much personal exposure, hardship and suffering as was incurred by any officer of the war, he stood at Morristown, in New Jersey, before a court-martial, as hereinafter detailed, to defend his honor. He thus speaks of his condition when the war began:

"When the present necessary war against Great Britain commenced, I was in easy circumstances, and enjoyed a fair prospect of improving them. I was happy in domestic connections, and blessed with a rising family who claimed my care and attention. The liberties of my country were in danger. The voice of my country called upon all her faithful sons to join in her defense. With cheerfulness I obeyed the call; I was one of the first in the field."[2]

He was a merchant of property, doing a large business. "He was possessor of an elegant house, storehouses and wharves and vessels," at New Haven.[3]

1. Letter of Arnold to B. Douglas, June 9, 1770; printed in Historical Magazine, April, 1867, p. 119.
2. Trial of General Arnold, p. 102.
3. See certificate of Jeremiah Miller, Jr., before Board of Claims, London, March 5, 1784, who estimates Arnold's property at New Haven at £2,400 currency, all of which, he says, was confiscated.

He and General Wooster, an officer in the then recent war against France, seem to have been the popular leaders. Wooster was an elderly gentleman, cautious and conservative, while Arnold was at the head of the ardent, zealous young men, who could with difficulty be restrained from open violence.

The Rev. Samuel Peters, in the appendix to his history of Connecticut, states that in 1774, while he "was being persecuted as a tory," by what he calls a mob, he applied to James Hilhouse for protection, and that Mr. Hilhouse replied, "I want protection myself against the mobs of Col. Wooster and Dr. Benedict Arnold." [1] Peters also relates that after he "had taken refuge in the house of the Rev. Dr. Hubbard, and armed it as his castle, with twenty muskets, and powder and balls, that Arnold and his mob came to the gate. Peters said: "Arnold, so sure as you split the gate, I will blow your brains out." Arnold retired, saying "I am no coward, but I know Dr. Peters' disposition and temper. * * * I have no wish for death at present."

The battle of Lexington was fought on the 19th of April, 1775. The news of this battle sent an electric shock throughout the Colonies. All New England was in an uproar. New York, Pennsylvania, Virginia, the Carolinas, everywhere the people were roused to action, and with one voice they echoed the cry of Virginia's great orator, Patrick Henry, "Liberty or death." The reports of the collision, like the vibrations of an earthquake, shook the whole continent. From the Merrimac to the Hudson, from the Mohawk to the Delaware and Potomac, from the Green Mountains to the Gulf of Mexico, from the Atlantic to the Alleghanies, the people flew to arms and shouted, "Let us march to the aid of our brethren in Massachusetts."

The news of this battle, fought on the nineteenth of April,

---

1. History of Connecticut, by Dr. Samuel Peters, 1781; re-published, 1877.

reached New Haven at mid-day of the twentieth. Arnold instantly called his company together in the public square, and addressing them with all the fervor of patriotic zeal, declared he was ready to lead them to Boston, and called for volunteers. A very large majority at once offered to go, and these being joined by some patriotic students, they numbered in all about sixty. The next morning, being ready to start, Arnold called upon the selectmen of New Haven for ammunition. They refused it, Gen. Wooster saying they had better wait for regular orders. This did not suit the impetuous temper of Arnold, so, marching his company to the place where the selectmen were in session, he sent them notice that unless the keys were produced in five minutes he would order his men to break open the doors of the magazine. The keys were given to him, the ammunition was obtained, and he and his men were off for Cambridge. Gen. Wooster tried to persuade him to wait for regular orders. Arnold exclaimed, "None but Almighty God shall prevent my marching." In passing through Pomfret they were joined by the veteran General Putnam,[1] who did not stay even to remove his plough from the furrow he was breaking.

On his arrival at Cambridge. Arnold took possession of and made his headquarters at the mansion of Gov. Oliver, who had fled. He and his company were well drilled, well uniformed and equipped soldiers, having been the pride of the city of New Haven. Their fine appearance caused their selection as a guard of honor to deliver to Governor Gage the body of a British officer, who had been wounded and taken prisoner at the Lexington fight, and who had died of his wounds.

It is a curious fact, which strikingly illustrates the high moral character of this band of volunteers, that before

1. Lossing's Field Book of the Revolution, p. 422.

starting for Boston, Captain Arnold and each of the officers and privates solemnly set their names to articles of agreement, in which, appealing—[1]

"To all Christian people believing and relying on that God to whom our enemies have forced us to apply; and having taken up arms for the relief of our brethren and for the defense of their and our just rights;" to prevent disorders, etc., each bound himself by all that is sacred to observe and keep this mutual covenant.

1st. That they would conduct themselves decently and inoffensively, both to their countrymen and to each other, and would obey all the rules and regulations.

2nd. Drunkenness, gaming, profanity and every vice, should be avoided and discountenanced.

3rd. Obedience to their officers was not to be enforced by blows, but if any person guilty of any offense, after being admonished, should persist, such incorrigible person should be expelled, "as totally unworthy of serving in so great and glorious a cause."[2]

The company marched with flags on which were emblazoned the arms of the colony, and upon each banner and drum they caused to be inscribed, in letters of gold, "*Qui transtulit sustinet*"—the motto of Connecticut—"He who brought us hither will support us;" or, "God, who transplanted us hither, will support us."

Such was the motto and such the covenant under which Benedict Arnold, the patriot, began his military career. No sooner had he reached the camp at Cambridge than he went before the Committee of Public Safety and proposed an expedition to capture Ticonderoga and Crown Point.[3]

These forts were the keys to the communications between Canada and New York. Here and in this neighborhood, had been the battle-fields of the old French and Indian wars. The shores and waters of Lake George and

---

1. Collections of Connecticut Hist. Society, Vol. II, pp. 215-217. American Archives, 1775; Vol. II, pp. 383, 384.
2. For the text of this agreement see collections of Connecticut Historical Society, Vol. II, p. 215.
3. See letter of Arnold, April 30th, to Mass. Committee, giving detailed statement of the condition of Ticonderoga, found in Force's American Archives, 4th Series, Vol. II, p. 450.

Champlain had been the scenes of conflict, adventure and romance, since the early settlement of the country. It was well known, and to none more clearly than to Arnold, that the British posts on these lakes were feebly garrisoned and carelessly guarded, and that they contained, what the colonies then most needed, military stores, arms and ammunition in large quantities.

The imagination of Arnold was fired with the idea of capturing these posts, and he was ambitious of the glory of striking a blow so important for his country. He had, when a boy, visited these lakes, and was familiar with the localities. Dr. Joseph Warren, "the first great martyr," as Daniel Webster called him, was then a member of the committee and entered warmly into the project of Arnold,[1] and here was formed a warm personal friendship between these two men, both of whom seem at that time to have been acting with "the utmost patriotic ardor." To the kindness of Warren on this occasion and the personal attachment then formed may be attributed the gratitude on the part of Arnold, which survived the death of his friend and was manifested in the generous aid furnished by him for the education of the orphan children of Warren, and which will be fully narrated hereafter.

Arnold presented the project so clearly, and such was the impression made upon the committee by his intelligence, energy and enthusiasm, that they immediately and eagerly commissioned him as colonel, and authorized him to raise four hundred troops for the service. He was instructed to leave a garrison at Ticonderoga, and return to Cambridge with the arms and stores that he might capture. The Congress of Massachusetts supplied him with money, powder,

---

[1] See letter of Warren, dated Cambridge, April 30th, 1775, quoted in Frothingham's Life of Warren, page 474. "Benedict Arnold proposed to lead an expedition to capture Ticonderoga. Warren was appointed on a committee on this subject, and took great interest in it."—*Frothingham's Life of Warren, p. 474.*

lead, flints and horses, and he set off on the expedition with the utmost speed. He was instructed to raise his men in Western Massachusetts.

Having been commissioned on the 3d of May, and arriving in Stockbridge on the 6th, he learned with surprise that an expedition for the same purpose had already started, and was on the way to the lakes. He himself had no men, and leaving some officers to raise troops, he hastened forward, and on the 9th overtook an expedition under command of Ethan Allen, leading a body of "Green Mountain boys" towards Lake George.[1]

Arnold exhibited his commission and claimed the command; but as he had no soldiers and was a stranger, the volunteers naturally preferred their own officers, and refused to recognize him.[2] A small party from Connecticut, and another from Berkshire county, under Colonel Easton, had joined Allen. Arnold has been censured for claiming the command. His manner of doing so may have been arrogant, but he certainly was the only officer who had then been commissioned to capture these posts by any recognized State authority. Allen's leadership was by the selection of his troops. Massachusetts, the leading New-England colony, and on whose soil the war had begun, had given to Arnold a regular commission, full instructions, and authorized him to raise the necessary troops, and in claiming the command he was hardly going beyond his authority; but while it was natural he should claim the command, it was equally natural that the "Green Mountain Boys" under Allen should refuse it to him. Arnold was compelled to yield the point and joined the expedition as a volunteer, insisting, however, upon his rank, but issuing no orders.[3] Early on the morning of the 10th of May,

[1] See Lossing's Field Book of the Revolution, Vol. I, p. 124.
[2] Sparks' Life of Arnold, p. 15.
[3] Sparks' Life of Arnold, p. 17.

the party reached the shore of Lake George, and were disappointed in finding very few boats with which to cross; but both Arnold and Allen appreciated the fatal consequences of delay: the fort must be surprised, if captured at all, and so they hastened across the water, with the small number of men their few boats would carry, and at the early dawn Allen, with Arnold at his side, and eighty-three men marched through a sally-port, and captured Ticonderoga! They were not disappointed in the arms and military stores found in the fortress—one hundred and twenty iron cannon, fifty swivals, two ten-inch mortars, ten tons of musket balls, three cart loads of flints, thirty gun carriages, shells, ten casks of powder, material for boat building, two brass cannon, and pork, flour, etc., were the valuable spoils taken.

After the surrender, Arnold again insisted on taking command of the post, affirming that no other person present was vested with an authority equal to that conferred on him by Massachusetts.[1] In order to comply with the instructions of that colony, to send the captured arms and ammunition to Cambridge, it seemed necessary that he should have command. In harmony with this idea, General Warren wrote to the Connecticut authorities, May 17th, asking them to appoint "Colonel Arnold to take charge of them (the arms, &c.,) and bring them down in all possible haste," and this, he suggests, "may be a means of settling any dispute which may have arisen between him and some other officers which we are always desirous to avoid, and now especially, at a time when our common danger ought to unite us in the strongest bonds of amity and affection."[2]

But the Connecticut committee which had followed the troops, instead of doing this, by a formal written instru-

---
1. Sparks' Life of Arnold, p. 18.
2. See letter of Warren in Frothingham's Life of Warren, p. 490

ment, appointed Colonel Ethan Allen commander of Ticonderoga until further orders from that State, or from the Continental Congress. Arnold protested, and sent a statement of his proceedings to the authorities of Massachusetts.

Four days after the surrender of Ticonderoga, the first detachment of about fifty men enlisted under the orders of Arnold, joined him at that place. They came by way of Skenesborough, and brought with them a schooner taken there from a Major Skene, "a dangerous British agent."[1]

Now, at last, Arnold had a few troops who recognized him as their commander. He immediately armed and took command of this vessel, and with a party of his soldiers, sailed down the lake to St. Johns, surprised and captured the garrison, capturing a king's sloop and crew; he seized also a number of batteaux, and putting on board the valuable stores from the fort, returned to Ticonderoga.

There seems to have been a race between Arnold and Allen, and this time Arnold beat, for on his return, when about fifteen miles from St. Johns, he met Allen on his way to attack the same place.[2]

Thus these brave spirits, led by Allen and Arnold, by "a series of daring exploits," had captured the keys to Canada, securing control of lakes George and Champlain, and obtaining a large amount of arms and military stores, so greatly needed by the colonies. All the sanguine representations of Arnold to the Massachusetts committee had been more than realized, not, it is true, by his own efforts alone; others as well as he, had appreciated the vast importance of this expedition. The idea seems to have occurred to him and to several others at about the

---

1. See Bancroft's History of the United States, Vol. VII, p. 340.

2. Warren writes, May 25th, 1775:
"Our worthy friend, Col. Arnold, not having had *the sole honor* of reducing Ticonderoga and Crown Point, determined upon an expedition to St. Johns, in which he happily succeeded."—*Letter of Warren, in Frothingham's Life of Warren*, p. 494.

same time; indeed, the moment hostilities commenced the obvious thing to do was to surprise and capture the British posts on the lakes. Governor Trumball, of Connecticut, speaking of the disputes on the subject of priority, says: "It is a matter of diversion with me to see the various competitors contending so strenuously about a matter in the execution of which all concerned justly deserve applause." If it were a matter of importance to settle, who first suggested the expedition, there is considerable evidence tending to show that the honor belongs to Arnold.

Col. Samuel H. Parsons, in a letter[1] to Joseph Trumball, April 26, 1775, speaking of what occurred, says: "On my way to Hartford I fell in with Captain Arnold *who gave me an account of the state of Ticonderoga, and that a great number of brass cannon were there.*" Governor Hall, of Vermont, speaking of this interview, says: "Captain Benedict Arnold spoke to Samuel H. Parsons, of the Connecticut Assembly of the importance and feasibility of its (Ticonderoga) capture and his desire to attempt it."[2]

"Colonel Samuel H. Parsons, returning from Massachusetts to Hartford, April 26, 1775, met Benedict Arnold, then captain of a company of volunteers, on his march to the Camp at Cambridge. At this interview the surprise of Ticonderoga was suggested."[3] Parsons' letter before referred to clearly shows that it was Arnold who made the suggestion, for he says: "He (Arnold) gave me an account of the state of Ticonderoga, and said that a great number of brass cannon were there," etc. Whoever first suggested the expedition, it was now accomplished, and the arms were soon on their way to the Colonial authorities; a portion of the

---

1. See Col. of Conn. Historical Society, Vol. I, p. 182.
2. Hall's History of Vermont, p. 199.
3. See "Origin of Expedition against Ticonderoga in 1775." A paper read before the Conn. His. Society, by J. H. Trumball, Jan'y, 1869. "The proposition came from Benedict Arnold, &c."

artillery and other stores reaching the camp of Washington at Cambridge, supplying the arms and ammunition which he so greatly needed.

Immediately after the capture, Arnold commenced the construction of boats for the transportation of the captured arms.[1]

These expeditions were none too quick, for soon after Arnold's capture of St. Johns, a reinforcement of more than four hundred British and Canadians arrived at that place, and it was rumored that an expedition would proceed up the lakes to re-take the forts. Arnold having had some experience in seamanship, collected the vessels he had taken and prepared to meet the enemy. The schooner captured from Major Skene, the King's sloop, and a flotilla of batteaux were armed, and, his force having been increased to one hundred and fifty men, he made vigorous preparations to repel any attack which might be made.

On the first of June the Congress of Massachusetts addressed him a letter, acknowledging the receipt of letters from him dated the 19th and 23d of May, and express "great satisfaction in the acquisitions you have made," * * and assure him that they place the greatest confidence in his fidelity, knowledge and good conduct, and they desire him to dismiss the thought of quitting his important command at Ticonderoga, Crown Point and Lake Champlain, adding, "You are hereby requested to continue your command over the forces raised by this colony."[2]

---

1. See Notes to the History of Fort George, by B. F. DeCosta.

2. See MSS. from Massachusetts Archives, quoted in DeCosta's Notes to History of Fort George, p. 10. Also, Am. Archives, 1775, p. 1882, as follows:

"COLLONY OF MASSACHUSETTS BAY,
WATERTOWN, June 1, 1775.

"SIR—This congress have Received yours of 19 & 23d May ult. a copy of which has been sent to N. Hampshire, and Capt. Brown and Capt. Phelps they highly approve of and take great satisfaction in the acquisitions you have made at Ticonderoga, Crown Point, on The Lake, etc.; as to the state you are in respecting your Provision, etc. we have advices from Connecticut and New York that ample prepara-

He sent messengers into Canada for the purpose of learning the feelings of the Canadians and the designs of the Indians. He also wrote to the Continental Congress, communicating all the facts he had thus ascertained, and expressing the conviction that it would not be difficult to take possession of all Canada, and detailing a plan of operations for that purpose, and offering to lead the expedition and be responsible for the result.[1] Meanwhile his enemies had been writing to Massachusetts, exaggerating his faults, and, as Sparks says, "his zeal and energy were passed over unnoticed." The Legislature or Congress (so-called) of Massachusetts, delegated three of their number to go to Lake Champlain and inquire into the " spirit, capacity and conduct "[2] of Colonel Arnold, and were authorized, if they thought proper, to order his immediate return to Massachusetts to render an account of the money, ammunition and stores he had received, etc. "If he remained he was to be subordinate to Colonel Hinman," an officer that Connecticut had sent forward to take the command.

They found Arnold at Crown Point, actively employed in preparing to defend the conquests which had been made, and maturing plans for future action. When they laid before him their instructions, he was exceedingly indignant, and complained of being treated with injustice and disrespect; "in which," says Mr. Sparks, "he was not entirely in the wrong." Silas Deane, a member of Congress from Connec-

---

tions is making with the Greatest Dispatch in those two collonies from whence you may Depend on being seasonably supplied — they are Sorry to meet with Repeated Requests from you that some Gentleman be sent to succeed you in command; they assure you that they place the Greatest Confidence in your Fidelity, Knowledge, Courage and Good Conduct, and they Desire that you at present Dismiss the Thought of Quitting Your Important Command at Ticonderoga, Crown Point Lake Champlain, etc., and you are hereby requested to continue your command over the forces raised by this Colony Posted at thos several Places, at least until the Collony of New York or Connecticut shall take on them the maintaining and commanding the same agreeable to an order of Continental Congress."—*MSS. in Mass. Archives.*

1. See Sparks' Life of Arnold, pp. 21-27.
2. See Sparks' Life of Arnold, p. 22.

ticut, writing from Cambridge, Aug. 10th, 1775, was more explicit: "Colonel Arnold has been in my opinion hardly treated by this colony, through some mistake or other. * * He has deserved much and received little or less than nothing."[1]

Arnold wrote a formal letter of resignation and discharged the men he had enlisted, and hastened back to Cambridge, arriving in July. Barnabas Deane, writing on the first of June from near Ticonderoga, to his brother, Silas Deane, then a member of the Continental Congress, says:

"Col. Arnold has been greatly abused and misrepresented by designing persons, some of whom were from Connecticut. Had it not been for him everything here would have been in the utmost confusion and disorder; people would have been plundered of their private property, and no man's person would have been safe that was not of the Green Mountain party. * * Col. Arnold has been twice fired at by them, and has had a musket presented at his breast by one of that party, who threatened to fire him through if he refused to comply with their orders; which he very resolutely refused doing, as inconsistent with his duty and directly contrary to the opinion of the colonies * * * Col. Webb and myself had an arduous task to reconcile matters between the two commanders at Crown Point, which I hope is settled for the present."[2]

As corroborating the foregoing statement, a large number of inhabitants prepared and presented to Arnold a memorial, expressing their gratitude for the great services he had rendered them and the colonies.[3]

Looking back calmly at these events and the differences between Arnold and Allen, and Arnold and the Connecticut committee, we perceive that they originated to a considerable extent in the local jealousies of the different colonies. It must be conceded that Arnold had the best legal authority to command, but he was compelled to, and did yield to Allen's popularity with the "Green Mountain Boys." He was decided, perhaps unconciliatory, and it may be, arro-

1. Losing's Life of Schuyler, Vol. I, p. 385.
2. See Col. of Conn. His. Society, Vol. II, p. 247.
3. Am. Archives, p. 1775.

gant in asserting his authority; possibly there may have been faults also of manner on the part of Allen. He was a rough diamond, and not famed for courtesy or subordination. After Allen's unfortunate dash at Montreal, in which he and his men were captured, General Schuyler wrote: "I always dreaded his impatience of subordination."

Washington, also, speaking of Allen, says: "His misfortunes will, I hope, teach a lesson of prudence and subordination to others who may be ambitious to outshine their general officers, and, regardless of order and duty, rush into enterprises which have unfavorable effects on the public."[1] Whatever may have been the faults of Arnold, none surpassed him at that time in zeal, activity and daring. He went into Ticonderoga by the side of Allen; he surprised and captured St. Johns and the king's ship and batteaux. The appearance at Crown Point of the Massachusetts committee, in the midst of his zealous labors and triumphs, to inquire into "his spirit, capacity and conduct," and with power to order his immediate return, to a sensitive soldier was as great an indignity as one can easily conceive. This was the first of a series of acts of injustice which resulted in his inexcusable crime. Had Washington possessed the power of appointing and promoting the officers of his army, from the beginning to the conclusion of the war, Arnold's treason would never have been committed. On the contrary, as a fighting general, for active service, he would have been the right arm of Washington. As it was, his honor as a soldier was severely wounded. When every British post on the New York lakes had been captured, none without his zealous co-operation, others by his own skill, daring and good conduct; in the midst of his success, while zealously planning the capture of Canada, he was superseded and compelled to return under a cloud to

1. See Irving's Life of Washington, Vol. II, pp. 396-7.

HIS PATRIOTISM AND HIS TREASON. 47

Cambridge, but fortunately he soon afterwards met Washington and secured his confidence and friendship; and from that time on, until his fatal fall, the Commander-in-chief was his steadfast friend.

On the 19th of June, and before Colonel Arnold's return from his campaign, his wife died, aged thirty years. Thus to the sense of bitter injustice was added this crushing domestic affliction.

"In the northeast corner of the new cemetery of New Haven is a dark stone, neatly carved, with an ornamental border, 'Sacred to the memory of Margaret Arnold, the first wife of Benedict Arnold.'"[1]

His sister Hannah took the place of his wife, and well discharged the duties of mother to his children. Three sons, aged seven, six and three, constituted her charge.

With a touching and devoted affection, honorable alike to herself and to her brother, she writes to him of these children; of "Ben," the eldest, "already eager," as she says, "to hear everything relating to his papa."[2]

Congratulating him on his "success in reducing Tyconderoga," and making himself "master of the vessels on the lakes;" and as "the cause is undoubtedly a just one," she hopes he may have health, strength, fortitude and valor for whatever he "may be called to;" and then she devoutly prays: "May the broad hand of the Almighty overshadow you; and if called to battle, may the God of armies cover your head in the day of it."

1. Lossing's Field Book of the Revolution, Vol. I. p. 429.

2. The following is the text of this beautiful letter, copied by the author from the original, in possession of Miss Varick, of New York city:

"N. HAVEN, June, 1775.

"DEAR BROTHER:

"Take this opportunity pr. Capt. Oswald, to congratulate you on your late success in reducing Ticonderoga, and making yourself master of the vessells on the lakes. Sincerely wish all your future endeavors to serve your country may be crowned with equal success. Pity the fatigue you must unavoidably suffer in the wilderness. But as the cause is undoubtedly a just one, hope you may have health, strength, fortitude and valor, for whatever you may be called to. May the broad hand of the Almighty overshadow you; and if called to battle, may the God of Armies

Then adding: "The men who went under your care to Boston give you the praise of a very humane and tender officer;" she hopes "those now with you may meet with an equal degree of tenderness and humanity. I doubt it not," says she, "for the truly brave are ever humane." All who read the letter will concur in the declaration, that few soldiers in modern times, few knights in the days of chivalry, ever went forth to battle borne up by a more holy or a more tender prayer than that uttered in this letter by his devoted sister.

It was on Colonel Arnold's return to Cambridge that Washington, more just than the Massachusetts committee, selected him to command one of the most difficult and perilous enterprises ever undertaken on the American continent—the expedition to Quebec; and it is not too much to say that his march through the wilderness was conducted with an ability and fortitude rarely if ever surpassed.

cover your head in the day of it. 'Tis to Him and Him only, my dear brother, that we can look for safety or success. His power is ever able to shield us from the pestilence that walks in darkness, and the arrows that fly by noonday. May a Christian resignation to His will strengthen your hands and fortify your heart. May you seek His aid and rest your whole confidence in Him; and then you will have no fear but that of offending Him; and if we are to meet no more in time, may a wise preparation for eternity secure to us a happy meeting in the realms of bliss, where painful separations are forever excluded. The men who went under your care to Boston, give you the praises of a very humane, tender officer. Hope those now with you may meet with an equal degree of tenderness and humanity.

"Your little family are all well. Benedict is eager to hear everything relative to his papa. Mr. Mansfield, contrary to all expectation, is again able to ride out; and his physicians think he is in a fair way of recovering a comfortable state of health. Mr. Harrison, you have undoubtedly heard, is dead by a fit of the apoplexy. We have numbers of people daily coming here from New York and Boston. Capt Sears, and Mrs. Brown and Platt, with several other families from York, are now here. The world seems a universal flutter and hurry. What the event will be God only knows. But in all its changes, of this I am certain: that your health and prosperity are dear to me as my own. "Your affectionate Sister,

"HANNAH ARNOLD."

CHAPTER III.

EXPEDITION TO QUEBEC.

"Qui Transtulit Sustinet."

EXPEDITION TO QUEBEC AND MARCH THROUGH THE WILDERNESS—ARNOLD PROPOSES THE EXPEDITION TO WASHINGTON—WASHINGTON APPROVES, AND SELECTS FOR IT THE "PICKED MEN" OF HIS ARMY, AND GIVES THE COMMAND TO ARNOLD—THEIR DIFFICULTIES, SUFFERINGS AND DANGERS—ENOS GETS FRIGHTENED AND ABANDONS HIS COMRADES—ARNOLD, WITH MORGAN, PUSHES ON—PROVISIONS EXHAUSTED—ARNOLD WITH SIX MEN MAKES A FORCED MARCH TO THE CANADIAN SETTLEMENTS, OBTAINS FOOD, AND SAVES THE DETACHMENT. (1)

QUEBEC has been called, perhaps with some exaggeration, the "Gibraltar of America." Seated on its rocky cliffs, overlooking and commanding the St. Lawrence, both France and England had ever regarded it as the stronghold of the Canadas, and the aid of art had been brought to add to its great natural strength. After the capture of the forts on lakes George and Champlain, the project of obtaining military possession of Canada, with a view of uniting the whole continent in opposition to the power of Great Britain, had, as we have seen, been presented to Congress by Arnold and others.

When Washington reached Cambridge and assumed command, on the 3d of July, 1775, he had already favorably

1. The details of this expedition are gathered from the letters and journal of Arnold See collections of Maine Historical Society, Vol. I, p. 446. Also manuscript journal of Arnold in possession of Mr. Barlow, of New York, the journals of Major Meigs, Judge Henry, Messrs. Thayer, Senter and others, who were in the expedition and kept journals. Also Spark's Life of Benedict Arnold, Lossing's Field Book of the Revolution, and Force's American Archives.

considered the project, was in correspondence with Schuyler on the subject, and Schuyler had been selected to lead an army into Canada by way of the Northern lakes. It was now proposed by Arnold that an expedition should march by way of the Kennebec river, through the wilderness over the mountains of Maine to Quebec, to capture that city by surprise, and thus co-operate with Schuyler.

The plan of reaching Quebec by this route is said in the introduction to Thayer's Journal, edited by Stone,[1] to have originated with Arnold, and to have been suggested to him by reading the Journal, written in 1760, of Colonel Montresor, an officer of the British Engineer Service. After careful study, and several conferences with Arnold, Washington heartily adopted the project. It was a most hazardous enterprise, full of difficulties and dangers, known and unknown, but if successful would realize results of the utmost importance.[2] Washington fully appreciated its difficulties, and there is a tone of gravity approaching to solemnity in his letter of instructions to Arnold. "You are entrusted with a command," writes he, "of the utmost consequence to the liberties of America; on your conduct and courage and that of the officers and soldiers detached on this expedition, not only the success of your present enterprise and your own honor, but the safety and welfare of the whole country may depend."[3]

Conscious of the difficulties to be encountered, he selected the best material in his army for the expedition. The field officers were Lieutenant Colonels Christopher Green, of Rhode Island, and Roger Enos, of Connecticut; Majors

---

[1] See Introduction to Thayer's Journal of the Expedition to Quebec.

[2] "The proposed expedition was wild and perilous, and required a hardy, skillful and intrepid leader. Such a one was at hand. Washington considered him (Arnold) the very man for the enterprise."—*Irving's Life of Washington* Vol. 2, p. 61.

[3] These carefully written instructions, and an address to the people of Canada, Washington prepared at his headquarters, now the residence of the poet Longfellow.

Return J. Meigs, of Connecticut, and Timothy Bigelow, of Massachusetts. Among the captains was the celebrated Daniel Morgan, the famous rifleman of Virginia.

Aaron Burr, afterwards Vice President of the United States, Mathew Ogden, and some other young men, eager for adventure, joined the expedition as volunteers.

That Arnold suggested this expedition to Washington appears from a letter of Gates, then adjutant-general of the force at Cambridge, dated Aug. 25th, 1775, in which he says: "I am directed by his Excellency, General Washington, to request you to await the return of the express (sent to Gen. Schuyler). I have laid your plan before the General, who will converse with you upon it when you next meet."[1]

The detachment consisted in all of eleven hundred men—ten companies of musketmen and three of riflemen. These riflemen were from the mountains of Virginia and Pennsylvania; men of whom Daniel Boone and David Crocket were examples; hunters and Indian fighters, familiar with woodcraft, the rifle, the hunting-knife and the birch-bark canoe; men who could endure hunger, exposure and fatigue; who knew how to find subsistence and shelter in the forests; who could supply themselves with food from the deer, the bear and other wild game, and from fish from the rivers and lakes; men with some of the sagacity, resolution and fertility of resource which Cooper has ascribed

---

[1]. The following is the letter:

HEAD QUARTERS, 25th Aug., 1775.

SIR: I am confident you told me last night that you did not intend to leave Cambridge until the express sent by your friend returned from General Schuyler. Lest I should be mistaken, I am directed by his Excellency, General Washington, to request you to wait the return of that express. I have laid your plans before the General, who will converse with you upon it when you next meet. Your answer by the bearer will oblige, sir,

Your affectionate and humble Servant,

HORATIO GATES, Adj't General.

To Col. Arnold, at Watertown.

Historical Magazine, Dec. 1857, Vol. 1. No. 12, p. 372.

to the Leatherstocking, equally at home on the trail of an Indian or the track of a wild beast—the picked men of the Colonies. Henry says,[1] "All these men were of as rude and hardy a race as ourselves, and as unused to the discipline of a camp, and as fearless as we."

Many of them were men of substance, well-to-do farmers, men of pride of character, zealous but independent, and with crude ideas of military discipline. It is obvious that no ordinary man could lead through unknown difficulties and dangers such a body. They could be controlled only by the personal qualities of their leader. He must be one whose character would compel their respect. He should be as bold, as manly, as plucky as the best of them, and they must believe he was their superior in skill and judgment. He should be a natural leader of men, and possess not only courage and capacity, but he should be able to inspire his men with confidence in his courage and ability. Washington believed Benedict Arnold to be such a man. This is proved not only by his selection to command this most hazardous expedition, but also from Washington's letters.

The three companies of riflemen were especially regarded as embodying the best material for the hard work expected of them. With Morgan's company from Virginia were associated a company from Cumberland, Pennsylvania, commanded by Captain William Hendricks, and another from Lancaster, in the same State, commanded by Captain Matthew Smith. "They were an excellent body of men, rude, hardy and fearless, * * formed by nature to be the stamina of an army, fit for tough, tight work."[2]

The riflemen, armed with a good rifle, a tomahawk, a long knife, a small axe, and dressed in a hunting shirt, moccasins and leggings, all of deer skin. This little army

---
[1]. Henry's Journal (Muncell), p. 11.
[2]. Henry's Journal.

started from Prospect Hill, near Cambridge, Massachusetts, on the 11th of Sept. 1775, and on the next day reached Newburyport. From there the detachment embarked in ten transports for the mouth of the Kennebec river, where, leaving the vessels, they were to go in batteaux, which Arnold had caused to be built, and thence proceed up the Kennebec to Fort Western, in Maine, opposite the present town of Augusta, at which place they arrived on the 23d of September.

All the information Arnold could obtain of the route, was what he could glean from the meagre journal of Montresor, who had passed from Canada to the Kenebec fifteen years before, some facts gathered from a party of St. Francis Indians, who had lately visited the camp of Washington, and a rude and imperfect map made by a surveyor of the Kennebec.

The route selected as the most feasible was to ascend the Kennebec to what was called the great carrying place, between it and the Dead river; then turning west, surmount the carrying place; thence on over the extreme summit which divides the waters of New England from those of the St. Lawrence. Crossing this, they hoped and expected to strike the head-waters of the Chaudiere, and from thence descend to the St. Lawrence and Quebec. With his very limited knowledge of the country and the route, the commander deemed it prudent to send forward a small exploring party in advance, who were expected to move with the utmost rapidity in bark canoes, to ascertain the obstacles and dangers, and explore and mark the best route. This party had instructions to go as far as Lake Magentic, or Chaudiere pond—the source or head-waters of the river of that name. Another pioneer party was sent to explore and survey the courses and distances of Dead river. Colonel Arnold selected Archibald Steele, a bold, active, hardy and resolute young soldier, to command the first party, and the result showed the selection to have been most judicious. His hardihood, resolution and ready skill carried him through, and enabled him to overcome the most formidable difficulties. Perhaps a brief recital of the adventures of this pioneer party will give as clear an idea of the obstacles and dangers which Arnold and his command encountered, as could be conveyed by any other means.

Steele selected for one of his companions John Joseph Henry, not then seventeen years of age, and he has left a narrative, which, though written late in life, and from memory, yet gives a most graphic and interesting sketch of their adventures.

Starting from Fort Western, on the 23d of September, in birch-bark canoes, the party passed on rapidly to Fort Halifax, and thence to Skouhegan Falls, four miles east of the village of Norridgewack. Here they met the first portage or carrying place around the rapids, and by *blazing* the trees marked the route of those who were to follow.

"Here," writes Henry, "the moose deer reigns master of the forest,"[1] and "monarch of the glen."

They ascended the river rapidly, *blazing* the trees at every carrying place. Leaving the last habitation of the white man at Norridgewack, the party passed on into the wilderness. Having passed many falls, rapids and carrying places, on the 29th of September they arrived at the great carrying place, distant about sixty miles from Skouhegan. The distance across the portage to Dead river was twelve miles, but there were three or four ponds which could be used to lessen the land carriage. Steele's party, leaving the Kennebec, struck out towards Dead river, and at evening encamped on the margin of the first pond, sleeping, as

---

[1] When the bull moose threw up their heads, the tips of their horns seemed to me to stand eighteen feet from the ground.—*Henry's Journal*, p. 21.

usual when on shore, on the branches of the fir, hemlock and other evergreens. The ground across this carrying place was rough, rocky and rugged, interspersed with bogs, in which the men often sunk to their knees. It was now decided by Steele to divide his little party, leaving the weakest and half the provisions, while he pressed forward with the strongest and most enduring of his men. Two days of very hard work brought him to the banks of Dead river.

Pressing on, each day meeting new difficulties, their provisions grew scant, and the party put themselves on short rations, and resolved to eat their pork raw, and to eat but twice each day, morning and evening. "Unacquainted" says Henry, "with the distance we had to go, without map or chart, yet resolved to accomplish our orders at the hazard of our lives; a half a biscuit, and half an inch square of raw pork was our evening meal."[1]

October 4th, brought the party to the deserted wigwam of Natanis, an Indian chief, then supposed to be in the pay of the English as a spy, but who with a part of his warriors was afterwards induced by Arnold to join the expedition, and who with his men faithfully accompanied him to Quebec. The country grew more and more rough and difficult as the party advanced, and having now reached nearly to the high lands dividing the waters which flow to the Atlantic, from those which empty into the St. Lawrence, the weather became bitterly cold, and snow and ice added to their difficulties. The lonely, inhospitable solitudes of these high and far-away regions, is strikingly illustrated by the fact, that in 1858 a musket which had been left in 1775, by one of Arnold's expedition, was first discovered. The stock had entirely decayed, and the mountings and barrel had fallen to the ground.[2] During this period of more than

---
1. Henry's Journal pp. 29, 31.
2. Henry's Journal. note to page 34.

eighty years, the Colonies had become a great nation; the pioneer had penetrated every bay and harbor of the great western lakes, and crossing the Mississippi, and scaling the rocky mountains, he had erected his settler's cabin along the shores of the Pacific; the far-off Columbia was dotted with his towns and villages, but into these gloomy solitudes of Maine, during all this time, no wanderer had gone!

For more than three-quarters of a century the adventurous step of no man, red or white, had trod these solitudes!

At length, on the 7th of October, the party of Steele, weary and worn, reached the end of their explorations—the head-waters of the Chaudiere. Gathering around the roots of a pine, which rose forty feet without a branch, Steele asked if any of the party could climb it?[1] Robert Cunningham, an athletic young soldier twenty-five years of age, instantly began the ascent, going up with the activity almost of a squirrel. From the top he could trace far away towards the north the meanderings of the river, until it expanded into Lake Chaudiere, fifteen miles distant. Elated with their success, the party turned their faces back towards their comrades, toiling far behind in the depths of the forests. Soon overtaken by a fierce storm, hungry, drenched with rain and sleet, they attempted to shelter themselves under the branches of the evergreens, and they were so exhausted they "slept, notwithstanding the pelting storm."[2]

"Rumaging my pocket," says Henry, "I found a solitary biscuit and an inch of pork." Far from their companions, and nearly famishing, where were they to obtain food to sustain life? They made all possible haste, looking constantly for game, and finding none until the 9th, when they fortunately shot a small duck called a diver. At night when they gathered around their camp-fire, they

[1] Henry's Journal, pp. 34, 35.
[2] Henry's Journal, p. 37.

anxiously discussed the question how this duck and their little pittance of remaining food could be most effectually used to prolong life. They decided to boil the duck in their camp kettle, each man putting in his last bit of pork, and each marking his own by running through it a small wooden skewer, marked with his own private mark. The broth so made was to be all the supper the poor fellows had, reserving the boiled pork for breakfast, and the duck to be divided and laid by. "My appetite," says Henry, "was as ravenous as a wolf," but the resolution to take no more than the broth was kept.[1] Rising early the next morning, each man took his mouthful of pork, and breakfast was over. The duck was then separated into ten parts, the number of the party, and divided in the hunter's usual way—that is, one of the party, turning his back—and then Steele asked of the man whose back was turned to the fragments, "Whose shall this be?" The man answered, naming the party. Henry says, "my share of the duck was one of the thighs." The day wore away, the party hastening on, the duck was eaten, and the party encamped and tried, when night overtook them, to sleep. Rising the next morning, they resumed their march with not a morsel of food. Traveling all the weary day, they lay down again supperless.

The next day, trying to hurry on with all the little strength left, they ran their canoe against a partially sunken tree, and the frail bark was torn open from stem to stern. To repair this by finding birch trees, stripping off the bark, digging cedar-roots for thread, and collecting pitch from the pine, delayed them some hours, and now, utterly exhausted with hunger and fatigue, and at an unknown distance from the main party, some of them began to despair. Henry says: "The thought came that the Almighty had

[1.] Henry's Journal, pp. 37-38.

destined us to die of hunger in the wilderness." Few will reproach the boy for saying: "The tears fell from my eyes as I thought of my mother and family in their far-off home." But the good Father who does not suffer the sparrow to fall to the ground unnoticed, had not destined this hapless party, without food for near forty-eight hours, to perish in this "wilderness," for as the sun went down, and Henry, whose struggling canoe from sheer exhaustion lagged some hundred yards behind, heard the sharp crack of a rifle, followed by a shout and a huzza, and pushing forward, he saw, with inexpressible joy, a moose deer struggle from the water and fall upon the bank. They were saved! The forest shores echoed with their shouts of exultation, as the whole party gathered around the game. Kindling a fire, the famishing men feasted.[1]

On the 17th this pioneer party and the advance of the main body met, and they were welcomed, as brave men welcome comrades who have escaped a fearful danger. More than three weeks had passed since they had left Fort Western.

The main body had followed as soon after these scouts as possible, moving in four divisions, one day's march apart, to avoid confusion in passing rapids and portages. The riflemen, with Morgan at their head, in advance; then came Green and Bigelow with three companies, followed by Meigs with four, and then Enos with the three remaining companies, brought up the rear.

Arnold remained at Fort Western to see all embarked, and then in a fast birch-bark canoe, paddled by Indians, he pushed rapidly forward, and, passing each party, overtook Morgan and the riflemen at Norridgewack falls. Here, just below the falls, more than half a century before, had been the site of an Indian village of the tribe for which

---

1. Henry's Journal, p. 47.

the falls were named; and here, in 1698, came the good Father *Ralle*, a French priest, as a missionary, who after twenty-three years of devoted self-denial among these red children, was, in 1724, cruelly slain in a sudden attack by a party from Massachusetts.[1] When Arnold arrived there, in October, 1775, he found an utter solitude. The only mementos of the once happy village were the ruins of the altar and the chapel, and a cross which marked the grave of the venerable priest. From this place the march was to be through a wild and uninhabited wilderness, without paths, and often without even an Indian trail. Across dismal swamps and deceptive bogs, up rocky precipices and almost inaccessible mountains, along streams full of rapids and falls, and along and over all these obstacles the rude batteaux, the arms and ammunition, with which to attack the strongest fortress in America, and all their provisions, supplies and clothing, to protect them from the rigor of a Canadian winter, now too rapidly approaching, were to be transported.

Draft animals could not be used to any considerable extent, as a large portion of this savage and desolate region was then inaccessible to any animals but those of the chase.

At the falls near Norridgewack, the first portage was encountered. Here the batteaux, ammunition, provisions, everything had to be taken from the water, and carried by hand a mile and a half around the falls. It was a task of great labor and fatigue, the banks being high, rocky and uneven. Upon unloading the boats it was found that a large portion of the provisions, especially the bread, had been spoiled by the leaks in the boats, and the various accidents and injuries which had happened in ascending the Kennebec. The carpenters were immediately set to work, and a week was expended in repairs, re-loading the boats, and getting ready to start.

1. Thayer's Journal, p. 50.

While the soldiers were busy crossing this portage, Colonel Arnold called a council of his officers, and with their concurrence letters were dispatched by a friendly Indian, to certain gentlemen in Quebec, believed to be friendly, informing them of the approach of the expedition.[1] Dispatches were also sent to General Schuyler, but they did not reach their destination, and are supposed to have fallen into the hands of the enemy.

As soon as the last boat was in the river, ready to start, Arnold in his bark canoe, still paddled by Indians, shot rapidly ahead of the rear division, and in two days came up with the first two divisions, at the great carrying place, some twelve miles below the junction of the Kennebec with the Dead river. Thus far, everything had been as favorable as he had anticipated, and although the force had been reduced by sickness and other causes to 950 men, yet both soldiers and officers were in good spirits, and all seemed as sanguine and hopeful as their leader. By this time they had learned what manner of man this leader was, and he had fully secured the confidence and respect of the men. Loud cheers welcomed and followed his Indian canoe, as it passed and repassed forward and backward along the lines of his patient, resolute and toiling soldiers. For physical endurance, activity and strength, he had few equals, and perhaps no superior in the expedition.[2]

The "great carrying place" was a distance of twelve or fifteen miles, across from the Kennebec to Dead river. The pioneer party had found this to be the most difficult part of the route. Rugged, rocky highlands, deep ravines, ponds, deep swamps, constantly succeeded each other. Still the faithful soldiers toiled on, sometimes rowing, sometimes pushing

---

[1] Journal of Isaac Senter, p. 50, Sept. 7. "By a council of the officers, it was thought advisable to send letters into Quebec."

[2] Manuscript letter of Rev. Mr. Leake.

their boats with poles; often jumping ashore and pulling them with ropes, and then wading in the water up to their arm-pits. At night they landed, kindled a fire in the forest, took their hard and scanty rations, sleeping on the ground, and with the early sunrise resumed their exhausting toil. Thus they worked their way, over the land, to the first pond, then in their boats floated down it, then another portage, then another pond, and again a portage, and a third pond and portage, until they reached the Dead River. Salmon trout were caught, and occasionally the hunters succeeded in bringing down a deer or an elk. Meanwhile Arnold caused an accurate account of provisions to be taken, and found that his supplies would last for twenty-five days, and he then confidently hoped to reach the waters of the Chaudiere in ten days.

But as a matter of prudence, many being sick, he caused a block-house to be built near the second portage, called "Arnold's[1] Hospital," at which the sick and exhausted were left. He had already given orders for another block-house near the Kennebec, as a depository for the provisions ordered up from Norridgewack.

As the soldiers pushed their boats up Dead river, passing around a bend, a high mountain covered with snow rose before them. Encamping near the foot of this mountain, Arnold raised his flag, and the incident has been commemorated by giving the name of "Flagstaff" to a village near by, and the mountain has been named Mt. Bigelow, after Major Bigelow, who is said to have climbed to the top, in the hopes of seeing Quebec.

Provisions were becoming scarce, and Arnold dispatched Lt. Colonel Greene with a party to the rear for supplies. Morgan and the riflemen had gone forward, and the commander followed with the second division. For three days

---

1. Senter's Journal, pp. 11 and 12.

they encountered cold, drenching rains, and every man was wet to the skin, and all the baggage soaked with water. One night, about the 23d of October, a fearful storm arose, the rain falling in torrents, so that the river rose eight to ten feet in this single night; the current became rapid, full of drift wood, and the channel difficult to find and follow, and portages frequent, and at length seven of the batteaux were upset, and their contents, including provisions, were lost. This was a very serious misfortune, for they were now in the very heart of the wilderness; weary, worn out, provisions poor and scanty, wintry winds howling around them, with unknown difficulties confronting them. Yet, in none of the journals is there any indication of despair; neither the men nor the officers, nor their leader, flinched from going forward, and it should be remembered that they were going towards and not from the enemy.[1] On the 24th of October it was supposed that they were within thirty miles of Chaudiere pond, and that their provisions might, with great care, hold out for twelve or fifteen days. Another council was called, and it was decided to send back to the hospital the sick and feeble, and that only the strong and hardy should go forward.

Arnold had written to Washington on the 13th of October, from the second portage, between the Kennebec and Dead river, when, after giving details of the expedition, he said:

"Your excellency may possibly think we have been tardy in our march, * * but when you consider the badness and the weight of the batteaux. the large quantity of provisions we have been obliged to force up against a very rapid stream, where you would have taken the men for amphibious animals, as they were a great part of the time under water; add to this the great fatigue in portage, you will think I have pushed the men as fast as could possibly be done."[2]

[1]. Henry's Journal, p. 52. Maine His. Col. Vol. II, p. 476.
[2] Collections of Maine His. So., Vol. I, pp. 471, 472.

The next day he wrote back "to hurry up the provisions as fast as possible." On the 17th he wrote to Lt. Colonel Enos from "Dead river, 20 miles above the portage:"

"I find Colonel Greene's division very short of provisions. I have ordered Major Bigelow, with thirty-one men out of each company, to return and meet your division, and bring up such provisions as you can spare, to be divided equally among the three. This will lighten the rear, and they will be able to make greater dispatch. * I make no doubt you will hurry on as fast as possible.[1]

On the 24th, Arnold, on Dead river, thirty miles from Chaudiere pond, writes again to Enos: "I have been delayed by the extreme rains and freshets; have provisions for twelve or fifteen days," and adds that in a council of the officers it had been decided to send back all the sick and feeble, and directing Enos to select as many of his best men as he could furnish with provisions for fifteen days, and the remainder, sick and well, should be sent back, and he concludes: "I make no doubt you will join with me in this matter, as it may be the means of saving the whole detachment and executing our plan, as fifteen days will doubtless bring us to Canada. I make no doubt you will make all possible expedition."

On the same day he wrote to Greene: "Send back all the sick, and proceed on with the best men. *Pray hurry as fast as possible.*"

Meanwhile Arnold himself was hurrying on with all possible dispatch. The rain changed to snow, ice covered the water, and the men wading and breaking through snow and sleet, at length reached the very summit which separates the waters of New England from those of Canada. Another portage of four miles brought them to a small stream, along which they passed to Lake Magentic, the Chaudiere pond. On the 27th Arnold addressed a letter to "Greene, Enos, and the captains in the rear," saying, "I

---

1. Maine His. Col., Vol. I, p. 473.

shall proceed as fast as possible to the inhabitants to send back provisions; pray make all possible dispatch." The day he reached Chaudiere pond he wrote to Washington, explaining the difficulties which had retarded his progress, saying, "I have this minute arrived." He explains how the provisions became short by losing a number of loaded batteaux at the falls; he had ordered all the sick and feeble to return. "I am determined," said he, "to set out immediately for Sartigan (the first French settlement) and procure a supply of provisions and send back to the detachment."[1] He adds that if he finds the enemy had not been apprised of his coming, he should attempt to surprise Quebec, "as soon as a proper number of men should arrive." He concluded by saying, "I have been deceived by every account of our route, which is longer, and has been attended by a thousand difficulties I never apprehended, but if crowned with success, I shall think it but trifling."

On the very day previous to the date of the above letter, Washington, writing to Schuyler, says: "My anxiety extends to poor Arnold, whose fate depends upon the issue of your campaign."[2] Again Washington writes to Schuyler: "I am alarmed for Arnold, whose expedition is built upon yours, and who will infallably perish if the invasion and entry into Canada is abandoned by your successor."[3]

On the 29th of October Arnold wrote "To the field-officers and the captains, and to be sent on, that all may see it," an encouraging letter, saying the scouts had reported that the French were rejoicing at his approach, and would gladly supply provisions; he tells them he had just met Steele and Church, and that he was going forward as fast as possible, and that he hoped in six days to send back provisions, and prays them to make all *possible dis-*

---

1. Maine His. Col. Vol. I, pp. 476–477.
2. Am. Archives, 4 S., Vol. III, p. 170.
3. Am. Archives, 4 S., 1875, p. 976.

patch. If any could spare provisions, they were to divide with those most needy.[1]

The same day he wrote again to Enos, unconscious that this officer had already abandoned the expedition, saying: "I hope soon to see you in Quebec."[2] About this time it seems that the order of march by companies was given up, and all were urged, in their extremity, to push on with all possible speed towards the French settlements, to which Arnold himself was hastening, to obtain supplies.

A few extracts from the journals of the soldiers will illustrate their condition better than any language I can use. Henry says:

"October 29th our provisions were exhausted. We had no meat of any kind. The flour was divided, and each man had five pints, and it was baked into five cakes, under the ashes, in the way of Indian bread."[3]

"We slept on fir branches, and on awakening in the morning, and the blanket thrown from my head, what was my surprise to find we had slept under at least four inches of snow."[4]

Henry gives the details of the misfortunes of a poor drummer named Shafer, who had defective eye-sight. His mishaps, sometimes ludicrous, often pathetic, were caused by his imperfect sight. Some mischievous or heartless soldiers had stolen all his last five cakes. The mess of which Henry was a party first laughed at him, and then gave him a cup full of flour and Henry gave him his own third cake. Often in crossing the gullies and ravines, the soldiers would cross on a log which had been blown down by the wind, or the ax men had felled. Often poor Shafer wou'd tumble off, drum and all, and he was, as Henry says, "the laughing stock" of the soldiers, but to Henry himself an object of compassion. Yet this poor drummer, half blind, starving, and almost, naked, "bore his drum uninjured to Quebec

---

[1] Maine His. Col., Vol. I, pp. 477-8.
[2] Maine His. Col., p. 478.
[3] Henry's Journal, pp. 59-62.
[4] Henry's Journal, p. 63.

when many strong and hale men died in the wilderness."[1]

Henry describes the endurance of the wife of Sergeant Greer, who was, he says, "a large, virtuous and respectable woman," accompanying her husband and the soldiers in their march. They encountered a pond frozen over with ice; breaking the ice with their hands and guns, they marched on and soon found themselves "waist deep in water." He was astonished by the endurance of Mrs. Greer, as she raised her clothes more than waist high, 'to keep them dry.' She waded before me to firm ground, and no one dared intimate a disrespectful idea of her."[2]

"Marching on, without even the path of the savage to guide us, we found a batteau to take us across which the providence of Col. Arnold had stationed there for our accommodation."[3]

"Thus we proceeded, the pale and meager looks of my companions tottering on their feeble limbs, * * and coming to a sandy beach of the Chaudiere, some men of our company were observed to dart from the file, and with their nails tear out of the sand roots which they deemed eatable, and eat them raw. Powerful men struggled, even with blows, for these roots, such was the extremity of their hunger. During the day's march (Nov. 2), I sat down on the end of a log, absolutely fainting with hunger and fatigue A party of soldiers were making a broth. They gave me a cup of it." It had a greenish hue, and Henry tasted it. It was made of a dog, a large black Newfoundland, which had belonged to Captain Dearborn, and though a great favorite, and the faithful companion of their march, it was given up to appease the cravings of their hunger. "They eat," says

[1]. Henry's Journal, p. 63.
[2]. Henry's Journal, p. 67.
[3]. Henry's Journal, p. 67.

Dearborn, "every part of him, not excepting his entrails,' and then collected the bones to pound up and make broth for another meal." There was only one other dog in the detachment. This, too, was killed and eaten. Old moose-hide breeches were boiled and then broiled on the coals and eaten. Some tried to make soup out of their old deerskin moccasins, but, although the poor fellows boiled them long, they were leather still. Many died from fatigue and hunger, frequently in four or five minutes after giving up and sitting down. Henry says these hardships produced among the men a willingness to die.' But why multiply details; nothing induced these resolute men to murmur or complain.

During all their sufferings and privations, such was Arnold's influence over them, and such the confidence he had inspired, there was no murmuring. He had shared every danger; they were satisfied he was doing the best that could be done, and they believed in his ability to take them through. The hour of supreme peril came at last, and speedy relief must be had, or the men would die by the hundred from absolute starvation. Selecting a small party of the strongest men, Arnold started at 10 o'clock for the French settlement, and he made twenty miles in two hours, passing down the Chaudiere with all the speed possible. The river was rocky, rapid and dangerous, and now three of his batteaux dashing against the rocks, were stove in, losing all their baggage and provisions, and the men barely escaping with their lives. This disaster saved them all from death, for a half a mile farther on was an unknown and terrible fall, over which no boat could safely pass, and, if it had not been discovered, all would have perished. This man of iron, however, was still hopeful and determined,

1. Letter of Dearborn, quoted in Thayer's Journal—note to page 15.
2. Henry's Journal.

and, dividing the small quantity of provisions still left, and taking with him but six men and two boats, he pressed on, conscious that the lives of hundreds of his brave, patient, devoted followers, depended on his success in procuring immediate succor.

On the 30th of October, at night, he reached the first house, eighty miles from the lake, and with the next morning's sun a supply of fresh provisions and flour had started and was hastening back, with all possible speed, yet none too soon to save the lives of his famishing soldiers.'

Says one: "When we saw the cattle coming up the river that Arnold had sent, it was the joyfullest sight I ever beheld, and some could not refrain from tears."

Arnold sent careful instructions that the needy should take sparingly, and those who had provisions, to let what was sent pass on to those most in need, so that all might be relieved. On the 8th of November he wrote to Washington, giving further details of his march, and saying that the detachment had all happily arrived within two or three day's march, except "Colonel Enos' division, which, I am surprised to hear, are all gone back,"[2] and in spite of this and all other disasters, he writes hopefully of the success of the enterprise.

The journals of these "forty days in the wilderness," including Arnold's letters and journal, give a plain but vivid picture of the sufferings endured and the difficulties overcome. The men had hauled or pushed their batteaux one hundred and eighty miles, and carried them and all their contents at least forty miles on their shoulders, and yet starving, half naked, nearly frozen, "fired with a love of liberty, the men pushed on with a fortitude superior to every obstacle."[3]

---

[1] Arnold to Washington, Maine His. Col. Vol. I, p. 482.
[2] Arnold to Washington, Nov 8, 1776. Maine His. Col. Vol. I, p. 482.
[3] Letter of Arnold; Maine Hist. Col., Vol. I, p. 406.

HIS PATRIOTISM AND HIS TREASON. 69

The desertion of Enos was very nearly fatal to the expedition. The party that returned took back with them, according to Dr. Senter, more than their proportion of the provisions, and thus contributed to the extreme scarcity of food.[1]

On his arrival at Cambridge, Enos was put under arrest by Washington, tried, and although acquitted (the witnesses against him, many of them, being where he ought to have been—in Canada), yet he never acquired again the confidence of the commander, and left the army.[2]

Washington writes to Schuyler: "In consequence of Enos' return, Arnold will not be able to make a successful attack on Quebec, without the co-operation of Montgomery."[3]

Nothing could exceed the indignation felt towards Enos, by those whom he had abandoned. Henry says, "Enos' desertion was worthy of punishment of the most exemplary kind."[4] "Enos got frightened, and with the greater part of the provisions turned back." It is somewhat surprising that the impetuous and passionate Arnold, in writing to Washington of this desertion, says only, "Colonel Enos' division, I am surprised to hear, are all gone back."[5] To which Washington replies, "Your surprise could not be greater than mine at Enos' return."[6] "I immediately put him under arrest, and had him tried for quitting your detachment without your orders."[7]

---

1. See Dr. Senter's Journal, p. 17. "We were left the alternative of accepting the small pittance, and proceed or return. The former was adopted, with the determined resolution to go through or die."
2. "His appearance excited the greatest indignation in the continental camp, and Enos was looked upon as a traitor for thus deserting his companions and endangering the whole expedition."—*Lossing's Field Book of the Revolution*, Vol. I, p. 182.
3. Force's Am. Archives, 4th S., Vol. III, p. 1708.
4. Henry's Journal, p. 182.
5. Appendix to Henry's Journal, p. 186.
6. Am. Archives, 4 S., Vol. III. p. 192.
7. Sparks' Writings of Washington, Vol. III, pp. 192-3.

70   LIFE OF BENEDICT ARNOLD.

Writing to Schuyler, Washington expresses his relief and joy at Arnold's safe arrival, and adds, "The merit of that officer is certainly great, and I heartily wish that fortune may distinguish him as one of her favorites. He will do everything which prudence and valor can suggest."[1]

Henry relates an incident, having reference to himself, illustrating the character of Arnold. As the army were approaching the St. Lawrence, Henry became so ill he could not march, and he seated himself on a log by the side of the road while the troops passed by. "In the rear," says he, "came Arnold on horseback." Seeing the young soldier sitting by the roadside, pale and dejected, Arnold halted and dismounted, ran down to the river, and hailed the owner of the house which stood opposite. The Canadian quickly came, and "took me into his boat, and Arnold placing two silver dollars in my hand, the Frenchman carried me to his house," and there he was kindly cared for until he was able to join his comrades.[2][3]

An officer in the expedition, writing from near Quebec, Nov. 21st, gives his impressions of Arnold. "Our commander," says he, "is a gentleman worthy of the trust reposed in him; a man, I believe, of invincible courage, of great prudence; ever serene, he defies the greatest danger to affect him, or difficulties to alter his temper; in fine, you will ever find him the intrepid hero and the unruffled Christian."[4]

Such appeared Arnold to his comrades on the march to Canada.

The candid student of history, after reading the various journals of this expedition, including the modest one of Arnold, and his letters to Washington, will not, I think,

[1] Am. Arch. 4 S., Vol. IV, p. 191.
[2] Henry's Journal, p. 77.
[3] The praise of the soldiers he led to Boston, of being "a very humane and tender officer," seems to have been well merited.
[4] Henry's Journal, appendix, p. 185.

withhold the conclusion that it was conducted with consummate ability. During all the difficulties I have attempted to describe, all testimony concurs in establishing that the leader possessed great executive ability; that he was resolute, ever thoughtful, vigilant and active, and sagacious in overcoming obstacles. He had such control over his men that none subject to the magnetism of his personal presence yielded to despondency. It was those only who were behind with Enos who harbored the thought of abandoning the enterprise. This power of inspiring men with enthusiasm, holding them up to a high purpose in the face of danger, is rare, and has always marked the great leaders of men. This power was exhibited by Arnold in a very remarkable degree, not only in this expedition, but in the hard battles which he afterwards fought. Washington, as we shall see in the progress of this narrative, recognized this power and sent him to the post of danger, not only on account of his courage, but also because of his power over the militia and his ability to make them fight like veterans.

In the midst of solitude, far from succor, cold, ill-clad, sometimes freezing, often nearly starved, nothing but enthusiasm for their cause, and perfect confidence in their leader, could have created and held them up to their resolute purpose. It is impossible to read the details of the expedition without being struck with wonder at the energy and perseverance which surmounted such obstacles. The intelligent and impartial foreign historian, Botta, speaks of the achievement as entitling its leader to be ranked "among the great captains of antiquity." But for Arnold's treason, this march and the assault upon Quebec would have been a favorite theme of poetry and eloquence, and the record thereof one of the brightest pages in American history. Is it just to his brave associates to say nothing of Arnold himself, to rob them of their well-earned glory, because it would illuminate a traitor's name! The sober and measured language of Washington warms into pathos, and almost passionate eloquence, when speaking of their exploits and sufferings. Indeed, such was the impression that Arnold's difficulties and conduct made upon him, that he closes his letter of December 5th with the prayer: "That the Almighty may preserve and prosper you, in the glorious work you have begun, is the sincere and fervent prayer of, dear sir, etc."[1]

This expedition has been compared to that of Napoleon crossing the Alps, the retreat of the 10,000 described by Xenophon, and to Bonaparte's retreat from Moscow; but in justice to the American soldiers, it should be remembered that this was an advance and not a retreat. Every difficulty overcome placed them nearer the enemy, and farther from their friends. Every obstacle they surmounted was a barrier against retreat. Taking it altogether, it is not extravagant to say that for tough endurance and unflinching courage, it is difficult to find its parallel.[2]

1. Sparks' Writings of Washington, Vol. III, p. 192.

2. In a letter dated Nov. 27, Arnold gives a brief summing up of the expedition: "Thus in about eight weeks we completed a march of near 600 miles, not to be paralleled in history; the men having, with the greatest fortitude and perseverance brought their batteaux up rapid streams, being obliged to wade almost the whole way, near one hundred and eighty miles; carried them on their shoulders near forty miles, over swamps and bogs almost impenetrable, and up to their knees in mire, being often obliged to cross them three or four times with their baggage. Short of provisions, part of the detachment disheartened and gone back, famine staring us in the face; an enemy's country and uncertainty ahead. Notwithstanding all these obstacles, the officers and men, inspired with a love of liberty and their country, pushed on with a fortitude superior to every obstacle, and most of them had not one day's provisions for a week."—*Maine His. Col. of Vol. I, pp. 495-6*

CHAPTER IV.

ASSAULT UPON QUEBEC.

"It is not in the power of any man to command success, but you have done more; you have deserved it."—*Washington to Arnold.* (1)

"'Tis not in mortals to command success,
But we'll do more, Sempronius, we'll deserve it."
—*Addison's Cato.*

ARNOLD HOLDS AN INDIAN COUNCIL—HIS SPEECH TO THE INDIANS—CROSSES THE ST. LAWRENCE—CLIMBS TO THE PLAINS OF ABRAHAM, AND MENACES QUEBEC—RECEIVES THANKS OF WASHINGTON AND SCHUYLER—MONTGOMERY AND ARNOLD ASSAULT QUEBEC—MONTGOMERY KILLED—ARNOLD SHOT WHILE LEADING THE "FORLORN HOPE"—MADE A BRIGADIER-GENERAL—BLOCKADES QUEBEC.

THE energy and activity of Colonel Arnold saved his detachment from actual starvation, but it taxed both to the utmost. A few hours more without relief would have seen many of his gallant men helpless and dying in the forest.

By the 8th of November nearly all of the detachment, except the rear division, had reached his camp at the French settlements. The men came straggling in, singly, in squads of small parties, and in companies. Their commander immediately set about re-organizing "the straggling and emaciated troops."[2] On the 4th of November, while the soldiers were coming in, a body of Indians occupying as their hunting grounds a part of the territory over which Arnold had marched, waited upon him at Sartignan, and with all the formality and dignity which characterize an

---
1. Sparks' Writings of Washington, Vol. III, p. 192.
2. Henry's Journal, p. 76.

(73)

Indian council, demanded the cause of his entering upon their territory.

Colonel Arnold made a formal reply, saying:

"FRIENDS AND BRETHREN:—I feel myself very happy in meeting with so many of my brethren from the different quarters of the great country, and more so, as I find we meet as friends, and that we are equally concerned in this expedition. Brothers, we are the children of those people who have now taken up the hatchet against us. More than one hundred years ago we were all as one family. We then differed in our religion, and came over to this great country by consent of the king. Our fathers bought land of the savages, and have grown a great people — even as the stars in the sky. We have planted the ground, and by our labor grown rich. Now a new king and his wicked great men want to take our lands and money without our consent. This we think unjust, and all our great men, from the river St. Lawrence to the Mississippi, met together at Philadelphia, where they all talked together, and sent a prayer to the king that they would be brothers and fight for him, but would not give up their lands and money. The king would not hear our prayer, but sent a great army to Boston and endeavored to set our brethren against us in Canada. The king's army at Boston came out into the fields and houses, killed a great many women and children while they were peaceably at work. The Bostonians sent to their brethren in the country, and they came in unto their relief, and in six days raised an army of fifty thousand men, and drove the king's troops on board their ships, killed and wounded fifteen hundred of their men. Since that they durst not come out of Boston. Now we hear the French and Indians in Canada have sent to us that the king's troops oppress them, and make them pay a great price for their rum, etc., press them to take up arms against the Bostonians, their brethren, who have done them no hurt. By the desire of the French and Indians, our brothers, we have come to their assistance, with an intent to drive out the king's soldiers; when drove off, we will return to our own country, and leave this to the peaceable enjoyment of its proper inhabitants.

Now if the Indians, our brethren, will join us, we will be very much obliged to them, and will give them one Portuguese per month, two dollars bounty, and find them their provisions, and the liberty to choose their own officers."[1]

This remarkable and curious speech had the desired effect. A treaty was entered into; the principal chief, Natanis, with his brother Sabatis, with about fifty war-

---

1. Journal of Dr. Isaac Senter, p. 23.

riors, joined the expedition, and served faithfully in the efforts against Quebec. The French and Canadians kindly welcomed "the Bostonians," as they called the soldiers of the United Colonies, furnished them with supplies, and gave such manifestations of friendship as encouraged the officers of the expedition to hope for their active aid and co-operation. The detachment being again organized, were not permitted to linger; for Arnold, ever sanguine, still entertained hopes of surprising Quebec. The beautiful valley of the Chaudiere spread out before them, and across the St. Lawrence was Quebec, the city and fortress, for the capture of which they had been so long toiling. The weary soldiers would gladly have lingered to recruit their exhausted strength; but, says an officer in his journal, "we were not permitted to tarry at any place, but marched as fast as our strength would admit, to Point Levi."[1] All along the march Arnold caused to be distributed a manifesto from Washington to the Canadians, which had been prepared, translated into French, and printed before his departure from Cambridge, assuring them of the friendship of the United Colonies, and asking their co-operation and assistance. The people were treated with the utmost kindness and respect, and nothing was left undone to conciliate their good will.

Such was the celerity of Arnold's movements, that within ten days after his arrival at the settlements with his five or six attendants, he had gathered in, and reorganized his men; had marched seventy-five miles to Point Levi, and by the thirteenth of December all his soldiers, except the sick and disabled, had gathered around him; and now across the St. Lawrence towered the citadel of Quebec. The walls of the city were bristling with heavy ordnance. The British authorities, apprised of his approach, had burned

---

1. See Appendix to Henry's Journal, p. 188.

every boat on the river, and sentineled the channel with vessels of war. Could he have found the means of crossing immediately on his arrival, it is probable Quebec would have fallen into his hands.[1] "We tarried at Point Levi nearly a week, during which time we were busy in preparing to cross the river; being obliged to purchase birch-bark canoes twenty miles distant and carry them by land, the regulars having burned all near them as soon as they heard of our approach."[2] During this time there had prevailed a terrible storm of wind and sleet, which rendered any attempt to cross impossible; meanwhile the garrison had been strengthened by troops from Newfoundland and from the Sorell, under McLain. The storm having abated, on the thirteenth, at nine o'clock at night, Arnold with his bark canoes succeeded in eluding a British frigate and sloop, and other vessels stationed in the river to intercept him; and before he was discovered, had landed five hundred men at Wolfe's Cove, leaving one hundred and fifty on the other side unable to cross.

At daybreak on the following morning, he and his troops had climbed the difficult path and formed his little army on the plains of Abraham. Here, sixteen years before, Wolfe had died at the hour of victory, repeating the lines of his favorite poet Gray,

"The paths of glory lead but to the grave."

His victory and death had given him a monument in Westminster Abbey, and his name had been added to the roll of heroes which illustrate the records of England's military glory. Were the Americans and their leader, now

---

[1] When Arnold appeared opposite Quebec, "this daring spirit was moved to an immediate advance. That instant of time was one of those which contain vast possibilities, and Arnold was a man peculiarly prompt to seize opportunities for daring adventure."—*Carrington's Battles of the Revolution*, p. 130.

[2] Letter of an officer of the expedition published in the appendix to Henry's Journal, p. 184.

standing on this historic "plain," less brave and meritorious than those who overcame Montcalm?

How did the enterprise of Wolfe and that of Arnold compare in point of difficulty and danger? When Wolfe led his troops to the plains of Abraham, his fleet consisting of twenty-two ships of the line, completely commanded the river, while Arnold had crossed in frail bark canoes and landed his soldiers by stealth, the St. Lawrence being absolutely controlled by British men-of-war.

Wolfe had an army of thousands of well trained, well equipped, well armed veterans, while the Americans did not exceed six hundred effective men—and these in rags, bare-footed, worn with fatigue, armed with damaged muskets, and without artillery; yet, with these few men, and relying on the friendly feeling of the people within the city, and of the Canadian militia, Arnold determined, if possible, to provoke a sally and an attack by the garrison, as Wolfe had done. He marched his men up to the walls, gave cheers. to which some of the citizens responded, and tried by every means to provoke an attack, but in vain; wiser but less chivalrous than Montcalm, the English kept within the shelter of their walls.[1] Arnold says, "my men were in want of everything but stout hearts, and would have gladly met the enemy, whom we endeavored in vain to draw out of the city."[2]

The garrison at this time, including regulars, marines and militia, were some eighteen hundred strong, but such were the fears felt by Lieutenant Governor Cramaha and Colonel McLain of the loyalty of the inhabitants and of the militia, and so great were the apprehensions created by the assailants,

---

[1] "Suppose the Marquis of Montcalm not to quit his intrenched lines to accept that strange challenge (of Wolfe) * * * and what becomes of the glory of the young hero?"—*Thackeray's Henry Esmond.*

[2] This act of Arnold has been condemned as "silly bravado," but a similar act of Montgomery, where the superiority of the garrison over his troops was equally great, has not been so characterized.

that with all their superiority of numbers, they would not venture outside the walls. Arnold then sent a flag demanding the surrender of the city, but the bearer of it was fired upon.[1] Hearing that Sir Guy Carleton was approaching with reinforcements from up the river, and after finding that he had ammunition only for five rounds to a man, Arnold thought it prudent to retire; and he succeeded in taking his troops to Point aux Trembles, twenty miles above Quebec, there to await the arrival of Montgomery, who was approaching. This retreat was none too soon, for he had scarcely reached his camp when the great guns of Quebec announced the arrival of Sir Guy Carleton, the same who had been a subaltern under Wolfe at the time of his victory over Montcalm. Washington, with a generous appreciation, never blind to the merits of his subordinates, wrote to Arnold, saying, "It is not in the power of any man to command success; but you have done more—you have deserved it." At this time, ignorant of his retreat from the walls of the city, he adds: "I hope you have met with the laurels which were due to your trials in the possession of Quebec." "My thanks are sincerely offered to you for your enterprise and persevering spirit." And on another occasion, Washington, after expressing his hopes for Arnold's success, says: "Then you will have added the only link wanting in the great chain of continental union, and rendered the freedom of your country secure."[2] General Schuyler, writing to Washington, says: "Colonel Arnold has great merit. He has been peculiarly unfortunate that one-third of his troops left him. If the whole had been with him when he arrived at Quebec, he would probably have had the sole honor of giving that important place to America."[3]

1. Maine His. Soc. Col. Vol. I, p. 494.
2. Am. Archives, 4th S., Vol. IV, p. 192.
3. Am. Archives, 4th S., Vol. IV, p. 226

The alarm of the Canadians on seeing these resolute men emerge from the wilderness, was very great. Their march through the forests and over the mountains seemed almost incredible, and the most exaggerated reports of their numbers, their skill with the rifle, and indomitable prowess, spread through the country.

This alarm—panic would describe it more accurately—prevented the English from attacking the Americans. Some acts of Arnold which have been criticised as "vanity" and "bravado," were among the means he used to keep up this alarm, he being one of those who act upon the principle that boldness, even to temerity, is sometimes prudence. "They best succeed who dare."

On the 19th of November Carleton arrived at Quebec, and his coming inspired the loyalists with hope and confidence. Montgomery, who had succeeded to the command of Schuyler's army, had thus far been brilliantly successful. He had captured St. Johns and Montreal, and came down the St. Lawrence, hoping to complete his career of triumph by taking Quebec. But his troops were undisciplined and sometimes turbulent, so that his authority over them rested largely upon his personal influence. The time of the enlistment of many of them having expired at the approach of winter, rendered them unwilling to remain, and he was left with eight hundred men only with which to garrison Montreal and go down to aid Arnold in the capture of Quebec. On the third of December he reached Arnold's camp at Point aux Trembles, and brought with him but three hundred men. He however brought clothing and stores, to relieve the necessities and sufferings of the hardy men who gladly welcomed him. He found only six hundred and seventy-five of those who had left Cambridge; these he relieved, and was impressed by them, as he says, "with a style of discipline much superior to what I have been used to see in this campaign." "Colonel Arnold's corps," says he, "is an exceedingly fine one, and he himself is active, intelligent and enterprising."[1]

Montgomery and Arnold seem, from their letters, to have inspired each other with mutual respect and confidence, and there was the most cordial co-operation between them. Both were young, enthusiastic, and fired with a love of glory. At the time of the assault Montgomery was thirty-seven, and Arnold thirty-four years of age.[2] On the 5th of December this little army, not exceeding one thousand men, with a regiment of two hundred Canadian volunteers, which Arnold had raised, and a few Indians who had followed him from the wilds of Maine, marched down towards Quebec, unquestionably the strongest fortified city in America, defended by two hundred cannon and a garrison of double the number of the assailants. The assault must be made at an early day, for the terms of the enlistment of a large number of the New England men would expire on the 31st of December, and many had left families at home to which they were impatient to return. Montgomery sent a flag demanding the surrender of the town. It was fired upon, as was that sent by Arnold, and refused admittance. Then, following the example of Arnold, he sent "a menacing and extravagant letter" to the commander, but Carleton refused to hold "any kind of parley with rebels."[3] "To the storming we must come at last," said the gallant Montgomery.

A council of war was called and the two leaders, sustained by their subordinates, resolved on the desperate and almost forlorn hope of an assault. It was arranged that Montgomery should attack the lower town by the way of Cape Diamond on the river, and Arnold on the side of St.

[1] Montgomery to Schuyler, Dec. 5th, 1775; Am. Archives, 4th S., Vol. IV, p. 189.
[2] The monument to Montgomery in St. Paul's church-yard, New York, states that he was aged 37 years at the time of his death.
[3] Lossing's Life of Schuyler, Vol. I, p. 486.

Roque, while two feigned attacks were to be made on other parts of the city. On the last day of the year, in the midst of a driving snow-storm, Montgomery and Arnold led in person the two assaulting parties. The troops were started at two A. M., and that they might recognize each other in the darkness and storm, each soldier wore on his cap a band of white paper, on which many wrote the electric words "Liberty or death." For many of those gallant fellows, there was to be no to-morrow, no *New Year's* day. Yet they were cheerful, confiding in their leaders and hopeful of success. Montgomery at the head of his party marched from his quarters at Holland house, to Wolfe's Cove, thence for two miles along the shore of the St. Lawrence to the barrier under Cape Diamond. The carpenters instantly began to saw off the pickets; entering the opening thus made, Montgomery found himself, with his aids, in advance of his troops, and sent back messengers to hurry them forward; continuing to press onward himself, until, directly in his front, a log house with loop-holes for muskets and a battery of two three-pounders intercepted his passage. This log house was held by a party of British soldiers and seamen, and as Montgomery and his party approached, "a part of the guard was seized with a panic; but the commander restored order and the sailors stood at their guns with lighted linstocks." Montgomery paused inside the pickets until about sixty of his men joined him, then shouting, "Men of New York, you will not fear to follow where your general leads; come on, my brave boys, and Quebec is ours!" he rushed forward towards the battery. As he and his party came running up, the cannon, loaded with grape-shot, were discharged into their breasts, and Montgomery, his aid McPherson, and young Cheeseman, and ten others, instantly fell. Their leaders killed, the column broke and fled. This left the garrison free to concentrate all its force upon the attack Arnold was making on the northeastern side of the town, he himself leading the "forlorn hope" of about twenty-five men.

Had Montgomery and Arnold made the assault with experienced soldiers, both would have been justly censured for the great personal exposure which resulted in the death of one and the severe wounding of the other; removing them at the moment their services were most needed. But each led militia, many of whom had probably never been under serious fire, and while these troops would cheerfully follow and obey the order—" Come on, boys "—they might hesitate and falter if told to " go ahead, boys." Arnold, therefore, as usual with him, led the forlorn hope, marching about one hundred yards before the main body.[1]

As he reached Palace Gate, in the midst of a wild storm, the alarm was ringing from all the bells of the city, drums were beating, and the artillery opened upon him. With their fearless leader at their front, the party ran along in single file, bending down their heads to avoid the storm, and covering their guns with their coats to keep their powder dry. Lamb, with a field-piece upon a sled, and Morgan, with his riflemen, followed. The first barrier was at the Sault au Matelot; approaching this the party found themselves in a narrow way, swept by a battery, with soldiers firing upon them from houses on each side of the passage. Arnold, advancing rapidly towards the barrier, cheering his men to the assault, was struck by a musket ball, at the moment of its capture. His leg was broken and he fell forward upon the snow. Rising with great effort, being able to use only one leg, he endeavored to press forward, and refused to be carried from the field until the main body came up. Dr. Senter, who accompanied the expedition as

---

[1]. "Arnold, leading the forlorn hope, advanced perhaps one hundred yards before the main body."—*Henry's Journal*, p. 107.

surgeon, says: "Daylight had scarcely made its appearance ere Colonel Arnold was brought in, supported by two soldiers, wounded in the leg by a piece of a musket ball."[1] "Now," says Henry, "we saw Colonel Arnold returning, wounded in the leg, supported by two gentlemen. Arnold called to the troops in a cheering voice as we passed, urging us forward."[2] His steps from the barricade to the hospital could be traced by the blood which flowed from his wound.

Meanwhile, Morgan, Porterfield, Greene, and others, pressing up and forward, carried the battery and took the guard prisoners; they pressed on to the second barricade, and the most heroic efforts were made to carry it, also. The voice of the gallant Morgan could be heard above the storm, cheering on his riflemen to the assault; but, unsupported by others, they were too few to succeed.

Some retreated; more, including Morgan, Greene, Meigs, Hendricks and others, of the gallant band who followed Arnold through the wilderness, were compelled to surrender. While his detachment was still fighing, Arnold, "not for a moment forgetful of his duty," writes from the hospital to Wooster, in command at Montreal, giving an account of the disaster as far as known, and asking for reinforcements.[3] As reports of continued disasters came into the hospital where he lay,

"We entreated Colonel Arnold," says Dr. Senter, "for his own safety to be carried back into the country, where they could not readily find him, but to no purpose. He would neither be removed nor suffer a man from the hospital to retreat. He ordered his pistols loaded, with a sword on his bed, adding, he was determined to kill as many as possible, if they came into the room. We were now all soldiers; even to the wounded in their beds were ordered a gun by their side, that, if they did attack the

1. "Two-thirds of the ball entered the outer side of the leg, about midway, and in an oblique course between the tibia and the fibula, and lodged in the muscle at the rise of the tendon Achilles."—*Dr. Isaac Senter's Journal*, p. 84.
2. Henry's Journal, p. 109.
3. Lossing's Life of Schuyler, Vol. I, p. 502.

hospital, to make the most vigorous defense possible. Orders were also sent out into the villages round the city, to the captains of the militia, to immediately assemble to our assistance."[1]

Carleton, still distrusting the loyalty of the people, sent out no troops in pursuit, and the American camp was undisturbed. On the sixth of January, Arnold, still in the hospital, writes:[2]

"The command of the army by the death of my truly great and good friend, General Montgomery, devolves upon me, a task I find too heavy under my present circumstances. I received a wound by a ball through my left leg, at the time I had gained the first battery at the lower town, which, by loss of blood, rendered me very weak. As soon as the main body came up, I retired to the hospital, near a mile, on foot, being obliged to draw one leg after me, and a great part of the way under the continued fire of the enemy from the walls, at no greater distance than fifty yards."

But, notwithstanding his wound, his eyes were fastened longingly on the walls of Quebec, "and," says this indomitable man, "I have no thoughts of leaving this proud town until I first enter it in triumph." * * "My wound has been exceedingly painful, but is now easy"; and "the Providence which has carried me through so many dangers is still my protection." * * "I am in the way of my duty and know no fear."

Had the ball that shattered his leg, pierced his heart, his would have been associated with the names of Wolfe and Montgomery, among the heroes who have died for their country. But there was work for him yet to do in aiding to achieve the independence of his country. Patriot blood still coursed through his heart, and he was destined, on still more sanguinary battle-fields, to shed that blood freely, for his country ; and then attempt to betray it. His

1. Senter's Journal, p. 35.
2. Am. Archives, 4th S., Vol. IV, p. 589.

services were effective—Providence rendered his treason abortive.

As soon as the news of the attack upon Quebec reached Congress, that body unanimously promoted him to the rank of Brigadier General, as a reward for his gallantry in the assault, as well as for his skill, address and energy in conducting his army through the wilderness. On the thirteenth of February, he wrote to Congress, returning thanks for his promotion, which, says he, "I shall study to deserve."[1]

Schuyler, writing to Washington, and referring to the attack on Quebec, says, with manly feeling: "The gallant Montgomery is no more! the brave Arnold is wounded, and we have met with a severe check in an unsuccessful attack upon Quebec."[2]

Washington replies with equal feeling: "I condole with you on the fall of the brave and worthy Montgomery," * * "and I am much concerned for the intrepid and enterprising Arnold."

Grateful for the kind consideration and good wishes which Washington's letters had expressed, Arnold replies: "I am greatly obliged for your good wishes and the concern you express for me. Sensible of the vast importance of this country, you may be assured, my utmost exertions shall not be wanting to effect your wishes in adding it to the United Colonies. I am able to hobble about my room, though my leg is a little contracted and weak; I hope soon to be ready for action."[3] Some historians, unwilling to commend and industriously seeking cause of complaint against Arnold, have criticised his conduct at Quebec, suggesting that if he had done this, or that he might have succeeded. To such critics, let Washington's letters reply. This calm,

1. Am. Archives, 4th S., Vol. IV, p. 1017.
2. Irving's Washington, p. 463.
3. Am. Archives, 4th S., Vol. IV, p. 1574.

just man, who understood all the facts and difficulties, had no language but that of unqualified praise and approbation. Had Arnold been killed instead of Montgomery, no words would have been too strong to have expressed the commendation of his country.

Sir Guy Carleton treated the prisoners he had captured with great kindness. Montgomery had been a fellow soldier with him in the British army, and both had been present at the storming of Quebec in 1759. Learning by a communication from Arnold that Montgomery had upon his person, when he fell, a watch which the widow of this gallant soldier desired to obtain, he sent it to her through the American commander.[1] The gallantry of Montgomery and Arnold; the death of one and the severe wound of the other, created a profound sensation throughout the United Colonies. As they had been joined as first and second in command, and as each had fallen at the head of his troops, their names were associated together, and both were for the time the popular idols.[2]

---

1. "Montgomery had a watch on his person which Mrs. Montgomery was very desirous of obtaining. She made her wish known to Arnold, who sent word to Carleton that any sum would be paid for it. Carleton immediately sent the watch to Arnold, and refused to receive anything in return."—*Lossing's Field Book of Revolution, Vol. I, p. 200.*

2. As one evidence of this the Pennsylvania committee of safety in March, 1776, fitted out a sloop-of-war, and named her "The Montgomery," and a floating battery which they named "The Arnold."—*Am. Archives, 4th S., Vol. V, p. 730.*

Also Oration of Dr. Smith before Congress, as follows:

Extract from "An Oration in memory of General Montgomery, and of the Officers and Soldiers who fell with him December 31st, 1775, before Quebeck; drawn up (and delivered February, 1776,) at the desire of the Honorable Continental Congress, by William Smith, D. D., Provost of the College and Academy of Philadelphia."—*Am. Archives, 4th S., Vol. IV, pp. 1775, 1776.*

After speaking of Montgomery in the highest terms, the orator says:

"Leaving him, therefore, for a while—alas, too short a while—to enjoy the noblest of all triumphs, the applause of his country, and the conscious testimony of his own heart, let us inquire after another band of brave and hardy men, who are stemming rapid rivers, ascending pathless mountains, traversing unpeopled deserts, and hastening through deep morasses and gloomy woods to meet him in scenes of another issue.

Arnold, though confined to the hospital with his wound, and surrounded with every imaginable difficulty, had no thought of giving up the enterprise. With a force less by half than the garrison of Quebec, he kept up the blockade. General Wooster, then in command, writes to Congress, February fourteenth: "General Arnold has, in a most surprising manner, kept up the blockade of Quebec, and that with half the number of the enemy." And on the twenty-fifth of February, he writes to Washington, saying: "General Arnold, to his great honor, kept up the blockade with

---

——————"Deserts in vain
Opposed their course, and deep rapacious floods,
And mountains in whose jaws destruction grinn'd,
Hunger and toil—*Armenian* shores and storms!
Greece in their view, and glory yet untouched,
They held their fearless way—oh! strength of mind
Almost almighty in severe extremes!"—*Thomson.*

This praise was paid to ten thousand heroes, sustaining every danger, in a retreat to their own country, and is certainly due, so far as heroism is concerned, to less than a tenth part of the number, marching through equal difficulties against a capital of a hostile country.

Even the march of *Hannibal* over the *Alps*, so much celebrated in history (allowing for the disparity of numbers,) has nothing in it of superior merit to the march of *Arnold;* and in many circumstances there is a most striking simititude. The former had to encounter the rapid *Rhone;* the latter the more rapid Kennebeck, through an immense length of country. The former, when he came to quit the river, found his farther passage barred by mountains, rearing their snowy crests to the sky, rugged, wild, uncultivated. This was also the case with the latter, whose troops, carrying their boats and baggage, were obliged to cross and recross the same mountains sundry times. At the foot of the mountains the former was deserted by three thousand of his army, desponding at the length of the way, and terrified at the hideous view of those stupendous heights, which they considered as impassable. In like circumstances, about a third part of the army of the latter, deserted, shall I say, or use the more courteous language, "returned home." The march of the former was about twelve hundred miles in five months. The Virginia and Pennsylvania rifle companies belonging to the latter, including their first march from their own habitations to Cambridge, and thence to Quebec, marched near the same distance in about three months.

Besides these rifle companies, *Arnold's* corps consisted of about five hundred New England troops, who sustained all the fatigues of the worst part of the march by land and water, with the utmost fortitude. And Gen. Montgomery, ever ready to do justice to merit, having joined them before Quebeck, gives their commander and them this character: "They are an exceedingly fine body of men; inured to fatigue, with a style of discipline among them much superior to what I have been used to see this campaign. He, himself, is active, intelligent and enterprising."

such a handful of men that the story when told hereafter will scarcely be believed."[1]

Washington, writing to Congress, says: "It (the blockade) exhibits fresh proofs of Arnold's ability and perseverance in the midst of difficulties."[2]

On the first of April, Wooster arrived from Montreal with reinforcements, and assumed the command. The day after, Arnold, only partially recovered from his wound, received a serious injury while visiting the outposts, by the fall of his horse. When somewhat recovered, being in favor of more active measures than General Wooster adopted, and impatient of inaction, he asked and obtained leave to report at Montreal, where, upon his arrival, he took command. In a letter to General Schuyler, dated April 20th, he explains his reasons for going to Montreal, and adds, "had I been able to take any active part, I should by no means have left camp, but as General Wooster did not think proper to consult me, I am convinced I shall be more useful here than in camp, and he very readily granted me leave of absence."[3] With the departure of Arnold from the camp, all vigorous efforts in the field to capture Quebec and unite the Canadas with the United Colonies terminated. Had the efforts of Washington, Schuyler, Montgomery, and Arnold been successful—had the Canadas joined the American Union—what changes in history would have ensued! Possibly the power of the free States thus strengthened might have prevented the extension of slavery, and slavery itself might possibly have been abolished without the great civil war.

[1] Am. Archives, 4th S., Vol, IV, p. 999; ditto, p. 1493.
[2] Sparks' Writings of Washington, Vol. III, p. 276.
[3] "Arnold was discontented at not being permitted to continue his authority at a season when he might have struck a daring and effectual blow."—*Introduction to Journal of Charles Carroll, of Carrollton*, p. 15.

CHAPTER V.

RETREAT FROM CANADA.

"I am content to be the last man who quits this country, and fall so that my country may rise."—*Arnold to Sullivan.*

THE AFFAIR AT THE CEDARS—VISIT OF FRANKLIN, CHASE AND CARROLL TO ARNOLD'S QUARTERS—THE SEIZURE OF GOODS IN MONTREAL—TRIAL OF COLONEL HAZEN BY COURT-MARTIAL—CONTROVERSY BETWEEN ARNOLD AND THE COURT—CHARGES AGAINST ARNOLD BY LIEUT. COL. JOHN BROWN—ACTION THEREON BY WOOSTER, SCHUYLER AND GATES—CHARGES DECLARED BY CONGRESS TO BE CRUEL AND GROUNDLESS—ARNOLD'S RETREAT FROM CANADA.

JOHN MARSHALL, Chief Justice of the United States, in his life of Washington, speaking of the expedition against Quebec, and summing up the case with judicial calmness and accuracy, says:

"It was a bold, and at one time promised to be a successful, effort to annex this extensive province to the United Colonies. The disposition of the Canadians favored the measure, and had Quebec fallen, there is reason to believe the colony would have entered cordially into the Union. Had Arnold been able to reach Quebec a few days sooner, or to cross the St. Lawrence on his first arrival, or had the gallant Montgomery not fallen in the assault on the thirty first of December, it is probable the the expedition would have been crowned with complete success. But the radical causes of the failure were the lateness of the season when the troops were assembled, a deficit in the preparation, and still more, the shortness of the term for which the men were enlisted."[1]

The means placed at the command of the officers never approached the estimates which they made as adequate to accomplish the result. Arnold, in one of his letters, says:

---
1. Marshall's Life of Washington, Vol. I, p. 66.

"We labor under almost as many difficulties as the Israelites did of old—obliged to make brick without straw." Yet he was the last to abandon the hope of success.

In April, 1776, the commissioners appointed by Congress to visit Canada, consisting of Benjamin Franklin, Samuel Chase, and Charles Carroll, of Carrollton, arrived at the camp of General Arnold, at Montreal. The Rev. John Carroll, brother of Charles, and the first Roman Catholic Arch-Bishop of the United States, accompanied the party, with the hope of enlisting the Roman Catholic clergy in Canada on the side of the United Colonies.[1] Carroll, in his Journal, says: "We were received by General Arnold in the most polite and friendly manner, conducted to headquarters, where a genteel company of ladies and gentlemen had assembled to welcome our arrival." A salute by the cannon of the citadel was fired. "We supped at the General's."[2]

Benjamin Franklin, then seventy years of age, honored and venerated as a sage and patriot on both sides of the Atlantic, Chase, and Carroll, of Carrolton, at supper, the guests of Benedict Arnold, grace being said by him who was the first Roman Catholic Arch-Bishop of the United States, would constitute a group for the artist. Modern reporting had not then been invented, otherwise we might have had the discussion of the Canadian campaign by these distinguished men.

In the Spring of 1776, a party of about four hundred Americans, led by Colonel Bedell, under the orders of Arnold, were holding a fortified position on the north bank of the St. Lawrence, some thirty-six miles above Montreal, on a point called "The Cedars." In May, Captain Foster, of the British army, came down the river from a place near

[1]. Journal of Charles Carroll, p. 30, Note.
[2]. Journal of Charles Carroll, p. 92, Maryland His. Society Centennial Memorial.

where Ogdensburgh now is, with about one hundred and fifty English and Canadians and five hundred Indians, under the celebrated Brant.

On hearing of their approach, not waiting for their arrival, Colonel Bedell fled to Montreal to obtain, as he said, reinforcements.[1] He left the post under the command of Major Butterfield, who, without making any efficient defense, was frightened by the threats of Indian barbarities to surrender. Both Butterfield and Bedell were afterwards tried by court-martial and cashiered for their conduct in this affair.[2] Arnold, as soon as he heard of the approach of the enemy, sent Major Sherburne, with one hundred and forty men, to strengthen the post, and prepared to follow himself. Major Butterfield, making no vigorous defense, surrendered the post the very day Sherburne would have arrived.

As the latter approached the Cedars, ignorant of the disgraceful surrender, he was caught in an ambuscade set for him by the Indians, and although surprised, he and his men fought gallantly until they were entirely surrounded and overpowered by numbers. Fifty-two were killed, many after they had ceased to resist. Arnold, indignant at Butterfield's surrender, and at the cruelties and barbarities perpetrated upon the soldiers, and on the way to their relief, hastened rapidly towards the scene of action to revenge the dead and re-take the post. Reaching St. Anne, at the western end of the island of Montreal, in advance of his boats, he was in time to see the savages conveying their prisoners from an island, almost three miles distant, to the main land. But his boats, not having yet arrived, he was without the means of instant pursuit. Dispatching messengers to hurry up the boats, he sent a friendly chief of the Caughnawaga

---

[1] See Letters of Messrs. Chase and Carroll, Am. Archives, 5th S., Vol. VI, p. 588.
[2] Am. Archives, 5th S., Vol. I, p. 747.

tribe to the hostile party, demanding the surrender of the prisoners, and declaring if the Indians injured them, he would destroy their villages, and pursue and put to the sword any one who fell into his hands. While he was waiting for his boats to come up, the Indian chief returned, bringing the reply: that they would not give up their prisoners, and that if Arnold attempted to follow and attack the British and Indians, the Indians would immediately put the prisoners to death.

Without a moments' delay, Arnold sprang into the boats which were now arriving, and proceeded as rapidly as possible to the island where the captives had been confined. All had been removed except five, and these had been robbed of their clothing, and were left nearly naked, and starving. The others, except two who were too feeble to endure the journey, had been taken to *Quince Chienze;* the two sick ones had been cruelly murdered. Arnold pushed directly for the enemy as rapidly as possible. As night approached, his flotilla of boats neared the place where the enemy were encamped, entrenched and fortified, and he was fired upon from the shore. As it was now dark, and the position of the enemy not known, he retired to St. Anne to wait for daylight; a council was held, and it was determined to attack in the morning as soon as it was light enough to see. At two o'clock at night a flag came from the British commander, bringing a cartel signed by Major Sherburne, proposing that as many British soldiers should be delivered up as there were American prisoners; but that the Americans should as soon as exchanged return to their homes, and never again bear arms against the British; hostages of American officers were to be sent to Quebec, and held until the agreement was fully executed; and Arnold was distinctly told that if he refused to ratify this agreement, the savages would put all the prisoners to death, and Captain

Foster declared his inability to prevent the execution of this terrible threat. It was a fearful dilemma. Arnold was extremely averse from entering into this agreement, and he had a force adequate to punish the barbarities already perpetrated; but he could not permit the prisoners to be sacrificed, and he finally, to save their lives, signed the agreement, after it had been so modified that the exchange of prisoners should be on equal terms. "I dispatched Lieutenant Parker," says Arnold, "to acquaint Captain Foster that I would enter into articles to exchange prisoners on equal terms—which if he refused, my determination was to attack him immediately; and if our prisoners were murdered, to sacrifice every soul which fell into our hands."[1] Arnold says, in his letter to the committee of Congress: "Words cannot express my feelings, * * torn by conflicting passions of revenge and humanity; a sufficient force to take ample revenge, raging for action, urged me on, on one hand; and humanity for five hundred unhappy wretches, who were on the point of being sacrificed if our vengeance was not delayed, plead strongly on the other."[2]

Foster yielded to the modification, and sent the agreement back signed; but Congress, regarding an agreement thus extorted by a threat of murdering prisoners of war as not binding, refused to sanction it; while Washington was inclined, though reluctantly, to execute it, because it had been entered into in due form. It was the subject of some correspondence between Washington and the British officers, but the latter finally dropt the subject. Arnold returned to Montreal, and it soon became quite clear that the forces of the colonies would soon be compelled to retire from Canada. The letters of the commissioners who had been sent by congress to that province, give a graphic picture of the condition of the army. Short enlistments, want of supplies,

[1] Am. Archives, 4th S., Vol. VI, pp. 595-6.
[2] Am. Archives, 4th S., Vol. VI, p. 596.

uncurrent paper money, and the terrible ravages of disease, especially of small pox, had finally broken the spirit of the brave men who had fought so desperately at Quebec.

The commissioners say:

"The army is in a distressed condition, and is in want of the most necessary articles—meat, bread, tents, shoes, stockings, shirts, etc. They say they were obliged to seize by force flour to supply the garrison with bread. But men with arms in their hands, will not starve when provisions can be obtained by force.[1] Soldiers without pay, without discipline, living from hand to mouth, grumbling for their pay; and when they get it, it will not buy the necessaries of life. Your military chest contains eleven thousand paper dollars, and you are indebted to your soldiers treble that sum, and to the inhabitants about fifteen thousand."

Meanwhile, England had been sending troops from Ireland, England and Germany, amounting to some thirteen thousand men; gathering strength with the purpose not only to drive the Americans out of Canada, but to follow by a powerful invasion of New York. The American troops under Thomas, who had succeeded Wooster in command, were driven from near Quebec, and pursued up the St. Lawrence to the Sorel, where Sullivan succeeded to the command.

On the thirteenth of June, Arnold wrote to General Sullivan, saying:

"The junction of the Canadas with the colonies is now at an end. Let us quit them and secure our own country before it is too late. There will be more honor in making a safe retreat than in hazarding a battle against such superiority; and which will be attended with the loss of men, artillery, etc., and the only pass to our country. * * * These arguments are not urged by fear for my personal safety; I am content to be the last man who quits this country, and fall, so that my country may rise. But let us not fall altogether."[2]

Sullivan retreated, Arnold still holding on to Montreal, that being the last place given up, and then he made a mas-

1. Am. Archives, 4th S., Vol. VI, pp. 588-590.
2. Am. Archives, 4th S., Vol. VI, p. 1104.

terly retreat to St. Johns. After seeing all the men embark, and the last boat leave the shore, he, with a single attendant, mounted his horse and rode back to reconnoitre the British army, advancing under Burgoyne. Coming in sight of the advancing columns, he satisfied himself of their numbers and character, then he wheeled his horse just in time to escape, and galloping rapidly back to the shore of the lake, stripping his horse of saddle and bridle, the animal was shot to prevent his falling into the hands of the enemy. With his own hands he pushed his boat from the shore, and leaping into it he was the last man to leave Canada. Darkness was now approaching, and it is not difficult to imagine the sad review of the incidents of the campaign which must have crowded his memory, as his boat was urged on in pursuit of his retreating soldiers. He overtook them during the night at Isle-aux-Noix.

General Sullivan, writing to Washington June 19th, says: "General Arnold pulled up the bridges on the road from Montreal, from which place he made a very prudent and judicious retreat with the enemy close at his heels."[1] He hastened on and proceeded to confer with General Schuyler, with whom all through the campaign he had kept up a constant and most friendly correspondence. Schuyler had been familiar with all his difficulties, and that officer's sympathy with his dangers had been often and most kindly expressed. Here he also met General Gates, with whom he then had the most friendly relations, as appears from the following, as well as many other letters which passed between them:

"CHAMBLAY, May 31st, 1776.

"MY DEAR GENERAL: I am a thousand times obliged to you for your kind letter of the 3d of April, of which I have a most grateful sense. I shall be ever happy in your friendship and society; and hope, with you, that our next winter-quarters will be more agreeable, though I must doubt it, if affairs go as ill with you as here. Neglected by Congress

[1] Am. Archives, 4th S., Vol. VI, p. 1104.

below; pinched with every want here; distressed with the small-pox; want of Generals and discipline in our Army—which may rather be called a great rabble—our late unhappy retreat from Quebeck, and loss of the Cedars; our credit and reputation lost, and great part of the country; and a powerful foreign enemy advancing upon us; are so many difficulties we cannot surmount them. My whole thoughts are now bent on making a safe retreat out of this country; however, I hope we shall not be obliged to leave it until we have had one bout more for the honour of America. I think we can make a stand at Isle-aux-Noix, and keep the Lake this summer from an invasion that way. We have little to fear; but I am heartily chagrined to think we have lost in one month all the immortal Montgomery was a whole campaign in gaining, together with our credit, and many men and an amazing sum of money. The commissioners this day leave us, as our good fortune has long since; but as Miss, like most other Misses, is fickle. and often changes, I still hope for her favors again; and that we shall have the pleasure of dying or living happy together.

In every vicissitude of fortune, believe me, with great esteem and friendship, my dear General, your obedient and humble servant,

"BENEDICT ARNOLD.

"To GENERAL GATES.

"P. S. For particulars respecting us I beg leave to refer you to the honourable Commissioners.

"B. A." [1]

General Gates had lately been sent by Congress to take command of the army in Northern New York, and Schuyler, Gates and Arnold now proceeded to Crown Point, to which place Sullivan had retreated. On consultation it was decided to abandon Crown Point and retreat to Ticonderoga, an act which was at first severely condemned, but in the end approved by all.

While here Arnold was involved in difficulties, growing out of the seizure of certain goods from the merchants of Montreal, for the use of the army, which have been made the basis of attacks upon his integrity. The facts are here set forth at some length, so that a just conclusion may be arrived at in regard to the charges growing out of the transaction.

1. Am. Archives, 4th S., Vol. VI, p. 649.

The condition of affairs at the time these goods were taken appears from a letter written by Arnold to the Committee of Congress, dated June second, in which he says: "I am making every possible preparation to secure our retreat. I have secured six tons of lead, ball, shot and merchandize. The inhabitants I have not as yet taken hold of; I intend to begin to-morrow. Everything is in the greatest confusion. Not one contractor, commissary or quarter-master. I am obliged to do the duty of all."[1]

It is not surprising that confusion and irregularity should exist. On the sixth of June he writes to Schuyler: "I have received your instructions respecting the tories and their effects; most of the former had absconded—great part of the latter is secured. I have sent to St. Johns a quantity of goods for use of the army, some bought, some seized."[2]

The goods were seized in accordance with orders for the use of the army; their seizure is referred to in the above letter, and the circumstances attending such seizure were fully and promptly reported by Arnold to Generals Schuyler and Sullivan. They were sent to Chamblay under the care of Major Scott, who, on his arrival there, was ordered to repair to Sorel, the guard had been ordered to return, and the goods were to be delivered to Colonel Hazen to be stored. Hazen refused to receive or care for them, and in consequence the boxes in which they were stored were broken open, and the goods plundered. What were left were sent to St. Johns, and delivered to one McCarthy, who received what was left of them, by orders of General Sullivan. Arnold's own account of the transaction is given in his reports to Generals Schuyler and Sullivan.[3]

---

1. Am. Archives, 5th S., Vol. I, p. 165.
2. Am. Archives, 4th S., Vol. VI, p. 925.
3.   "St. Johns, June 13th, 1776.
"Dear General:—I wrote you a few days since from *Montreal* that I had seized a parcel of goods for the use of the army by particular orders from the Commis-

98   LIFE OF BENEDICT ARNOLD.

Charges were made by General Arnold against Colonel Hazen for his refusal to receive and take care of these goods. A court-martial was ordered for his trial. The

<blockquote>
sioners of Congress. Our hurry and confusion was so great when the goods were received, it was impossible to take a particular account of them; every man's name was marked on his particular package, with intention to take particular account of them at *Chambly* or *St. Johns*, where the goods were ordered to be stored. Major *Scott* was sent with them, with orders to have them stored under the care of Colonel *Hazen*, who commanded at *Chambly*. On his arrival there he received orders from General *Sullivan* to repair to *Sorel*. Col. *Hazen* refused taking the goods into store, or taking charge of them. They were heaped in piles on the bank of the river. Colonel *Hazen* finally received them, and placed sentinels over them. They were, however, neglected in such a manner that great part were stolen or plundered. On receiving this intelligence, I repaired to *Chambly*. The goods were sent to *St. Johns* by Col. *Hazen*, in different parcels, all under the care of a *French* corporal; and through them I found the goods broken open, plundered and mixed together in the greatest confusion, and great part missing. Mr. *McCarthy* has General *Sullivan's* orders, and is now receiving the goods. I have sent over to *Ticonderoga* a quantity of nails and goods, the property of *Thomas Walker*, Esq., and ordered them to be stored there, and delivered to his order."—*Am. Archives*, 4th S., Vol. VI, p. 1088.

See also report to Gen. Sullivan, as follows:

"* * The junction of the *Canadians* with the Colonies—an object which brought us into this country—is now at an end. Let us quit them, and secure our own country before it is too late.

"There will be more honor in making a safe retreat than hazarding a battle against such superiority, which will doubtless be attended with the loss of men, artillery, etc., and the only pass to our country.

"These arguments are not urged by fear for my personal safety; I am content to be the last man who quits this country, and fall, so that my country rise. But let us not all fall altogether.

"The goods I seized in Montreal & sent to Chambly, under care of Major *Scott*, have been broken open, plundered and huddled together in the greatest confusion. They were taken in such a hurry it was impossible to take particular account of them. Each man's name was marked on his packages.

"When Major Scott arrived at Chambly he received your positive orders to repair to Sorel; the guard was ordered to return, and the goods to be delivered to Colonel *Hazen* to be stored. He refused receiving or taking any care of them; by which means, and Major *Scott's* being ordered away, the goods have been opened and plundered, I believe, to a large amount. It is impossible for me to distinguish each man's goods, or even settle with the proprietors. The goods are delivered to Mr. McCarthy. This is not the first or last order Colonel Hazen has disobeyed. I think him a man of too much consequence for the post he is in. I have given him orders to send directly to St. Johns all the heavy cannon, shot, powder and batteaux, valuable stores, and the sick.

"I go to Montreal immediately, and beg to have your orders as soon as possible for my future conduct.

"I am, with respect and esteem, dear General, your most obedient, humble servant,
"B. ARNOLD."

—*Am. Archives*, 4th S., Vol. VI, p. 1105.
</blockquote>

important and only witness beside himself to sustain the charges was Major Scott, who was offered by General Arnold, and the court refused to receive his testimony. This decision was palpably erroneous, and Arnold was naturally indignant, and thereupon filed his protest, saying: "As the court have refused accepting my principal evidence, Major Scott, * * I do solemnly protest against their proceedings and refusal as unprecedented, and I think unjust."[1]

Thereupon the court made an entry on their records in these words:

"General Arnold having offered a protest to the court, for the entry of it, in their minutes, which appears to them illegal, illiberal and ungentlemanlike; for these reasons they have objected to its entry and refuse the same." The court likewise directed the President to demand satisfaction of the General, which he did in the following words:

"SIR:

"As you have evidently called in question not only the honor, but the justice of this court, by the illiberal protest you exhibited, the court have directed me—and as President of this court I deem it my duty—to inform you that you have drawn upon yourself their just resentment, and that nothing but an open acknowledgment of your error will be considered as satisfactory."[2]

To which Arnold haughtily replied: "The very extraordinary vote of the court, and directions given to the President, and his still more extraordinary demand, are in my opinion ungenteel and indecent reflections on a superior officer; which the nature and words of my protest will by no means justify; nor was it designed as you have construed it. I am not very conversant with courts-martial, but this I may venture to say: they are composed of men not infallible; even you may have erred. Congress will judge between us; to whom I will desire the General to transmit the proceedings of this court. This I can assure you, I shall ever in public or private, be ready to support the character of a man of honor; and as your very nice and delicate honor in your apprehension is injured, you may depend as soon as this disagreeable service is at end (which God grant may soon be the case,) I will by no means withhold from any gentleman of the court, the satisfaction his nice sense of honor may require. Your demand I shall not comply with."[3]

1. Am. Archives, 5th S., Vol. I, p. 1272.
2. Am. Archives, 5th S., Vol. I, p. 1273.
3. Am. Archives, 5th S., Vol. I, p. 1273.

The court sent a letter to General Gates, giving their reasons for refusing to hear the evidence of Major Scott, every one of which went to affect his credibility and not his competency as a witness. The case is this:—Charges were presented by General Arnold against Colonel Hazen, and the General offered as the principal witness to sustain the charges, Major Scott; the court refused to hear the evidence; Arnold protests, and says he thinks the refusal "unprecedented and unjust."

This language can hardly be considered as disrespectful, or going beyond an earnest protest: certainly the court go much farther when they declare the protest of their superior officer, "illegal, illiberal and ungentlemanlike"; but when the court goes farther still, and directs its president "to demand satisfaction," and dictate an "open acknowledgement of error," as the only satisfaction the court will accept, they certainly exhibit a strange spectacle of judicial dignity. The answer of Arnold, except the last part, is dignified and certainly not uncourteous. He disclaims the construction they put upon the words of his protest—reminds them that courts are composed of men who are not infallible, and then says: "Congress, to whom the proceedings will be transmitted, will judge between us." Had he stopped there no exception could have been taken to his reply; but the extraordinary resolution, that the President "should *demand satisfaction* of the General," were words to which Arnold was ever too ready to respond: and his response that when the service was over he would by no means withhold any "satisfaction any gentleman of the court might require," was undignified and unworthy of his position.

The court sent the papers to General Gates, demanding the arrest of Arnold. Thereupon Gates issued an order dissolving the court, and transmitted all the papers to Congress, with the following comment:

"The warmth of General Arnold's temper might possibly lead him a little farther than is marked by the precise line of decorum to be observed before and towards a court-martial. *Seeing and knowing all the circumstances*, I am convinced, if there was fault on one side, there was too much acrimony on the other. I was obliged to act dictatorially, and dissolve the court-martial the instant they demanded General Arnold to be put under arrest. The United States must not be deprived of that excellent officer's services at this important moment."[1] There is no evidence in the case reflecting upon the integrity of General Arnold. Mr. Sparks, perhaps the most accurate of American annalists, and one who tries to do justice to Arnold, but whose just prejudice against him for his treason rendered it difficult, and sometimes impossible, says the "letters of Arnold alone sufficiently prove that he was not practicing any secret manœuvre in the removal of the goods, or for retaining them in his possession."[2]

It will be observed that General Arnold reports that the goods were seized by order of the commissioners. In this connection, I quote a paragraph from a letter from him to Chase, one of the commissioners, dated the 15th of May, in which he says, "I believe I know your sentiments in regard to provisions, and I shall not let the army suffer.' * * * * Most of our men returned from below naked. Will it not be advisable *to seize on all* such goods in Montreal as we are in absolute necessity for, and pay them the value? This I submit to your better judgment."[4]

Carroll, of Carrollton, was one of the commissioners, by whose orders Arnold alleges the goods were seized. He was one of the Board of War, which investigated these charges, as hereafter particularly detailed.

[1] Am. Archives. 5th S., Vol. I, p. 1268.
[2] Sparks' Life of Arnold, 69.
[3] Am. Archives, 4th S., Vol. VI, p. 581.
[4] Am. Archives, 4th S., Vol. VI. p. 581.

If the allegation of General Arnold, that the goods were seized by order of the commissioners was untrue, Carroll must have known it. When, therefore, he who had been in Canada and knew all the facts, reports that these charges were "cruel and groundless," I think we may safely concur in his conclusion.[1]

This affair created a prejudice in the minds of some members of Congress, and probably contributed to bring about the acts of injustice towards Arnold, which will be hereafter detailed.

It was also the misfortune or the fault of Arnold, that he had a difficulty with Lieutenant-Colonel John Brown. Their difference seems to have originated at the capture of Ticonderoga, in 1775, when Brown was a subordinate of Colonel Easton, and opposed Arnold in his claims to command. Brown went to Quebec with the troops under Montgomery, and after the death of that officer, Arnold wrote a letter to Congress, charging Brown with having been "publicly impeached with plundering the officers' baggage taken at Sorel," * * * and adding, "I think it my duty to say the above charge is the topic of public conversation at Montreal," and he protested against Brown's promotion until these matters were cleared up; and with his usual frankness, he adds: "The contents of the enclosed letter I do not wish kept from the gentleman mentioned therein; the public interest is my chief motive in writing. I should despise myself were I capable of asserting a thing to the prejudice of a gentleman without sufficient reasons to make it public."[2] Brown declared, in a letter dated June 26, 1776, addressed to Congress, that the charge was false, scandalous and malicious, and on first hearing of the charge at Quebec, he "challenged General Arnold to prove it," and demanded a court of inquiry, which was refused.[3]

1. Journal of Congress, Vol. III, p. 199.
2. Am. Archives, 4th S., Vol. I, pp. 12-20.
3. Am. Archives, 4th S., Vol. I, pp. 12-20.

He also alleges that on the arrival of General Wooster at Quebec, he again demanded a court of inquiry, "who likewise refused." He made the same demand "of the committee sent to Canada from Congress, who refused." He made, he says, the same demand of General Schuyler, at Fort George, "but the General thought it inexpedient."[1] One can scarcely help concluding that the action taken by Generals Wooster and Schuyler, and the committee of Congress, who were on the ground, must have been just; and that there were circumstances existing why Lieutenant Colonel Brown's demand should not be granted. Schuyler was eminently a just man, and Wooster was not particularly friendly to Arnold, and the committee of Congress, consisting of Franklin, Chase and Carroll, would unquestionably have interfered to correct a wrong, if satisfied of its existence.

On the first of December, 1776, Colonel Brown sent a paper to General Gates, presenting thirteen charges against General Arnold, expressed in very intemperate language, and asking that he be ordered "in arrest for the following crimes;"[2] and then enumerated thirteen specifications of offenses, running back to the affair at Ticonderoga, in 1775, and following him to Cambridge, Quebec, and through Canada. The language is violent, and discloses "a warmth which," in the words of Mr. Sparks, "indicates too great a degree of excited feeling."[3]

Gates treated Brown with coolness, and in reply to repeated applications, which he characterized as "importunate," he at length said: "I shall lay your paper before Congress, who will, when they think proper, give such orders as they think necessary thereupon."

Schuyler, writing to Gates, says: "If courts-martial

---

[1] Am. Archives, 4th S., Vol. I, p. 1220.
[2] See paper in full. Am. Archives, 5th S., Vol. III, p. 1159.
[3] Sparks' Life of Arnold, p. 71.

would severely punish officers for illiberal abuse of their superior officers, such violent and ill-founded complaints as you mention to be made by Lieutenant Colonel Brown against General Arnold, would soon cease. The latter gentleman will always be the subject of complaint, because his impartiality and candor will not suffer him to see impropriety of behavior with impunity."[1]

The reply of Arnold and the action of Congress will be more fully set forth hereafter. Suffice it to say now, that the papers were referred to the Board of War, who reported that they were entirely satisfied as to the character and conduct of General Arnold, which, in the language of the Board, had been "so cruelly and groundlessly aspersed." The report was confirmed by Congress.[2]

The difficulties and embarrassments of the officers of the army in the expedition to Canada, and other military movements, many of them growing out of violent passions and discordant interests, induced John Adams to say, "It requires more serenity of temper, a deeper understanding, and more courage than fell to the lot of Marlborough to ride in this whirlwind."[3]

If Arnold was sometimes unjust, if he did not at all times maintain, amidst all these trials and vexations, the "serenity of temper" which Adams speaks of, it would have been generously excused and forgiven and long ago forgotten, but for his subsequent treason.

Col. Brown met an honorable death in the service of his country. Had such been the fate of Arnold, the controversy between these officers would never have been recalled. It is now difficult, if not impossible, to determine the exact merits of the quarrel. But for Arnold's treason, the action of Wooster, the judgment of Schuyler and Gates, and the action of Congress, would have been accepted.

1. Am. Archives, 5th S., Vol. II, p. 250.
2. Spark's Life of Arnold, page 94. See, also, Journals of Congress, Vol. III. p. 199
3. Am. Archives, 4th S., Vol. V, p. 1112.

CHAPTER VI.

NAVAL BATTLE OF VALCOUR ISLAND.

"The conduct of Arnold in these naval affairs gained him new laurels. He was extolled for the judgment with which he chose his position, and brought his vessels into action; for his masterly retreat; for the *self sacrificing* character with which he exposed himself to the overwhelming force of the enemy in covering the retreat of part of his flotilla."—*Washington Irving.*

THE BRITISH, GREATLY SUPERIOR IN NUMBERS AND IN GUNS, ATTACK THE AMERICAN FLEET UNDER ARNOLD ON LAKE CHAMPLAIN—THE FIGHT CONTINUES FROM NOON UNTIL NIGHT, WHEN THE BRITISH RETIRE—THE AMERICANS ESCAPE THROUGH THE BRITISH LINE—ARE OVERTAKEN, AND ARNOLD, IN THE CONGRESS, FIGHTS AND RETARDS THE ENEMY UNTIL HIS OTHER VESSELS ESCAPE—HE RUNS THE CONGRESS ASHORE, BURNS HER, AND WITH HIS MEN, REACHES TICONDEROGA.

LAKE CHAMPLAIN, named after one of the early French explorers, was very early known in English and French colonial history. It is a narrow sheet of blue water, lying between Vermont and New York, and in many parts presenting a landscape of exceeding beauty. From it may be seen, in the distance, the varied outlines of the Green Mountains on the east, and the Adirondacks on the west. This lake, with its still more beautiful adjunct, Lake George, the "Horicon" of the graphic pen of Cooper; the St. Sacramento of the French; and connected by water communication with the St. Lawrence, formed the natural route and easy highway from Canada to the interior of New York.

As the Americans were compelled to retreat from Canada, as stated in the preceding chapter, the British closely followed, occupying St. Johns. Sir Guy Carleton early saw the importance of obtaining naval supremacy on these waters, that he might bring the English troops to Ticonderoga, within convenient distance of Albany, looking to a junction ultimately with the King's force from the city of New York, and thereby separating and isolating New England from the other states. These Lakes and their connections formed the most practical route by which the United States could be invaded from Canada; and both parties, in the summer of 1776, prepared vigorously to contest their control.

Carleton, the British leader, had many advantages over Gates and Arnold in the race of preparation. First, and of immense importance, he could draw upon the rich treasury of Great Britain. He had contractors and ship-builders from England, and naval stores in abundance from the fleet in the St. Lawrence and from Quebec. The English admiralty contributed liberally in material for ship-building, and in naval equipments. It sent out three vessels of war fully prepared for service; more than two hundred flat-bottomed boats were built at Montreal and taken to St. Johns; and the larger vessels, unable to ascend the rapids, were taken to pieces and reconstructed at the last mentioned place. One of these, the Inflexible, was a three masted ship, carrying twenty twelve-pound guns, and ten smaller guns. About seven hundred experienced sailors and the very best of young naval officers, were selected from the vessels of war and transports to man and command the lake fleet.

The Americans had to cut from the forest every stick of timber for the additions to their small fleet. All their naval stores and material had to be brought from tide water and the Atlantic, over roads nearly impassable. They lacked money, skilled ship-builders, naval stores—everything; still they were zealous, active, hopeful, and energetic. General Arnold, having some knowledge of ships, shipbuilding and navigation, was selected to superintend the construction of the fleet, and to command it when ready for service.

On the twenty-ninth of July, Gates wrote to the President of Congress, saying:

"General Arnold (who is perfectly skilled in naval affairs,) has most nobly undertaken to command our fleet on the lake. With infinite satisfaction I have committed the whole of that department to his care, convinced that he will thereby add to the brilliant reputation he has so deservedly acquired.[1] * * * General Arnold, ever active and anxious to serve his country, is just returned from Skenesborough, where he has been to give life and spirit to our dock-yard."

General Schuyler, writing to Gates, August third, says: "I am extremely happy that General Arnold has undertaken to command the fleet. It has relieved me from very great anxiety, under which I labored on that account."[2] Washington, looking anxiously to the naval control of Lake Champlain, on the fourteenth of August, and before he had learned that Arnold had been assigned to this duty, writes to Gates: "I trust neither courage nor activity will be wanting in those to whom the business (the command of the fleet) is committed. If assigned to General Arnold, none will doubt of his exertions."[3] Gates, writing to Washington, July 29th, says: "Our little fleet already built is equipping under the direction of General Arnold, with all the industry which his activity and good example can inspire."[4]

It thus appears that such was Washington's appreciation of Arnold's qualities, ignorant that he had been

1. Am. Archives, 5th S., Vol. I, p. 649.
2. Am. Archives, 5th S., Vol. I, p. 474.
3. Am. Archives, 5th S., Vol. I, p. 952.
4. Sparks' Writings of Washington, Vol. 4, p. 12.

already appointed to this service, he suggests it to Gates, and that both Schuyler and Gates felt "infinite satisfaction" and relief from "very great anxiety" when he undertook the command. These distinguished officers did not overrate his zeal, activity and energy. He did, indeed, give "life and activity to the dock-yards," and to every branch of the business of preparation.

He was constantly going to and fro, urging on the work, making requisition for mechanics, for seamen, for naval stores, for ordnance, for everything necessary to build, equip, arm and man his little fleet. But no degree of energy and activity could enable him to equal the armament which Sir Guy Carleton could bring from the St. Lawrence to the theatre of conflict. The resources of a mighty empire with untold wealth; the naval stores of the the then acknowledged "mistress of the seas," was behind Carleton, and her rulers had the ability and disposition to supply his every want. On the other hand, the feeble Colonies, with their depreciated "continental" paper money, with comparatively few seamen; all naval stores and needed supplies and material difficult to obtain on the sea coast, and when obtained, to be transported far inland—these were difficulties which no energy could overcome. On the 18th of September, Arnold, writing to Gates, says:

"I beg at least one hundred good seamen as soon as possible; we have a wretched motley crew in the fleet. The marines, the refuse of every regiment, and the sailors, few of them ever wet with salt water—we are upwards of one hundred men short."[1]

On the 1st of October, Arnold, writing to Gates, complains that the seamen have not been sent, and hopes he shall be excused, "if with five hundred men, half naked," he should not be able to beat the enemy in their overwhelming numbers and complete preparation. He sends for shot,

[1] Am. Archives, 5th S., Vol. II, p. 481.

musket balls, buckshot, grenades, clothing, and "one hundred seamen, no land-lubbers."[1]

Gates replies on the third, and sends what he can, but says: "What is not to be had, you and the princes of the earth must go unprovided with."[2]

Gates, writing to Schuyler, speaking of the want of supplies and the difficulty of obtaining them, says: "Succeed or fail, we have done our best."[3] Arnold, on the seventh of October, complaining that those in authority on the Atlantic had failed to send much needed supplies, says: "Is it possible my countrymen can be callous to their wrongs, or hesitate one moment between slavery or death? * * That Being in whose hands are all human events, will doubtless turn the scale in favor of the just and oppressed."[4]

Gates gave to Arnold careful instructions, and among other directions, said: "Should the enemy come up the lake and attempt to force their way through the pass you are stationed to defend, in that case you will act with such cool, determined valor as will give them reason to repent of their temerity."[5]

Arnold kept Gates, who was at Ticonderoga, constantly advised of his position and movements. On the 21st of September, he announced his intention to go to Valcour Island, and says, "if you do not approve, will return."[6]

On the 28th, he writes to Gates from "Isle Valcour," giving a detailed statement of the position of the fleet.[7]

On the 12th of October, Gates says to Arnold: "I am pleased to find you, and your armada, ride in Valcour Bay, in defiance of our foes in Canada."[8]

1. Am. Archives, 5th S., Vol. II, p. 835.
2. Am. Archives, 5th S., Vol. II, pp. 859-860.
3. Am. Arch ves 5th S., Vol. II, p. 481.
4. Am. Archives, 5th S., Vol. II, p. 933.
5. Am. Archives, 5th S., Vol. II, p. 896.
6. Am Archives, 5th S., Vol. II, p. 140.
7. Am. Archives, 5th S., Vol. II, p 591.
8. Am. Archives, 5th S., Vol. II, p. 1017.

The correspondence at this time between Arnold and Gates, and Arnold and Schuyler, had ceased to be formal. Engaged in a common cause, and struggling with difficulties which taxed their energies and patience to the utmost, and sharing common responsibilities, they had been drawn close to each other, and during all the campaign of 1776, their correspondence is frank, friendly, cordial, and sometimes playful. Gates writes to Arnold: "That the blessing of the Almighty may prosper all your undertakings is the sincere prayer of, dear General, your affectionate, humble servant."[1]

Arnold, writing to Gates for a surgeon for his fleet, says: "The surgeon's mate of Colonel St. Clair's regiment, has a good box of medicines, and will incline to go with the fleet. I wish he could be sent here, or some one who will answer to kill a man *secundum artem*."[2]

He closes with expressing his compliments to the gentlemen of the family of Gates, and his "affection" for that officer. These kind relations, unfortunately, were afterwards broken by Arnold's adherence to Schuyler, and the jealousy of Gates.

While the fleet was being exercised, and the raw material out of which Arnold was trying to make sailors and gunners were being trained, an instance of gross disobedience of orders on the part of one of his subordinates occurred, which in its treatment illustrates the character of Arnold and Gates. A certain commander, Wyncoop, flatly refused to obey the orders of Arnold. Arnold reported the facts to Gates, who immediately sent back a peremptory order that Wyncoop should be placed in arrest and sent a prisoner to Ticonderoga. Arnold, in complying with the order, writes a note to Gates, and after saying this was the

1. Am. Archives, 5th S., Vol. II, p. 187.
2. Am. Archives, 5th S., Vol. I, p. 968.

only case of insubordination, adds: "Wyncoop is sorry for his disobedience, * * * and if it could be done with propriety, I wish he may be permitted to return home without being cashiered."[1] His kind request was granted.

The time at which the desperate struggle for supremacy between the fleet of Arnold and that of Sir Guy Carleton approached, Schuyler, Gates, Washington — all were conscious of the great superiority of the British. All were anxious, but each indulged hope, arising mainly from the desperate valor of Arnold. Knowing his inferiority in ships, in weight of metal, and in men, Arnold avoided the possibility of an encounter on the open lake, where he might have been flanked or surrounded by anchoring his fleet in a line between Valcour Island and the western shore. In this position, the rear being unapproachable, and his line extending across the channel, he could be attacked in front only. This was the first time an American fought a British fleet.

There have been three notable battles between the United States and the British on the lakes. The battle on Lake Erie, known in American history as "Perry's Victory," and fought between Commodore Perry and the British Admiral Barclay; the battle on Lake Champlain, in which the Americans, under Macdonough, triumphed. In neither of these was there any such great disparity of force, as between that of Arnold and Sir Guy Carleton.

The British fleet consisted of the Inflexible, a large, three-masted ship, two schooners, the Lady Mary, and the Carleton, a floating battery called the Thunderer, twenty gun-boats, besides long-boats and transports. "They had," says Bancroft,[2] "more than twice his (Arnold's) weight of

1. Am. Archives, 5th S., Vol. I, p. 1078.
2. Bancroft's History, Vol. IX, p. 154.

metal, and twice as many fighting vessels, and skilled seamen and officers against landsmen." As has been stated, the British armed vessels were manned by about seven hundred selected seamen and well-trained gunners. Captain Pringle, of the British navy, commanded, but Carleton was himself on board, and among the many young officers was Edward Pellew, afterwards distinguished as Admiral Viscount Exmouth. This fleet carried ninety-three guns, some of them of heavy calibre. The fleet of Arnold consisted of three schooners, two sloops, three galleys and eight gondolas, carrying in all seventy guns.[1]

Early on the morning of the 11th of October, the guard boats, stationed as sentinels, gave notice that the British fleet was approaching, and it soon appeared off Cumberland Head, moving before a fair wind up the lake. Carleton came on, conscious of his greatly superior strength, with his battle-flags proudly flying, and when the fleet of Arnold was discovered, moored in the passage behind Valcour Island, Captain Pringle expressed his belief that they would not encounter much resistance, and he anticipated an easy victory; but Carleton, remembering Quebec, knew that Arnold would fight to desperation. As the enemy approached, the Americans made ready to receive them. As they advanced around the southern point of Valcour Island and attempted to beat up towards the channel in which the Americans had formed their line of battle, the large ships fell behind. Arnold, who rarely waited to be attacked, determined to take advantage of the wind, and attack the smaller vessels which were in advance, before the large ones could beat up to their assistance. With the schooner Royal Savage, and three galleys, he went to meet the British, and opened a rapid fire, but was gradually pushed back by superior force, and attempting to return to the line, in

[1] Sparks' Life of Arnold, p. 75, and Lossing's Field Book of Revolution, Vol. I, p. 163.

beating back, the Royal Savage, with its inexperienced crew, went aground and was abandoned; Arnold losing his baggage, and all his papers, but the men were saved.[1]

At half-past twelve the British, having brought all their gun-boats and schooners within musket-shot of the American line, the action became general, and from the shore of the mainland to the island, the hostile fleets fired at close range. Arnold, in the Congress galley, to which he had gone after abandoning the Royal Savage, anchored in the hottest part of the fire, and here, with obstinate determination, he held his position against all odds until five o'clock in the afternoon, when the enemy retired. During this long afternoon, a terrific cannonade of round and grape shot was continually kept up, and a constant blaze of rifles by a large body of Indians in the covers of the forest, on the shores of the island and the mainland. But as Arnold had taken the precaution to protect his men and his ships by fascines attached to the sides of the vessels, the rifles did little execution. So terrific was the cannonade, that the roar of the heavy guns is said to have been heard at Crown Point. The Congress and the Washington galleys received the most injury. Arnold, in the former, which was armed with two eighteen-pounders, two twelves, and two sixes, fought with desperate heroism. In the absence of experienced gunners, he pointed most of the pieces himself, passing rapidly from gun to gun, and firing as fast as they could be loaded.[2] This vessel received seven shots between wind and water, was hulled twelve times, the mainmast was wounded in two places, the rigging cut to pieces; yet, in this condition, and with dead and wounded all around him, he refused to yield or retreat; but hour after hour, for five

---

[1] General Richard Arnold, of the U. S. Army, has a table made of the oak lately taken from the wreck of the Royal Savage.

[2] "So deficient was the fleet in gunners, that Arnold pointed almost every gun that was fired from his vessel."—*Sparks' Life of Arnold*, p. 76.

hours, cheered on his men by word and example, until, as night approached, the British withdrew—retiring from an enemy commanded by a man who would never know that he was beat, and who would rather go down with flags flying than surrender.

The Washington galley was nearly as badly shattered as the Congress; the first lieutenant killed, and the captain and master wounded. The New York lost all her officers except her captain. The Philadelphia was hulled in so many places that she sunk one hour after the engagement. The whole number of killed and wounded was about eighty.

Never has there been exhibited a more striking illustration of Arnold's wonderful power of leadership and ability to inspire his men with heroic bravery, and power to make militia fight with unflinching courage, than on this occasion.

As darkness fell over the scene of this terrible conflict, the British commander posted his fleet across the channel, through which Arnold must pass to effect his escape, with the expectation that in the morning, with his greatly superior force, he would capture the whole American flotilla. Arnold, however, determined to make an effort to escape, and if he failed, to destroy his ships, land his men, and fight his way through the Indians to Crown Point. He called to him for consultation his two able and efficient subordinates, Colonels Waterbury and Wigglesworth, and, he says, as their "ammunition was three-fourths spent,"[1] and the enemy greatly superior in ships and men, they resolved to make an effort to pass through the hostile lines. It was a hazy night, and a fair wind had sprung up from the north, and so, each vessel putting out every light except a single signal lantern in the stern, to guide the ship that followed, attempted to pass through the British lines.

[1] Am. Archives, 5th S., Vol. II, p. 1117.

As the darkness of the misty night gathered over the waters, the first vessel started, and in breathless silence one by one the whole flotilla glided through, between the hostile vessels: Arnold, in the Congress bringing up the rear, and, as usual, the last to leave, as he was ever the first to reach, the post of danger. They were undiscovered. It was skillfully, gallantly, admirably done—and now with a fresh breeze, the crippled vessels bore away as rapidly as possible up the Lake. Using all possible expedition, the fleet reached Schuyler's Island, some twelve miles from the scene of the battle; and here they were compelled to lay to, and stop the leaks in their vessels and repair damages. Arnold instantly sent off a dispatch to Gates, saying: "As soon as our leaks are stopped, our whole fleet will make the utmost dispatch for Crown Point." Well might he add: "We have great reason to return our humble and hearty thanks to Almighty God, for preserving and delivering so many of us from our more than savage enemies."

Two of the gondolas were so badly injured they had to be abandoned and sunk. In the afternoon the remainder of the crippled flotilla again got under way; but the wind gradually ceased, and soon a breeze sprung up from the south, retarding their advance, so that very little progress could be made by beating and rowing. The next morning, as the fog rose and the sun came out, the whole British fleet, with every sail set, was seen crowding down upon them! The crippled Congress, with Arnold on board, the Washington and some gondolas, were in the rear. All the others, with every inch of canvass spread, and urged to the utmost, were flying towards Crown Point. It was but a short time, however, before the enemy came up and opened fire on the Congress, the Washington and the gondolas. After receiving a few broadsides the Washington struck her colors; but

Arnold had no thought of surrender. He determined, with the Congress and the crippled gondolas, to fight the whole fleet of the enemy, and so retard their advance, that the remainder of his vessels might make good their escape— to sacrifice himself if necessary to their safety. He received the whole fire of the hostile fleet. A ship mounting twelve eighteen-pound guns, a schooner of fourteen six-pounders, and another of twelve sixes, two under her stern and one on her broadside, poured their concentrated fire of round and grape shot into the already disabled Congress. These vessels kept up an incessant fire for four hours upon this one ship, which Arnold returned as best he could. Thus the English fleet was delayed, and the remainder of his own was making good their escape. The Congress was so disabled she could not fly, and Arnold would not surrender. Her sails, rigging and hull were shattered and torn to fragments; the Lieutenant killed; the crew, many of them killed and wounded. Still her stern commander had no thought of striking his flag, and continued the contest, until still other vessels of the enemy arrived, and he found himself surrounded with seven sail, each pouring in upon the hapless Congress broadside after broadside; and still, in the openings of the enemies' sails, and of the smoke of their guns, which thickly enveloped him, his flag could be seen still flying.[1]

His ship was now a complete wreck, and, as he could fight no more, he managed to break through the vessels which surrounded him, and ran the Congress and the gondolas into a small creek; and ordering the marines to leap

---

1. From "the shore dimly seen, through the mists of the deep,
　Where the foe's haughty host in dread silence reposes,
What is that which the breeze o'er the towering steep,
　As it fitfully blows, half conceals, half discloses?
Now it catches the gleam of the evening's last beam
　In full glory reflected—now shines on the stream—
'Tis the star-spangled banner; O, long may it wave
O'er the land of the free and the home of the brave!"

overboard and wade ashore with their small arms, he then set fire to the ship and the gondolas, and protected from the approach of small boats by the muskets of the marines, he lingered until the fire had extended too far to be extinguished, and then—his flag still flying—and ordering all his men ashore, he himself the last to leave, leaped from the bowsprit to the beach, and both he and his men, escaping an Indian ambuscade by taking an unusual route, arrived in safety at Crown Point, and passed on to Ticonderoga.

"From Salamis to Trafalgar,"

Where has there been a braver fight? Well may the sober Mr. Sparks, roused by the magnetism of such conduct, exclaim: "There are few instances on record of more deliberate courage and gallantry than were displayed by him, from beginning to end of this action."[1]

The country rang with praises of his heroism, and his brilliant achievements were in every man's mouth. "Such were the skill, bravery and obstinate resistance of Arnold and his men against a vastly superior force; the event was hailed as ominous of great achievements when such fearful odds did not exist."[2]

"General Arnold covered himself with glory, and his example appears to have been nobly followed by most of his officers and men. Even the enemy did justice to the resolution and skill with which the American flotilla was managed, the disparity of force rendering victory out of the question, from the first. The manner in which the Congress was fought, until she had covered the retreat of the galleys, and the stubborn resolution with which she was defended until destroyed, converted the disasters of this part of the day into a species of triumph."[3] This lan-

---
1. Life of Arnold, p. 79.
2. Lossing's Field Book of Revolution, p. 165.
3. J. Fennimore Cooper's Naval History U. S., Vol. I, p. 75.

guage of Lossing and Sparks and Cooper is not extravagant. Search the naval history of our English ancestors, from Frobisher to Nelson, and our own, from Paul Jones to Perry and Decatur, down to Farragut, and there is no instance of more desperate valor. Arnold lost some of his ships, but by his own desperate fighting he saved the others and his flag, added to his fame, and in the language of his instructions, he met the enemy "with such cool, determined valor," as taught them the difficulty of conquering such a people.

The battle of Bunker Hill was an American defeat, but its moral influence on both the contending nations, was equal to an American victory. The battle of Valcour Island resulted in the defeat of the American fleet, but if every battle was to be thus bloody and desperate, how long would the British ministers desire to continue the conflict?

How the conduct of Arnold was regarded by Gates and other officers appears from extracts from their letters and orders.

On the fifteenth of October, Gates encloses Arnold's report of the engagement to Schuyler, and adds:

"It has pleased Providence to preserve General Arnold. Few men ever met with so many hair-breadth escapes in so short a space of time."[1]

---

1. The following is Arnold's report of the fight:

"TICONDEROGA, Oct. 15, 1776.

"DEAR GENERAL:—I make no doubt before this you have received a copy of my letter to General Gates, of the 12th instant, dated at Schuyler's Island, advising of an action between our fleet and the enemy the preceding day, in which we lost a schooner and a gondola. We remained no longer at Schuyler's Island than to stop our leaks and mend the sails of the Washington. At two o'clock P. M., the 12th, weighed anchor, with a fresh breeze to the southward. The enemy's fleet at the same time got under way; our gondola made very little way ahead. In the evening the wind moderated, and we made such progress that at six o'clock next morning we were about off Willsborough, twenty eight miles from Crown Point. The enemy's fleet were very little way above Schuyler's Island; the wind breezed up to the southward, so that we gained very little by beating or rowing; at the same time the enemy took a fresh breeze from the northeast, and by the time we had reached Split Rock, were along side of us. The Washington and Congress were in the rear, the rest of our fleet were ahead, except two gondolas sunk at Schuyler's

Richard Varick, writing to General Gates, October 17th, after alluding to the defeat of the fleet, adds:

"But among the *favors* of Providence we have the blessing of General Arnold's safe return. I feared much for him. I hope, however, he will still humble the pride and arrognace of haughty Britain, and convince them that one defeat does not dispirit Americans."[1]

On the twenty-second of October, General Gates, writing to Gov. Trumball, says:

Island. The Washington galley was in such a shattered condition, and had so many men killed and wounded, she struck to the enemy after receiving a few broadsides. We were then attacked in the Congress galley by a ship mounting twelve eighteen-pounders, a schooner of fourteen sixes, and one of twelve sixes, two under our stern and one on our broadside, within musket shot.

"They kept up an incessant fire on us for about five glasses, with round and grape shot, which we returned as briskly. The sails, rigging and hull of the Congress were shattered and torn in pieces, the First Lieutenant and three men killed, when, to prevent her falling into the enemy's hands, who had seven sail around me, I ran her ashore in a small creek ten miles from Crown Point, on the East side, when, after saving our small arms, I set her on fire, with four gondolas, with whose crews I reached Crown Point through the woods that evening, and very luckily escaped the savages, who waylaid the road in two hours after we passed. At four o'clock yesterday morning I reached this place, exceedingly fatigued and unwell, having been without sleep or refreshment for near three days. Of our whole fleet we have saved only two galleys, two small schooners, one gondola, and one sloop. General Waterbury, with one hundred and ten prisoners, were returned by Carleton last night. On board of the Congress we had twenty-odd men killed and wounded Our whole loss amounts to eighty odd. The enemy's fleet were last night three miles below Crown Point; their army is doubtless at their heels. We are busily employed in completing our lines, redoubts, which, I am sorry to say, are not so forward as I could wish. We have very few cannon, but are mounting every piece we have. It is the opinion of Generals Gates and St. Clair, that eight or ten thousand militia should be immediately sent to our assistance, if they can be spared from below. I am of opinion the enemy will attack us with their fleet and army at the same time. The former is very formidable, a list of which I am favored with by General Waterbury, and have enclosed.

",The season is so far advanced, our people are daily growing more healthy. We have about nine thousand effectives, and if properly supported, make no doubt of stopping the career of the enemy. All your letters to me of late have miscarried. I am extremely sorry to hear by General Gates you are unwell. I have sent you by General Waterbury a small box, containing all my public and private papers and accounts, with a considerable sum of hard and paper money, which I beg the favor of your taking care of.

"I am, dear General, your most affectionate humble servant,

"B. ARNOLD.

"To Hon. Major-General Schuyler."

Am. Archives, 5th S., Vol. II, p. 1080.

1. Am. Archives, 5th S., Vol. II, p. 1102.

"It would have been happy for the United States had the gallant behavior, and steady good conduct of that excellent officer (Arnold), been supported by a fleet in any degree equal to the enemy."[1]

On the 14th of October, General Gates in general orders "returns his thanks to General Arnold and the officers, seamen and marines of the fleet for the gallant defense they made against the great superiority of the enemy's force."[2] The conduct of the Americans extorted the admiration even of their enemies. A gallant young English officer, named Dacre, was sent to England with dispatches, and in giving an account of the conflict "does justice to Arnold, and acknowledges that the disposition of his force, and the defense he made against a superior enemy, and the management of his retreat, did him great honor."[3]

The above extracts are given to show the judgment of the officers and fellow-soldiers of Arnold at the time of the action, and before their opinion could be changed by his subsequent conduct.

I am not unaware that, after Arnold's treason, and since it has become the natural inclination of our historians to discredit him, it has been stated "that he recklessly sacrificed his fleet without public benefit."[4] Such was not the opinion of his comrades, and Chief Justice Marshall, with more judicial fairness, expresses the judgment of the officers of the Revolution, when he says: "Arnold's fleet was very advantageously posted, and forming a strong line to defend the passage between Valcour Island and the western main; and his defeat did not dispirit the Americans, nor diminish his reputation.[5]

1. Am. Archives, 5th S., Vol. II, p. 1192.
2. Am. Archives, 5th S., Vol. III, p. 525.
3. Am. Archives, 5th S., Vol. III, p. 1,227.
4. Bancroft's History of the United States, Vol. IX, p. 156.
5. Marshall's Life of Washington, Vol. III, pp. 8-10. See also Irving's Life of Washington, Vol. II, p. 444.

CHAPTER VII.

ARNOLD SUPERCEDED, AND HIS FIGHT AT RIDGEFIELD.

"I am anxious to know whether General Arnold's non-promotion was owing to accident or design; and the cause of it. Surely a more active, a more spirited, and sensible officer fills no department of your army."—*Washington.* 1

"May the broad hand of the Almighty overshadow you; and if called to battle, may the God of armies cover your head in the day of it."—*Hannah Arnold to her Brother.*

ARNOLD IN WASHINGTON'S CAMP—SENT TO RHODE ISLAND—ADVANCES £1,000 TO AID LAMB IN RAISING HIS REGIMENT—OFFERS HIMSELF TO THE BEAUTIFUL MISS DEBLOIS—FIVE JUNIOR BRIGADIERS PROMOTED OVER HIM—HE WITHHOLDS HIS RESIGNATION AT WASHINGTON'S REQUEST—HIS DESPERATE BATTLE, AND ESCAPE AT RIDGEFIELD—CONGRESS VOTE HIM A HORSE, AND COMMISSION HIM A MAJOR-GENERAL—DECLARE THE CHARGES OF BROWN TO BE CRUEL ASPERSIONS UPON HIS CHARACTER—WASHINGTON BEGS CONGRESS TO SEND HIM NORTH TO AID IN REPELLING BURGOYNE.

ON his arrival at Ticonderoga, Arnold was most cordially welcomed by General Gates. His popularity had been greatly increased by his conduct in the battle upon Lake Champlain. Mr. Sparks says:

"Some writers have commented on the execution of this enterprise in a tone of captious criticism, which can by no means be sustained by an impartial view of the subject.² Arnold was sent out to meet the enemy. Whether he should fight or not, it is true, was left to his discretion. He chose the former, and was beaten; but not until he had maintained a combat for half a day, with a force nearly double his own, and caused the enemy to retire. This fact is enough to prove that his position was

---
1. Letter to Richard Henry Lee. Sparks' Writings of Washington, Vol. IV, p. 351.
2. Life of Arnold, pp. 80-81. See Bancroft's History of U. S., Vol. IX, p. 156.

judiciously chosen, and that the action on his part was skillfully fought. * * With consummate address, he then penetrated the enemy's lines, and brought off his whole fleet, shattered and disabled as it was, and succeeded at last in saving six of his vessels, and it might be added, most of his men. * * *

The conduct of Arnold was at the time approved by his military superiors, by Congress, and the whole nation."

Therefore, when he joined the army again at Ticonderoga, his fellow-soldiers cordially welcomed him, and regarded his escape, in the language of Colonel Varick, as "a blessing from Almighty God." Carleton did not attack Ticonderoga. The lateness of the season, and the manner in which Arnold had resisted his attack on the American fleet, doubtless influenced him. Arnold had exhibited thus far in his military career a brilliant heroism, an energy and determination, certainly unsurpassed by that of any officer in the service. He had from the first enjoyed the unqualified confidence of Washington and Schuyler. Warren, while he lived, was his devoted friend, and Chase, and Carroll of Carrollton the commissioners from Congress to Canada, who had visited him in his camp, certified to his good conduct. Yet he had bitter and influential enemies. Lieutenant Colonel Brown and Colonel Easton probably prejudiced some of the members of Congress from New England against him. Chase had written to him in August, on his return to Philadelphia from Canada:

"I am distressed to hear so many reports injurious to your character about the goods seized at Montreal. I cannot but request all persons to suspend their opinion, to give you an opportunity of being heard. Your best friends are not your countrymen. * * * Mr. Carroll requests his compliments, etc.[1]   Your affectionate and obedient servant,
"SAMUEL CHASE."

Possibly the warm friendship manifested for him by Schuyler, who early suggested his name for an important position, and who was very unpopular with most of the

1. Am. Archives, 5th S., Vol. I, p. 810.

New England delegates in Congress, may have prejudiced some of the members from that section against him.

"A prophet is not without honor, save in his own country."

As he now came up the lake to Ticonderoga, with the glory won in the wilderness of Maine, at Quebec, at Valcour Island, honored by his associates as the hero of the hour, there was a great contrast between his condition, when in May 1775, he marched by the side of Ethan Allen into the sally-port of the old fortress. If his memory reverted, as it doubtless did, to the time when as a runaway boy he had sought on the shores of these same waters, adventure in the ranks, he must have felt some satisfaction in what he had already accomplished. Intensely ambitious, had he possessed the wonderful self-control and poise of Washington, his career would have been as brilliant in its termination as it had thus far been bright and promising. But, while respectful to his superiors, and placable to those who made friendly advances to him, there is probably no instance—I know of none—in which this proud and haughty soldier sought to conciliate an enemy. To those who injured him, and to those he believed desired to injure him, he was stern and defiant. Hence he had many and powerful enemies, and he was too proud to take any step to conciliate them. They who became unfriendly from any cause, or without cause, were apt to continue so; and prejudice was easily created against a man of his haughty spirit, and these enemies finally drove him to desperation and a terrible crime.

On the twenty-seventh of November, Arnold and Gates were at Albany, and Gates wrote to the President of Congress, saying:

"General Arnold, who is now here, is anxious after his long absence to see his family, and settle his public accounts. Should the motions of the enemy make his presence necessary, I know his zeal for the service will outweigh all other considerations, and induce him to take the route that leads to them."[1]

On the fourteenth of December, 1776, Washington writes to Governor Trumball, of Connecticut:

"I have ordered General Arnold, on his way down from Ticonderoga to Norwich, or wherever his presence will be most necessary;"[2] and to General Gates: "I wrote to General Arnold to go to the eastward on account of intelligence from that quarter. His presence will be of infinite service."[3]

This order missed him on his route, and he had the pleasure of visiting Washington at his camp, on the banks of the Delaware, where he remained three days, a short time before the battle of Trenton.

The British were threatening the coast of New England, and Arnold was now sent to Rhode Island to co-operate with General Heath in rallying the militia, and making preparations to repel them. General Green, writing to the Governor of Rhode Island, says: "General Spencer and General Arnold are coming to take the command in Rhode Island. Arnold is a fine spirited fellow, and an active General."[4] On his way, Arnold visited his sister, and his children, then under her motherly care. The British landed and took possession of Newport. The winter was passed by him in New England. He visited Boston, and spent some time there in consulting leading men and the Legisture, with a view of raising a force with which to attack the enemy in Rhode Island. Washington wrote to him several times during the winter, and in reply to letters from him desiring permission to attack, Washington discouraged him,

1. Am. Archives, 5th S., Vol. III, p. 875.
2. Am. Archives, 5th S., Vol. III, p. 1215.
3. Am. Archives, 5th S., Vol. III, p. 1217.
4. Am. Archives, 5th S., Vol. III, p. 1343.

on the ground that his force was insufficient to make success "morally certain."[1]

In the campaign against Quebec, Arnold had formed a strong attachment for a comrade, Capt. John Lamb, who in the assault commanded the artillery; and who had been severely wounded and taken prisoner. While at Washington's headquarters, on the Delaware, he had made strong and successful interest with the commander-in-chief to have Lamb exchanged. Soon after the exchange, Lamb was authorized to raise a regiment of artillery, and among his captains he selected Samuel Mansfield, the brother of General Arnold's deceased wife.[2]

Colonel Lamb was very much embarrassed in raising his regiment for want of funds, Congress neglecting to furnish them. After exhausting his own means, and borrowing of his friends, he

"Fell in with General Arnold, who, upon being acquainted with the failure of the government to furnish funds for enlistment, offered the loan of one thousand pounds, and sent to Colonel Lamb an order on his sister Hannah, who had taken charge of his family after the death of his wife. The order was accepted, and that excellent and patriotic woman advanced, with alacrity, the money."[3]

It was during this winter, and while at Boston, that Arnold met and fell in love with the beautiful Miss Deblois, then a distinguished and much admired belle of that city. The following is a curious letter of his to Mrs. Knox, wife of General Knox, and presents a new phase of his character:

"WATERTOWN, 4th March, 1777.
"DEAR MADAM:—
"I have taken the Liberty of Enclosing a letter to the heavenly Miss Deblois, which I beg the favor of your delivering with the trunk of gowns, etc., which Mrs. ⸺ promised me to send to you. I hope she

[1]. See letter of Washington to Arnold, Feby. 6, 1777. Sparks' Writings of Washington, Vol IV, p 313; also, letter of March 3d, Vol. IV, p. 344.
[2]. Leake's Life of Lamb, p. 150.
[3]. Leake's Life of Lamb, p. 153. This act does not tend to prove the penuriousness with which Arnold has been charged.

will make no objection to receiving them. I make no doubt you will soon have the pleasure to see the charming Mrs. Emery, and have it in your power to give me the favorable intelligence. I shall remain under the most anxious suspense until I have the favor of a Line from you, who, if I may judge, will from your own experience consider the fond anxiety, the glowing hopes and chilling fears that alternately possess the heart, of dear Madam, Your obedient and most humble Servant,

"BENEDICT ARNOLD.

"Mrs. KNOX, Boston."[1]

Perhaps the brilliant soldier would have been more successful if he had made love in person. What was the reply of Miss Deblois, we are not informed; but it may be inferred from the fact that she never married.

While Arnold was actively engaged in New England in trying to raise a force with which he could attack the British, an event occurred which had "an important bearing on his future destiny."

On the 19th of February, 1777, Congress elected five Major Generals, namely: Stirling, Mifflin, St. Clair, Stephen and Lincoln. Arnold was passed over, and the above named five, every one his junior in rank, and one of them, Lincoln, was promoted from the militia. Whatever may have been the merits of Stephen, Stirling, and their associates, no one will assert that in service or merit as soldiers, there was anything in their past history to justify their promotion over such an officer as Arnold, with the military record he had made. He was astonished and in-

---

[1] W. H. Sumner, who communicates the letter to the Register, says: "The original letter in Arnold's own handwriting, was accidentally found among the papers of General Knox. It is written in a handsome hand, free and unaffected." Mr. Sumner says:

"The impassioned language of Arnold shows that he made love as he fought, and did everything else, with all his might and main, and one cannot help reflecting how very different might have been the history of this brave but passionate and ill-disciplined man, had he succeeded in this, perhaps his first love affair." (Mr. Sumner forgets his attachment and marriage to Miss Mansfield, at New Haven.) "He was then," says Sumner, "at the zenith of his fame, just subsequent to his brilliant career in Canada and on the lakes."—*New England Historical and Genealogical Register, Vol. II, p. 75.*

HIS PATRIOTISM AND HIS TREASON. 127

dignant, but acted with dignity and self-control. Washington was concerned and equally astonished; he feared the army would lose the services of a general he was accustomed to look to for hard work and severe service. He could not think it credible that this indignity could have been inflicted upon Arnold by design. "This measure," says Sparks, "was deeply regretted by Washington, who valued highly the military abilities of Arnold, and who considered the good of the service to require a strict regard to the customary rewards for professional merit."[1]

Washington wrote to Arnold, saying:

"I am at a loss to know whether you have had a preceding appointment, as the newspapers announce, or whether you have been omitted through some mistake. Should the latter be the case, I beg you will not take any hasty steps, but allow proper time for recollection, which I flatter myself will remedy any error that may have been made; my endeavors to that end shall not be wanting."[2]

Arnold's reply, dated March 11th, was manly and dignified, but indicated that his feelings were deeply hurt.

"I am greatly obliged to your Excellency," he wrote to General Washington, "for interesting yourself so much in my behalf in respect to my appointment, which I have had no advice of, and know not by what means it was announced in the papers. I believe none but the printer has a mistake to rectify. Congress, undoubtedly, have a right of promoting those whom, from their abilities, and their long and arduous services, they esteem most deserving. Their promoting junior officers to the rank of major-generals, I view as a very civil way of requesting my resignation, as unqualified for the office I hold. My commission was conferred unsolicited, and received with pleasure only as a means of serving my country. With equal pleasure I resign it. when I can no longer serve my country with honor. The person who, void of the nice feelings of honor, will tamely condescend to give up his right, and retain a commission at the expense of his reputation, I hold as a disgrace to the army, and unworthy of the glorious cause in which we are engaged. When I entered the service of my country my character was unimpeached. I have sacrificed my interest, ease and happiness in her cause,

1. Note of Sparks to Writings of Washington, Vol. IV, p. 345.
2. Sparks' Writings of Washington, pp. 345-6.

It is rather a misfortune than a fault, that my exertions have not been crowned with success. I am conscious of the rectitude of my intentions. In justice, therefore, to my own character, and for the satisfaction of my friends, I must request a court of inquiry into my conduct; yet every personal injury shall be buried in my zeal for the safety and happiness of my country, in whose cause I have repeatedly fought and bled, and am ready at all times to risk my life. I shall certainly avoid any hasty step (in consequence of the appointments which have taken place,) that may tend to the injury of my country."

Again:—

" In my last I intimated to your Excellency the impossibility of my remaining in a disagreeable situation in the army. My being superseded must be viewed as an implied impeachment of my character. I therefore requested a court of inquiry into my conduct. I believe the time is now at hand when I can leave this department without any damage to the public interest. When that is the case, I will wait on your Excellency, not doubting my request will be granted, and that I shall be able to acquit myself of every charge which malice or envy can bring against me."[1]

On the 6th of March, Washington writes to his confidential friend, Richard Henry Lee, member of Congress from Virginia, saying:

"I am anxious to know whether General Arnold's non-promotion was owing to accident or design, and the cause of it. Surely a more active, a more spirited and sensible officer fills no department in your army. Not seeing him, then, in the list of Major-Generals, and no mention made of him, gives me uneasiness, as it is not to be presumed, being the oldest brigadier, that he will continue in the service under such a slight."[2]

On the third of April, Washington again wrote to Arnold on this subject, as follows:

"MORRISTOWN, 3d April, 1777.

" DEAR SIR: It is needless for me to say much upon a subject which must undoubtedly give you a good deal of uneasiness. I confess I was

---

1. Spark's Writings of Washington, Vol. IV, pp. 345–346.
2. Sparks' Writings of Washington, Vol. IV. p. 351. As an illustration of Congress' disregard of Washington's wishes, he wrote to Richard Henry Lee, in regard to the appointment of Conway as Major General: "I think it will be a fatal blow to the existence of the army;" and yet Congress appointed Conway. Writings of Washington, Vol. V, p. 484.

surprised when I did not see your name in the list of Major-Generals, and was so fully of opinion that there was some mistake in the matter, that, as you may recollect, I desired you not to take any hasty step before the intention of Congress was fully known. The point does not now admit of a doubt, and is of so delicate a nature that I will not even undertake to advise. Your own feelings must be your guide. As no particular charge is alleged against you, I do not see upon what ground you can demand a court of inquiry. Besides, public bodies are not amenable for their actions. They place and displace at pleasure; and all the satisfaction that an individual can obtain when he is overlooked, is, if innocent, a consciousness that he has not deserved such treatment for his honest exertions. Your determination not to quit your present command while any danger to the public might ensue from your leaving it, deserves my thanks, and justly entitles you to the thanks of your country.

"General Greene, who has lately been at Philadelphia, took occasion to inquire upon what principle the Congress proceeded in their late promotion of general officers. He was informed that the members from each State seemed to insist upon having a proportion of general officers adequate to the number of men which they furnish, and that, as Connecticut had already two Major-Generals, it was their full share. I confess this is a strange mode of reasoning, but it may serve to show you that the promotion, which was due to your seniority, was not overlooked for want of merit in you. I am, dear sir, yours, etc."[1]

Arnold, in consequence of the advice of Washington, did not resign, saying, "Every personal injury shall be buried in my zeal for the safety and happiness of my country, in whose cause I have repeatedly fought and bled, and am ready at all times to risk my life."

He was not, more than other officers, unduly or unusually sensitive about his rank and promotion. Later in the year 1777, a report reached camp that a French officer, named Ducondray, had been appointed by Congress a Major-General in the American army, and was to command the artillery. Without waiting to learn whether the report was true, Generals Greene, Sullivan and Knox, each wrote to Congress a laconic letter, dated on the same day, and each requesting, if the report was true, permission to retire. General

[1] Sparks' Writings of Washington, Vol. IV, pp. 377-8.

Nathaniel Greene says: "If the report be true, it will lay me under the necessity of resigning my commission, as his appointment (Ducondray's) supercedes me in command."[1]

Ducondray was not appointed, but the incident is introduced to show the feeling among the American officers on the subject. An opportunity soon occurred to test Arnold's sincerity, when he declared his readiness, notwithstanding the indignity put upon him, "to risk his life for his country."

Smarting under this injustice, on his route from Providence to Philadelphia—to ask an investigation of his conduct,—in passing through Connecticut he stopped at New Haven to visit his sister and his children. While there he heard of the invasion of that State by Governor Tryon with two thousand British troops. They had landed near Fairfield, marched towards Danbury where a large amount of public stores had been collected. They reached Danbury on the 26th, at four P. M., and burned the stores and a part of the town. Generals Wooster and Silliman had hastily collected a few hundred militia, and about one hundred continentals; amounting in all to some six hundred, and pushed forward in pursuit of Tryon. Hastening from New Haven, Arnold joined them at Reading, and they all marched to Bethel, four miles from Danbury, arriving there at two o'clock at night. Here they learned that Danbury had been burned, with all the public stores, and that the British were preparing to retire to their ships.

"At day-light on the following morning, Arnold and Silliman proceeded with four hundred men to Ridgefield, with the design of intercepting the enemy on their return; and Wooster with two hundred men took another route to harrass the rear of the enemy." Wooster soon came up with the British, and a skirmish ensued in which the brave old general received a mortal wound.

1. Sparks' Writings of Washington, note on page 490 of Vol IV

By the time Arnold arrived at Ridgefield, the militia of his State, proud of his fame, and eager to fight under his leadership, had flocked to his standard, so that his numbers exceeded five hundred men.

He hastily constructed a barricade of carts, logs, stones and earth, across the highway along which the British were coming. His position was well chosen, the street narrow, and flanked on the one side by a ledge of rocks, and on the other by a house and barn. Behind this barricade, he formed his men, and awaited the approach of the enemy. At three o'clock Tryon approached at the head of nearly two thousand troops, marching in solid column, and as soon as he discovered the position of Arnold, he opened a heavy fire in front, and sent out detachments on each flank, to turn them and get into the rear of the Americans. The British fire was returned with great spirit, and Arnold with his small force, held his position against four times their number, for some time. At length, the British flanking party, under General Agnew, gained the summit of the ledge of rocks, when Arnold ordered his men to retreat. At about the same time, a whole platoon of General Agnew's infantry, who had gained the rocks above him, came running down, and when not more than thirty yards distant, all fired at him. His horse received nine balls and instantly fell dead.[1] He, strange as it seems, was not hit. For a moment, his feet being entangled in his stirrups, he was unable to rise. Seeing his position, a soldier rushed forward with fixed bayonet to run him through; approaching Arnold, as he sat still entangled on his dead horse, the soldier called out: "Surrender! you are my prisoner!" "Not yet," exclaimed Arnold, coolly, and drawing a pistol from his holster, he shot the soldier dead. At the same moment, extricating

---

1. Lossing's Field Book of the Revolution Vol. I, p. 409. See note in which it is stated that nine bullet holes were found in Arnold's dead horse, as he was skinned by some neighboring farmers.

himself, he sprang upon his feet, and leaped away into a thickly wooded swamp near by, followed by a shower of balls—but again he escaped untouched. "So remarkable an exhibition of cool and steady courage in a moment of extreme danger has rarely been witnessed."[1] The British went into camp within a mile of Ridgefield until the following morning, when they resumed their march towards their ships, at Compo.

As Tryon approached Norwalk, he learned that the indefatigable, and apparently invulnerable, Arnold, was again in the saddle, and was rallying the scattered militia to cut him off.

"Being reinforced, he hung upon their flanks and rear, throughout their entire march to their ships, attacking them at every assailable point."[2] At Compo, aided by a portion of Lamb's artillery, it is probable the whole detachment would have been captured, had not Sir William Erskine landed a party of marines from the ships, and with these fresh troops drove the Americans back. During all this fighting, Arnold, reckless of danger, at the head of the attacking party, led the militia in person, encouraged them by voice and example, until his horse—his second horse—was wounded in the neck and disabled. Arnold still escaped, although a bullet passed through the collar of his coat. In such a manner did he make good his words to Washington, that he was still, notwithstanding the indignity put upon him—"ready at all times to risk his life for the safety and happiness of his country."

The news of these exploits passed rapidly to Congress, and extorted from that body the promotion, which, in the judgment of Washington, had been so unjustly withheld. Congress, on the twentieth of May, also passed the following resolution:

1. Sparks' Life of Arnold, p. 91.
2. Sparks' Life of Arnold, p. 91.

"That the Quarter-Master General be directed to procure a horse, and present the same, properly caparisoned, to Major-General Arnold, in the name of this Congress, as a token of their approbation of his gallant conduct in the action against the enemy, in their late enterprise to Danbury, in which General Arnold had one horse killed and another wounded."[1]

Congress also, on the same day, ordered, "That the letter from General Arnold, with the papers enclosed, be referred to the Board of War, together with such complaints as had been lodged against him." This referred especially to the charges of Lt.-Colonel Brown, and all other "complaints" against him. On the 23d of May, the Board of War reported that they had had a conference with General Arnold concerning the imputations of Brown; had examined original letters, orders and papers, giving an account of his conduct; confirmed by the relations of Mr. Carroll, one of the late commissioners to Canada, then a member of the Board of War, and that this evidence had given entire satisfaction to the Board, concerning the General's character and conduct, *so cruelly* and *groundlessly* aspersed.[2]

Congress immediately confirmed the report. But notwithstanding all this, for some reason Congress did not give him his proper rank; he was still out-ranked by the five Major Generals, by whom he had been superceded on the 19th of February. He who had been the senior Brigadier General, was now at the foot of the Major Generals,

1. Journals of Congress, Vol. III, p. 194.
2. The text of the resolution is as follows: "The Board of War reported that they had had a conference with Major-General Arnold, concerning the imputations cast upon his character, contained in a hand-bill, dated Pittsfield, April 12th, 1777, and subscribed, John Brown—laid before Congress by the General in his letter to the Pr sident—that the General laid before the Board a variety of original letters, orders and other papers, which, together with the General's account of his conduct, confirmed by the relation of Mr. Carroll, one of the late commissioners to Canada— now a member of this Board—have given entire satisfaction to this Board, concerning the General's character and conduct, *so cruelly and groundlessly aspersed in the publication.*

"*Resolved*, That the said report be confirmed." Ditto p. 199.

all his late juniors outranking him. There is an inconsistency and a mystery in regard to this action of Congress, difficult to understand. General Washington himself could not understand it. On the 5th of May, he wrote to the President of Congress, saying: "General Arnold's promotion gives me much pleasure. He has certainly discovered in every instance, where he has had an opportunity, much bravery, activity and enterprise. But what will be done about his rank? He will not act, most probably, under those he commanded but a few weeks ago."[1]

Washington, sensible of the delicacy of Arnold's position, gave him the command on the Hudson, which was then regarded as honorable a post as any officer could hold. On the 7th of May, Washington writes to General McDougal, saying: "I have desired him (General Arnold) to come immediately to Peekskill. * * You will find him a man of judgment." * *[2]

Arnold however did not accept this position, but asked and obtained leave to go to Philadelphia, and ask the restoration of his proper rank and that his accounts should be settled. Washington gave him a letter to the President of Congress stating the object of his visit, and requesting that Arnold should have "an opportunity of vindicating himself, and his innocence."[3] He adds "It is needless to say anything of this gentleman's military character. It is universally known that he has always distinguished himself as a judicious, brave officer, of great activity, enterprise and perseverance."

On his arrival, he addressed a letter to Congress, which shows how deeply he felt wounded and grieved:

"I am exceedingly unhappy," said he, "to find that after having made

---

1. Sparks' Writings of Washington, Vol. IV, p. 406.
2. Sparks' Writings of Washington, Vol. IV, p. 410.
3. Sparks' Writings of Washington, Vol. IV. p. 416.

every sacrifice of fortune, ease and domestic happiness to serve my country, I am publicly impeached (in particular by Lt.-Colonel Brown,) of a catalogue of crimes, which, if true, ought to subject me to disgrace, infamy, and the just resentment of my countrymen. Conscious of the rectitude of my intentions, however I may have erred in judgment, I must request the favor of Congress to point out some mode by which my conduct, and that of my accusers, may be inquired into, and justice done to the innocent and injured." [1]

This was the letter which, with the other papers, were referred to the Board of War, as above set forth.

On the day this petition was presented, May 20th, Richard Henry Lee wrote from Congress to Mr. Jefferson, saying: "One plan, now in frequent use, is to assassinate the characters of the friends of America, in every place and by every means; at this moment they are now reading in Congress an audacious attempt of this kind against the brave General Arnold." [2]

But Congress did not restore his proper rank—nor was any action taken on the letter "of General Washington." Congress had declared that they were entirely satisfied with the conduct of General Arnold; they declared the charges against him "cruel and groundless," and yet they did not do him the justice to restore his rank. Those who knew him best, and whose opportunities for learning his true character were most favorable, were his warmest friends. Washington, Schuyler and Gates, up to and after this time, the commissioners of Congress to Canada, Chase and Carroll, of Carrollton, who had been in his camp, and among the troops in Canada, sent there to investigate and correct wrongs and abuses—all bear testimony to his merits, and all at this time were his friends. To what extent his treatment by Congress is to be attributed to envy, jealousy, or other unworthy motives, it is now perhaps impossible to determine.

1. Sparks' Writings of Washington, Vol. IV, p. 417.
2. Sparks' Writings of Washington, Vol. IV —note to page 418.

While in Philadelphia, Arnold presented his accounts, and asked the appointment of a committee to investigate and audit them. These accounts were voluminous, running back to the time when he started from Cambridge on the expedition to Quebec, through all his campaigns in Canada and on Lake Champlain, down to the battle of Valcour Island. During all this time the army was very imperfectly organized, the supply of money was inadequate—what was furnished often un-current; the business of purchases, payments, and money affairs generally, rested in a very large degree with the commanders of detachments.

In June, 1776, in a letter from St. Johns, writing to General Sullivan, Arnold says: "I have borrowed several sums of hard money. * * The poor soldiers receive no benefit from their pay (it being in uncurrent paper), and starve in the midst of plenty, with their pockets full of money."[1] Writing to the commissaries of Congress, June 2nd, 1776, Arnold says: "Everything is in the greatest confusion." Not one contractor, commissary or quarter-master. I am obliged to do the duty of all."[2] In May, 1776, at Sorel, he had to purchase for the troops beef, wheat, flour, blankets, tents, clothing, etc. He says: "A quarter-master and commissary are much needed here; I have so much on hand I can hardly get one minute to write."[3] To Chase, one of the commissaries, he says, May 15th: "Will it not be advisable and justifiable to seize on all such goods in Montreal as we are in absolute necessity for, and pay them the value? This I submit to your better judgment."[4]

Arnold had sometimes used his own means, and his credit, which at that time seems to have been good in Canada, to relieve the most pressing needs of the suffering soldiers. At

---
1. Am. Archives, 4th S., Vol. VI, p. 931.
2. Am. Archives, 5th S., Vol. I, p. 165.
3. Am. Archives, 4th S., Vol. VI, pp. 579-580.
4. Am. Archives, 4th S., Vol. VI, pp. 580-581.

the commencement of the war he was in easy circumstances, a prosperous and enterprising merchant. He said that in the service of his country he had sacrificed the "greater part of a handsome fortune." He was always profuse in his expenditures, and was a man who, if he had means or credit, would never hesitate one moment in using both for the relief of his soldiers, and to promote his ruling passion for military success. Undoubtedly the accounts of his expenditures, seemed to the committee of investigation very large; and he had enemies who did not hesitate to charge him with an attempt to defraud the country, for which he had been so freely exposing his life. In the absence of any proof of fraud, it is more charitable—probably more just—to attribute the large claims which he presented, to the confusion in which affairs had been managed, and to the necessities of the service—the sufferings of the soldiers, which had induced him to use his own means and credit to the utmost.

While the committee of Congress were examining his accounts, he was appointed to the command of the army then gathering in the neighborhood of Philadelphia, to watch the movements of General Howe. When this officer made a demonstration towards Philadelphia, Arnold was sent forward to the Delaware above Trenton, to co-operate with Washington in opposing his advance. This duty he discharged with his usual zeal, and was as usual eager to fight. Writing to Mifflin, June 12th, 1777, he says: "Fight the enemy we must, whenever our reinforcements are in. We cannot avoid it with honor; our men are in high spirits."[1] But the British General retired to Brunswick, and Arnold returned to Philadelphia, and again sought a settlement of his accounts. The committee having the matter in charge did not report, nor did Congress act upon his reiterated request that his proper rank should be

1. Remembrancer, Vol. V, p. 268.

restored. His patience became exhausted, and his wounded pride and impetuous temper would not submit. He wrote a letter to Congress tendering his resignation, but declaring that he was driven to it only by a sense of injustice; and professing an ardent love for his country, and his readiness to risk his life in her cause; but added: " Honor is a sacrifice no man ought to make; as I received, so I wish to transmit it to posterity."

On the very day this letter from Arnold was presented to Congress, that body received a letter from General Washington, dated July 10th, 1777, communicating the fact that General Burgoyne was advancing along the old war path from Canada, determined to possess himself of all our posts in that quarter, and threatening to advance still further to Albany and the Hudson, and earnestly recommending that they should send Arnold to the field of danger. He says:

" * * Upon this occasion I would take the liberty to suggest to Congress the propriety of sending an active, spirited officer to conduct and lead them on. If General Arnold has settled his affairs, and can be spared from Philadelphia, I would recommend him for this business, and that he should immediately set out for the northern department. He is active, judicious and brave, and an officer in whom the militia will repose great confidence. Besides this, he is well acquainted with that country, and with the routes and most important passes and defiles in it. I do not think he can render more signal services, or be more usefully employed at this time than in this way. I am persuaded his presence and activity will animate the militia greatly, and spur them on to a becoming conduct. I could wish him to be engaged in a more agreeable service, to be with better troops, but circumstances call for his exertions in this way, and I have no doubt of his adding much to the honors he has already acquired."[1] * *

And again, on the 12th, Washington says to Congress: " In my last I took the liberty of suggesting the propriety of sending an active officer to animate the militia that may assemble for checking General Burgoyne's progress, and mentioned General Arnold for that purpose. * * Being

[1] Sparks' Writings of Washington, Vol. IV. pp. 485, 487.

more and more convinced of the important advantages that will result from his presence and conduct, I have thought it my duty to *repeat* my wishes on the subject, and that he may *without a moment's loss of time*, set out from Philadelphia for that purpose."[1]

These letters from his chief soothed the wounded feelings of Arnold, and the mention of a campaign against Burgoyne was to him like the sound of the trumpet to the war-horse.

Instantly he asked leave to suspend his request for permission to resign, only adding that he would leave it with Congress, and made no doubt they would listen to it when the service was over. He had determined to drive Burgoyne back to Canada or die. He went even farther, and "volunteered," says Sparks, "an act of magnanimity, which certainly must extort praise if it cannot win esteem."[2] Knowing that St. Clair was in command in the northern army, and that he was one who had been his junior, and one of the five promoted over him, he generously waived all considerations of rank and pride, and declared he would "do his duty faithfully in the rank he then held, and trust to the justice of his claims for a future reparation."

Such was the spirit with which Arnold left Philadelphia to join Schuyler in the campaign against Burgoyne.

The thrilling story of that campaign, and the part that Arnold bore in it, will be the subject of the following chapters.

1. Sparks' Writings of Washington, Vol. IV, pp. 489-490.
2. Sparks' Life of Arnold, p. 99.

CHAPTER VIII.

CAMPAIGN ON THE MOHAWK, AND RELIEF OF FORT STANWIX.

> "He (Arnold) is active, judicious and brave, and an officer in whom the militia have great confidence."—*Washington.*
>
> "In my last I suggested an active officer to animate the militia who may assemble, for checking General Burgoyne's progress, and mentioned General Arnold. Being more and more convinced of the important advantages of his presence, I have thought it my duty to repeat my wishes, that he may without one moment's loss of time set out."—*Washington.* 1

ST. LEGER INVESTS FORT STANWIX—HERKIMER GOING TO ITS RELIEF, FALLS INTO AN AMBUSCADE, AND AT THE BATTLE OF ORISKANY IS MORTALLY WOUNDED—ARNOLD VOLUNTEERS TO GO TO THE RELIEF OF GANSEVOORT—REACHES GERMAN FLATS, AND ALTHOUGH A COUNCIL OF WAR RESOLVE THAT THEY MUST WAIT FOR REINFORCEMENTS, HE DETERMINES TO "PUSH FORWARD AND HAZARD A BATTLE," RATHER THAN SEE THE GARRISON FALL—HE RESORTS TO A RUSE—FRIGHTENS THE INDIANS, WHO ABANDON THE SIEGE, AND STANWIX IS RELIEVED.

THE third year of the war was now opening, and as yet no decisive results had been reached. No great victories had been achieved, nor had any large army been captured on either side. Washington's wise Fabian policy would in time tire out an enemy fighting three thousand miles from home. The English began to realize this, and the British ministry meant to make the campaign of Burgoyne in 1777 decisive. The plan was simple, but skillful, and if successful, might in its results have realized the hopes of its projectors. The principal feature was the expedition of Burgoyne, which was to move from Quebec by the St. Lawrence,

---

1. Washington to Congress. Writings of Washington, Vol. IV. p. 457-459.

Lake Champlain, and the banks of the Hudson, to Albany. Auxiliary and co-operative with this, was another expedition under St. Leger, which, passing up the St. Lawrence and Lake Ontario to Oswego, was to push through by way of Wood Creek and the Oneida Lake, into the rich valley of the Mohawk, capturing on its way old Fort Stanwix, then called Fort Schuyler, where the city of Rome now stands; thence along the Mohawk to join Burgoyne at Albany. Meanwhile, General Howe was to advance up the Hudson from the city of New York, and form a junction with the combined forces of St. Leger and Burgoyne. With St. Leger was a large body of Indians, under Sir John Johnson and Joseph Brant (Thayandenega), one of the ablest and most celebrated of the Indian chiefs. The fall of Fort Schuyler, and the success of the expedition, would expose all the settlements west of Albany, most of which were then organized, as Tryon county, to the barbarous cruelties of the savages. How appalling these would have been, the massacre of men, women and children at Wyoming, Cherry Valley and other places, but too well indicate.

The success of Burgoyne's campaign would have cut off New England from the other States, and have placed the powerful State of New York in the complete control of the British. It is not, therefore, surprising that both the friends and foes of American independence, looked upon the result, as likely to be extremely important, perhaps absolutely decisive. "This campaign will end the war," said Reidesel, one of Burgoyne's most distinguished officers.

The theater of conflict was one of the most picturesque in America; and has been long known as hereinbefore stated, as the battle ground on which the fate of America between France and Great Britain had been often contested. The lakes of the north, as well as the valleys of the Mohawk and the Hudson, had often been the pathway of French, English,

Colonial and Indian armies. Composed of lakes and mountains, rivers and valleys, dark forests and fertile flats, the country was interesting, not only for its strategic importance, but for its picturesque beauty. Most of this vast region, now among the most thickly settled and highly cultured parts of New York, was in 1777 a wilderness. Settlements west of Albany were scattered and weak; the people exposed alike to the wild animals and still wilder and more savage Indians. Block-houses for defense were still common among the settlers; and along the Mohawk the little stone church was often used as a substitute in case of attack.

The Tory element was of considerable strength. In the Valley of the Mohawk, there had lived for several years in baronial style, in "Johnson Hall," the family of Sir William Johnson, and the influence of this family over the Indians, with whom they were allied by marriage, was very strong.

Far greater differences in social rank and condition existed at that time in New York than in most of the New England States. Grants of lands in large areas had been made to various individuals, and as the law of entail and primogeniture then existed, these lands were still held in very large tracts by the descendants of the grantees, and the landlords lived in considerable state, and exercised large influence over their tenants and dependants. Some of these large land-holders were adherents of Great Britain, but most of the historic families of the colonial days were patriots, exercising controlling influence in their State, and they made themselves felt in the national government. The Clintons, the Livingstons,[1] the Van Rensselaers, the Ganevoorts, the De Lanceys, the Duers, the Jays and the Schuy-

---

1. Livingston "informed me he held 300,000 acres of land."—*Journal of Charles Carroll to Canada, in 1776.* Van Rensselaer had a grant of twenty miles on each side of the Hudson.

lers, and their associates, were very important personages at the Colonial and Revolutionary period.

In no part of the Republic are the changes and advance of our country more strikingly illustrated than in this valley. A hundred years ago, and Fort Stanwix was the frontier post; the bark canoe of the Mohawk and Oneida Indians, and the flat-boat of the pioneer, bore the few supplies and exchanges taken to and from Albany to the settlers. Now the journey from the site of Fort Stanwix at Rome, past Utica, through this picturesque valley to Schenectady and Albany, is along a canal and railway that convey the travel and the trade of the continent, and over which pass a number of passengers and an amount of commerce nowhere exceeded in the world.

John Burgoyne, the leader of the expedition, which it was confidently hoped would end the war, had seen service and won a brilliant reputation as a soldier, in Portugal. He was connected by marriage with the noble house of Derby; was popular with the people, a favorite at court and in the army; and every means was placed at his command which could contribute to the success of his enterprise. His troops, grenadiers, infantry and artillery were of the best in the British army. He had under him Major-General Phillips and General Fraser, a gallant Scotchman, both regarded as possessing extraordinary skill and ability; about four thousand German troops, commanded by General Rediesel, and a large number of Canadians, Indians and Royalists, made up a force numbering in all nine or ten thousand men. In arms and appointments, in everything which could make his army effective, nothing was omitted.

On the 24th of June, this carefully prepared engine of destruction moved along the old historic war path towards Crown Point. General St. Clair occupied Ticonderoga and

Mount Independence—the former the old fortress into which Ethan Allen and Arnold had marched side by side, on the 10th of May, 1775. Fort Independence had been constructed since that time. Together, these two posts commanded a narrow passage of the lake, and this had been so obstructed as, it was believed, would prevent the passage of vessels; but unfortunately both these fortifications were themselves completely commanded by high and accessible elevations, called Sugar Loaf Hill and Mount Hope, and through a strange oversight these commanding positions had been left unoccupied.

The British arrived in the neighborhood of Ticonderoga on the 2nd and 3d of July, and discovering that Sugar Loaf Hill was unoccupied, and finding on investigation that it was practicable to place a battery on its summit, during the night of the 4th a road was made and a battery placed on the top, and it was then christened by the British " Mt. Defiance," as from it the guns of the Americans in Ticonderoga could be defied. At dawn of day on the 5th, St. Clair was startled by the intelligence that the British flag was floating from the top of the mountain, and the scarlet uniform of British soldiers could be seen placing heavy guns in battery which overlooked and commanded his position. A council of war was called, which decided the position of the Americans to be untenable, and arrangements were immediately made for retreat. The forts were abandoned. St. Clair attempted to escape by stealth, but his movement was discovered and he was hotly pursued by the enemy, who captured guns, material of war, baggage and stores in large quantities.

Farther up the lake at Skenesborough, the troops hearing that Ticonderoga had been abandoned, set fire to the vessels, the fort, the mills and block-houses, and retreated to Fort Anne. Burgoyne reported to Lord Germain that the American army at Ticonderoga "was disbanded and totally ruined." This was an exaggeration; the pursuit was checked at Hubberton, by Warner and Francis, and St. Clair reached Fort Edward with fifteen hundred continental troops.[1] But the retreat and abandonment of the defenses, which were supposed to be strong, and before which the country confidently believed the enemy would be checked and held at bay, if not repulsed, cast a deep gloom over the people. Both Schuyler and St. Clair were severely censured.

The Indians who accompanied the expedition, emboldened by this success, and thirsting for blood and plunder, began to bring in scalps, and hanging on the out-posts of the advancing columns, frequently murdered unarmed parties, and their ferocity was often exhibited in the ruthless scalping of the settlers, not sparing women and children.

On the 27th of July, Jane McCrea, a beautiful girl of twenty years of age, betrothed to David Jones, a loyalist and Lieutenant in the British service, while riding from Fort Edward to the British camp, escorted by two Indians, was cruelly killed and scalped. This sad tragedy, made more touching by the beauty of the victim, has for a century been the theme of poetry and romance. The horrid drama has been told in various and conflicting narratives, and the exact truth is involved in some obscurity; but that it touched the heart and nerved the arm of every loyal father, brother, and lover in the American settlements, far and near, there is no dispute. Each realized the possibility that such might be the fate of his own wife, daughter, sister or betrothed; and the story told at the fireside of so many homes, aroused a hatred toward the British, then accused of exciting the savages against the Americans, which, in the neighborhood of the tragedy has not died out to this day The accusation, so far as Burgoyne was

1. Lossing's Field Book of the Revolution.

concerned, has long been known to have been unjust. He was shocked by the event, caused "the assassin to be hunted out, and threatened him with death, but pardoned him on being told that the total defection of the Indians would have ensued from putting his threat into execution."[1] But the touching story of poor Jenny McCrea brought hundreds of volunteers to oppose Burgoyne, who might otherwise have remained at home.

The fall of Ticonderoga and the retreat of St. Clair alarmed the patriots, gladdened the loyalists, and fixed the wavering Indians to what they now regarded as the strongest side. Yet heavy as was the loss, it is not clear but that in the end it was for the advantage of the American cause. If Burgoyne had been repulsed from the fortifications at Ticonderoga, having command of the lake, he could at all times have made good his retreat; but he was now advancing so far into the interior that he must either get through to Albany or be captured. His advance south and beyond water communication with Canada, secured the capture of his whole army. Yet at the time the disasters of the Americans in the north, and the approach of Burgoyne with his Indian allies, caused a depression and anxiety scarcely equalled during the war. In this dark hour it appears that both Washington and Schuyler, each of whom knew Arnold well, thought of him as the fittest officer to send forward to lead, and as Washington said in his letter to Congress, "to animate the militia that may assemble for checking General Burgoyne's progress;" and he adds: "being more and more convinced of the important advantages that will result from his presence and conduct, I have thought it my duty to repeat my wishes, that he may set out without a moment's loss of time for that purpose."[2] "He is active,

[1] Bancroft's History of the United States, Vol. IX, p. 372.
[2] Sparks' Writings of Washington, Vol. IV, p. 490.

judicious and brave," and " I have no doubt of his adding to the honors he has already acquired."[1] Congress, notwithstanding the strong prejudice which some of the members entertained against Arnold, yielded to these repeated requests of Washington, and he was ordered to the northern frontier.

Pleased with such an endorsement, which soothed his wounded pride, and flattered by being selected for the post of danger, Arnold instantly set forward, declaring he would serve under anybody or anywhere, so that he could serve his country, and that he would trust to the justice of his claims for future reparation. How much Washington expected from him appears from a letter to General Heath, dated July 19, 1777: "I have sent General Arnold up to join Schuyler. * * I hope with Arnold's assistance, in whom the army, and militia particularly, have great confidence, matters will be put in a more forward train."[2]

On the 16th of July, 1777, Washington writes to Schuyler from "The Clove:"

"Upon my requisition, General Arnold, waiving for the present all dispute about rank, left Philadelphia, and arrived here last evening, and this day proceeds on his journey to join you. Although he conceives himself, if his promotion had been regular, as superior in command to General St. Clair, yet he generously, upon this occasion, lays aside his claim and will create no dispute, should the good of the service require him to act in concert. I need not enlarge upon the well-known activity, conduct and bravery of General Arnold. The proofs he has given of all these have gained the confidence of the public, and of the army—the Eastern troops in particular."[3]

On the same day Washington, to encourage the officers of the militia, announced to them that their favorite, General Arnold, was to command them. He addressed a letter

"To the Brigadier Generals of Militia in the western parts of Massachusetts and Connecticut," saying: "General Arnold, who is so well

[1] Sparks' Writings of Washington. Vol. IV, p. 487.
[2] Mass. His. Vol.. Vol. IV, p. 67. Heath Papers.
[3] Writings of Washington, Vol. IV, pp. 498-9.

known to you all, goes up at my request to take the command of the militia in particular, and I have no doubt but you will, under his conduct and direction, repel an enemy from your borders who has brought savages with the avowed intent of adding murder to desolation." [1]

Starting without delay from the camp of Washington and traveling rapidly, he arrived in July at Fort Edward, and joined General Schuyler. The army was preparing to move a few miles down the Hudson and take a position near Moses Creek. The forces were divided into two divisions, one of which was put under the command of Arnold. Schuyler retreated to Stillwater, the British taking possession of Fort Edward. While here, intelligence reached Arnold that the question of his rank had been brought up in Congress, and on the ayes and nays—then for the first time *called* in the Continental Congress—decided against him.[2] In the face of the letters of Washington to Congress in reference to Arnold, his military record, and his conduct in the present expedition, this action seems very strange and cruel. Indignant, mortified and wounded, he asked permission to resign, but by the persuasion of his old friend, General Schuyler, who represented to him the "absolute necessity" of his services at so critical a moment, he, with a magnanimity and patriotism rivaling that of Schuyler himself, withdrew his request. He was yet, by his heroic services and by his blood, to extort from Congress the rank which in the judgment of Washington was so unjustly withheld.[3] Writing to Gates, then his friend,

---

1. Writings of Washington, Vol. IV, p. 500.
It was at this time, while Arnold was the guest of Washington, and being "*Brother Masons*," they visited together a Masonic Lodge. They received a brotherly welcome, and each signed his name on the records of the Lodge. The record is in existence, and the name of Washington stands, but some zealous patriot, in his hatred of his treason, has drawn black lines across the name of Arnold. How deplorable that Arnold should have caused the alienation of Washington—separating forever these "*Brothers of the Mystic tie.*"

2. Journal of Congress, Vol. III, p. 319.

3. Washington to Lincoln, advising him that Arnold had been restored to his rank, says: "Arnold is *restored* to a violated right."—*Sparks' Writings of Washington*, Vol. V, p. 217.

Arnold says, alluding to the action of Congress, "No public or private injury or insult shall prevail on me to forsake the cause of my injured and oppressed country until I see peace and liberty restored to her, or nobly die in the attempt."[1]

While at Stillwater, intelligence reached Schuyler that St. Leger, accompanied by Sir John Johnson and the celebrated Mohawk chief, Joseph Brant, in command of the Indians, had reached and closely invested Fort Schuyler. Peter Gansevoort, a brave, active, firm and determined officer, was in command. When he heard of the approach of St. Leger and his Indian and tory allies, he appealed to Schuyler for aid, setting forth the dreadful condition of the inhabitants of Tryon County, if the fort should be taken, and the scattered and defenseless settlers given up to the cruelties and atrocities of the Indians. The garrison had been strengthened by Colonel Marinus Willett, a brave and skillful officer, from the city of New York, with his regiment and provisions and military stores.

St. Leger had arrived on the 3d of August, and surrounding the fort with Indians, who, by their yells and war whoops, sought to intimidate the garrison, demanded a surrender, which Ganesvoort peremptorily refused. Meanwhile, General Herkimer having heard that the enemy were approaching across Oneida Lake towards the valley, called on the militia of Tryon county to rally to the rescue. They responded zealously, and from the scattered hamlets and settlements gathered in and met at Fort Dayton, on the German Flats in the Valley of the Mohawk, and on the day when St. Leger invested Fort Schuyler, Herkimer was at Oriskany marching to its relief.

The sister of the Mohawk chief sent word to him that

---

[1] Letter from Arnold to Gates. Aug. 5, 1777. Manuscript letter in Gates' papers, Vol. IX. p. 42, in the New York Historical Society.

Herkimer was approaching, and this skillful warrior on consultation with Sir John Johnson and St. Leger, determined to go out and meet Herkimer, and in accordance with Indian modes of war, prepared an ambush for his destruction.

Herkimer, on the 5th of August, sent messengers apprising Ganesvoort of his approach, and requesting him to signal the arrival of the messengers by the rapid discharge of heavy guns, and that he should also make a sortie from the fort, thus co-operating with Herkimer, who would advance at the sound of the guns, and fight his way to the garrison.

The morning of the 6th came, and Herkimer waited impatiently for the signal, but no guns were heard. The officers of Herkimer, eager to go forward, pressed him to advance; but the brave, yet cautious old soldier, then sixty-four years of age, still waited for the signal. Some of his subordinates still urged him, and a quarrel ensued, in which the officers called him a "tory and a coward," and at length provoked him to give orders for the advance. Herkimer's messengers had been delayed, and did not reach the fort until ten or eleven o'clock of the morning of the 6th. Most of the Indians and tories called "The Greens," had left their camp to intercept Herkimer. Ganesvoort had noticed the quiet in St. Leger's camp, and the arrival of Herkimer's messengers explained the ominous silence. The Indians and their allies had gone to waylay and ambush the Americans. Ganesvoort ordered Colonel Willett to sally out and co-operate with Herkimer. That officer (Herkimer), at about mid-day, marching without much precaution through the defiles of the forest, was suddenly assailed on every side by Brant and his followers. The war-whoop of the Mohawks, the Senecas, the Onondagas, and of all the Six Nations except the Oneidas, resounded through the forests, and there now occurred one of the most bloody conflicts of the war. "The slaughter was dreadful."

The Indians and their allies had arranged the ambush with great skill. Hiding in the forests, they had formed nearly a circle, leaving an opening for Herkimer and his troops to enter, and when, unaware of danger, all had passed in except the rear-guard, which fled, the Indians closed the gap, shutting the trap, and then, with a yell that thrilled the hearts of the assailed, a thousand rifles blazed upon the surprised and doomed Americans. It seemed at first that the whole force would be annihilated, but many of these men were accustomed to Indian warfare. Instantly seeking cover behind trees, those who survived the first onset fought with desperate valor. Herkimer, although his horse was shot dead under him, and his leg broken just below the knee by a musket ball, behaved with the greatest heroism. He ordered his saddle removed from his dead horse, and placed beneath a large beech tree, and seating himself upon the saddle, with his back against the tree, he continued to issue his orders, and animate his men to maintain the fight. After nearly an hour's hard fighting, and great slaughter on both sides, the enemy began to close in and concentrate upon the Americans; the "Greens" and "tory rangers" charging with the bayonet, the patriots forming themselves into circles and repulsing the charges. Thus the bloody work went on, with a fury and rancour which rarely was stayed for mercy or quarter, and was checked only when a clap of thunder silenced for a moment the crack of rifles and the yells and shouts of the combatants. This was followed by such a deluge of rain as instantly to render the fire-arms unserviceable. Both parties paused and sought shelter under the trees. During this pause the leaders were busy preparing to renew the conflict as soon as the rain should cease. When the rain slackened the battle raged again with undiminished fury. In the midst of this conflict, guns were heard from the direction of Fort Schuyler; it was the attack of Colonel Willett on the partially deserted camp of Sir John Johnson. Willett captured a large quantity of clothing, stores, camp equipages, five British flags, and carried them into the Fort without the loss of a man. The British flags were immediately run up on the flag-staff and hung under the colors of the United States, a flag of stripes of red and white, lately improvised and rudely made up from the garments of the soldiers and their wives. The firing from the direction of the Fort caused the Indians to falter, and they soon gave way and fled in all directions. This bloody battle, known as the "Battle of Oriskany," was, in proportion to the numbers engaged, one of the most destructive during the war. It was not a decisive victory for either party. The Americans remained in possession of the field, but the conflict did not relieve Fort Schuyler; the British and Indian forces returning to the siege, so closely invested it that no reliable information of the battle reached Gansevoort. The gallant Herkimer was taken to his home near the Little Falls, on the Mohawk, and died a few days after the battle. His name has been appropriately given to the village and county of his residence, where his memory is still cherished.

St. Leger claimed a victory at Oriskany, and again demanded a surrender of the fort, declaring to Ganesvoort that nothing could save the garrison from massacre by his savage allies but immediate surrender. Ganesvoort indignantly refused, and determined to hold out to the last extremity. He dispatched Colonel Willett, with Lieutenant Stockwell as guide, to General Schuyler for relief. At night, in the midst of a violent storm, they left the fort; crossing the Mohawk upon a log, and crawling upon their hands and knees, they passed the line of sentinels undiscovered, and after many hardships, on the 12th of August reached the headquarters of General Schuyler.[1] He had already heard of the battle, and was devising means for the succor of Gansevoort. He fully appreciated the sufferings which would follow the fall of Fort Schuyler. He knew that the tomahawk, the scalping knife and the midnight torch, would desolate, scatter and destroy the patriot settlements all along the Valley of the Mohawk, and through Tryon county, and that the victorious Indians and tories, flushed with success, would come down "like an avalanche" upon Schenectady and Albany, and swell the approaching army of Burgoyne.

Arnold, writing to Gates, says:

"These infernal savages, painted like furies, are continually harrassing and sca'ping our people, and the miserable, defenceless inhabitants. Whole families of the latter have been inhumanly butchered, without distinction of age or sex; and some (I am credibly informed) have been roasted alive in the presence of the polite and humane British army. * * * This is the protection many poor deluded wretches have experienced from the British arms, who remained quietly in their homes, agreeably to General Burgoyne's proclamation."[2]

Schuyler, therefore, from motives alike of compassion for the settlers who appealed to him as to a father for protection, as also for military reasons, determined to relieve the beleaguered garrison. He called a council of war, and proposed to the officers assembled, to send a detachment up the Mohawk. Most of the officers, except Arnold, opposed this proposition, on the ground that the entire army was already too weak to resist Burgoyne.

Schuyler became very much excited by their opposition. Walking rapidly up and down the council room, and smoking vehemently, he overheard some one say, "*he means to weaken the army!*" He had been charged with

[1]. Lossing's Pict. Hist. of the Revolution, Vol. I, p. 250.
[2]. From Gates' Papers, Vol. IX, p. 42, in New York Historical Society.

cowardice, and even with treason, by his prejudiced enemies. Crushing into fragments with his teeth the clay pipe which he was smoking, he paused, raised his head, and looking over the group of officers, said with dignity: "Gentlemen, I shall take the responsibility upon myself; Fort Stanwix and the Mohawk Valley shall be saved!! Where is the Brigadier who will command the relief? I shall beat up for volunteers to-morrow." Arnold, though a Major-General, and second in command, indignant that his friend should be so wronged, instantly volunteered. Impulsive, ever ready for deeds of daring, knowing how false and cruel were the imputations cast upon Schuyler, he at once offered his services, and they were most gratefully accepted. On the next morning the drums were beating through the camp for volunteers, and it was announced that Major-General Arnold had offered to lead them, and before noon eight hundred men had volunteered to follow him to the rescue of Gansevoort. Schuyler, giving Arnold his instructions, says: "It gives me great satisfaction that you have offered to go and conduct the military expedition in Tryon County."[1]

Many of Arnold's volunteers were of the brigade under General Learned, some of which had already been sent by Schuyler into the valley of the Mohawk.

Washington, writing to Schuyler August 21st, says: "If the militia keep up their spirits * * * they will, with the reinforcements under General Arnold, be enabled to raise the siege of Fort Schuyler, which will be a most important matter just at this time."[2]

With such portion of his troops as could move rapidly, Arnold pushed on with his usual energy to Fort Dayton, on the German Flats, arriving on the 20th of August. On

[1] Lossing's Schuyler, Vol. II, p. 288.
[2] Sparks' Writings of Washington, Vol. V, p. 37, and Carrington's Battles, p. 325.

the 21st he called a council of war, consisting of Brigadier-General Learned and the six Colonels who commanded the regiments which constituted his command. By a friendly Oneida Indian, corroborated by Colonel Willett, the council was informed that the force before Fort Schuyler was not less than seventeen hundred men, besides tories, while the force under Arnold was only nine hundred and thirty-three. Under the circumstances, the council resolved that it would be "imprudent" and "too hazardous" to attempt the relief of Fort Schuyler until reinforcements had arrived.[1]

[1] The following is a copy of the proceedings of the council, from Gates' papers in manuscript, Vol. IX. p. 70, in New York Historical Society:

"At a council of war held at Fort Dayton, German Flats, August 21st, 1777, present: The Honorable Major-General Arnold, President; the Honorable Brigadier-General Learned, Col. Bailey, Col. Livingston, Col. Wesson, Lt. Col. Van Dyck, Lt. Col. Brooks, Lt. Col. Willett, members.

"The General informed the council that previous to his leaving Albany, Gen. Schuyler had sent a belt and message to the Oneidas to meet at Albany, and had intrusted him (Gen. Arnold) to engage as many of them as possible in our service, and had furnished him with some presents for them, in consequence of which he had dispatched a messenger to them, requesting they would meet him at the German Flats; as yesterday they did not arrive, he had given orders for the army to march for Fort Schuyler this morning, since which a deputation from the Oneidas and Tuscaroras had arrived, acquainting him that the chief of both tribes with their families would be here the day after to-morrow, requesting a meeting with us; one of the Oneidas who had lately been at the enemy's encampment, also informed that all the Six Nations, except the two tribes above mentioned, had joined the enemy, the whole with foreign Indians amounting to fifteen hundred, by the enemy's account. The Oneida, who is known to be a fast friend of ours, says, that from viewing their encampment, he is fully convinced there is upwards of one thousand Indians, and from the best authority their other forces are near seven hundred, besides some tories who have joined them since their arrival. Col. Willett, who lately left the Fort, being present, is fully of opinion the above account is nearly true.

"The General then acquainted the Council that by the returns delivered this morning, our whole force, rank and file, effectives, are nine hundred and thirty-three, and thirteen artillery men, exclusive of a few militia, the whole not exceeding one hundred, on whom little dependence can be placed; at the same time requests the opinion of the Council whether it was prudent to march with the present force and endeavor to raise the siege of Fort Schuyler, or to remain at this place until a reinforcement can be solicited from below, and more of the militia turned out to join us, and until the Oneidas had determined if they would join us, of which they give encouragement.

"*Resolved*, That in the opinion of this Council, our force is not equal to that of the

High-sounding proclamations had been issued early in the campaign by both Burgoyne and St. Leger, and that of St. Leger had been signed also by Sir John Johnson and others, holding out inducements to the inhabitants to join the royal cause, and containing fearful threats against those who should refuse.

Learning that these proclamations had had some influence upon the people, on his arrival at the German Flats, Arnold issued a counter-proclamation, modeled somewhat after those which had been issued on the other side. The severity and plainness of his language may doubtless be attributed in part to the Indian outrages, of which the murder of poor Jane McCrea, which had been lately perpetrated, was an instance. He denounced St. Leger's force as "a banditti of robbers, murderers and traitors, composed of savages of America, and more savage Britons." He offers "all concerned pardon, provided within ten days they lay down their arms, sue for protection, and swear allegiance to the United States of America;" but declares if they "persist in their wicked career, determined to draw upon themselves the just vengeance of Heaven and of this exasperated country, they must expect no mercy from either."[1]

---

enemy, and that it would be imprudent and putting too much to the hazard to attempt to march to the relief of Fort Schuyler, until the army is reinforced; the Council are of the opinion that an express ought immediately to be sent to Gen. Gates, requesting he will immediately send such a reinforcement to us as will enable us to march to the relief of the Fort, with a probability of succeeding, and that in the meantime the army remain at the German Flats, at least until an answer can be had from Gen. Gates, and that all possible method be taken to persuade the militia and Indians to join us.

"B. ARNOLD, *President*."

1. The following is a copy of the proclamation:

"By the Hon. Benedict Arnold, Esq., Major General and Commander-in-Chief of the Army of the United States of America, on the Mohawk River.

"Whereas, a certain Barry St. Leger, a British General in the service of the —— George of Great Britain, at the head of a banditti of Robbers, Murderers and Traitors, composed of Savages of America and more savage Britons. among whom is a noted Sir John Johnson, John Butler and Daniel Claus, have lately appeared on the frontiers of this S'ate, and have threatened ruin and distruction to all the inhabitants of the United States.

Meanwhile, some of the garrison at Fort Schuyler, hearing nothing from Colonel Willett, and seeing no signs of relief, began to consider whether it would not be wiser to save themselves from threatened massacre by surrender; but their determined commander resolved that if no succor reached him, when his provisions were exhausted he would march out some dark night with his troops, and cut his way through his besiegers, or die in the attempt. But this desperate expedient was rendered unnecessary by the skill and strategy of Arnold. He had been detained a short time at Fort Dayton for supplies, baggage and ammunition, to overtake him, and for the "militia, who were now coming in in great numbers."[1] He now sent word to Gansevoort that he was coming. On the 22nd, having heard that St. Leger's approaches had reached very near the fort, notwithstanding the supposed superiority in numbers on the part of St. Leger, and notwithstanding the resolutions of the council of war, that it would be imprudent to attempt to relieve Fort Schuyler until reinforcements should arrive, he determined "to push forward and hazard a battle rather than see the garrison fall a sacrifice."[2] On the 21st of August he wrote to General Gates: "I leave this place (the German Flats) this morning with 1200 Continental

---

"They have also, by artifice and misrepresentation, induced many of the ignorant and unwary subjects of these States to forfeit their allegiance to the same, and join them in their atrocious crimes and parties of treachery and parricide Humanity to these poor deluded wretches, who are hastening blindfold to destruction, induces me to offer them and all others concerned, whether savages, Germans, Americans or Britons, *pardon*, provided they do wi hin ten days from the date hereof, come and lay down their arms, sue for protection, and swear allegiance to the United States of America But if, still blind to their own safety, they obstinately persist in their wicked courses, determined to draw on themselves the just vengeance of Heaven, and of this exasperated country, they must expect no mercy from either.

"B. ARNOLD, Major-General.
"Given under my hand at Head Quarters, German Flats, 20th of August, 1777."
—*Gates' Papers, N. Y. His. Society.*

1. Letter from Arnold to Gansevoort, Aug. 22, 1777.
2. Stone's Campaign of Burgoyne, p. 212.

troops and a handful of militia, for Fort Schuyler, still besieged by a number equal to ours. You will hear of my being victorious or no more. * * As soon as the safety of this part of the country will permit I will fly to your assistance." On the 23d he wrote again to Gates, inclosing copy of the proceedings of the council of war, and saying that he had determined to hazard a battle rather than suffer the garrison to fall a sacrifice, and that he was marching for Fort Schuyler."[1]

On the morning of the 23d he was making a forced march up the Mowhawk with a part of his force, and had proceeded about ten miles from his camp when he met an express from Gansevoort announcing that the siege had

1. The following is the text of his letter:

"MOWHAWK RIVER, 10 MILES ABOVE FORT DAYTON,
Aug't 23, 1777, 5 O'clock P. M.

DEAR GENERAL:

"I wrote you the 21st Inst. from the German Flatts, that from the best intelligence I could procure of the Enemy's strength, it was much superior to Ours; at same time Inclosed you Coppy of the resolutions of a Council of Warr, and requested you to send me a reinforcement of One thousand Light Troops. As the Enemy had made their approaches within Two hundred yards of the Fort, I was determined at all events to hazard a Battle rather than suffer the Garrison to fall a sacrifise; this morning I marched from the G. Flatts for this place; the excessive bad roads and necessary precautions in Marching thro' a thick wood retarded us so much that we have but thi- moment reached this place, where I have met an Express with the Inclosed Letter from Colo. Gansevoort, acquaints me the Enemy had yesterday retired from Fort Schuyler with great precipitation; I am at a loss to Judge of their real intentions; whether they have returned home or retired with a view of engaging us on the road; I am inclined to the former from the acco't of the Deserters, and from their leaving their Tents and considerable Baggage, which our people have secured.

"I shall immediately Detail Abt. Nine hundred Men and make a forced March to the fort in hopes of coming up with their rear, and securing their Cannon and heavy Baggage.

"My Artillery, Tents, &c., &c., I shall leave here; the Batteaus with Provisions follow me. As soon as the security of the Post will Permit, I will return with as many Men as can be spared. As I come down in Batteaus, shall be able to make great dispatch.

"I have sent an Order for the Light Troops if you have sent any, to return to you immediately, and the Militia to go home.

"I am, Dear General, Your Affectionate, "Obed., Hble. Srvt.,
"B. ARNOLD.

"Honble. Major-General Gates."

—*Gates' Papers, Vol. IX, p. 90, N. Y. Hist. Society.*

been raised. Gansevoort did not at first understand it, but Arnold grimly smiled at the success of a *Ruse De Guerre*, which he had practiced. It was this : His troops had captured a Mohawk Dutchman named HonYost Schuyler or Cuyler, whose residence was near the Little Falls. In company with Lieutenant Butler and some others, he had been arrested within the American lines at a public meeting at which Butler, making a speech, was endeavoring to persuade the people to join the Royal cause. The parties so taken were tried by court-martial as spies, and both Butler and HonYost convicted and sentenced to death. HonYost is said to have been a singular combination of cunning and shrewdness in some things, with a want of sense approaching idiocy in others; so that the Indians on the Mohawk regarded him as one stricken by the Great Spirit. They regarded him with the mysterious respect and wonder mingled with awe, with which the red man regards the insane and the idiot. Those thus stricken by the Great Spirit they always treat with a certain respect. Living much with the Indians, HonYost had joined the tories. His aged mother and his brother hearing that he was a prisoner and had been sentenced to be hung, hastened to Arnold at Fort Dayton, and implored him to spare his life. It is a touching trait of a mother's love that her devotion to her child, so unhappy as to be physically a cripple, or mentally defective, is greater than that for her more fortunate children not thus afflicted. The mother of poor HonYost was not an exception, and the touching pathos and eloquence with which she plead for the life of her afflicted son, are told to this day in the legends of the Mohawk Valley.[1] Arnold for a time affected to be firm against all her pleadings, but finally said that he would spare the prisoner's life on one condition. Knowing how HonYost was regarded by the Indians, Arnold proposed

[1] Stone's Campaign of Burgoyne, p. 213.

that he should hasten to the camp of St. Leger, and alarm the besiegers by the report of Arnold's near and rapid approach with overwhelming numbers, and thus raise the siege. If HonYost accomplished this, his life should be spared. He and his mother gladly accepted the proposal, and she offered herself as a hostage for his good faith. This Arnold declined, but insisted that his brother Nicholas should be retained as such hostage, knowing that while he held him he had all the security which the influence of both mother and brother could give in favor of the good faith of the prisoner. This was assented to, and Nicholas went into the prison in place of his brother, pledging his life for HonYost's fidelity.

An arrangement was also made with an Oneida Indian to aid in the experiment. Before they started several bullets were shot through the coat of the Dutchman, to give color and probability to the story that, a prisoner, he had escaped at the hazard of his life.

Thus prepared, he and the Oneida started, it being arranged that the Indian, as he approached the camp of St. Leger, was to separate from his companion and go in alone, corroborating the Dutchman in his story of the vast numbers who were approaching, and thus aid in creating a panic.

The Indians in St. Leger's camp were already impatient to get away; they had suffered severely in the battle of Oriskany; they had been disappointed in the success and plunder they had anticipated; and rumors of Arnold's approach had already reached them. It is said they had met and were in council to consult the *Manitou* as to their future movements, when at the very moment HonYost, the mysterious and Manitou-stricken one, was suddenly brought before the council. He was cunning, and his life and that of his brother, as he believed, depended on his success.

Exhibiting his garments riddled with bullets, he declared he had barely escaped death from the approaching foe, and had hastened on to tell his red brethren of the coming enemy and of their danger. The chief inquired the number of Arnold's troops and he pointed to the leaves of the trees. He was taken to the tent of St. Leger, and repeated his story, cunningly mixing truth and falsehood; he gave St. Leger an account of his capture with Lieutenant Butler, of which that officer had already heard, then of his trial and condemnation. He said on his way to the gallows, knowing he could but die in the attempt, he had made his escape; a whole volley had been fired at him, but fortunately the balls had passed through his clothes without wounding him. By this time the Oneida arrived in the camp bringing a belt, and told the Indians that the Americans were approaching in great numbers under their war-chief Arnold; that they did not wish to fight the Indians, but were determined to destroy the British troops, tories, rangers and Greens.

These stories had the desired effect; the Indians prepared to leave. St. Leger tried in vain to induce them to remain. The tales started by HonYost, corroborated by the Oneida, flew throughout the camp, a panic arose, and the whole body of the Indians fled. The tories and troops followed, and a rumor reaching them that Arnold was just behind them, they threw away their knapsacks, arms, and whatever would encumber their flight. Perhaps Curtis was somewhat extravagant in saying that "Arnold, volunteering to relieve Fort Stanwix, had by the mere terror of his coming blown St. Leger away."[1] Yet it is clear that there was at that time no name among the American officers whose approach would be more likely to produce such a result than his. HonYost, after going with the flying Indians a short

1. Centennial Address of Geo. W. Curtis at Bemis' Heights, Oct. 7, 1877.

distance, fell behind and returned to Fort Schuyler, and gave Gansevoort the first information he had that Arnold was approaching by forced marches.'

Then he hastened back to Arnold, his brother Nicholas was set at liberty, and the old mother returned home joyfully with both her sons.

Arnold pushed on to Fort Schuyler, hoping to overtake and capture the fugitives. He was received with a salute of artillery, and the cheers of the brave garrison. Gansevoort had followed the retreating St. Leger, but so precipitate had been his flight, that he could not be overtaken, but his tents, artillery, provisions, and camp equipage fell into the hands of the Americans. Thus ended the siege of Fort Schuyler, and thus, through the efforts of Herkimer, Willett, Gansevoort and Arnold, the right arm of Burgoyne's expedition, from which so much had been expected, was lopped off, and the British commander's reliance for aid and co-operation from St. Leger and his powerful Indian and tory allies, in all the Mohawk Valley and west to Lake Ontario, was destroyed. It was a hard blow for Burgoyne, and contributed largely to his final overthrow. Arnold returned in triumph to the main army on the Hudson, receiving as he passed, the thanks of the settlers, whose homes and families his success had rendered safe.

1. " FORT SCHUYLER, 22nd August, 1777.
" DEAR SIR:

"This morning at 11 o'clock I began a Heavy Canonade upon our Enemies' Works, which was immediately returned by a Number of Shells and Cannon. About 3 O'clock several Deserters came in, who informed me that General St. Leger with his Army was retreating with the utmost precipitation; soon after which I sent out a party of About Sixty Men to enter their camps, who soon returned and confirmed the above Accounts.

"About 7 O'clock this Evening, Hon Yost Schuyler Arrived here and informed me that General Arnold, with Two Thousand Men, were on their March for this Post, in Consequence of which I send you this information.

" I am, Dr. Sir, yours, &c.,
" PETER GANSEVOORT, Colo.

" To the Hon'ble General Arnold,
or Officer Commanding
the Army on their March to Fort Schuyler.

" pr. favour of }
Serj't Myres." }
—*Gates' Papers, Vol. IX, p. 75, in N. Y. His. Soc.*

CHAPTER IX.

FIRST BATTLE NEAR SARATOGA.

"But for Arnold that eventful day, Burgoyne would doubtless have marched into Albany at the autumnal equinox, a victor."—*Lossing.*

BATTLE OF 19TH OF SEPTEMBER—ARNOLD LEADS THE TROOPS TO VICTORY—ERROR OF BANCROFT—TESTIMONY OF COLS. VARICK AND LIVINGSTON, GENERALS SCHUYLER, BURGOYNE, AND OTHERS—VERDICT OF IRVING, LOSSING, AND OTHERS.

THE decisive campaign of the American Revolution approached its crisis. The battles of Saratoga, resulting in Burgoyne's surrender, have been selected by a distinguished English historian [1] as the conflict in American history to be ranked among the fifteen great battles of the world.

Arnold returned from his successful expedition up the Mohawk in high spirits. He had been absent twenty days, and had succeeded without loss, in raising the siege of Fort Schuyler, dispersing the Indians and tories, and driving St. Leger back to the Lakes.

Now he arrived in the camp of the main army, sanguine of success, full of zeal, and impatient for the approaching conflict. His sagacious military eye perceived that Burgoyne, the brave and chivalric soldier, and the courtly gentleman, with his small but magnificently appointed army, was doomed to defeat and capture.

Eager for military glory, still young and full of hope, and

---

1. Creasy.

yet proudly and bitterly recalling the refusal of Congress to give him the rank which Washington thought he had so well earned, he was determined to connect his name with the approaching conflict. Many an English sailor and soldier besides Nelson, has gone into battle with the sentiment, "Victory, or Westminster Abbey."

Arnold's desperate valor and reckless personal exposure in both the battles which resulted in the surrender of Burgoyne, indicate that with him it was a fixed determination to extort from Congress his proper rank, or die on the field.

Two events had occurred while he had been absent on the Mohawk, both of great importance to his country, and one influencing largely, perhaps fatally, his own future, the defeat and capture of Colonel Baum, near Bennington, and the change in the command of the army from Schuyler to Gates.

Burgoyne, suffering for provisions himself, learned that there had been collected at Bennington a depot of beef, corn and other needed supplies intended for the American army. Bennington was about twenty miles from the Hudson, and was guarded by militia only, and Burgoyne, in need of these very supplies, hoped to surprise Bennington and capture the stores. He ordered Colonel Baum with about five hundred men, to march to Bennington for that purpose, and soon after sent Lt.-Colonel Breyman to Batten-kill to be within supporting distance, as he supposed, of Baum.

The approach of the British was discovered by Colonel Stark at Bennington, and he immediately called on Colonel Warner at Manchester, to hasten to his aid. At the same time he appealed to the militia and yeomanry of the surrounding country to rally to his assistance, and he soon found himself at the head of a force considerably outnumbering that of Baum, and he determined to attack.

On the sixteenth of August, after a severe battle, in which Stark and his men behaved with great courage, Cololonel Baum and his whole force were compelled to surrender.

Breyman came up while the Americans were collecting the spoils of victory, and for a moment threatened to turn the tide of success against them; but Colonel Warner, arriving at the critical moment, drove the enemy from the field, and pursued them over hills and through forests, until night put an end to the conflict, capturing guns and baggage. At daylight, on the morning of the seventeenth of August, Burgoyne was awakened by the tidings that Baum was killed, and that his command were all prisoners, and that Breyman was struggling to make good his retreat to the main army.

While Arnold had been absent, Schuyler occupied the islands at the fords of the Mohawk, where it empties into the Hudson. He had been making every effort in his power to gather together the means of successfully repelling the menacing enemy. Many of the members of Congress from New England entertained strong prejudice against Schuyler, and were very slow to recognize his noble character and sterling virtues.

On the nineteenth of August Gates arrived in camp, and by command of Congress (Washington declining to make the ungrateful selection), superseded Schuyler in command of the northern army. Nothing could be more magnanimous and patriotic than the conduct of Schuyler on the execution of this cruel order. He had prepared the means of victory, and now when the hour of triumph approached, an intriguer, who, Bancroft declares, "had no fitness for command, and wanted personal courage,"[1] was placed at the head of this army which Schuyler had contributed so

[1] Bancroft, Vol. IX, p. 407.

largely to raise, and he was now about to gather the laurels which Schuyler was prepared to win; but such was the patriotism and generosity of Schuyler, that he manifested no resentment, and did everything in his power to contribute to the success of his unworthy rival.

It will be remembered that in the campaign of 1776, Gates and Arnold had been very intimate, but the careful reader of the correspondence between them, and between Schuyler and Arnold, will observe that while there is familiarity between Gates and Arnold, there is in the letters of Arnold to Schuyler a tone of respect not to be discerned in the letters to Gates. Still there was as yet no coldness on the part of Arnold towards Gates. So far from it, he says, writing to Gates from the German Flats, "as soon as the safety of this part of the country will permit, I will fly to your assistance."[1]

Arnold was now with the main body, ready to assist and co-operate with Gates to the utmost. The left wing of the army was at Loudon's Ferry, on the south bank of the Mohawk, five miles above its junction with the Hudson. Two brigades and Morgan's famed riflemen were there. Soon after Arnold's arrival in camp the entire army was concentrated on and near Bemis' Heights, Arnold commanding the left wing, composed of the same troops which had been at Loudon's Ferry.

The British were approaching, and Gates was about to throw his army across Burgoyne's path, and intercept his march towards Albany. It was deemed important to select with care the best position to check such advance and receive the attack. Arnold therefore, says Irving, "reconnoitered the neighborhood in company with Kosciusko, the Polish engineer, in quest of a good camping ground, and

---

[1]. Irving's Life of Washington, Vol. III, p. 196.

at length fixed upon a ridge of hills called Bemis' Heights, which Kosciusko proceeded to fortify."[1]

During the few days which preceded the battle of the nineteenth of September, Arnold continually annoyed the enemy by skirmishing and attacking the parties engaged in repairing roads and bridges.[2] A German officer says: "We had to do the enemy the honor of sending out whole regiments to protect our workmen."

"It was Arnold," says Irving, "who provoked this honor. At the head of fifteen hundred men he skirmished with the superior force sent out against him."[3,4]

1. Irving's Washington, Vol. III, p. 239.
2. Lossing's Schuyler, Vol. II, p. 343.
3. Irving's Washington, Vol. III, p. 242.
4. Manuscript letter of Vol. Varick to Schuyler, Sept. 15, 1777, as follows:

"HEAD QUT'S, SEPT. 15th, 1777.

"DEAR GENERAL:—Yesterday Afternoon I had the pleasure of attending General Arnold on a Reconnoitering party, to pick out Ground for a New Camp. We took our Departure in Company with Mr. Lansing, Col. Chris. Yates, and three light Horse, all along the heights on the West of the River, up Hill and down Dale, till we came to Sword's House, where we fell in with Colo. Morgan's Party of Riflemen and Infantry, and the Genl's Aids, and took the road along the river till we reached the House on this side Blind Morris—here the troops were halted, and Livingston, with Lansing and two horse, advanced till they should discover some person or movement of the enemy; agreable to orders they advanced till near Colo. Van Vechten, and were followed by the Genl's Aids, and there discovered a party supposed to be the advanced picket of the enemy, of about 100, on the Hill North of Van Vechten. I went In pursuit of the Young Gentlemen as far as the Bridge between the Hill and the Bridge at Colo. Van Vechten's, where I met them on their return. I found the Bridge in the same Plight in which our Army left it on their retreat from Saratoga.

"The enemy discovered our party, and we had a fair prospect of them from the hill beyond Morris on the banks of the *Dove-Gat*—they appeared to be parading without the beat of drums.

"On our return we were in hopes of the Genl's ordering a party to attack them, but it being near Evening, the Gen'l tho't more prudent to return. When we returned at   we heard our Evening Gun, but none from the Enemy.

"Upon the whole it is supposed that Burgoyne will advance this way and attack us. It may be that this manouvre of his is to cover the Retreat of his Cannon and baggage; however it is hardly probable. On my Return I am honored with your polite favor of the 14th, for which I am much obliged to you. I suppose by this time you have rec'd two of my letters of the 13th, giving you an account of Colo. Wilkinson's Expedition.

"I most sanguinely expected to have been at Saratoga by this day, but am much disappointed, and am now convinced that no Carriages can pass the Road in less

He was generally successful, and took many prisoners, and thus encouraged and animated the troops.

At this time there began to appear a coolness on the part of General Gates towards General Arnold. Gates having succeeded in his intrigue against Schuyler, was already dreaming of superseding Washington himself.[1] Washington's kindness to Arnold, his efforts with Congress for his promotion, and for the restoration of his proper rank, were well known; and Gates naturally and rightly assumed that Arnold could not be induced to become a partisan of his against the Commander-in-Chief.[2] Besides, Arnold was known to be a friend of Schuyler, Colonel Henry Brockholst Livingston, who had been on the staff, and Colonel Varick, the Secretary of General Schuyler, when their chief left for Albany remained in camp, and the former was now acting as aid to General Arnold.[3]

than two or 3 days. As soon as I am happy Enough to get there, I shall cheerfully comply with your requests, and prevent any injury being done to your buildings and fences as far as my influence with the Genl. and other Gentlemen will extend. I have no doubt of Gen. Gates complying with the request.

"Gen. Arnold is this day gone out with a large party. I don't know his intentions; probably to try the east side of the river, as he seemed very desirous to have a prospect of the enemies' camp from the high hill on that side. If he proceeds on this side, he may fall in with some of the Enemy.

"We found no height yesterday large enough for our camp.

"Mr. Lansing and Livingston join in their respects to you. Be good enough to make them to Mrs. Schuyler and Miss Peggy. I am much obliged to them for their good wishes.

"I am, with every respectful,
"faithful sentiment,
"Your most obliged,
"RICHARD VARICK.

"To the Hon. M. Genl.,
"SCHUYLER."

The Schuyler papers. This and other letters quoted from the Schuyler manuscripts are now, for the first time, printed in full. These Schuyler papers are of great historic value.

1. "He (Gates) aspired to the chief command of the continental armies, indulged in the egotistical idea that he knew better how to move them than did the Virginian General, and that the New England delegates would support him in such preposterous claims.' —*Lossing's Schuyler*, Vol. II, p. 182.

2. The scheme to supersede Washington by Gates "originated with three men," Conway, Gates and Mifflin, the latter one of the junior Brigadiers, who had been promoted over Arnold.—*Spark's Writings of Washington*, Vol. V, pp. 390 and 483.

3. Lossing's Schuyler, Vol. II, p. 341.

Varick was also much of the time with Arnold, and these young officers, known to be in the confidence of Schuyler, excited the jealousy of Gates.

Livingston writes to Schuyler on the twenty-third of September, after the quarrel between Gates and Arnold had become open and notorious, "the reason for the present disagreement between *two old cronies, is simply this: Arnold is your friend.*"[1]

Varick, writing to Schuyler on the 22nd of September, says: "He (Arnold) has the full confidence of the troops, and they would fight gallantly under him."[2]

Having stated these circumstances, I now proceed to detail the events of the nineteenth of September:

The army was at Bemis' Heights. The camp, which had been, as before stated, carefully selected by Arnold, and fortified by Kosciusko, was situated on the west bank of the Hudson, and extending from the margin of the stream across a narrow flat, and then across a ridge of hills called Bemis' Heights, and thence on to other hills still farther west. Kosciusko had caused breastworks to be thrown up in front three-quarters of a mile long, with a strong battery at each end and one in the center; on the right across the low ground near the river, an entrenchment was thrown up, and on the bank was a strong battery protecting a floating bridge which crossed the river. On the morning of the eighteenth, Burgoyne moved down within two miles of the American camp, and prepared for battle. He was surrounded by a brilliant array of distinguished officers—Major-General Philips, Generals Fraser, Hamilton and Powell, and the German General, Riedesel, the Earl of Balcarras, Colonel Breyman, Major Ackland—all officers of great merit and distinction.

1. Lossing's Schuyler, Vol. II, p. 851.
2. Schuyler papers.—MSS.

Gates' head-quarters were some distance south of the line of breastworks, and behind Bemis' Heights; Arnold's were north and west of Gates' quarters, and west of the line of breastworks.

The morning of the nineteenth the sun rose bright, and the air was clear and bracing; a hoar frost whitened the ground. The hostile armies now confronting each other, were so near that the morning gun and drum-beat of each could be distinctly heard by the other. Each army extended from the bank of the river westward over the hills. The right wing of the Americans, under the immediate command of Gates, and composed of Glover's, Nixon's and Patterson's brigades, occupied the hills near the river and the flats on its margin.

The left, under the command of Arnold, consisting of Poor's brigade, made up of Cilleys', Scammel's and Hales' New Hampshire troops, and Van Courtland's and James Livingston's New York regiments, the Connecticut militia, Morgan's riflemen and Dearborn's infantry.[1] These were posted on the hills, three-quarters of a mile west of the river. The center was composed of Learned's brigade, of Massachusetts, and New York troops.

The left wing of the British, with the very powerful train of artillery, rested on the flats near the river; the center and right wing composed largely of German troops, extended west on the hills, and were commanded by Burgoyne in person, and with them were Fraser and Breyman with the light infantry. The front and flanks were covered by the Indians, Canadians and Loyalists.

Philips and Riedesel were to march down the road on the bank of the river. The Canadians and Indians were to attack the outposts of the Americans, while Burgoyne and Fraser, with the grenadiers and light infantry, were to

1. Irving's Washington, Vol. III, p. 241.

march through the forests behind the hills, and assault the left flank and rear of the Americans. As most of the ground was covered with a dense forest, the movements were to be regulated by signal-guns. When Burgyone and Fraser had effected a junction, three heavy guns were to be fired as a signal for an attack on the flank and rear of the American left, and for a general assault along the whole line. American lookouts were stationed in the tops of trees on high ground, and the unusual activity in the British camp was soon reported to the American officers. The glitter of moving arms, the bright scarlet uniforms, and the moving of flags, indicating that the enemy was forming his line of battle, were observed and reported at the headquarters of Arnold and Gates, and at ten A. M. it was announced that the British were coming, moving down in three divisions. Philips and Riedesel with the artillery, were marching down the river road; Burgoyne with the center followed the stream now forming Wilbur's Basin, south and west; and Fraser and Breyman started on their circuitous route to reach the flank and rear of the American left.

Arnold, watchful and eager for the fight, to whom these movements were known, was anxious to go out and meet the enemy. "Gates," says Lossing, "gave no orders and evinced no disposition to fight."[1] His officers were impatient. Arnold "urged, begged and entreated"[2] permission to lead his troops to the attack, and at length he obtained permission to send Morgan's riflemen and Dearborn's infantry out to meet the enemy.

They soon met the Canadians and Indians and dispersed them. Following their advantage with too much eagerness, they became scattered, and a strong reinforcement of the enemy coming up, they were obliged to fall back, and the

1. Lossing's Schuyler, Vol. II, p. 344.
2. Colonel Varick. Letter quoted hereafter.

brave partisan, Morgan, for a moment thought his renowned corps was "ruined;" but sounding loudly his shrill woodman's whistle—known to them as the "turkey call"—the riflemen gathered around their chief, and the regiments of Scammel and Cilley coming up, the fight was kept up with equal fury. Meantime Burgoyne and Fraser were moving rapidly to fall on the front and flank of the American left. The center under Burgoyne reached a clearing called Freeman's farm, while Fraser, farther west, marched rapidly south, hoping to turn the American left. Arnold at the same time attempted to cut Fraser off from his connection with Burgoyne. Arnold and Fraser met about sixty yards west of Freeman's cottage,[1] and a bloody conflict ensued. "Arnold led the van of his men and fell upon the foe with the fury and impetuosity of a tiger. By voice and action he encouraged his troops."[2]

He was met by overwhelming numbers. Fraser rapidly turned and attacked Arnold's right. Arnold rallied his troops, and being reinforced, and now leading the regiments of Cilley and Scammel, and Dearborn, Hale and Brooks, attempted to break through the British lines and separate Fraser from the center. "He made a rapid counter-march, and his movements being masked by the wood, suddenly attempted to turn Fraser's left." Here he threw himself upon it with a boldness and impetuosity which threatened to cut the wings of the army asunder.[3] But the grenadiers and Breyman's riflemen hastened to its support, and General Philips, hurrying through the thick woods and over the hills, came hastening up from the extreme left, and just at the moment when victory seemed to be crowning the efforts of the Americans.

1. Lossing's Field Book, Vol. I, p. 52.
2. Lossing's Field Book, Vol. I, p. 52.
3. Irving's Washington, Vol. III, p. 244.

Now Burgoyne, Fraser and Philips were leading and encouraging their forces, and Sergeant Lamb, a British writer, says: "For four hours a constant blaze of fire was kept up, and both armies seemed to be determined on death or victory."[1] Arnold had brought his whole division into action and called for re-enforcements, but they were refused. Lossing says: "Had he (Arnold) been seconded by his commander, and strengthened by re-enforcements * * he would doubtless have secured a complete victory." He adds: "But for Arnold, on that eventful day, Burgoyne would doubtless have marched into Albany at the autumnal equinox, a victor."[2] Night put an end to the conflict, which the British themselves declare to have been the most obstinate and hardly fought of any ever experienced in America.

Arnold rode a grey horse during the conflict, and near night ("evening," as Wilkinson says), went himself to the camp of Gates for re-enforcements. Wilkinson states the incident as follows:[3]

"Gates and Arnold were together in front of the camp. Major Lewis came in from the scene of action, and announced that its progress was undecisive. Arnold immediately exclaimed: 'By G—d! I will soon put an end to it'—and clapping spurs to his horse galloped off at full speed. I was instantly dispatched by Gates after Arnold, overtook and ordered him back, lest he might do some 'rash act.'"

Arnold having blackened by his treason the fame hitherto so brilliant as a soldier, some historians[4] and writers have denied that he was on the battle-field of Saratoga at all!

1. Lossing's Life of Schuyler, Vol. II, p. 349
2. Lossing's Life of Schuyler Vol. II, p. 348.
3. Wilkinson's Memories, Vol. I, p. 245.
4. Notably Bancroft.

Let us inquire who led the American forces on this eventful day; or was the battle fought without any leader?

It is not claimed by any one that Gates was on the field, or that he had anything to do with the battle, except to yield to Arnold's importunity and permit him to send Morgan and Dearborn to the front; when he saw Scammel's battalion marching out, "he asked where the troops were going, and on being told, he declared no more troops should go—he would not suffer the camp to be exposed."[1]

Who then did lead? This battle was full of skillful maneuvers and evolutions, beginning at mid-day and lasting till night; and Burgoyne and Phillips, and Fraser and Riedesel, skillful and able men, were all on the field skillfully guiding and directing the British troops. Was the battle on the American side fought without a leader? Was there no guiding spirit? Such an improbable statement would never have appeared on the pages of any respectable writer, if the man who ably led and valiantly fought that battle had not afterwards betrayed his country.

But let us be just to this man, even though his name be Benedict Arnold.

A brilliant and fascinating, but not always accurate, historian, has said: "Arnold was not on the field."[2]

If so, this was the first time he was ever near a battle-field and not at the head of his troops. He commanded the left wing, and this was the object of Burgoyne's skillfully arranged attack; his troops fought gallantly, maneuvered skillfully, met and foiled by skill and valor every attempt of Burgoyne for five long hours; and we are told they did so without their leader, without any leader? The statement is utterly incredible, and can be demonstrated to be untrue.

This is Mr. Bancroft's language:

1. Colonel Varick, Lossing's Schuyler, Vol. II, p. 349.
2. Bancroft's History of United States, Vol. IX, p. 411.

"On the British side three Major-Generals came on the field; on the American side not one, nor a Brigadier till near its close;" and in a note he adds: "Arnold was not on the field. So witnesses Wilkinson, whom Marshall knew personally and believed. So said the informer of Gordon."[1] Let us examine the evidence: Wilkinson was the Adjutant-General of Gates. He was then a young man of twenty, an enemy of Arnold, pert, officious and vain. Gates' headquarters were behind Bemis' Heights, and from these quarters the battle-ground could not be seen.[2] More than thirty years (1816) after the battle, Wilkinson published his memoirs, and while the just indignation against Arnold for his treason was fresh, and when everything to his prejudice and nothing to his credit, found its way into print, makes this statement:

"It is worthy of remark, *that not a single general officer was on the field of battle on the nineteenth of September*, until the evening, when General Learned was ordered out. About the same time General Gates and Arnold were in front of the center of the camp, listening to the peal of small arms, when Colonel M. Lewis returned from the field and reported the indecisive progress of the action, at which Arnold exclaimed: 'By G—d, I will soon put an end to it,' and clapping spurs to his horse, galloped off at full speed. Colonel Lewis observed to Gates, 'You had better order him back; he may, by some rash act, do mischief.' I was instantly dispatched, overtook, and remanded Arnold to camp."[3]

This was at "evening." It was the first time Wilkinson speaks of seeing Arnold that day. Arnold's intelligence of Burgoyne's approach was received at mid-day. Colonel Varick says, "It is evident to me he (Gates) never intended to fight Burgoyne till Arnold urged, begged and entreated him to do it."[4] Where had Arnold been from noon until

---

1. Bancroft's History of United States, Vol. IX, p. 410. But Marshall himself says: "Arnold with nine Continental regiments and Morgan's corps was completely engaged with the whole right wing of the British army."—*Life of Washington, Vol II, p. 275.*
2. Stone's Burgoyne's Campaign, p. 71.
3. Wilkinson's Memoirs, Vol. I, pp. 245-6.
4. Losing's Life of Schuyler, Vol. II, p. 349.

"evening" during the four or five hours in which his whole division had been fighting?

At "evening" Arnold appears "mounted" in front of the center of the camp, finds Gates, and the moment a report is brought in that the action is "indecisive" he exclaims: "By G—d, I will soon put an end to it," and clapping spurs to his horse, gallops off at full speed, and is only restrained by the peremptory order of Gates. This conduct certainly does not indicate a man who had been for four hours away from the field of battle on which his own soldiers were hotly engaged. It was a strange spectacle for the chief to arrest the second in command when spurring to the front under circumstances above stated. It may well be that Wilkinson did not *see* Arnold on the field of battle during the day. The battle-ground was uneven, and most of it covered with forest, so that no general view could be had of the field.

Neither Arnold's head-quarters, nor any considerable portion of the battle-field were visible from Gates' head-quarters.[1] Wilkinson's proper position when not executing an order, was near his chief, and Gates, somewhat rudely reminds his staff-officer of this; as Wilkinson says, "about half past twelve o'clock, a report of small arms announced Morgan's corps to be engaged in front of our left. The General and his suite were examining the battery, which had been commenced on our left. I asked leave to repair to the scene of action, but was refused, with this observation:" "It is your duty, sir, to await orders." If he had repaired to the scene of action, he would doubtless have seen Arnold in the fight as usual. But not being permitted to go to the scene of action, he did not, and could not see Arnold until the incident at "evening," already described.

But let us examine and see what is implied by the corres-

1. Burgoyne's Campaign, by Charles Neilson, p. 149.

pondence of these officers at that time. On the twenty-second of September, Arnold having heard that Gates, in his report of the engagement transmitted to Congress, had made no mention of his division, nor of himself, indignant at this treatment, writes to Gates, saying: "On the nineteenth, when advice was received that the enemy was approaching, I took the liberty to give it as my opinion that *we* ought to march out and attack them. You desired *me* to send Colonel Morgan and the Light Infantry, and *support them; I obeyed your orders*, and before the action was over, *I* found it necessary to send out the whole of my division to support the attack. No other troops were engaged that day except Colonel's Marshall's regiment."[1] These facts, not denied by Gates, are entirely inconsistent with the statement of Wilkinson, and show that Arnold obtained leave to "march out and attack, and that to that end he had obtained leave to send Colonel Morgan and the Light Infantry, and that he did "support them;" and that before the action was over, he found it necessary to "support" them by "the whole of my (his) division."

These statements of Arnold, made three days after the battle, in a letter complaining of Gates' injustice to his troops, *if true*, establish the fact that the battle of the nineteenth of September was fought by Arnold's division, under his leadership. Is it likely that Arnold, in the camp of Gates, and in the presence of the whole army, would make statements which, if untrue, would be instantly known to be false, and stamped as such? And if he had been guilty of such folly, would not Gates—then Arnold's bitter enemy—and his Adjutant-General, have then and there contradicted the statement? But the statement was not contradicted by Gates; it was not until more than thirty years had gone by, that Wilkinson says that not a single

---

1. Arnold to Gates, Wilkinson's Memoirs, Vol. I, p. 254.

general officer was on the field. As criticisms of Wilkinson's statements, by various historians and writers, will be quoted hereafter, I forbear further comments, and will proceed to present the clear and positive testimony of impartial eye-witnesses, showing that Mr. Bancroft's allegation—based on Wilkinson's—that Arnold was not on the field, is erroneous. Wilkinson was a bitter enemy of Arnold, and a partizan of Gates, but there were in the camp at the time of the battle, two gentlemen of high personal character, and every way entitled to full credence—Colonel Richard Varick,[1] who had been the secretary, and Colonel Livingston, who had been the aid of General Schuyler. Colonel Livingston was now the aid of General Arnold, and of course, as such, knew perfectly well what Arnold was doing on the day of the battle. Three days thereafter, and when Arnold, indignant at Gates' treatment of his division and of himself, threatened to leave, Livingston, in a letter to Schuyler says:

"When the general officers and soldiers heard of it, they were greatly alarmed. * * * They had lost confidence in Gates, and had the highest opinion of Arnold.[2] To induce him (Arnold) to stay, General Poor proposed an address from the general officers and Colonels of his division, returning him thanks for his services, and *particularly for his conduct during the late action*, and requesting him to stay.[3] The address was framed and consented to by Poor's officers. Those of General Learned refused. They acquiesced in the propriety of the measure, but were afraid of giving umbrage to General Gates,"[4]—a paltry excuse for officers of rank to allege for not doing their duty. Finally a letter was written to Arnold, and signed by all the general officers, excepting Lincoln, urging him to remain, for another battle seemed imminent.[5]

1. Afterwards on the staff of Washington, Mayor of the city of New York, and Attorney-General of the State.
2. Quoted from Schuyler papers, in Lossing's Life of Schuyler, Vol. II, p. 351.
3. Schuyler Papers.
4. Livingston to Schuyler, September 23d.
5. Lossing's Life of Schuyler, Vol. II, p. 351.

HIS PATRIOTISM AND HIS TREASON.   179

Col. Varick, writing from Arnold's camp to Schuyler on the 22nd, three days after the battle, says:

"Gates seemed to be piqued that Arnold's division had the honor of beating the enemy on the 19th. This I am certain of: Arnold has all the credit of the action; and this I further know, that Gates asked where the troops were going when Scammel's battallion marched out, and upon being told, he declared no more troops should go; he would not suffer the camp to be exposed. Had Gates complied with Arnold's repeated desires, he would have obtained a general and complete victory over the enemy. But it is evident to me he never intended to fight Burgoyne until Arnold urged, begged and entreated him to do it."[1]

Colonel Varick, in another letter, alluding to the quarrel between Arnold and Gates, says: "I apprehend if Arnold leaves us we shall move, unless the enemy moves up the river. He has the full confidence of the troops, and they would fight gallantly under him."[2]

Writing to Schuyler, Varick says:

"CAMP, WEDNESDAY, 9 O'CLOCK A. M.,
"Sept. 24, 1777.

"Your very polite favor of the 21st was delivered me yesterday by Maj. Franks. I have anticipated the answer in mine of 22d at 11 o'clock P. M., and the 23d in the morning, with reference to Arnold and Lincoln. The former will, I believe, remain till the action we expect this day or to-morrow, is settled, although he had received his permit to go down yesterday morning. * * I am happy that Arnold has decided to stay. I have no doubt of some hot work this day. Many discharges have already happened in the woods."[3]

In another letter of the 24th, Varick says:

"General Arnold is so much offended at the treatment Gates has given him, that I make not the least doubt the latter will be called on, as soon as the service will admit."[4]

On the 25th September, Schuyler, replying to Varick's letter of 21st, says:

1. Schuyler Papers—MSS. I refer also to Lossing's Life of Schuyler. Vol. II, p. 849.
2. Schuyler Papers—MSS. Varick to Schuyler, Sept. 22, 1777.
3. Schuyler Papers. Varick to Schuyler, Sept. 24, 1777.
4. Schuyler Papers—MSS.

"A report prevails that a second fracas has happened between Gates and General Arnold, and I hope it is not of such a nature as to oblige that gallant officer to leave the army. If he does, I shall be far, very far from being so easy as I feel myself, in the reflection that he is with you."[1]

And on the 25th of September, Schuyler, in reply to Varick, says:

"I am pleased to hear that our gallant friend, General Arnold, has determined to remain until a battle shall have happened, or General Burgoyne retreats. Everybody that I have conversed with on the subject of the dispute between Gates and him, thinks Arnold has been extremely ill-treated. He (Gates) will probably be indebted to him (Arnold) for the glory he may acquire by a victory; but perhaps he is so very sure of success that he does not wish the other to come in for a share of it."[2]

Such are the statements of Colonel Varick. Colonel Livingston's statements are not less explicit and conclusive.

In a letter to Schuyler dated "Camp, Bemis' Heights," Sept. 23d, 1777, he says:[3]

"I am much distressed at General Arnold's determination to retire from the army at this important crisis. His presence was never more necessary. He is the life and soul of the troops. Believe me, Sir, *to him alone is due the honor of our late victory*. Whatever share his superiors may claim, they are entitled to none. He enjoys the confidence and affection of officers and soldiers. They would to a man follow him to conquest or death. His departure will dishearten them to such a degree as to render them of little service."

1. Schuyler Papers—MSS.
2. Schuyler to Varick, Sept. 25, 1777. Schuyler MSS.
3. Schuyler MSS.

This is the text of the letter:

"CAMP AT BEMIS HEIGHTS, }
"Sept. 23, 1777. }

"DEAR SIR:

"I am this moment honored with your favor of the 21st by Major Franks. General Lincoln arrived here last night, and part of his infantry came to-day; the remainder are expected to-morrow. I wrote to you some time since of his having detached two parties to Ticonderoga and Fort Independence. Colonel Varick has given you the particulars of their success. I cannot persuade myself that the mount will be taken.

"I am much distressed at General Arnold's determination to retire from the Army

The next day, Sept. 24th, Arnold having in consequence of the expectation of an engagement, determined to remain, Livingston hastens to write to Schuyler, saying, "as

at this important crisis. His presence was never more necessary. He is the life and soul of the troops. Believe me, Sir, to him alone is due the honor of our late Victory; whatever share his superiors may claim, they are entitled to none. He enjoys the confidence and affection of his officers and soldiers. They would, to a man, follow him to conquest or death. His departure will dishearten them to such a degree as to render them of little service.

"The difference between him and Mr. G. has arisen to too great a height to admit of a compromise. I have for some time past observed the great coolness, and in many instances, even disrespect, with which General Arnold has been treated at He dquarters. His proposals have been rejected with marks of indignity. His own orders have been frequently countermanded, and himself set in a rediculous light by those of the *Commander-in-Chief*. His remonstrances on those occasions have been termed presumptuous. In short, he has pocketed many insults for the sake of his country, which a man of less pride would have resented. The repeated indignities he received at length roused his spirit and determination again to remonstrate. He waited on Mr. Gates in person last evening. Matters were altercated in a very high strain. Both were warm—the latter rather passionate and very assuming. Towards the end of the debate Mr. G. told Arnold 'He did not know of his being a Major-General. He had sent in his resignation to Congress. He had never given him the command of any division of the Army. General Lincoln would be here in a day or two, and that then he should have no occasion for him, and would give him a pass to Philadelphia, whenever he chose.'

"Arnold's spirit could not brooke this usage. He returned to his quarters, represented what had passed, in a letter to Mr. G., and requested his permission to go to Philadelphia. This morning, in compliance to his letter, he received a permit by the way of a letter directed to Mr. Hancock. He sent this back, and requested one in proper form, which was complied with. To-morrow he will set out for Albany. The reason of the present disagreement between two cronies is simply this: *Arnold is your friend*. I shall attend the General down, chagrining as it may be for me to leave the army when an opportunity for any young fellow to distinguish himself. I can no longer submit to the command of a man whom I abhor from my very soul. His conduct is disgusting to every one, except his flatterers and dependants, among whom are some who profess to be your friends. A cloud is gathering, and may ere long burst on his head. * * Lt. Arden is just returned with eight Tory prisoners. He made a tour as far as Saratoga—was in your house, which he found is much damaged. The glasses are entirely gone, the paper ruined and frame much injured. The barn and other out-buildings are safe. Two letters were taken from one of the Tories are from Burgoyne to Brig. Pond, in which he says: 'We left 500 dead on the field.' He is silent as to his own loss. He begs that St. Leger may be hastened on. The Indians you have sent us are of great service; not a day passes without their taking some prisoners. Make my best respects to Mrs. Schuyler and family.

"I am, dear General, &c.,
"HENRY B. LIVINGSTON.

"General Philip Schuyler."

the enemy are hourly expected, General Arnold cannot think of leaving camp."[1]

On the 26th of September, Livingston wrote again to Schuyler, saying:

"It gives me pleasure to inform you that General Arnold intends to stay. When the general officers found him determined to go, they thought it necessary to take some measures to induce him to continue in the army. They have accordingly written him a letter (signed by all but Lincoln), requesting him not to quit the service at this critical time. He has consented, though no accommodation has taken place."

In the same letter he speaks of an attempt being made to have the writer turned from Gen. Arnold's family.

---

[1] Schuyler MSS. The following is the text of the letter of 24th Sept:

"CAMP AT BEMIS' HEIGHTS,
"Sept. 24, 1777.

"DEAR SIR:

"I wrote you last evening and was in hopes to have had the pleasure of seeing you to-day, *but as the enemy are hourly expected, General Arnold cannot think of leaving camp.* Three deserters came in this morning, and it was rumored in the camp when they came off, that we were to be attacked this day. Burgoyne yesterday harrangued the soldiers, and told them he was determined to leave his bones on the field or force his way to Albany. He has about one month's salt provisions in his camp. Three Tories were just now brought in by the Oneidas; they confirm the report of the deserters, and add that the enemy acknowledged publicly to have lost 700 killed and wounded in the late battle, and plume themselves with a confidence that our loss might have been at least double.

"General Arnold's intention to quit this department is made public, and has caused great uneasiness among the soldiers. To induce him to stay, General Poor proposed an address from the general officers and colonels of his division, returning him thanks for his past services, and particularly for his conduct during the late action, and requesting him to stay. The address was framed and consented to by Poor's officers. Those of General Learned refused. They acquiesced in the propriety of the measure, but were afraid of giving umbrage to General Gates—a paltry excuse for officers of rank to allege in excuse for not doing their duty. As this method has failed, I see no other way left to bring about a reconciliation but by the interposition of the General officers. This has been proposed to Lincoln. He is now anxious for Arnold's stay, and will push the matter. I hope he may succeed, as I think he is an officer of too much moment to be neglected—though it may be a mortifying situation for any Gentleman of spirit to submit to the petulent humors of any man, be his rank ever so high.

"I am with due respect and esteem, Sir,
"Your friend,
"HENRY B. LIVINGSTON.

"Major General Schuyler."

"Maj. Chester," [1] says he, "attempted to bring about a reconciliation. For this purpose he consulted with the Deputy Adjutant-General, and in the course of their conversation was told that some overtures were necessary on Arnold's side; that Gen Gates was jealous of me, and that I had influenced Arnold's conduct, and that of course it was necessary to get rid of me to open a way for accommodation. When this was told to Arnold, he could not contain himself, and desired Chester to return for answer: 'that his judgment had never been influenced by any one, and that he would *not sacrifice a friend for the 'face of clay.'*" [2]

1. The same Maj. Chester with whom Livington fought a duel in defense of Arnold, or about a matter growing out of the quarrel between Gates and Arnold.

2. The following is the text of Livingston's letter (letter of Sept 26).

"CAMP AT BEMIS HEIGHTS, }
"Sept. 26, 1777. }

"DEAR SIR:

"I am favored with yours of the 25th, and am much obliged for the intelligence you gave me; I am particularly happy to hear that the enemy have left New Jersey. That state has had its share of the calamities of war, and needs some respite to recover itself.

"It gives me pleasure to inform you that General Arnold intends to stay. When the General Officers found him determined to go, they thought it necessary to take some measures to induce his continuance in the army. They have, accordingly, wrote him a letter (signed by all but Lincoln) requesting him not to quit the Service at this critical moment. He has consented, though no accommodation has taken place. * *

"I find myself under the necessity of returning to Albany, merely to satisfy the caprice and jealousy of a certain great person. It has been several times insinuated by the Commander-in-Chief to General Arnold, that his mind has been poisoned and prejudiced by some of his family, and I have been pointed out as the person who had this undue influence over him. Arnold had always made proper replies on these occasions, and despised the reflection. But since the last rupture, another attempt has been made in a low, indirect manner, to have me turned from General Arnold's family. Major Chester (who, by the way, is an impertinent pedant) attempted to bring about a reconciliation. For this purpose he consulted with the Lieu't-Adj't-General, and in the course of their conversation was told that some overtures were necessary on Arnold's side; that General Gates was jealous of me, and thought I had influenced Arnold's conduct, and that of course it was necessary to get rid of me to open a way for accommodation. When this *was told to Arnold he could scarcely contain himself*, and desired Chester to return for answer: that his judgment had never been influenced by any man, and that he would *not sacrifice a friend to* please the 'Face of clay.'

"Arnold told me what had passed, and insisted on my remaining with him. As I find this cannot be done consistently with the harmony of these two gentlemen, I shall leave camp to-morrow. I purposed to have set off to day, but Arnold insisted on my staying at least this day, lest it should appear like a concession on his part. I have taken no pains to cure any one of these jealousies but let their own feelings prompt them.

"Two deserters have come in this morning; they say, this is the day fixed to attack us. I believe these will be (paper torn). General Arnold sends his best wishes

The statements of Varick and Livingston, that Arnold *was* on the field and led his troops, settle beyond controversy the facts in relation to Arnold's conduct on the 19th of September, and show the estimation in which he was held by his fellow soldiers. One cannot read the glowing testimony of Judge Livingston in regard to Arnold's

to you. He would write, but is prevented by business. Mine wait on Mrs. Schuyler and family. I am with great esteem.

"Your affectionate humble servant,
"HENRY B. LIVINGSTON.

"Major General Schuyler."
—*Schuyler MSS.*

Also letter of Colonel Varick, as follows:

"CAMP, SEPT. 25TH, 1777,
"7 o' clock, P. M.

"DEAR GEN'L:

"This afternoon I was honored with your very polite favor of this Date.

"As to the subject of Dispute between the Gentlemen mentioned in Yours, the enclosed from Major Livingston will inform you further. It seems that it is a heartsore to your success, or that our Major should live with Arnold. He has thrown out in an unmanly manner, that Arnold's mind was poisoned by some of those about him—here I feel myself touched, although the person alluded to in mine of (I think) the 19th, who affects great friendship for you, was polite enough to tell Major Chester, Livingston's antagonist, that the first step towards an accommodation will be to get rid of Livingston. This Arnold was informed of, but disdained so ignoble an act. Livingston has too much regard for his country to remain, when by sacrificing his own pleasure, he may possibly promote its weal; this however is but ostentation. As I conceive the hint to be intended (by Gate's friend) for me also, I shall avoid as much as possible going to Arnold's, lest I may be the ostensible cause of Dispute. Livingston will go down to-morrow, and if there is no probability of an action by Saturday or Sunday, I shall follow him, though it would give me more pleasure if I could see Saratoga first; this pleasure I fancy I should have this day enjoyed, if General Gates had either furnished Arnold with troops on the 19th, or permitted us to go out on the 20th while the Enemy were in confusion, and are now in high spirits and rejoicing in their *past* Victory, A Victory I will not call it when we drove them from the field of battle, which was of no further use to us when night came on, and we retired deliberately to our camp, leaving them to bury our Dead the *next* day—A day, the loss of which we may severely regret.

"The enemy are strongly encamped and fortified, and I do not imagine Gates will attack them, nor will it be prudent for them to attack us.

"If our army moves by Saturday noon or Sunday, I shall continue here; if not, my Duty will oblige me to return to Albany and sign the Muster Rolls, before I see Saratoga.

"It is said the Enemy have fortifyed the Ground we fought on with a work 12 or 16 feet high. What use this can be of unless it be for a Garrison and safe Guard for his stores. It is hardly practicable to take it 'coup de-main' as it is a high ground surrounded by vallies.

services, and the extent to which he enjoyed the confidence and affection of officers and soldiers, and the declaration that "they would, to a man, follow him to conquest or death," without being convinced that he must have possessed other qualities which soldiers love, besides courage.

It is proper to add that Colonel Livingston, after being on the staff of Schuyler and Arnold, went to Spain as the Secretary of John Jay, whose sister he married. Afterwards he was Judge of the Supreme Court of New York, and then Justice of the Supreme Court of the United States.

I cite also the testimony of Charles Neilson.[1] He gives as his authority his father, who was in the engagement as a guide, and had occupied a portion of the battle-field as a farm, and this statement of an eye witness is as Neilson says, corroborated by many officers and soldiers who were present. Neilson says:

"About the time General Philips arrived on the field with the artillery, General Arnold, on a gray horse and under full speed from the scene of action, rode up to General Gates," * * and said: "General, the British are reinforced—we must have more men." General Gates re-

---

"I believe you are not much in the wrong in your conjectures that Gates was sure of success, and wished to ascribe all the honor to himself, as no other officer (except Arnold) had enough of a Gentleman's spirit to dispute it with him.

"This morning the enemy's picket of German's in the rear were attacked and would have been all secured had not the Fogg (which was very intense) prevented it: six were killed and one prisoner; the rest escaped. The prisoner had a *ral* and the end of his title, but he did not know whether he was a *General* or a *Corporal*.

"General Gates said this afternoon that his army was at least 3,000 stronger than 8 days since; that Lincoln had 1,600 Rank and file.

"As this is like to be a rainy night, Burgoyne may possibly be fool enough to make a tryal to push on, or try our pickets. (Paper torn—illegible.)

"I am exceedingly happy in the Good Wishes of your family. I need not assure you that they have ever had mine. I wish my best respects to Mrs. Schuyler, with thanks for the Butter she has been so good as to send me. Miss Peggy and the Young Gentleman also claim my best regards.

"I am, dear sir,
"Very sincerely and affectionately Yours,
"RICH'D VARICK.
"To Hon. Gen'l Schuyler."
—*Schuyler MSS.*

1. Burgoyne's Campaign, by Charles Neilson, published by Munsell, 1844, p. 161.

plied, "You shall have them," and immediately ordered Learned's brigade, when Arnold hurried back on a full gallop, and the men after him in a double-quick time.

He adds: "These incidents were well known at the time, and often spoken of afterwards to this day, and the author relates them in contradiction to what was said by Wilkinson respecting Arnold." [1]

If any further proof is desired, it may be found in the account of the battle, sent by express from General Gates' headquarters, on the afternoon of September 21st, by Major Cochran to the Council of Safety, at Bennington, Vermont, as follows:

"General Arnold with his division, attacked a division of Burgoyne, in which General Arnold gained the ground; when the enemy were reinforced by the main body, when General Arnold was obliged to retreat; but being reinforced, recovered his own, so that the ground remained at eight o'clock yesterday divided between them. This account came by express from General Gates' head-quarters yesterday afternoon by Major Cochran." [2] [3]

The English commander and his officers do not mention any other general officer on the field in the battle of the 19th September, except Arnold. General Burgoyne, in his account of the campaign, before the House of Commons, in 1779, says:

"Mr. Gates had determined to receive the attack in his lines. Mr. Arnold, who commanded on the left, forseeing the danger of being turned, advanced without consultation with his general, and gave enstead of receiving battle. The stroke might have been fatal on his part had he failed. But confident I am, upon a minute examination of

---

[1]. Burgoyne's Campaign, by Charles Neilson, pp. 148-9—150-151. See Preface, p. 8. Ditto p. 153. "The fact of Arnold's being present on the field during the action of the 19th, and actually heading the troops that engaged Fraser's division, is also confirmed by a number who were present and who were engaged in the battle."

[2]. Vermont Historical Society Collections, Vol. I, p. 239.

[3]. See, also, Magazine of Am. History, May, 1878, p. 278: "Col. Philip Van Courtlandt, who commanded a New York regiment engaged in the fight, says that after he had left his parade and was marching towards the enemy, he received his orders from Gen. Arnold."

the ground since, that had the other idea been pursued, I should in a few hours gained a position, that in spite of the Ennemy's numbers would have put them in my power."[1]

It would be difficult to find any account of the battle, written before his treason, in which Arnold is not mentioned as leading the American troops, for no man ever discovered that he was not on the field until after his conspiracy.

The testimony now to be cited of historians and writers, is important only as showing how candid and impartial judges have regarded the evidence. In the face of the just and universal prejudice against him, the proof has compelled, often against their inclination, a very large majority of the ablest writers to give the credit and the glory of the battle of the nineteenth of September to General Arnold.

Washington Irving, in his Life of Washington, delineates the battle and the generalship of Arnold, as follows:

" * * * The American officers grew impatient. Arnold especially, impetuous by nature, urged repeatedly that a detachment should be sent forth to check the enemy in their advance, and drive the Indians out of the woods.

"At length he succeeded in getting permission, about noon, to detach Morgan with his riflemen and Dearborn with his infantry, from his division. They soon fell in with the Canadians and Indians, which formed the advance guard of the enemy's right, and attacking them with spirit, drove them in, or rather dispersed them. Morgan's riflemen, following up their advantage with too much eagerness, became likewise scattered, and a strong reinforcement of royalists arriving on the scene of action, the Americans, in their turn, were obliged to give way. Other detachments now arrived from the American camp, led by Arnold, who attacked Fraser on his right, to check his attempt to get in the rear of the camp. Finding the position of Fraser too strong to be forced, he sent to headquarters for reinforcements, but they were refused by Gates, who declared that no more should go; 'he would not suffer his camp to be exposed.'"[2]

1. Burgoyne's Expedition. Gen. Burgoyne's Narrative, London, 1780, p. 26. See also, p. 60.
2. Irving's Life of Washington, Vol. III, p. 243.

"* * * Arnold now made a rapid counter-march, and his movements being masked by the woods, suddenly attempted to turn Fraser's left. Here he came in full conflict with the British line, and threw himself upon it with a boldness and impetuosity that for a time threatened to break it, and cut the wings of the army asunder. The grenadiers and Breyman's riflemen hastened to its support. General Phillips broke his way through the woods with four pieces of artillery, and Riedesel came on with his heavy dragoons. Reinforcements came likewise to Arnold's assistance; his force, however, never exceeded three thousand men, and with these, for nearly four hours, he kept up a conflict almost hand to hand with the whole right wing of the British army. Part of the time the Americans had the advantage of fighting under the cover of a wood, so favorable to their militia and sharpshooters. Burgoyne ordered the woods to be cleared by the bayonet. His troops rushed forward with a hurrah! The Americans kept within their entrenchments, and repeatedly repulsed them; but if they pursued their advantage, and advanced into open field, they were in their turn driven back.

"Night alone put an end to a conflict which the British acknowledged to have been the most obstinate and hardly-fought they had ever experienced in America. * * * * Arnold was excessively indignant at Gates' withholding the reinforcements he had required in the heat of the action; had they been furnished, he said, he might have severed the line of the enemy and gained a complete victory. He was urgent to resume the action on the succeeding morning and follow up the advantage he had gained, but Gates declined, to his additional annoyance."[1]

Lossing, in his Field Book of the Revolution,[2] says:

"Let us pause a moment and render justice to as brave a soldier as ever drew blade for freedom. * * I mean Benedict Arnold. * *"

Botta, who was acquainted with many of the foreign officers who served in the war, and whose sources of correct information were very ample, observes:

"'Arnold upon this occasion exhibited all the impetuosity of his courage. He encouraged his men by voice and example.'

"Steadman, a British officer, says in his History of the American War:

"'The enemy were led to the battle by General Arnold, who distinguished himself in an extraordinary manner.'"

Lossing, in his life of Schuyler, says:

"To Arnold's skill and daring, which animated his

[1] Irving's life of Washington, Vol. III, pp. 344-345.
[2] Lossing's Field Book of the Revolution, Vol. I, p. 55.

troops, was chiefly due the credit of successfully resisting the inroads at Bemis' Heights."[1]

Colonel Varick, writing to Schuyler from Albany, says: "During Burgoyne's stay here he gave Arnold great credit for his bravery and his military abilities; especially in the action of the nineteenth, whenever he speaks of him, and once in the presence of Gates."[2]

[1.] Lossing's Schuyler, Vol. II, p. 849.
[2.] A very late, accurate and able professional writer,'General Carrington, Professor of Military Science, etc., in his "Battles of the American Revolution," says, p. 342:

"* * * * To what extent General Arnold accompanied the successive portions of his division, which bore the brunt of this day's fight, is not clearly or uniformly defined by historians. That contemporaneous history gave his division credit is nowhere questioned; and that he was a listless observer, or remained in camp regardless of the fact that he was responsible for the entire left wing, which was then assailed, is perfectly inconsistent with his nature and the position he occupied.

"Wilkinson, Adjutant-General of Gates, and by virtue thereof '*prima facia*' good authority as to the acts of Gates, makes the remarkable statement that 'not a single general officer was on the field of battle the nineteenth of September until evening,' and states the execution of this wonderful military exploit, that 'the battle was fought by the general concert and zealous co-operation of the corps engaged, and sustained more by individual courage than military discipline.'

"Bancroft states that 'Arnold was not on the field;' and adds, 'so witnesses Wilkinson, whom Marshall knew personally and believed.' But Marshall says, 'Reinforcements were continually brought up, and about four o'clock Arnold, with nine continental regiments and Morgan's corps, was completely engaged with the whole right wing of the British army. The conflict was extremely severe, and only terminated with the day.' * * * There was little disposition on the part of historians, who wrote just after the war, to do Arnold justice for real merit; but Stedman, equally good authority with Gordon, in most respects, says: 'The enemy were led to battle by General Arnold, who distinguished himself in an extraordinary manner.' Dawson, *who has few superiors in the careful examination of American history*, and Lossing, who has devoted his life to this class of specialties, and Tomes, concur with Marshall; while Colonel Varick, writing immediately from the camp, and Neilson and Hall, and many other writers, give to Arnold not merely the credit of superintending the field operations of his division, but of leading them in person. It is difficult to understand how the withdrawal of troops from Fraser's front, and their transfer to the British centre, with the consequent movements described by General Burgoyne, which required such rapid and exhaustive employment of the whole force which he brought into action, could have taken place undirected, and with no strong will to hold the troops to the attack and defense.

"It is material that other facts be considered in order to appreciate the value of Wilkinson's statement. He was a young man about twenty years of age, restless, migratory in the camp, and like a boy in his eagerness to see everything everywhere. He exercised his functions as Assistant Adjutant-General, as if he were the duplicate of his chief, and repeatedly gave orders as if the *two persons* made the

Perhaps too much space has been given to a question which would never have been raised at all but for Arnold's treason, and would scarcely have deserved serious consideration, but that Mr. Bancroft has, without careful investigation, never having seen, as I am compelled to believe, the letters of Varick and Livingston, permitted himself to be misled by the dictum of Wilkinson.

The whole army, as is clearly shown by the letters of Varick and Livingston, gave to Arnold the glory of bravely and skillfully fighting this battle. An old soldier who was with him in the battle, quaintly but clearly expresses the verdict of his comrades, saying:[1]

"Arnold was our fighting general, and a bloody fellow he was. He didn't care for nothing; he'd ride right in. It was 'come on boys,' 't'want 'go boys.' He was as brave a man as ever lived. They didn't treat him right. He ought to have had Burgoyne's sword. But he ought to have been true;" and the old soldier seemed to grieve over the defection of his commander, as a father mourns over the dishonor of a son.

general commanding. * * * * * * Arnold also, in his objections to the transfer of Morgan from his command, and neither Gates nor Wilkinson dissent from his statement, thus addresses General Gates: "On the 19th inst., when advice was received that the enemy were approaching, I took the liberty to give it as my opinion that we ought to march out and attack them. You desired me to send Colonel Morgan and the Light Artillery to support them. I obeyed your orders, and before the action was over I found it necessary to send out the whole of my division to support the attack.' * * *

' It is a fact that General Gates did not pass under fire, neither was it necessary for him to do so; but the whole conduct of that officer, and of his Adjutant General, savors of the disgust with which in an earlier war, King Saul heard the shouts that 'Saul had slain his thousands, but David his tens of thousands.' Arnold must stand credited with personal valor, and a gallant defense of the left wing of the American army on the nineteenth day of September, 1777.

"There is no method of determining the details of his conduct, and the student of history must unite with Sparks and Irving and Marshall, in the general sentiment that Morgan only, of American officers, can compete with Arnold for the brightest laurels of the Saratoga campaign."

1. Samuel Downing, heretofore quoted.

CHAPTER X.

SECOND BATTLE OF SARATOGA.

"Gates will be indebted to him (Arnold) for the glory he may acquire by a victory."—*General Philip Schuyler.*

QUARREL BETWEEN GATES AND ARNOLD—ACTION OF OCTOBER 7TH—HEROISM OF ARNOLD—GATES TRIES IN VAIN TO RECALL HIM FROM THE FIELD—MORGAN, BY DIRECTION OF ARNOLD, ORDERS HIS RIFLEMEN TO FIRE AT FRASER—FRASER SHOT—SENATOR FOSTER'S ACCOUNT OF ARNOLD'S CHARGE, AS WITNESSED BY HIS FATHER—ARNOLD SHOT—SAVES THE LIFE OF THE SOLDIER WHO SHOT HIM—CONGRESS VOTES HIM THANKS AND THE RANK HITHERTO REFUSED—WASHINGTON SENDS HIM HIS NEW, ANTE-DATED COMMISSION, AND DECLARES HE IS RESTORED "TO A VIOLATED RIGHT."

IT is difficult to conceive a more painful position than that of General Arnold after the battle of the 19th of September. If his subsequent crime could be forgotten, it would not be possible to withhold from him the sympathy and admiration which is always felt for a man of ability suffering from undeserved misfortune. Thus far his military career had been brilliant—almost without a parallel.

He had seen as much or more hard service—had done as much downright hard fighting—as any man, Washington always excepted, of his rank in the American army. The brightest laurels of Greene, so nobly won, were acquired later in the war.

In the spring of 1777 he went to Philadelphia, from a short volunteer campaign in Connecticut, in which his soldierly qualities, his zeal, his energy, his activity, his coolness in the hour of supreme peril, had literally extorted praise and promotion from his bitter enemies. When intelligence reached Schuyler that Burgoyne was approaching from the north, he called for Arnold, and Washington urged Congress to send him without "one moment's delay," because, to use Washington's own words, he was "active, judicious and brave," and because "his zeal and activity will animate the militia greatly." Leaving his unsettled accounts, offering to serve under juniors, who had been promoted over him, some of them without a military record, he had hastened to Schuyler, volunteered to lead the force sent out along the bloody trail of Oriskany to relieve old Fort Stanwix, and, this accomplished, he had hastened back, to find Gates in command, but taking the left wing of the army, he had skirmished heavily and successfully with the enemy. He had fought the battle of the 19th of September, and now he found himself in the camp of the soldiers he had so lately led to victory *without a command!* Gates' jealousy, Wilkinson's hatred, Arnold's faithful friendship for Schuyler, the praises and encomiums of Washington, and probably his own imperious and unyielding temper, were the causes which resulted in his humiliation.[1]

---

1. As an illustration of the injustice done to Arnold even in the most minute details, by some historians, Bancroft says, Vol. IX, p. 407, "Arnold, who *assumed* the part of Schuyler's friend, was quarrelsome and insubordinate." Let us see what his "*assumption*" was. We have already shown that Col. Livingston, late on Schuyler's staff, in a confidential letter to Schuyler, says: "The reason of the disagreement between *two cronies* is simply this—*Arnold is your friend.*" Schuyler speaks of "our gallant *friend*, Gen. Arnold." The truth is, that Arnold and Schuyler were warm and faithful *friends* all through the campaigns of 1776 and 1777, and afterwards. If Arnold had not been faithful to Schuyler, he might have continued the favorite of Gates, and then he would have been the acknowledged *hero* of *Saratoga*. But he was independent enough to be Schuyler's friend, in the camp of Gates, and Gates punished him for it, and yet Mr. Bancroft says that he "*assumed*" to be Schuyler's friend. The treatment of Arnold by some historians suggests the spirit of one who, when a friendless and obnoxious man was struck, cried out "hit him again, he has no friends here!" Yet to state or suggest a falsehood against Arnold, while it may please popular feeling, and add to popular hatred, has neither chivalry nor Christianity to excuse it.

The coolness, or more than coolness of Gates and his Adjutant-General towards the second in command, had become an open quarrel when Morgan's corps, which had been attached to the left wing under the command of Arnold ever since his return from Fort Schuyler, was now, without consultation or even notice, withdrawn from his division by general orders. "This," says Sparks, "was supposed to have been owing to the officious interference of Wilkinson."[1]

In his official report to Congress of the late battle, Gates was so unjust that he did not mention, or even allude to Arnold, nor to his division, but merely said the battle was fought by "detachments from the army." This was unmanly, unsoldier-like and ungenerous, and as unjust to Arnold's gallant troops as to their commander. Arnold naturally complained and expressed in strong language his sense of the injustice done to his soldiers.[2]

Gates, knowing Arnold's temper, and obviously seeking to provoke and drive him from the service, went so far as to say sneeringly, he thought Arnold of little consequence in the army; that when General Lincoln arrived he would take away his command; and that he would with all his heart give him a pass to leave the army—very different language from that he used Sept. 2d, 1776, when he was urged to put Arnold in arrest, and replied: "The United States must not be deprived of that excellent officer's services at this important moment."[3]

But as Gen. Schuyler suggests, Gates was now "so very sure of success that he did not wish the other (Arnold) to come in for a share of the glory he may acquire" from a victory.[4] Then followed an angry correspondence. Arnold

[1]. Sparks' Life of Arnold, p. 114.
[2]. Arnold's letter to Gates, Sept. 22, 1777; Wilkinson's Memoirs, Vol. I, pp. 254-6-7.
[3]. Gates to the President of Congress, Am. Archives, 5th S., Vol. I, p. 1268.
[4]. Schuyler to Varick, Sept. 25, 1777.

wrote the letter of Sept. 22nd before mentioned. Gates was irritating, arrogant and vulgar; Arnold indiscreet, haughty and passionate. Gates succeeded in provoking Arnold to demand a pass to Washington, which Gates was but too ready to give. When the officers and soldiers heard what was passing they became excited and indignant. "They had," as Lossing says, "lost all confidence in Gates, and had the highest opinion of Arnold."[1]

By personal entreaty, and in a written address, Arnold's officers begged him not to leave them, "for another battle seemed imminent."[2]

"As the enemy are hourly expected, General Arnold cannot think of leaving camp," as Livingston wrote to Schuyler.

Arnold had asked a pass to Washington in the heat of passion, and he was willingly persuaded to remain. On the first of October he had addressed a letter to Gates, in which he says: "Conscious of my own innocency and and integrity, I am determined to sacrifice my feelings and continue in the army at this critical juncture."[3] But Gates was inexorable; his rival was now without a command, and Gates meant to keep him in that condition, and therefore he had not the grace to restore him to his former position, but took the division under his own charge, placing Lincoln in command of the right wing. A day or two after Lincoln's arrival, Arnold still claiming to command his old division, observing Lincoln giving some directions in regard to it, inquired if he was doing so by order of General Gates, and Lincoln replying in the negative, Arnold observed that the left division belonged to him (Arnold) and that he believed that Lincoln's proper

1. Lossing's Life of Schuyler, Vol. II, p. 351.
2. Lossing's Life of Schuyler, Vol. II, p. 351.
3. Letter to Gates, Oct. 1, 1777. Wilkinson's Memoirs, Vol. 1, pp. 259-260.

station was on the right, and that of Gates ought to be the center.[1] "Arnold requested Lincoln to mention this to Gates and have it adjusted." Lincoln wisely sought to reconcile their differences, but without success. "Arnold is determined," says Varick, "not to suffer any man to interfere in his division, and says it will be death to any officer in action."[2]

He remained in camp, receiving the sympathy of his brother officers, but never consulted. Gates did not issue a formal order, depriving him of command, but ignored him.

Meanwhile two thousand troops, lately under Lincoln, had arrived in camp, and the gates to Canada were being shut against the British retreat; the bridges in their rear were being destroyed by the Americans, and the toils were closing around Burgoyne. He looked anxiously towards New York for a diversion in his favor by Sir Henry Clinton. Provisions were growing scarce, and his troops, constantly harrassed by skirmishes, were now put on short allowance. Burgoyne fortified his camp, and the American militia came flocking in to take a hand in the capture of the British army, now regarded as morally certain. Its leader realized that he must fight or fly, and that without delay. In the early days of October the question of a rapid retreat, or a vigorous attack, was much considered and discussed by the British officers. Burgoyne, in the beginning of the campaign, proud and sanguine of success, had in his proclamation said: "This army must never retreat!" Now an escape by retreat would have been a relief to his anxiety. Philips proposed to make a rapid, circuitous march and fall upon the American left. Riedesel advised a retreat to Fort Edward. Fraser was ready and willing to fight.

On the morning of the 7th of October, it was decided to

[1] Irving's Life of Washington Vol. III, p. 249.
[2] Varick to Schuyler. Schuyler papers.

make preparations for battle, and that a reconnoissance in force should be executed, and if there should be found an opportunity for an attack, with reasonable prospects of success, it should be given; if otherwise, preparations to retreat should be made.

At 10 A. M., Burgoyne, aided by Philips, Riedesel and Fraser, led 1,500 picked men to high ground, three-fourths of a mile to the west of the American line, and behind a screen of dense forests formed his line of battle. At the same time he despatched a party of five hundred rangers, loyalists and Indians, to steal through the forests and attack the rear of the left of the Americans, while he should attack their front and flank. The movements of the British were quickly discovered. The American center beat to arms, and the whole army prepared for battle. "Order out Morgan to begin the game," said Gates. At Morgan's suggestion he was directed to take possession of the heights to the right of the enemy. General Poor with his brigade, and a part of Scammels, were sent against the left of the British line; meanwhile the party of rangers, loyalists and Indians had gained the rear of the Americans, driven in the pickets, and being joined by the grenadiers, drove the Americans within their lines; here they rallied, and being joined by Morgan and his riflemen, they in turn drove the British to the main line of battle now being formed, consisting of grenadiers under Major Ackland, with artillery under Major Williams on the left; the center was composed of the Germans under Riedesel, and British under Philips, while the light infantry under Earl Balcarras formed the extreme left. General Fraser, with five hundred picked men, was placed in advance of the right, ready to attack the Americans in the flank when the action should begin. It was now two o'clock in the afternoon, and Morgan, as has been stated, at his own suggestion, was sent with his riflemen to take possession of some high ground on the extreme right of the enemy, to watch and attack Fraser at the moment when an attack should be made on the British left by Poor's brigade and a part of Learned's. At half past two the battle began. The troops of Poor and Learned marched up the slope to attack the grenadiers and the artillery under Ackland and Williams, and with orders not to open fire until after the first discharge of the enemy. Silently and steadily they marched forward, and were recived by a discharge of musket balls and grape shot, which passed over their heads into the branches of the trees. Instantly, with a shout, they rushed forward and delivered their fire. Then followed a fierce assault and conflict. The Americans charged up to the very mouths, and among the cannon, and were met with a stubborn resistance. Cannon were taken and re-taken; one of the field-pieces was captured and re-captured four times, until finally Colonel Cilley, who led his regiment, leaped upon the captured gun, and waving his sword, dedicated it to the patriot cause, and whirling it towards the enemy, discharged it upon them; the act was dramatic, and the effect electric. Finally, after a terrible struggle, and when Major Ackland was severely wounded and Williams taken prisoner, the grenadiers and artillery fled, and the Americans held the field. While the battle was raging on the right Morgan led the attack upon Fraser and drove him back within the British lines; then falling upon their right flank, he broke their lines and put them to confusion. Dearborn with fresh troops attacked their front, which was broken, but rallied and made a stand under the Earl of Balcarras. The center of the British still held their ground. And now Arnold on his black horse was seen approaching at full speed. Chafing in his tent, he had early heard the sounds of the conflict, and no stag-hound chained in his kennel, when he hears the music of the pursuit, was ever more eager to join the chase than was Arnold to join his comrades in the field. "No man," exclaimed he to his aids, "shall keep me in my tent to-day. If I am without command, I will fight in the ranks; but the soldiers, God bless them, will follow my lead. Come on," said he, "victory or death!" and leaping into his saddle he plunged into the thickest of the fight, and the soldiers welcomed their old and beloved commander with shouts and cheers, which rose above the din and roar of the conflict.[1] His gallant, thorough-bred horse bounded over the field with a motion as elastic and nearly as rapid as the deer springs from the hounds. Arnold was a splendid rider, and the martial spirit which animated him, and the magnetism of the rushing, powerful animal beneath him, thrilled his whole frame almost to frenzy as he dashed through the storm of smoke and fire and lead.[2]

"Fast, fast, with heels' wild spurning,
The dark brown charger sped;
He burst through ranks of fighting men;
He sprang o'er heaps of dead."

"General Arnold," says Lossing, "had watched with eager eye and excited spirit the course of the battle thus far. Deprived of all command, he had no authority even to *fight*, much less to *order*. Smarting under the indignity heaped upon him by his commander, thirsting for that glory which beckoned him to the field, burning with a patriotic desire to serve his country, now bleeding at every pore, and stirred by the din of battle around him,

---

1. He enjoys the confidence and affection of officers and soldiers. They would to a man follow him to victory or death.'—*Livingston Letter quoted.*

2. His conduct recalls Scott's fine description of Marmion, in the battle of Flodden Field:

"Like a thunderbolt,
"First in the vanguard made a halt,
When such a shout there rose
Of 'Marmion! Marmion!' that the cry
Up Flodden mountains shrilling high,
Startled the Scotish foes."
—*Canto VI.*

the brave soldier became fairly maddened by his emotions, and leaping upon his large brown horse, he started off on a full gallop for the field of conflict. Gates immediately sent Major Armstrong after him to order him back. Arnold saw him approaching, and anticipating his errand, spurred his horse and left his pursuer far behind, while he placed himself at the head of the regiments of Learned's brigade, who received their former commander with loud huzzas. He immediately led them against the British center, and with the desperation of a madman, rushed into the thickest of the fight, or rode along the lines in rapid and erratic movements, brandishing his broad-sword above his head, and delivering his orders everywhere in person. Armstrong kept up the chase for half an hour, but Arnold's course was so varied and perilous that he gave it up.

"The Hessians received the first assault of Arnold's troops upon the British center with a brave resistance; but when, upon a second charge, he dashed furiously among them at the head of his men, they broke and fled in dismay. And now the battle became general along the whole lines. Arnold and Morgan were the ruling spirits that controlled the storm on the part of the Americans, and the gallant General Fraser was the directing soul of the British troops in action. His skill and courage were everywhere conspicuous. When the lines gave way, he brought order out of confusion; when regiments began to waver, he infused courage into them by voice and example. He was mounted upon a splendid iron-gray gelding, and, dressed in the full uniform of a field officer, he was a conspicuous object for the Americans. It was evident that the fate of the battle rested upon him, and this the keen eye and sure judgment of Morgan perceived. In an instant his purpose was conceived, and calling a file of his best men around him, he said, as he pointed toward the British right, 'That gallant officer is General Fraser. I admire and honor him, but it is necessary he should die; victory for the enemy depends upon him. Take your stations in that clump of bushes, and do your duty.'[1] Within five minutes Fraser fell mortally wounded, and was carried to the camp by two grenadiers. Just previous to being hit by the fatal bullet, the crupper of his horse was cut by a rifle ball, and immediately afterward another passed through the horse's mane, a little back of his ears.

"The aid of Fraser noticed this and said, 'It is evident that you are marked out for particular aim; would it not be prudent for you to retire from this place?' Fraser replied, 'My duty forbids me to fly from danger,' and the next moment he fell."

[1] Lossing's Field Book of the Revolution, Vol. I, pp. 61-2; also Life of Schuyler, Vol. II, p. 366.

In regard to the death of Gen. Fraser, it is proper to state that Samuel Woodruff, of Windsor, Connecticut, a sargeant in the American army, and a participator in the battle, gives the following account of the death of that gallant officer:

"Soon after the commencement of the action, Gen. Arnold, knowing the military character and efficiency of Gen. Fraser, and observing his motions in leading and conducting the attack, said to Colonel Morgan, 'that officer upon the gray horse is of himself a host, and must be disposed of; direct the attention of some of the sharpshooters among your riflemen, to him.'' Morgan nodded his assent, repaired to his riflemen, and made known to them the hint given by Arnold. Immediately upon this the crupper of the gray horse was cut by a rifle ball,[1] and soon Fraser received his mortal wound."

This statement is corroborated by Neilson.[2]

This account does not, it will be observed, conflict with the statement in regard to Morgan, but only adds, that the cruel, but perhaps in a military point of view, important suggestion, originated with Arnold. It is difficult not to condemn this order. The impulse of every generous heart is, that the gallant soldier should have the chance of escape without being singled out for death. But the American officers were fighting for their country. Arnold and Morgan believed the death of Fraser was necessary, and therefore gave the fatal order. When Fraser fell, a panic seized the British, and the whole line gave way and fled behind their entrenchments. The Americans followed, and, I again quote from the Field Book of the Revolution:

"The conflict was now terrible indeed, and in the midst of the flame, and smoke, and metal hail, Arnold was conspicuous. His voice, clear as a trumpet, animated the soldiers, and as if ubiquitous, he seemed to be everywhere amid the perils at the same moment. With a part of the brigades of Patterson and Glover, he assaulted the works occupied by the light infantry under Earl Balcarras, and at the point of the

1. Stone's Campaign of General Burgoyne, pp. 324-325.
2. "Morgan, *at the suggestion of Arnold*, took a few of his riflemen aside," and gave them the order to pick off Fraser as stated.—*Burgoyne's Campaigns, by Charles Neilson.*

bayonet drove the enemy from a strong *abatis*, through which he attempted to force his way into the camp. He was obliged to abandon the effort, and dashing forward toward the right flank of the enemy, exposed to the cross-fire of the contending armies,[1] he met Learned's brigade advancing to make an assault upon the British works at an opening in the *abatis*, between Balcarras' light infantry and the German right flank defense under Colonel Breyman. Canadians and loyalists defended this part of the line, and were flanked by a stockade redoubt on each side.

"Arnold placed himself at the head of the brigade, and moved rapidly on to the attack. He directed Colonel Brooks to assault the redoubt, while the remainder of the brigade fell upon the front. The contest was furious, and the enemy at length gave way, leaving Breyman and his Germans completely exposed. At this moment Arnold galloped to the left and ordered the regiments of Wesson and Livingston and Morgan's corps of riflemen to advance and make a general assault. At the head of Brooks' regiment, he attacked the German works. Having found the sally-port, he rushed within the enemy's intrenchments. The Germans, who had seen him upon his steed in the thickest of the fight for more than two hours, terrified at his approach, fled in dismay, delivering a volley in their retreat which killed Arnold's horse under him and wounded the General himself very severely in the same leg which had been badly lacerated by a musket ball at the storming of Quebec, two years before.

"Here, wounded and disabled, at the head of conquering troops led on by his valor to the threshold of victory, Arnold was overtaken by Major Armstrong, who delivered to him Gates' order to return to camp, fearing he 'might do some rash thing!' He indeed did a rash thing in the eye of military discipline. He led troops to victory without an order from his commander. His conduct was rash, indeed, compared with the stately method of General Gates, who directed by orders from his camp what his presence should have sanctioned. While Arnold was wielding the fierce sickle of war without, and reaping golden sheaves for Gates' garner, the latter (according to Wilkinson) was within his camp, more intent upon discussing the merits of the Revolution with Sir Francis Clark, Burgoyne's aid-de-camp, who had been wounded and taken prisoner, and was lying upon the commander's bed at his quarters, than upon winning a battle all-important to the ultimate triumph of those principles for which he professed so warm an attachment. When one of Gates' aids came up from the field of battle for orders, he found the General very

---

1. Wilkinson says: "This would have been deemed incredible if Gen. Scott had not performed the same '*mad prank*' at Lundy's Lane."

angry because Sir Francis would not allow the force of his arguments. He left the room, and, calling his aid after him, asked as they went out, 'Did you ever hear so impudent a son of a b—h?' Poor Sir Francis died that night upon Gates' bed.

"It is a curious fact," says Sparks, "that an officer who really had not command in the army, was the leader of one of the most spirited and important battles of the Revolution. His madness or rashness, or whatever it may be called, resulted most fortunately for himself. The wound he received at the moment of rushing into the arms of danger and of death, added fresh lustre to his military glory, and was a new claim to public favor and applause."[1]

The following is the account of Arnold's conduct in the action, given by General Carrington in his "Battles of the American Revolution."

"At this stage of the battle, Arnold, no longer under self-control, burst from the camp, and, like a meteor, rode to the front of Learned's brigade, which had been so recently under his command, and dashed into the fight. He was cheered as he rode past, and like a whirlwind the regiments went with him upon the broken British lines. Fraser fell mortally wounded in this assault, and swiftly behind the half crazy volunteer came Tenbroeck with a force nearly double that of the whole British line. That line was now in full retreat. Phillips and Riedesel, as well as Burgoyne, who took command in person, exhibited marvelous courage in an hour so perilous, and withdrew the troops with creditable self possession and skill, but nothing could stop Arnold. Wherever he found troops he assumed command, and by the magnetism of his will and passion, he became supreme in daring endeavor. With a part of the brigades of Patterson and Glover, he assaulted the intrenchments of Earl Balcarras, but was repulsed. To the right of Earl Balcarras, the Canadians and Royalists were posted under cover of two stockade redoubts. Arnold here again met Learned's brigade, took the lead, and with a single charge cleared these works, leaving the left of Breyman's position entirely exposed. Without waiting for the result of the further attack at this point, he rode directly in front of Breyman's intrenchmens under fire, and meeting the regiments of Wesson and Livingston and Morgan's rifle corps, which had made the entire compass of the British right, he ordered them forward, and then riding on with a portion of Brooks' regiment which joined at that moment, he turned the intrenchments of Breyman, entered the sally-port and was shot, with his horse, as the victory was achieved."[2]

1. Lossing's Field Book of the Revolution, Vol. I, p. 63.
2. Carrington's Battles of the American Revolution, p. 348.

Sparks, perhaps the most careful of all writers upon Revolutionary history, and who is never extravagant in his language, says:

"The brilliant manoeuvre with which the engagement was closed, the assault of the enemy's works, and driving the Hessians from their encampment, was undoubtedly owing in the first case to Arnold. He gave the order, and by his *personal* bravery set an example to the troops which inspired them with ardor, and hurried them forward. He was shot through the leg while riding gallantly into the sally-port, and his horse fell dead under him. The success of the assault was complete, and crowned the day with victory."[1]

"Gates was not on the field, nor indeed did he leave his encampment during either of the battles of Bemis' Heights."[2]

There is little doubt that Arnold went to the field on this day reckless of his life, and perhaps intending to seek death by the most hazardous exposure, but he meant to die victorious, and death at the moment of victory would have been welcome. When on the morning of the twenty-first of August, he started from German Flats to march across the bloody field of Oriskany to relieve Fort Schuyler, expecting to meet a superior force, he says: "You will hear of my being victorious, or—*no more!*"[3]

His conduct on the field the seventh of October, shows that his excitement amounted almost to frenzy. During the progress of the battle, wishing to pass rapidly from the right to the left, "he dashed through the fire of the two lines, and escaped unhurt."[4]

It is said by Wilkinson, that while encouraging his troops, Arnold, in a state of furious distraction, struck an officer with his sword, "believed to be Captain Ball, of Dearborn's infantry." Sparks, alluding to the incident, says when the

1. Sparks' Life of Arnold, p. 118,
2. Sparks' Life of Arnold, p. 119.
3. Gates' Papers. Letter from Arnold to Gates, Aug. 21, 1777. MSS.
4. Wilkinson's Memoirs, Vol. I, p. 273.

officer, on the following day, "demanded redress, Arnold declared his entire ignorance of the act and expressed his regret." [1]

Foster, of New London, late a Senator of the United States from Connecticut, at the Centennial celebration of this battle, on the 7th of October, 1877, relates an interesting incident in relation to Arnold. Senator Foster's father was adjutant of a Connecticut regiment made up in part of recruits from New London and Norwich, Arnold's birthplace. He says: "The earliest recollection of my boyhood was sitting on my father's knee and listening to the stories of the march, the camp and the battle-field. I well recollect hearing my father say that Arnold came dashing along the line, the speed at which he rode leaving his aid far behind him, and as he came up to my father's regiment he called out, 'Whose regiment is this?' My father replied: 'Colonel Latimer's, sir.' 'Ah!' said Arnold, 'my old Norwich and New London friends. God bless you! I am glad to see you. Now come on, boys; if the day is long enough, we'll have them all in hell before night.' General Arnold was a native of Norwich, and was born within fifty yards of my house in that town." [2]

As Arnold's horse fell under him, and he received a shot through his thigh, breaking the bone, he cried to his sol-

---

1. Life of Arnold, p. 118. It has been suggested that in the fury and frenzy of his desperate charge, that this blow may have been accidental.

2 Manuscript letters from Senator Foster to the author, dated Oct. 27th, 1777: "The *Daily Saratogian*, which I enclose, contains a pretty full statement of what I have heard my father say of General Arnold's conduct on the battle-field. I recollect further hearing my father speak of Arnold's impatience and fretfulness with the surgeon, who on looking hastily at his wounded leg, expressed some apprehension that amputation might be necessary. * * * He led the party that stormed Burgoyne's camp, after his men fell back to it; although it was not taken. He certainly inspired the men with a large portion of his own impetuousity, for they rushed on to the assault with shouts and cheers and yells; so I have heard my father and uncle both say.

"Very truly your friend, etc.,

"L. F. S. FOSTER."

diers, "Rush on, my brave boys, rush on!"[1] According to a statement of Nicholas Stoner, Arnold was shot by a wounded German private. An American soldier, seeing his General fall, rushed forward and was about to run the wounded German through with his bayonet, but Arnold, though prostrate and bleeding, seeing that the soldier was helpless, cried, "Don't hurt him, he did but his duty ; he is a fine fellow!"[2] Thus he saved the life of this soldier who had just shot him. This, Stone justly characterizes as an act of "true chivalry."[3] He who could thus save the life of a helpless enemy, while writhing from a wound just inflicted by that enemy, could not have been wanting in generosity. This was the hour for Benedict Arnold to have died! Had he been so fortunate as to have died of the wound received at the moment of victory, and immediately following an act of chivalry, of which I can recall no parallel, few soldiers in American history would have achieved a prouder fame. Arnold was mounted on this day, upon a beautiful dark horse named "Warren," after his old friend, the hero and "martyr" of Bunker Hill.[4] Wilkinson says, "It may be remembered by several who now live that Arnold rode on that day a black or dark brown horse, * * * and I well recollect observing the body of the horse the morning after, in the rear of the German encampment."[5]

1. Letter of E. Mattoon, quoted in Stone's Campaign of Gen. John Burgoyne, p. 375.
2. Stone's Campaign of Burgoyne, p. 66.
3. "A private by the name of John Redman, seeing his General wounded, ran up to bayonet the offender, but was prevented by Arnold, who, with true chivalry, exclaimed, 'He is a fine fellow—do not hurt him.' This was told, in 1848, to I. R. Simons, by Nicholas Stoner, the celebrated scout, who was an eye-witness of the circumstance."—*Stone's Burgoyne's Campaign*, p. 66.
4. Headley's Washington and his Generals, p. 183.
5. Wilkinson's Memoirs, Vol. I, p. 274.
There is a conflict in the statements by Col. Wilkinson and Major Lewis, in regard to the horse which Arnold rode at the battle of Saratoga Wilkinson, as we have quoted, says the one rode on the 7th of October was a black horse, belonging to Leonard Chester; and Lewis, as quoted by Mr. Sparks, states the animal was a

The British officers killed were Colonel Breyman, Sir Francis Clarke and the gallant and lamented General Fraser. Burgoyne himself had a very narrow escape, two rifle balls passing through his clothes; while of the Americans,

beautiful Spanish horse, which had belonged to Gov. Skene, but now was the property of Col. Lewis, and borrowed for the occasion. Wilkinson says he saw the horse the next day dead, and is probably correct. How Arnold came to ride a borrowed horse is explained in the following note from Arnold to Colonel Lamb: "My sister writes me she sent one of my horses to Peekskill, about 25th of July, to be forwarded to me, and that she intended sending another the last of July. I have received neither, and beg the favor of Col. Oswald to make inquiries for them, as he knows the horses,—the one a sorrel stallion, and the other a sorrel mare. I wish him, if they can be found, to send them to Albany, to the Dept. Quartermaster-General.
—*See Life of Lamb* p. 172.   "Yours,   B. A."

Arnold, it is said, gave an order to Lewis on the Quartermaster for the mare, in place of the one shot, and it is said none was there. It is not improbable the above note will explain this order consistently with his integrity, and if so, show how liable all persons are to do injustice who hear only one side of a case, without explanation.

It is quite clear that previous to his treason, while Arnold had enemies, his friends were as warm and devoted as his enemies were bitter. Among the former was General Lamb, who afterwards, while condemning his treason with the utmost severity, would never suffer the reputation of Arnold as a soldier to be questioned, or his courage and conduct on the field impeached without defending both.

"Some years afterwards, when dining at Putnam's headquarters, in company with one of Gates' brigadiers who had served at Saratoga, the name of Arnold was introduced, when '*confusion to the traitor*' was drank with great unanimity. And when his demerits had been freely discussed, Colonel Lamb remarked that it was a pity so good a soldier, and a man of such consummate courage should become so despicable a villain."

"'Consummate courage, sir!' said Gen. G.: 'where has he ever exhibited any proof of such quality?' 'Sir,' said Col. Lamb, 'you astonish me by the question. In my judgment, it would be more difficult to point out an instance where he has not given ample evidence of bravery, than to enumerate the instances of his intrepidity. I was with him at the storming of Quebec, and at the battle of Compo; and am somewhat qualified to judge; and if these exploits are not sufficient, the battle of the 7th Oct., in 1777, and the storming of the German intrenchments, would add strength to my testimony.' 'Pshaw! Sir,' was the rejoinder; 'mere Dutch courage: He was drunk, sir.' 'Sir.' said Col. Lamb, 'let me tell you, that drunk or sober, *you* will never be an Arnold, or fit to compare with him in any military capacity.' 'What do you mean by that, sir?' exclaimed Gen. G. 'Literally and emphatically what I say,' was the answer. Here Putnam (who lisped) broke in: 'Whath all thith?' he said; 'God, cuth it, gentlemen, let the traitor go! Here's Washington's health in a brimmer.' This ended the conversation, and the matter was not pushed to farther arbitrament."—*Life and Times of Lamb*, p. 262.

General Arnold was the only commissioned officer who received a wound.[1]

"During all the fight," says Bancroft, "neither Gates nor Lincoln (second in command) appeared on the field."[2]

The gallantry of Arnold, his reckless exposure, his severe wound, added fresh lustre to his fame. Even Gates, coerced by the sympathy and enthusiastic admiration of the army, created by Arnold's heroism, now mentioned his name in his report of the battle to Congress,[3] and that body, as we shall detail more fully hereafter, at last gave him his proper rank.[4]

There are many touching incidents connected with the details of this battle; none more so than the death and burial of General Fraser. He lingered after being wounded until the 8th, and a short time before his death expressed a wish to be buried at six o'clock in the evening in a redoubt

---

1. Lossing's Field Book of the Revolution, Vol. I, p. 64.
2. Bancroft's His. of United States, Vol. IX, p. 418.
3. Bancroft's History of United States, Vol. IX, p. 418. "In his report of the action Gates named Arnold with Morgan and Dearborn."
4. There was little disposition in those who wrote immediately after the war, to do Arnold justice, and some later historians have been so blinded by prejudice as to deny him all honor, and therefore I shall be excused for quoting the eloquent words of George W. Curtis, in his Centennial Oration, in regard to his conduct: "The British, dismayed, bewildered, overwhelmed, were scarcely within their redoubts, when Benedict Arnold, to whom the jealous Gates, who did not come upon the field during the day, had refused a command, outriding an aid whom Gates had sent to recall him, came spurring up; Benedict Arnold—whose name America does not love, whose ruthless will had dragged the doomed Canadian expedition through the starving wilderness of Maine, who volunteering to relieve Fort Stanwix had, by the mere terror of his coming, blown St. Leger away, and who on the 19th of September had saved the American left. Benedict Arnold, whom battle stung to fury, now whirled from end to end of the American line, hurled it against the great redoubt, driving the enemy at the point of the bayonet; then flinging himself to the extreme right, and finding there the Massachusetts brigade, swept it with him to the assault, and streaming over the breastworks, scattered the Brunswickers, who defended them, killed their Colonel, gained and held the point which commanded the entire British position, while at the same moment his horse was shot under him, and he sank to the ground wounded in the leg that had been wounded at Quebec. Here, upon the Hudson, where he tried to betray his country; here upon the spot, where, in the crucial hour of the Revolution, he illustrated and led the American valor that made us free and great, knowing well that no earlier service can condone for a later crime, let us recall for one brief instant of infinite pity, the name that has been justly execrated for a century."

which had been built on the top of a hill near the battle-ground. At sunset, followed by General Burgoyne and the staff officers, his body was borne by the grenadiers of his division to the grave.[1] The Americans, seeing indistinctly through the twilight a movement of soldiers, and not knowing what it meant, pointed their artillery upon the funeral cortége, and as it proceeded up the hill balls struck the ground near the new-made grave. Undisturbed and forgetful of all but the duties of his sacred office, the chaplain, with "unaltered" voice read the sublime service, "Dust to dust; ashes to ashes," though often himself covered with the dust thrown up by the shot which fell around him.[2]

Amidst the cheers and shouts of the triumph to which he had so gallantly led his troops, Arnold was borne bleeding and helpless to his quarters. The victory was won, and Burgoyne's surrender was now a question only of time. Arnold was soon made to realize that the words of Schuyler

1. "Slowly and sadly we laid him down,
    From the field of his fame fresh and gory;
    We carved not a line, we raised not a stone,
    But we left him alone in his glory."

2. Burgoyne has himself very eloquently and feelingly described the scene—"The incessant cannonade during the ceremony; the steady attitude and unaltered voice with wh ch the chap'ain officiated, though frequent y covered with dust which the shot threw up on all sides of him; the mute, but expressive mixture of sensibility and indignation upon every countenance; these objects will remain to the last of life upon the mind of every man who was present. The growing darkness added to the scenery, and the whole marked a character of that juncture which would make one of the finest subjects for the pencil of a master that the field ever exhibited. To the canvas and to the faithful page of a more impor ant historian, gallant friend! I consign thy memory. There may thy talents, thy manly virtues, their progress and their period, find due distinction and long may they survive; long after the frail record of my pen shall be forgotten."—*Irving's Life of Washington, Vol. III, p. 277*

The following is the tribute from the poetic pen of Bancroft to the memory of Fraser, and is scarcely surpassed by anything in Ossian?

"Never more shall he chase the red deer through the heather of Strath Frrick, or guide the skiff across the fathomless lake of central Scotland, or muse over the ruins of the Stuarts on the moor of Drum Mossie, or dream of glory beside the crystal waters of the Ness. Death in itself is not terrible; but he came to America for selfish advancement, and though bravely true as a soldier, he died unconsoled."—*Bancroft's History of the United States, Vol. IX, p. 419.*

were true. "Gates will be indebted to him for the glory he may acquire by the victory."[1] Arnold's blood watered the laurels which now encircled the brow of Gates. There is, says De Quincy, a Nemesis which haunts the steps of those who become illustrious by appropriating the trophies of their brothers. Gates ungenerously appropriated the honors due to Arnold and to Schuyler, and has passed into merited disgrace.

Burgoyne abandoning his sick and wounded, attempted to retreat to Saratoga. Here he found himself completely surrounded. Stark, with two thousand men, held the river at Fort Edward, and his whole camp was exposed to cannon and rifle shot, and the firing upon him was constant. On the 17th the terms of capitulation were signed, and his whole army surrendered, the Americans obtaining forty-two pieces of the best brass ordnance then existing, a large quantity of ammunition, and 4,600 muskets. The British loss in this campaign is estimated at ten thousand men.[2]

On Monday, Nov. 4th, Colonel Wilkinson laid before Congress the papers in relation to the surrender of Burgoyne.[3]

1. Letter from Schuyler to Varick, before quoted.
2. In a letter to General Schuyler from Col. Varick, dated "Albany, October 30th, 1777,' (Schuyler Papers) he says:

"General Arnold is growing better very fast. He requests his compliments to you He is in expectation of accompanying you to Congress. *He is not* satisfied with *Gates' convention* (with Burgoyne). He thinks we m'ght have caught them on more advantageous terms than we have." * * (Burgoyne and his army did not become absolute prisoners to be exchanged, only agreeing not to serve again during the war.)

"Great part of Gates' army is still here. They have destroyed 'almost all the fences. Among others you have a great share of loss. Mrs. Schuyler's poultry and garden have suffered in defiance of every order and threat."

And again he writes:

"Nov. 1, 1777

"General Arnold is growing better daily. So is also Major Ackland. The former censures Gates detaining the troops. He says they ought to have joined General Washington. Gates is billiting 150 ' in and about this place."—*Schuyler P pers.*

3. "Colonel Wilkinson, Adjutant General in Gates' army, was made by him the bearer of dispatches to Congress, communicating the official intelligence of the surrender of Burgoyne, and the articles of capitulation. Wilkinson arrived at

14

On Tuesday Congress passed a vote of thanks to Generals Gates, Lincoln and Arnold, and "the other officers and soldiers," for "their brave and successful efforts."[1]

On the 29th General Washington was directed to issue a new commission to General Arnold, of such a date as to give him the precedence to which he was entitled.[2]

It will be remembered that his first promotion, from Colonel to Brigadier-General, was given as a reward for his efforts in leading the army through the wilderness to Canada, and for his gallantry in the assault on Quebec. He was made a Major-General for his heroism at Ridgefield, where one horse was killed under him and another wounded, and when he escaped as by a miracle, but his proper rank had been hitherto refused by Congress.

The victory at Saratoga, where, at each of the battles, he was the only Major-General on the field, his last brilliant and triumphant charge and his severe wound, brought to him the rank he had long before won, and now, at last, Washington enclosed his commission, saying: "You are restored to the rank you claim in the line of the army. This (the commission) I transmit by direction of Congress."[3]

Writing to Lincoln, a junior who had been promoted over Arnold, he says: "General Arnold is restored to a *violated right*, and the restitution I hope will be considered by every

Easton, in Pennsylvania, on the 24th of October, and wrote from that place a line to General Washington, merely stating the fact of the surrender, the number of prisoners taken, and the nature of his errand to Congress, but not intimating that he had any authority from General Gates to make this communication to the Commander-in Chief, nor enclosing a copy of the articles.

"Wilkinson did not reach the seat of Congress till the 31st of October, fifteen days after the convention of Saratoga was signed, and then it took him three days to put the papers in order which he was to lay before Congress. It was on this occasion that one of the members made a motion in Congress that they should compliment Colonel Wilkinson with the gift of a pair of spurs."—*See Sparks' Writings of Washington Vol. V, p.* 114.

1. Journals of Congress, Vol. III. p. 469, 1777.
2. Journals of Congress, Vol. III. p. 548, 1777.
3. Sparks' Writings of Washington, Vol. V, p. 216.

gentleman concerned, as I am sure it will by you, as an act of necessary justice."[1]

Thus ended these battles near Saratoga, and the campaign which secured American independence. It was decisive; it disheartened the enemy, it fixed the wavering, and filled the patriots with new hope and energy, and it brought active aid from France and Spain to the patriot cause.

It was a brilliant success, and some one is fairly entitled to the honor of achieving it. Who? Schuyler's wise preparation and magnanimity cannot be too highly honored. But who fought the battles? Gates did not see the face of the enemy during the campaign. To what extent did Arnold contribute to the triumph of the Americans? Washington sent him North to rally the militia and lead them. They flocked to his standard, and he led them to victory. His expedition up the Mohawk was a perfect success, and if Stanwix had not been relieved, and St. Leger had come down to Albany and formed a junction with Burgoyne, the result would probably have been changed. Returning from Fort Stanwix, Arnold skirmished successfully, and restored the spirits of the army, depressed by the retreat from Ticonderoga. He selected Bemis Heights for the battle-ground, and fought the battles of the 19th of September and the 7th of October.

If this is, indeed, true, and if the conflict at Saratoga was one of the great battles which have influenced the fate of nations; if this was the decisive contest of the Revolution; if it was fought by Arnold, and his blood contributed to the victory, should he not have the credit, so dearly earned? Give all honor to Schuyler; give to Morgan, Stark, Dearborn, and others, all praise as brave partisans, but let history be just and truthful, and record that Benedict Arnold was the hero of the campaign of 1777, and of the battles of Saratoga.

[1]. Sparks' Writings of Washington, Vol. V, p. 217.

CHAPTER XI.

WASHINGTON'S FRIENDSHIP—ARNOLD'S GENEROSITY.

"I take the liberty of presenting these (epaulettes and sword-knotts) as a testimony of my sincere regard and approbation of your conduct."—*Washington to Arnold.* 1

ARNOLD'S WOUND—HE IS CARRIED TO ALBANY, THENCE TO CONNECTICUT—RECEPTION AT NEW HAVEN—RECEIVES PISTOLS, EPAULETTES AND SWORD KNOTS FROM WASHINGTON—HE SUPPLIES MONEY FOR THE EDUCATION AND MAINTENANCE OF THE ORPHANS OF GENERAL WARREN—GOES TO VALLEY FORGE—WASHINGTON ASSIGNS HIM TO COMMAND OF PHILADELPHIA.

The wound of General Arnold received at the battle of the 7th of October, was very severe and painful. In a letter written from Albany on the evening of October 8th, it is said: "The brave General Arnold is badly wounded in his left leg, having received a compound fracture, which endangers the loss of the limb."[2]

Ex-Senator Foster says: "I recollect, further, hearing my father speak of Arnold's impatience and fretfulness with the surgeon, who, on looking hastily at his wounded leg, expressed some apprehension that amputation might be necessary. This, according to my recollection, was on the field. Arnold thought he should stand "no such d——d nonsense, and that if that was all the surgeon had to say, the men should lift him upon his horse, and he would see the action through."[3]

---
1. Sparks' Writings of Washington, Vol. V, p. 361.
2. Connecticut *Courant* of Oct. 15th, 1777.
3. MSS. letter of Hon. L. F. S. Foster, to the author, Oct. 29th, 1877.

Arnold's impatience and chagrin must have been increased by the unmerited honors lavished by Congress upon Gates. So elated was Gates by the victory which had been secured by the wise preparation of Schuyler and by the valor and the skill of Arnold and Morgan, and their associates, who fought the battles of Saratoga, that, in his arrogance, he made no report of the surrender of Burgoyne, to Washington, the Commander-in-Chief, but passed him by, in contemptuous neglect, reporting directly to Congress, and that body, instead of rebuking the insubordination, on the 4th of November voted that a gold medal should be struck in his honor: "HORATIO GATES, *Duci Strenuo, Comitia Americana*"—The American Congress to Horatio Gates, the gallant leader.[1]

Arnold was carried in a litter from the camp at Saratoga to Albany, and remained there, completely disabled, during the autumn and much of the winter of 1777-8. On the 24th of December, 1777, Dr. J. Brown, a surgeon in the Continental Army, writing of a visit to the hospital, says: "General Lincoln is in a fair way of recovery. * * He is the patient Christian, etc. * * Not so the gallant General Arnold, for his wound, though less dangerous in the beginning than Lincoln's, is not in so fair a way of healing. He abuses us for a set of ignorant pretenders.[2]

Late in the winter or early spring, he was able to be moved to Connecticut, and it is said that on his way, in passing through Kinderhook, New York, his wound was still in such a condition that a door post had to be removed to make room for his litter to enter the house where he was to pass the night.[3]

He spent some time in Middletown, Connecticut, and on

---

[1] "General Gates was to be exalted upon the ruins of my reputation and influence."—*Washington to Patrick Henry, Sparks' Writings of Washington*, Vol. V, p. 515
[2] New England Historical and Genealogical Register, Vol. XVIII, p. 84.
[3] Henry C. Van Schoick, His. Magazine, Sept. 1778, p. 525.

the 1st of May, was able to reach his sister and his old home in New Haven. A few days more than a year had passed since (April 27, 1777,) he had made the desperate fight at Ridgefield, and during that time he had made the campaign up the Mohawk, fought the battles near Saratoga, and he now returned to his friends and neighbors the popular hero of the campaign of 1777. But the recognition of his great services by Congress was cold. Gates, who had not been under fire, was loaded with honors bought by Arnold's blood. The people, however, impulsive and generous, received their "fighting general" on his return to his native State with acclamations. The officers of the army, the militia, the cadet company, and a throng of the most respectable citizens of New Haven went out to welcome the gallant and still suffering soldier, to testify their esteem and conduct him to his home. A salute of thirteen guns announced to his devoted sister and to his proud and eager sons his approach.[1]

From the campaign of 1777, and the surrender of Burgoyne, the name of Arnold became a familiar word at many a home and beside the fireside of many a log cabin on the banks of the Hudson, the Mohawk and the New York lakes, as well as in New England, and was honored and cherished until he himself brought disgrace upon it.

I have spoken of the cold recognition of Arnold's services by Congress, but it was otherwise with the Commander-in-Chief. Thatcher, in his "American Revolution," says:

"It is but justice to confess that by his military phrensy, or romantic heroism, Arnold contributed to the honor and success of that day (battle of Oct. 7th). General Washington had a high sense of his gallantry, and presented him with a pair of elegant pistols."[2]

And on the 20th of January, when transmitting the

[1]. Connecticut Journal, May 6th, 1778.
[2]. Appendix to Thatcher's American Revolution, p. 468.

ante-dated commission, so long withheld by Congress, conferring upon Arnold the rank he had claimed, and directed to him at Albany, where he was still confined by his wounds, Washington closes his letter by saying:

"May I venture to ask whether you are upon your legs again? If you are not, may I flatter myself that you will be soon? There is none who wishes more sincerely for this event than I do, or who will receive the information with more pleasure. * * * As soon as your situation will permit, I request that you will repair to this army, it being my earnest wish to have your services the ensuing campaign."[1]

A few days after Arnold reached New Haven, he received the following letter from Washington:

"VALLEY FORGE, 7 May, 1778.
"DEAR SIR:—

"A gentleman in France having very obligingly sent me three sets of epaulettes and sword-knots, two of which, professedly, to be disposed of to any friends I should choose, I take the liberty of presenting them to you and General Lincoln, as a testimony of my sincere regard and approbation of your conduct. I have been informed by a Brigade-Major of General Huntington's, of your intention of repairing to camp shortly; but, notwithstanding my wish to see you, I must beg that you will run no hazard by coming out too soon.

"I am sincerely and affectionately your obedient, etc."[2]

This testimony of Washington's "sincere regard and approbation" of Arnold's "conduct" and of his sympathy and affection, were very gratifying, and it seems to me, coming from one who knew him so well, is entitled to great consideration in judging of Arnold's character and conduct previous to his treason.

I now come to other incidents in the life of Arnold which show that, with all his faults, his heart was warm with gratitude and generosity; and that he had formed a friendship for General Warren, which survived the death of that heroic man, and was manifested in a most liberal manner towards his children.

1. Sparks' Writings of Washington, Vol. V, p. 216.
2. Sparks' Writings of Washington, Vol. V, p. 361.

It will be remembered that General Warren, at the time of Arnold's visit to Cambridge, in 1775, was chairman of the Committee of Safety, and was an active friend of Arnold's in his expedition to Ticonderoga and St. Johns. The friendship then formed, and Arnold's grateful recollections of Warren's kindness, were not obliterated by time nor by the vicissitudes of a soldier's life. Warren, when killed at Bunker Hill, left four children, Elizabeth, Joseph, Mary and Richard, all of them under twelve years of age, and their only inheritance was the name made so illustrious by the patriotism and death of their father.[1] In the spring of 1778, Arnold learned that these children of his friend were in want, and that no one had as yet made any provision for them. He was not at this time a rich man; he had expended large sums of his own money in the public service, and his accounts had not been settled and paid by Congress; yet he did not hesitate in affording liberal aid. In a letter to Miss Mercy Scollay, he says:

"About three months ago I was informed that my late worthy friend General Warren, left his affairs unsettled, and that, after paying his debts, a very small matter, if anything, would remain for the education of his children, who, to my great surprise, I find have been entirely neglected by the State. Permit me to beg your continuing your care of the daughter, and that you will at present take charge of the education of the son. I make no doubt that his relations will consent that he shall be under your care. My intention is to use my interest with Congress to provide for the family. If they decline it, I make no doubt of a handsome collection by private subscription. At all events, *I* will provide for them in a manner suitable to their birth, and the grateful sentiments I shall ever feel for the memory of my friend. I have sent to you by Mr. Hancock five hundred dollars for the present. I wish you to have Richard clothed handsomely, and sent to the best school in Boston. Any expense you are at, please call on me for, and it shall be paid with thanks."[2]

The above letter was written July 15th, 1778. In the following letter to Dr. Townsend, dated Aug. 6th, 1778, there are interesting details on the same subject.

1. Life of Joseph Warren, by Frothingham. pp. 542-43.
2. Sparks' Life of Arnold, p. 127.

"I wrote you some time since, respecting the children of my late worthy friend, and requested the favor of your putting Richard to a school, and soliciting Miss Scollay to keep Betsey. Soon after I was informed you had left Boston, and as it was uncertain if you would receive my letter, I wrote Miss Scollay by Mr. Hancock, and sent her five hundred dollars, requesting her to take particular care of the education of Betsey, and prevail, if possible, with the relations to have Richard sent to the best school in Boston at my expense. Mr. Hancock has promised to me his interest to have the children taken care of. I shall apply to Congress soon. If they decline, make no doubt of a handsome collection by private subscriptions. At all events, am determined they shall be provided for, which fortune has put in my power to effect. I shall be glad to hear from you at all times and am, Dr. Townsend,

"Your Friend and Humble Servant,
"B. ARNOLD."[1]

From a letter written by Samuel Adams to Elbridge Gerry and James Lovell, dated Dec. 20th, 1779, I make the following extract:

"The two younger children, a boy of about seven years, and a girl somewhat older, are in the family of John Scollay, Esq., under the particular care of his daughter, at her most earnest request; otherwise, I suppose, they would have been taken care of by their relations at Roxbury, and educated as farmer's children usually are. Miss Scollay deserves the greatest praise for her attention to them. She is exceedingly well qualified for her charge; and her affection for their deceased father prompts her to exert her utmost to inculcate in the minds of these children those principles which may conduce 'to render them worthy of the relation they stood in' to him."[2]

"General Arnold has assisted, by generously ordering five hundred dollars towards their support. This I was informed of when I was last in Philadelphia. I called on him, and thanked him for his kindness to them. Whether he has done more for them since I cannot say."[3]

The generous sentiments of Arnold for the children of Warren continued to be manifested by occasional supplies of money, as promised in his letter to Miss Scollay.

1. New England Historical and Genealogical Register. Vol. IX, p. 122.
2. Miss Scollay is said to have been engaged to be married to General Warren, as his second wife at the time of his death.
3. Frothingham's Life of Warren, p. 458.

"Arnold made application to Congress for provision for these children, and the application was referred to a committee who reported 'that the three younger children of General Warren should be maintained at the public expense, in a manner suitable to their rank in life, till they should come of age, and at that time one thousand pounds should be given to each as a portion.' If this report was ever called up, it did not receive the sanction of Congress. Arnold persevered, however, in his solicitation, and at last the point was carried to allow for the support of these chi·dren the half-pay of a major general from the date of their father's death till the youngest should be of age.

"General Warren had been dead five years, and the annual amount of half-pay was somewhat more than thirteen hundred dollars, making the sum due nearly seven thousand dollars, besides the future stipend. In the congratulatory letter which Arnold wrote to Miss Scollay on this event, only six weeks before the consummation of his treachery, he reiterated his ardent concern for the welfare of the children, but complained that his application to Congsess had been opposed from the beginning by all the Massachusetts delegates except one. They looked upon the case as appertaining only to the State of Massachusetts, and as not coming within the jurisdiction of Congress. Others had the same opinion The success of the measure, which every benevolent mind must heartily approve, may be fairly ascribed to the zeal and perseverance of Arnold." [1]

The letter of General Arnold to Miss Scollay, referred to by Sparks in the preceding quotation, is as follows:

"PEAKS HILL, Augt. 3rd, 1780.
"DR. MADAM:—

"I must ask pardon for not answering your several letters before, in particular the one of the 7th inst. I do assure you it was not inattention, but a hope (deferred from time to time) of giving you an accot. of the success of my application to Congress in favor of the orphans of the late General Warren, which I hope you will admit as an apology. I now have the pleasure to inform you that my application has so far succeeded (notwithstanding it has been opposed from the beginning by the Delegates of the State of Massachusetts Bay, except by Mr. Holton. Mr. Gerry, in particular, did everything in his power to prevent the Success of the Appli'n), that Congress have at last Resolved that the three youngest children (the oldest being provided for) shall receive the Half pay of a Major-General from the Death of the General untill they are of age, which will amount to three hundred pounds pr. annum, C. (Continental) money, in Specie or an equivalent, so that there is five

1. Spark's Life of Arnold, p. 128.

years' pay due, amtg. to the Sum of £1500 in Specie, which the States is by the Resolution of Congress requested to pay, and to provide the Education and clothing, &c., of the Children.

When application was made to Congress, Mr. Gerry opposed it as disagreeable to the Southern States, and a provision which ought to be made by the State of Massachusetts Bay; when a private subscription was handed about, he opposed it as dishonorable to the State and the particular friends and relations of the late General, so that a trifle was subscribed and nothing collected. It has not been want of Inclination, but want of ability which has prevented my remitting you the ballance for the expense of the children. The Public are indebted to me for a considerable Sum which I advanced for them in Canada, and for four years pay which I cannot obtain. I must request you will present the Acco't of expenses incurred to the Presid't and Council of Massachusetts Bay without any mention of my name, and request payment, which I make not the least doubt, they will not only Comply with but reimburse the Sum advanced. In a hurry I forgot the Resolution of Congress; I have this day wrote to Philadelphia for it. When it arrives I will Inclose it to you. If the State refuses to pay the Acco't., I shall esteem myself obliged to. But as the Resolution of Congress makes ample provision for them, they will not stand in need of the assistance of Individuals in future. The General Officers of the Army have within a few days presented a Spirited Memorial to Congress in behalf of the Widows and orphans of all those who have fell in the Service of their Country since the Commencement of the war, and I am not without hopes of our Succeeding in it. Your observations on the Charitable disposition of People of oppulence is very Just. Charity, urbanity, and the Social Virtues Seem swallowed up in the tumult and Confusion of the times, and self wholly engrosses the nabobs of the present day. I am much obliged to you for your tender of services, and shall be happy at any time to receive a letter from you, and to hear of the welfare of your charge, as I feel myself greatly interested in their happiness, and hope you will be enabled to resume the charge of them soon. Please to present my love to them, and believe me, with great regard and esteem, Madam,

"Your Obed., Hble. Svt.,
"B. Arnold."

"I wish you would be good enough to consult with your Friends, as a proper method of obtaining the Ballance due you of the State; which I think they cannot, with any Face of Justice, refuse when they have the Resolution of Congress. But if that should be the Case, you will please to make out a particular acco't in Specie of the whole Sum you have advanced, and credit the Sum you have received, that the Ballance may appear. For which I may possibly honor an order of Congress for payment.

"B. A.[1]

"Miss SCOLLAY."

The action of Congress referred to was as follows: on the first of July, 1780.

"On motion of Mr. Livingstone, seconded by Mr. Adams, Congress came to the following resolutions:

"WHEREAS, Congress have thought proper to erect a monument to the memory of Major-General Warren, in consideration of his distinguished merit and bravery, and to make provision for the education of his eldest son; and whereas, it appears no adequate provision can be made out of his private fortune for the education and maintenance of his three younger children: therefore,

Resolved, That it be recommended to the Executive of Massachusetts Bay to make provision for the maintenance and education of the said three children of the late Major-general Warren.

Resolved, That Congress will defray the expense thereof, to the amount of the half-pay of a major-general, to commence at the time of his death, and continue until the youngest of the said children shall be of age." [2]

---

1. Certified from Department of State at Washington.
2. Frothingham's Life of Joseph Warren, p 544.

The following is a statement of monies advanced and paid to Miss Mercy Scollay, copied from the day-book of General Benedict Arnold, in his own handwriting, now in the office of the Secretary of the Commonwealth of Pennsylvania, at Harrisburg, p. 8.

"1778. Miss Mercy Scollay to cash   Dr.
July 15. To 500 dollars for expenses on acct. of the late Genl. Warren's
children,   £150."
(This appears by Arnold's letter to Miss Scollay to have been sent by Hancock.)
         [Page 16.]
"Feb. 19, 1779. Miss Mercy Scollay,   Dr.
"To cash 500 dollars for the use of the late Gen. Warren's children, sent by Lieut. Peter Richards."

There are several accounts of curious interest in this book; among others, one with Gen. Washington. There are accounts with ships "Mars" and "Jonathan," the sloop "Active," the "Charming Nancy," and schooner "General Arnold."

Among the charges are items for arms furnished. There are large transactions with his sister, Hannah Arnold, showing that she was entrusted with important business affairs for him."

There are accounts with "Hon. Silas Deane," and items with him about the time, or soon after, his marriage, for brocades, striped satin, silk, white and green, linen, cambric, etc.; also accounts with his butler, Ben Provost, for family expenses. Also,

Such was the action of this so-called "sordid," "avaricious" "and grasping" man towards the children of a friend, who "had rendered him some, and the State great service."

In the diary of the eminent surgeon, John C. Warren, who was a near relative of Joseph Warren, dated 1799, at "Margate, England," is written: "I met General Arnold, the "traitor," so called. He was there with his family; I recollect a son, very handsome, and a daughter. Arnold was rather a stout man, broad shouldered, large black eyes. He walked lame from a wound received at the attack on Quebec, I think."

In May, Arnold arrived at the camp of Washington, at Valley Forge. His wound still rendered him unfit for active service in the field, and as it was expected that the British would very soon evacuate Philadelphia, the Commander-in-Chief determined to give him the command of that city. This would be a new and untried theatre for one whose true place was on the battle-field. Happy would it have been for him if he could have remained with Washington, and shared with his chief the perils and the glory of the war until the contest closed at Yorktown.

The drama which now opened in the city of Penn, then the metropolis of the Union, presenting this brave soldier in the character of an ardent lover and successful suitor of the belle of Philadelphia, the young, fascinating and beautiful Peggy Shippen, and which ended so darkly at West Point, I will not enter upon until the next chapter.

"April 2, 1779. Rev. Mr. Barth'w Booth, Dr.
"To cash £600 lawful money, for schooling and boarding Ben and Richard two and a half years. To £300 for their expenses." These were his two children by his first wife.

CHAPTER XII.

ARNOLD'S COURTSHIP AND MARRIAGE.

"She loved me for the dangers I had passed,
And I loved her that she did pity them."

PHILADELPHIA DURING THE REVOLUTION—ARNOLD ASSUMES COMMAND AND SUCCEEDS SIR WILLIAM HOWE IN OCCUPYING THE PENN HOUSE—THE SHIPPEN FAMILY—MAJOR JOHN ANDRE—THE "MISCHIENZA"—PEGGY SHIPPEN, THE BELLE OF PHILADELPHIA—ARNOLD AS HER SUITOR—HIS COURTSHIP—SETTLES UPON HER MT. PLEASANT—HIS MARRIAGE AND DOMESTIC LIFE—LETTER OF HANNAH ARNOLD TO MRS. ARNOLD AT WEST POINT.

ON the 18th of June, 1778, the British army retired from Philadelphia, and on the 19th General Arnold, by direction of Washington, assumed command of that city. During the British occupation, the headquarters of Sir William Howe, commanding the British force, had been the mansion which was once the home of Governor Richard Penn, the grandson of William Penn. This house was afterwards repaired by Robert Morris, and occupied by President Washington, while the seat of government was at Philadelphia, and thus it became known as the "Washington Mansion."

The British army had taken possession of Philadelphia on the twenty-sixth of September, 1777, and for the headquarters of the commander they had selected what was then regarded as the finest house in the city. It was built of brick, and stood on the south-east corner of Front and Market streets, "a large, double house, and which with its offices extended back one hundred and twenty-one feet," and Rush, in his reminiscences says of it, that in 1790 few, if any, equaled it in Philadelphia.[1] Here General Howe and his brilliant staff of officers and associates, passed a gay winter in 1777-'8.

To such an extent were the gayeties and dissipations carried in this old Quaker city during that time, that Dr. Franklin said: "General Howe has not taken Philadelphia; Philadelphia has taken General Howe." He and his associates certainly seemed much more interested in the amusements which occupied their time than in efforts to capture the army of General Washington. Philadelphia was then the most important city in America, and its social circles were among the most cultivated and aristocratic. The gentry consisted largely of the old Quaker families and those connected with the Anglican church, and many of them possessed wealth, culture, courtly manners and dignified deportment. The ladies were already distinguished for their beauty, grace and intelligence. Chastellux, a French traveler, says they were graceful and fascinating, and dressed with elegance. The majority of the so-called fashionable society people adhered to the crown, and cordially welcomed General Howe; and during his stay the young English officers were the leaders and favorites in social gayeties and amusements. While the British were living in luxury in the city, and indulging in all sorts of dissipation, the American army under Washington were enduring with heroic fortitude the hardships of Valley Forge. Among the former, dinner-parties, cock-fights, amateur theatrical performances, and every amusement and dissipasipation idle men could desire, occupied their time. Among these gay and dashing young soldiers Major John André was a favorite. He was young, handsome and

[1] The Historic Mansions of Philadelphia, p. 250. Rush's Reminiscences.

graceful, and of purer morals and a more refined taste than many of his associates. He was a welcome guest in the house of Edward Shippen, a gentleman of rank, character and fortune, and of one of the most respected families in Philadelphia, and who, although he took no very decided part on either side during the war, and was generally regarded as a loyalist, yet such was his high personal character, that he was, after its termination, elected Chief Justice of Pennsylvania. André, though a brave and efficient soldier, was still more distinguished as a favorite in society, and was ever ready, both with his pen and pencil, to contribute to its amusements. He wrote graceful verses, arranged plays for exhibition, painted scenery and drop-curtains, and was himself an accomplished actor.

Among the amusements and gayeties of the winter of 1778, was the celebrated *Mischienza*, a pageant, play and mock tournament, gotten up in honor of General Howe. It was a novel and splendid entertainment, and in consequence, perhaps, of the very prominent part taken in its preparation and performance by the unfortunate Major André, and the appearance in it of Miss Peggy Shippen, afterwards the wife of General Arnold, it has always been regarded with historic interest. The scene of this brilliant pageant, which took place on the eighteenth of May, 1778, was at Walnut Grove, the country seat of Joseph Wharton,[1] a fine old country house, surrounded by a noble park of venerable trees, the grounds extending to the banks of the Delaware.

The Queen of the *Mischienza* has represented André as "the charm of the company." He seems to have been the leader of the whole affair, and his costumes, verses, etc., were all very clever. The knights and ladies who appeared were divided into two parties; one designated as that of

---

1. Historic Mansions of Philadelphia, p. 466.

the "Burning Mountain," and the other as the "Blended Rose."

Among the other incidents of the spectacle was a tournament, arranged and conducted in accordance with the customs and usages of ancient chivalry. Knights, mounted on trained horses and armed as in the olden time; ladies dressed in brilliant costumes, with favors with which they were to reward the knights who contended in their honor. The party designated as "The Knights of the Blended Rose," were led by Lord Cathcart, and with him were associated six knights, each with his squire, and each selected one of the ladies in honor of whom he was to contend in the lists.

Third on the list of this party was Captain John André, in honor of Miss P. Chew; his device, two game cocks fighting; motto, *No Rival*. The sixth knight of this party was Lieutenant Sloper, in honor of Miss M. Shippen; device, a heart and sword; motto, *Honor, and the Fair*.

Captain Watson, of the guards, was the chief of the party, designated as "The Knights of the Burning Mountain," supported by six knights, each attended by his squire, and each to contend in honor of the lady of his choice The second knight of those making up the party of "The Burning Mountain" was Lieutenant Winyard, in honor of Miss Peggy Shippen; device, a bay-leaf; motto, "*unchangeable.*"[1] These two parties, superbly mounted—those of the Blended Rose on gray, and those of the Burning Mountain on black horses—now contended in the lists, according to the rules of chivalry, with lance and shield and sword, for the honor of their several ladies, "as superior in wit, beauty and accomplishment to those of the whole world." After the tournament followed the bestowal of favors, a brilliant ball, splendid fireworks and illumina-

---

[1] Sargent's Life of Andre, p. 172, etc.

tions. Among these gay and brilliant actors André and Miss Shippen, afterwards Mrs. Arnold, were conspicuous. This gay young soldier, and this lovely maiden, then only eighteen years of age, bright and joyous, mingling in scenes of romance and mimic chivalry, happy in the present, and hope lighting up all the future; happy that the veil was drawn, shutting out from the one his tragic death upon the scaffold, and from the other her clouded life, her exile from home and friends—yet a life devoted to duty in soothing the perturbed spirit of a bitterly disappointed man, a life which opened so brilliantly to go out in darkness. The spectacle was altogether a very brilliant affair * * but provoked much ridicule, and the inquiry was often made what had General Howe done, during his more than half-year's indolent and luxurious occupation of the city, to merit such an ovation ?

As the British retired from the city, Arnold entered and assumed command, and took possession, as his headquarters, of the same Penn House which Howe had so lately occupied.

Whatever may have been the character of those who preceded him, and however effeminate their amusements, he was no "carpet-knight." Not in the tilting yard, nor at the tournament, nor in any form of mimic war, had his laurels been won. In the wilderness, by the severest hardships and sufferings, beneath the walls of Quebec, on the Lake, against the most decisive odds, on the field, in the midst of carnage and blood, had he earned the character which induced Washington to express a desire to have "his services the ensuing campaign," [1] and to ask him to join the main army, as soon as his wounds would permit active field service.

[1] Washington to Arnold, January 20th, 1778, Sparks' Writings of Washington Vol. V, p. 216.

It has already been stated that the Shippen family was, at the time of the Revolution, one of the most distinguished and respected in Philadelphia. Edward Shippen had three daughters who took part in the *Mischienza*—Miss S. Shippen, Miss M. Shippen, and Miss Peggy Shippen, who became Mrs. Arnold.[1] The latter was the "darling of the family circle." Young, extremely beautiful and graceful, and with a magnetism of person and manner which drew to her in love and admiration, every one who came within her influence. Washington said to Lafayette, "Ah, Marquis, you young men are all in love with Mrs. Arnold."[2] Tarlton and other returning officers, after she went to London, reported that "she was the handsomest woman in England." The enthusiasm with which Hamilton, in his letter to Miss Schuyler, describes her will not be forgotten. I have read her letters to her father, husband and family, from the time of her marriage to her death, and there is throughout an exhibition of filial tenderness and respect; a conjugal devotion, purity, elevation and dignity, which indicate a warm and affectionate heart, a Christian fortitude, and a cultivated intellect, rare as beautiful.

While Philadelphia was held by the British, as has been stated, courtesies were reciprocated between the families of wealth and social position and the British officers, and the brilliant Major André was a frequent and welcome visitor at the Shippen's; and there is yet preserved among them as an heir-loom, a pen-and-ink sketch of Miss Peggy Shippen, in the costume of the *Mischienza*, drawn by André. When Arnold took command in Philadelphia, crippled with honorable wounds in the service of his country, few soldiers in the American army had a higher reputation for skill, and none were more distinguished for personal cour-

[1] Sargent's Life of Andre, pp. 171-2.
[2] Irving's Washington, Vol. IV, p. 137.

age. These are qualities which the people always appreciate, and those possessing them have in all ages been the especial admiration of women. Arnold was still young, only thirty-six, of manly bearing, splendid physique, and yet bore visible marks, both in his appearance and his movements, of the wounds he had received. It is not surprising that he should have captivated the fancy and won the heart of the beautiful and fascinating Miss Shippen.

A member of the Shippen family says "there can be no doubt the imagination of Miss Shippen was excited, and her heart captivated by the oft repeated stories of his gallant deeds, his feats of brilliant courage, and traits of generosity and kindness, such as his contributions towards the education of the orphan children of General Warren."[1]

It was not long before he was the declared suitor for the hand of Miss Shippen. In a note to her father, asking his permission to address his daughter, Arnold says, among other things:

"My fortune is not large, though sufficient (not to depend upon my expectations) to make us both happy. I neither expect nor wish one with Miss Shippen. * * My public character is well known; my private one is, I hope, irreproachable. If I am happy in your approbation of my proposa s of an alliance, I shall most willingly accede to any you may please to make consistent with the duty I owe to three lovely children. Our difference in political sentiments, will, I hope, be no bar to my happiness. I flat er myself the time is at hand when our unhappy contests will be at an end, and peace and domestic happiness be restored to every one." * *

On the 25th of September, he made to her the following formal declaration of his love and offer of his hand:

"DEAR MADAM:—

"Twenty times have I taken up my pen to write to you, and as often has my trembling hand refused to obey the dictates of my heart—a heart which, though calm and serene amidst the clashing of arms and all the din and horrors of war, trembles with diffidence and the fear of

---

[1]. Shippen Papers.

giving offence when it attempts to address you on a subject so important to its happiness. Dear madam, your charms have lighted up a flame in my bosom which can never be extinguished; your heavenly image is too deeply impressed ever to be effaced.

"My passion is not founded on personal charms only: that sweetness of disposition and goodness of heart, that sentiment and sensibility which so strongly mark the character of the lovely Miss P. Shippen, renders her aimiable beyond expression, and will ever retain the heart she has once captivated. On you alone my happiness depends, and will you doom me to languish in despair? Shall I expect no return to the most sincere, ardent and disinterested passion? Do you feel no pity in your gentle bosom for the man who would die to make you happy? May I presume to hope it is not impossible I may make a favorable impression on your heart? Friendship and esteem you acknowledge. Dear Peggy, suffer that heavenly bosom (which cannot know itself the cause of pain without a sympathetic pang) to expand with a sensation more soft, more tender than friendship. A union of hearts is undoubtedly necessary to happiness; but give me leave to observe that true and permanent happiness is seldom the effect of an alliance founded on a romantic passion; where fancy governs more than judgment. Friendship and esteem, founded on the merit of the object, is the most certain basis to build a lasting happiness upon; and when there is a tender and ardent passion on one side, and friendship and esteem on the other, the heart (unlike yours) must be callous to every tender sentiment if the taper of love is not lighted up at the flame.

"I am sensible your prudence and the affection you bear your amiable and tender parents forbids your giving encouragement to the addresses of any one without their approbation. Pardon me, Dear Madame, for disclosing a passion I could no longer confine in my tortured bosom. I have presumed to write to your Papa, and have requested his sanction to my addresses. Suffer me to hope for your approbation. Consider before you doom me to misery, which I have not deserved but by loving you too extravagantly. Consult your own happiness, and if incompatible, forget there is so unhappy a wretch; for may I perish if I would give you one moment's inquietude to purchase the greatest possible felicity to myself. Whatever my fate may be, my most ardent wish is for your happiness, and my latest breath will be to implore the blessing of heaven on the idol and only wish of my soul.

"Adieu, dear Madame, and believe me unalterably, your sincere admirer and devoted humble servant,

"B. ARNOLD.

"Sept. 25, 1778.
"Miss Peggy Shippen."

This is not the language of a man whose attentions had been wasted upon unworthy objects, but the words express a genuine, manly, honest attachment. This letter warmly expresses a passion, ardent, sincere, and so true and generous, that he is unwilling to purchase his own supreme happiness at the expense of hers. "May I perish," says the blunt soldier, "if I would give you one moment's inquietude to purchase the greatest possible felicity to myself."

It has been said that her father opposed their marriage; if so, the opposition was not persistent. On the 21st of December, 1778, Mr. Shippen says:

"I gave my daughter Betsy to Neddy Burd last Thursday evening, and all is jollity and mirth. My youngest daughter is much solicited by a certain General on the same subject. Whether this will take place or not depends on circumstances. If it should, it will not be till spring."[1]

On the second of January, 1779, Edward Shippen, senior, grand-father of Peggy, writes to Colonel Burd, from Lancaster, "We understand that General Arnold, a fine gentleman, lays close siege to Peggy; and if so, there will be another match in the family."[2] It appears that his ardent passion was soon reciprocated, for on the eighth of February, 1779, he writes to her with the fervor of an accepted lover:

"CAMP AT RARITAN, February 8th, 1779.
"MY DEAREST LIFE:—

"Never did I so ardently long to see or hear from you as at this instant. I am all impatience and anxiety to know how you do; six days' absence, without hearing from my dear Peggy, is intolerable. Heavens! what must I have suffered had I continued my journey—the loss of happiness for a few dirty acres. I can almost bless the villanous roads, and more *villanous men*, who oblige me to return. I am heartily tired with my journey, and almost so with human nature. I daily discover so much baseness and ingratitude among mankind that I almost blush at being of the same species, and could quit the stage without regret was it not for some gentle, generous souls like my dear Peggy, who still retain the

1. Historic Mansions of Philadelphia, pp. 221-222.
2. Historic Mansions of Philadelphia, p. 222.

lively impression of their Maker's image, and who, with smiles of benignity and goodness, make all happy around them. Let me beg of you not to suffer the rude attacks on me to give you one moment's uneasiness; they can do me no injury. I am treated with the greatest politeness by General Washington and the officers of the army, who bitterly execrate Mr. Reed and the Council for their villanous attempt to injure me. They have advised me to proceed on my journey. The badness of the roads will not permit, was it possible to support an absence of four weeks, for in less time I could not accomplish it. The day after to-morrow I leave this, and hope to be made happy by your smiles on Friday evening; 'till then all nature smiles in vain; for you alone, heard, felt, and seen, possess my every thought, fill every sense and pant in every vein.

"Clarkson will send an express to meet me at Bristol;[1] make me happy by one line, to tell me you are so; please to present my best respects to your mamma and the family. My prayers and best wishes attend my dear Peggy. Adieu! and believe me, sincerely and affectionately thine.

"B. ARNOLD.
"Miss PEGGY SHIPPEN."

On the twenty-second of March, 1779, General Arnold, in anticipation of his marriage, purchased the fine old country seat called Mount Pleasant, situated on the east bank of the Schuylkill, and made a settlement of the estate on himself for life, "remainder to his wife and children." Two weeks thereafter General Arnold and Peggy Shippen were married at the residence of her father, a fine substtantial mansion on the west side of Fourth street.[2]

He was still so far disabled by the wound received at Saratoga, that during the marriage ceremony he was compelled to lean upon the arm of a fellow soldier, and when seated his limb was supported by a camp stool.[3] His condition rendered him only the more interesting to the lovely bride. To her he was then and ever a hero.

The beautiful country seat of Mount Pleasant, which he settled upon his wife and children, is still standing in Fairmount Park. The mansion stands on a bluff, overlooking

1. Major Mathew Clarkson, of New York, was one of Arnold's aids.
2 Historic Mansions of Philadelphia, p. 223.
3. Watson's Annals, Vol. III, p. 445.

the Schuylkill, to which the grounds extended. A broad walk from the front led down to the banks of the river; a carriage drive passed around the house; out-houses for coachman and gardner, and carriage house and barn were in the rear, and the whole situated in extensive grounds, well wooded with grand old oaks, sycamores, and evergreens. John Adams, dining at this mansion in October, 1775, says it is "the most elegant seat in Pennsylvania."[1]

Here, and at his house in the city, Arnold resided until his removal to West Point. Here he gave those splendid entertainments, costly beyond his means, which involved him in debt, and which ultimately contributed to his ruin. He kept his coach and four, and lived altogether in a style of ostentation and expense entirely beyond his fortune, and unbecoming the officer of a country so poor and struggling with poverty as ours then was.[2] His entertainments were frequent, and his guests were numerous, and embraced nearly all the members of Congress and the officers of the army, as well as the fashion of the city. "When M. Gerard, the French Embassador, first arrived in Philadelphia, he was entertained at a public dinner given by General Arnold, and for several days afterwards the Embassador and his suite occupied apartments at his house."[3] On his trial by court-marshal, when charged with entertaining tories and neglecting the friends of his country, he says: "With respect to the gentlemen in civil life and the army, I can appeal to the candor of Congress and the Army, as scarcely a day has passed but many of both were entertained by me;" and in regard to the reproach of entertain-

---
[1]. Historic Mansions of Philadelphia, p. 214.
[2]. In a schedule of his property confiscated in Philadelphia, are mentioned among other things, "horses and carriages, "furniture, bedding and linen, &c., of the value of £300, books, electrical machine, mycroscope of the value of £200, china. glass, etc., etc. £50."
[3] Sparks' Life of Arnold, p. 144.

ing those who adhere to the crown, he said : " It is enough for me, Mr. President, to contend with *men* in the *field*." [1]

Here, on the nineteenth of March, 1780, was born to him a son—Edward Shippen. His domestic life while in Philadelphia, notwithstanding his difficulties and annoyances with the authorities of Pennsylvania, was a very happy one. The affection between himself and wife seems to have been tender, constant and uninterrupted. His sister, Hannah, with his youngest son, Henry, by his first wife, visited him, and remained some time in his family, while his two older sons, Ben and Richard, were away at school. A letter from the sister to Mrs. Arnold, dated September tenth, 1780, gives a vivid picture of the affection and happiness of this family, and shows how devotedly attached to each other were all its members.

"MONDAY, September 10, 1780.

" I address you, my dear Mrs. Arnold, from the regions of gloom and solitude; but when this splenatic scrawl will reach you, know not, for at present have not the shadow of a conveyance for it.

" This is Monday, the fourth day since your departure, and I have not once in the whole time step'd my foot over the threshold of our own door, and have scarcely been off the bed two hours together; have had the slight but troublesome fever that has so indiscriminately attact'd all orders of people (old maids not exempted.) Mrs. Burd has been in the same situation with myself, so that we have as yet not seen each other. Mr. Burd has kindly called once or twice; if you could conceive how we miss you and the dear little bantling, you would pity us. Harry was inconsolable the whole day you left us, and had, I believe, not less than twenty the most violent bursts of grief; his little brother Edward seems to be the principal theme of the mournful song—not one day has escaped without his sheding tears at his absence; he laments that just as he began to know and love his brother, he must be removed so far from him that he cannot even hear how he does ; this day with a falling tear, he observ'd to me that he thought it very hard when he had so few relations, that they shoul1 all be at such a distance from him; must own the observation call'd forth a sympathetic drop from my eyes. Am extremely anxious to know how you perform your journey; am very

1. Court-marshal Trial of General Arnold, p. 132.

fearful for the poor little sore-headed boy, and am surpriz'd that I have not heard a syllable from you, but comfort myself with the thought that no news is good news, as I cannot imagine but I should have heard it, if any material accident had befallen you. Yesterday got a letter from your anxious husband, who, lover-like, is tormenting himself with a thousand fancied disasters which have happened to you and the family; however hope by the day after to-morrow you will be able to remove all his distressing fears. Heaven guard you safely to him, for in your life and happiness his consists.

"Your papa was in yesterday; the family at the Cottage were all well, and had just heard your mamma was gone down to your aunt Pierce's— my head aches, and as I am sleepy, will close my letter for to-night; sweet re‚ose to you and yours.—

"*Monday Morning*—Had wrote the above, hoping some opportunity would present for sending it; and left it unseal'd to make whatever additions I found proper; but none presenting, had left it *in statu quo;* was just dressing myself, with an intent to creep out and make Mrs. Huntington a morning visit, when Punch[1] came tripping up stairs (showing his teeth), with a letter in his hand from mistress: I broke the seal with eager solicitude, and am more than hapyy to find you performed your journey as far as Brunswick with so much ease and pleasure; may they both attend in your train to the end of it;—am rejoic'd at the account you give me of Edward; hope the little rogue holds out as well as he began; reckon he will this night finish his first grand tour.—

"Sent just now to see how Mrs. Burd was; have for answer that she is much better; if my morning's visiting don't make me sick, design seeing her in the evening.—

"*Thursday*—Nothing new to-day. Saw Mrs. Burd last night, and we have made an appointment to Mrs. Morris's to-morrow.[2]—family affairs go on smooth; find I have got a steady, clever, industrious old cook; she has been out only once to church, and seems to have no inclination for gadding; your papa keeps Mrs. Allen's house for you, or himself; which takes it will be determined soon; he thinks Mrs. Allen's, on some accounts, most convenient for him, and knows the one we are now in, most so for you; for my part, wish he may find it most convenient to take Mrs. Allen's himself.

"*Friday Evening*—Am just returned from Mrs. Morris's where I drank tea with Mr. and Mrs. Isaac Cope, two Miss Marshalls, Miss Nellie

---

1. A Negro servant.
2. Mrs. Robert Morris, wife of the financier.

McCall,[1] Mrs. Harrison,[2] Mrs. Burd,[3] Miss Sally Morris,[4] of New Jersey, and another Miss—name unknown, the two Mr. Coxes,[5] all the beaux we had to help ourselves with. Hear nothing from the little boys at Maryland.[6] Mr. and Mrs. Mead are just annonc'd; adieu for to-night.

Saturday Evening—The day has passed off without hearing one lisp from you; I cannot account for it, unless by delays on the road; promise myself you are now happy with my brother; hope you have by this reach'd, and Edward quite well of his sore head. Your papa has been unwell for a few days, but is better; he went from here two hours since; all well at the cottage. Your mamma is not yet return'd. Harry desires his duty to papa and mamma, his love to Edward and Betsy; he says he wishes mamma would please to kiss Edward one hundred times for him, and when her hand is in, she may, if she pleases, give him fifty for his aunt; make my love to my brother, if you please. I shall expect letters the first and all opportunities, and am with sincere esteem and regard.   Yours,   H. ARNOLD.

"I have nothing to say in excuse for this ill pen'd scrawl, but that writing is not my talent.   H. A."[7]

1. Daughter of Samuel McCall.
2 Mrs. Henry Harrison. Her husband was mayor of Philadelphia in 1762. She was the daughter of Mathias Aspden. Her half-brother, Mathias Aspden, was a loyalist. His daughter was the wife of Bishop White.
3. Elisabeth, eldest daughter of Chief Justice Shippen, wife of Edward Burd.
4. Sister of Governeur Morris, and who was probably in charge of her brother's household, as he was then unmarried.
5. The two Messrs. Coxe must have been John D. Coxe, and his brother Tench Coxe. *Vide* Sabine's Loyalists. Hildeburn, of Philad.
6. Gen. Arnold's sons, Ben and Richard.
7 Autograph letter from State Department at Washington.

As an illustration of the care and tenderness of General Arnold towards his wife and child, I copy from a paper in the office of the Secretary of State at Washington, in Arnold's own hand-writing:

"Directions for Mrs. Arnold on Her way to West Point:

"You must by all means get out of the Carriage, Crossing all Ferries, and going over large Bridges to prevent accidents.

"Your first night's stage will be at Bristol, Mr. Coxe's, 20 miles.

"The second at Trenton, Banagers, unless you (go) to G. Dickinson's or Col. Caduc., 10 miles.

"The third night to Brunswick, Mrs. Mamners, a good house, 28 miles. If the weather is warm, and this stage too long, you can lodge at Princeton, 12 miles from Trenton.

"The fourth night at Newark, 26 miles. If this stage is too long you can stop 6 miles short, at Elizabethtown, or if any danger is apprehended from the enemy, you will be very safe riding a few miles out of the common road.

"The fifth night at Paramas. 12 miles.

"The sixth night, Judge Coe's, 14 miles; and, if not fatigued, to John Smith, Esqr.,

Thus I have given a phase of General Arnold's domestic life in Philadelphia—his courtship and marriage. This has been done without mingling with it his public conduct. In the next chapter I shall return to his public life, and endeavor to give a truthful narrative of his difficulties with the authorities of Pennsylvania, his trial by court martial, and his reprimand by Washington.

6 miles further, and only three from King's Ferry, where you will be hospitably received and well accommodated. You will get tolerable beds at Coe's, and from thence on south can reach West Point next day with ease, as you will go from King's Ferry by water, so that in seven days if the weather is cool, you will perform the journey with ease. At Paramas you will be very politely received by Mrs. Watkins, Mrs. Provost, very genteel people. 1 Let me beg of you not to make your Stages so long as to fatigue yourself and the Dr Boy, if you should be much longer in coming."

1. Mrs. Provost was a Loyalist of social distinction, and was afterwards married to Aaron Burr.

CHAPTER XIII.

ARNOLD'S CONTROVERSY WITH THE AUTHORITIES OF PENNSYLVANIA.

"His (Arnold's) brilliant services spoke eloquently in his favor. His admirers repined that a fame won by such daring exploits on the field should be stifled down by cold calumnies in Philadelphia, and many thought dispassionately that the State authorities had acted with excessive harshness towards a meritorious officer in widely spreading their charges against him, and thus in an unprecedented way putting a public brand upon him."—*Washington Irving*.

ARNOLD'S CONDUCT IN COMMAND OF PHILADELPHIA—HIS CONTROVERSY WITH PRESIDENT REED AND THE AUTHORITIES OF PENNSYLVANIA—THE ACTION OF CONGRESS—REPORTS OF COMMITTEE EXONERATING HIM—A COURT-MARTIAL ORDERED FOR HIS TRIAL.

It is my purpose, in the following pages, to examine the conduct of General Arnold in Philadelphia, and the charges made against him by the authorities of Pennsylvania, and endeavor to determine how far he was guilty of conduct indicating a want of integrity as a man, and honor as a soldier. The most unqualified language of condemnation has generally been used against him, and the decision of the court-martial by which he was tried, has been cited as establishing his guilt. So far from this, the judgment of the court though in form guilty on two charges, was substantially an acquittal. The so-called reprimand of Washington was an eulogy, such as has rarely been bestowed upon a public officer, and its warm commendation and generous sympathy—following the severe charges so widely circulated—

were intended to, and did, express Washington's confidence and respect. Washington Irving, who hated Arnold's treason, but loved justice, in his life of Washington, says: "We have considered the particulars of *this trial attentively*, discharging from our minds, as much as possible, all impressions produced by Arnold's subsequent history, and we are surprised to find after the hostility manifested against him by the Council of Pennsylvania, and their extraordinary measures to possess the public mind against him; how venial are the trespasses of which he stood convicted." [1]

"In regard to both charges nothing fraudulent on the part of Arnold was found." [2]

Let us then, forgetting his treason, endeavor to investigate the facts fairly, and see whether Irving's conclusions were just or otherwise.

Arnold, as the military commander of the confederation at Philadelphia, held a very difficult and delicate position. The jealousy which has always existed between State rights and National authority, was at that time peculiarly sensitive, and the line separating the one from the other was not clearly defined. This city, during the period of British occupation, had been the residence of a large number of loyalists and active tories. In it was much property and merchandise belonging to those who were unfriendly to the cause of National independence. By a resolution of Congress, adopted June 5th, 1778, the Commander-in-Chief was directed to suspend the removal, sale or transfer of goods in Philadelphia, until a joint commission of that body, and of the Executive Council of Pennsylvania, should determine whether it was the property of the King, or any of his subjects. General Washington, in his instructions to General Arnold, dated on the 18th of June,

[1] Irving's Life of Washington, Vol. IV, p. 22.
[2] Irving's Life of Washington, Vol. IV, p. 22.

enclosed this resolution, and directed him to see that the resolution of Congress was enforced.[1]

Arnold, on the 19th of June, issued his proclamation, reciting the resolution of Congress, the instructions of General Washington, and ordering the shops and stores closed. This was done at the suggestion of leading patriots of Philadelphia, and the proclamation was written by General Reed himself, one of the Executive Council of Pennsylvania, and Arnold's chief accuser.[2]

This proclamation was an arbitrary exercise of military authority, and produced great dissatisfaction, and rendered General Arnold personally unpopular; but it was simply an obedience of orders; and yet this, with other acts on his part, led to the controversy between him and the Executive Council of the State, and to their presenting charges to Congress against him, some of which were referred to a court-martial for trial. But inasmuch as the court-martial found that though the shops and stores were shut by General Arnold's orders, they were of opinion that he was justified by the resolution of Congress of the 5th of June, and the Commander-in-Chief's instructions on the 18th of June, these orders are only important in this connection as showing the origin of the unfortunate controversy. It was Arnold's misfortune that it became his duty to execute an arbitrary and very unpopular order, and in doing so he became the object of a personal hostility, which his own haughty and unyielding temper did little to conciliate. His style of living aggravated the dislike which his military orders had created.

As stated on a preceding page, he kept a splendid establishment, had his carriages and horses, gave expensive entertainments, and exhibited an ostentatious display which

---
1. See Trial of Arnold, for Resolution of Congress. Washington's Instructions, etc., pp. 18-19.
2. Arnold's Trial—testimony of Major Franks.

was beyond his means, and unbecoming his position.[1] He was at the same time an open and avowed suitor of Miss Shippen—having obtained the sanction of her father to his addresses, and her family were not friendly to the cause of independence. Indeed, it was said that "he had courted the loyalists from the start."[2]

General Joseph Reed, who was then one of the Executive Council, and who led the State authorities against Arnold, writing to General Greene, says: "Will you not think it extraordinary that General Arnold made a public entertainment the night before last, of which not only tory ladies, but the wives and daughters of persons proscribed by the State, and now with the enemy at New York, formed a considerable number."[3]

Irving, in commenting upon this, says:

"Regarded from a different point of view, this conduct might have been attributed to the courtesy of a gallant soldier, who scorned to carry the animosity of the field into the drawing room, or to proscribe and persecute the wives and daughters of political exiles."[4]

Yet all who have witnessed the violence of party spirit in time of war, will understand how little such "courtesy" would be appreciated by heated partisans, and how extremely obnoxious a person exercising it, would become in a city where party feeling was intense and bitter. The feeling towards General Arnold growing out of these various causes, became so hostile and annoying that he seems to have formed the idea of retiring from the army, and becoming a large landholder and leading a country life. His approaching marriage with Miss Shippen, and the prospect of a home in the country with her, doubtless added to the at-

1. Irving's Life of Washington, Vol. IV, p. 12.
2. Irving's Life of Washington, Vol. IV, p. 14.
3. Irving's Washington, Vol. IV, p. 14.
4. Irving's Washington, Vol. IV, p. 15.

tractions of this project. His plan was to obtain a grant of land in western New York, and to establish there a settlement of the officers and soldiers who had served under him, and with whom he was always personally popular. With these and such others as might join the enterprise, he hoped to build up a successful settlement, retrieve his pecuniary embarrassments, and realize the kind of life he had witnessed on the part of General Schuyler, and other large and wealthy land owners of New York. A country house surrounded by a large landed estate, the building up of a prosperous settlement, was to him very attractive, and such was his power over men, that he would most probably have been successful. In a letter to Schuyler he declares his ambition is to be "a good citizen rather than shining in history."

The enterprise was submitted to the delegation in Congress from New York, and to the pure-minded John Jay, its President, by all of whom it was cordially approved. The delegation wrote a joint letter to Governor Clinton, requesting his aid and council in obtaining the favorable action of the Legislature. "To you, Sir," they say, "and to our State, General Arnold can require no recommendation; a series of distinguished services entitle him to respect and favor."[1]

President Jay, writing to Governor Clinton, said:

"I wish that in treating with him (Arnold), they (the Legislature) may recollect the services he has rendered to his country, and the value of such a citizen to any State that may gain him. Several other general officers have thoughts of settling in our State, and the prevailing reason they assign for it is, the preference for our Constitution to that of other States. They consider it as having the principles of stability and vigor as well as of liberty; advantages which the loose and less guarded kinds of government cannot promise. I have no doubt but that generosity to General Arnold will be justice to the State."[2]

1. Spark's Life of Arnold, p. 135.
2. Sparks Life of Arnold, p. 135.

Alas! who will not join in the regret that this enterprise was not successful, and this man, who then numbered among his warm and devoted friends, some of the purest and best patriots of the Revolution, have been diverted from the dark crime which lay in the future.

But it was not so to be; while on his way to New York, in furtherance of this enterprise, he stopped at the camp of Washington on the Raritan, and there received intelligence of the attack made upon him by General Reed and the Council of Pennsylvania, and of the charges they had printed and circulated against him, and he hastily returned to meet these charges, and became involved in a long and irritating controversy, which led to his ruin. From the camp of Washington he wrote the impassioned letter to Miss Shippen, of February 8th, 1779, set forth in the preceding chapter.

Almost immediately after his departure from Philadelphia on this trip, the Executive Council of Pennsylvania sent to Congress their complaints and grievances, embodied in eight charges of misconduct and culpability on the part of General Arnold. Printed copies of these charges were widely circulated, one of which reached him in the camp of Washington. They were published in the newspapers of Pennsylvania and Maryland.

In the absence of General Arnold, Major Clarkson, his aid, immediately on the 8th of February, published a card to the public, asking them to suspend their judgment, "and complaining of the injustice of condemning an absent man unheard," and of the cruelty of those who, having made the charges, ordered them to be published and circulated before trial." General Arnold's first solicitude was to prevent any stain upon his honor in the mind of Miss Shippen, to whom he wrote as before stated. On the day following his letter to her, from the camp at Raritan, he sent a card to the public, in which, after referring to his services in the cause of his country for nearly four years, he complains of the "cruel and malicious charges" which the President and Council of Pennsylvania had preferred against him to Congress; and also of their having ordered copies of the charges to be printed, and dispersed through the several States, for the purpose of prejudicing the minds of the public, while the matter is in suspense.[1]

The personal hostility in which these charges originated may be inferred from the circular signed by Joseph Reed, addressed to the Governor of each of the States, enclosing the charges, and asking that they be communicated to the Legislature of each State. It is not surprising, I think, in view of this action, that Irving should call attention to the hostility manifested by the Council of Pennsylvania, and "their extraordinary measure to prepossess the public mind against him.[2] "Many thought, dispassionately, that the State authorities had acted with extreme harshness towards a meritorious officer in widely spreading these charges against him thus in an unprecedented way, putting a public brand upon him."

Arnold promptly requested Congress to direct a court-martial to inquire into his conduct.

The following are the charges preferred against General Arnold :[3]

"*First*—That while in the camp of General Washington at Valley Forge, last Spring, he gave permission to a vessel belonging to persons then voluntarily residing in this city with the enemy, and of disaffected character, to come into a port of the United States without the knowledge of the authority of the State, or of the Commander-in-Chief, though then present.

"*Second*—In having shut up the shops and stores on his arrrival in the

1. See Trial of Arnold, for cards of Major Clarkson and General Arnold in full, pp. 153-154.
2. Irving's Life of Washington, Vol. IV, p. 17.
3. Trial of Arnold, pp. 5, 6, 7, etc.

city, so as even to prevent officers of the army from purchasing, while he privately made considerable purchases for his own benefit, as is alleged and believed.

"*Third,*—In imposing menial offices upon the sons of freemen of this State, when called forth by the desire of Congress to perform militia duty, and when remonstrated to, hereupon, justifying himself in writing, upon the ground of having power so to do ; for that, "when a citizen assumed" the character of a soldier, the former was entirely lost in "the latter ; and that it was the duty of the militia to obey "every order of his aids (not a breach of the laws and Constitution), as his (the General's), without judging of the 'propriety of them.' "

Fourth.—For that, when a prize was brought into this port by the Convention brig, of this State, whereupon a dispute arose respecting the capture, which would otherwise, in great probability, have been amicably adjusted between the claimants, General Arnold interposed, by an illegal and unworthy purchase of the suit, at a low and inadequate price, as has been publicly charged by a reputable citizen; to which may, in some degree, be ascribed the delay of justice in the courts of Appeal, and the dispute in which the State may probably be involved with Congress hereupon.

Fifth.—The appropriating the wagons of this State, when called forth upon a special emergency last autumn, to the transportation of private property, and that of persons who voluntarily remained with the enemy last winter, and were deemed disaffected to the interests and independence of America.

"*Sixth*—In that Congress, by a resolve of the 21st of August last, having given to the executive powers of every State an exclusive power to recommend persons desirous of going within the enemy's lines, to the officer there commanding, General Arnold in order, as may reasonably be inferred, to elude the said resolve, wrote a letter, as appears by comparison of hands and the declaration of the intended bearer, recommendatory for the above purpose, and caused his aide-de-camp, Major Clarkson, to sign the same. But the said device not taking effect, through the vigilance of the officers at Elizabethtown, General Arnold, without disclosing any of the above circumstances, applied to Council for their permission, which was instantly refused, the connection, character and situation of the party being well known and deemed utterly improper to be indulged with such permission, thereby violating the resolve of Congress, and usurping the authority of this Board.

" *Seventh*—This Board having upon the complaint of several inhabitants of Chester county, through the late Wagon-Master General, *requested* of the said General Arnold to state the said transaction respecting the wagons, in order that they might satisfy the complainants, or explain the same without farther trouble, received in return an indecent and disrespectful refusal of any satisfaction whatsoever.

"*Eighth*—The discouragement and neglect manifested by General Arnold during his command to civil, military and other characters who have adhered to the cause of their country—with an entire different conduct towards those of another character, are too notorious to need proof or illustration. And if this command has been, as is generally believed, supported by an expense of four or five thousand pounds per annum to the United States, we freely declare we shall very unwillingly pay any share of expenses thus incurred."

On the 16th of February (the communication from President Reed, and the charges having been referred to a committee) the letter of General Arnold, asking an investigation, was referred to the same committee. This committee having been instructed to inquire into the grounds of said charges, about the middle of March made a report exculpating him from all criminality in the matter charged against him.[1]

1. The following is a report of the Committee in full:

"Report of the Committee of Congress on the charges exhibited against General Arnold by the President and Council of Pennsylvania:

"The first, second, third and fifth charges are offences triable only in a court-martial; that the fourth charge is an offence only of a civil nature, and triable only in a court of common law; that the sixth, seventh and eighth charges are offences not triable by a court-martial or common law court, or subject to any other punishment than the displeasure of Congress and the consequences of it; that the committee are furnished with evidence by the supreme executive council on the fifth and seventh charges, to which they beg leave to refer; that the committee of the said executive council, though repeatedly applied to, declined to give any evidence on the rest of the charges, after fruitless application for three weeks, during which time several letters passed between the said executive council and committee, in which letters the supreme executive council even threaten the committee and charge them with partiality.

"*Resolved*, That as to the first and second charges, no evidence appears tending to prove the same; that the said charges are fully explained, and the appearances they carry of criminalty fully obviated by clear, unquestionable evidence. The third charge, admitted by General Arnold in one instance, to be transmitted to the Commander-in-Chief. The fourth charge, there appears no evidence to prove the same, and that it is triable only in a common law court. The fifth charge be transmitted to the Commander-in-Chief.

"*Resolved*, That the recommendatory letter in the sixth charge is not within the spirit of the resolve of Congress, or an usurpation of authority.

"*Resolved*, That the letter in the seventh charge, though not in terms of perfect civility, yet it is not expressed in terms of indignity; and that after the conduct

The first charge relating to the alleged improper issuing of a pass, the second in regard to the closing of the shops of Philadelphia, the third in regard to imposing menial offices upon the sons of freemen performing military duty, and the fifth, in regard to the use of wagons furnished by the State for the transportation of private property—each of these, they repeat, "are triable only in a court-martial." The fourth, which relates to a prize and prize-money, the committee say is triable only in a court of common law. They add that the committee were furnished with evidence in regard to the fifth and seventh charges, which relate to the use of the wagons and Arnold's alleged refusal to give any explanation thereof; and that in regard to the other charges, the committee of the executive council, though repeatedly applied to, declined to give any evidence, after fruitless application for three weeks. They therefore resolved, that in regard to the first and second charges (those relating to the pass and the use of the wagons,) no evidence appears tending to prove the same; that the said charges are fully explained, and the appearances they carry of criminality are fully obviated by clear and unquestionable evidence. In regard to the fourth charge (in relation to the prize), they say there appears no evidence to prove the same, and it is triable only in a common law court. That the fifth charge be transmitted to the Commander-in-Chief, and they

"*Resolved*, that the letter in the seventh charge (claimed to be disrespectful), though not in terms of perfect civility, yet it is not expressed in terms of indignity; and that after the conduct of the said supreme executive council towards General Arnold, and the unexampled measures they took to obtain satisfaction, totally and absolutely preclude all right to concessions or acknowledgment."[1]

of the said supreme executive council towards the said General Arnold, and the unexampled measures they took to obtain satisfaction, totally and absolutely preclude all right to concessions or acknowledgment.

"*Resolved*, On the eighth charge, that there is no evidence to prove the same."— *Arnold's Trial by Court Martial*. pp. 133-4-5.

1. Trial of Arnold, p. 135. See also Sparks' Writings of Washington, Vol. VI, pp. 516-517.

Arnold, as soon as this report was brought in, considered his name vindicated, and resign'd the command of Philadelphia, for which he had already obtained permission from Washington. On the 17th of March he addressed a letter to Congress, begging that body to examine and decide upon the report of the committee without delay.[1] But the Executive Council of Pennsylvania were not satisfied, and, although in their circular they had said, "the proofs were ready to be exhibited, and that Arnold had departed from the State, pending the complaint," yet after his prompt return and demand of inquiry, they complained there had been a misunderstanding which prevented them from presenting their testimony.

General Reed and the Executive Council represented the great State of Pennsylvania, and were entitled to and received extraordinary consideration, and Congress, at their instance, instead of acting upon the report of their own committee exculpating Arnold, referred the whole subject to a joint committee of that body and the Council of Pennsylvania. This joint committee reported several resolutions intended to soothe Pennsylvania, as represented by the executive committee; and also recommended that the first, second, third and fifth charges be referred to a court-martial to be appointed by the Commander-in-Chief. Arnold was indignant at this action, but said, in a letter addressed to Congress :

"If Congress have been induced to take this action for the public good, and to avoid a breach with this State—however hard my case may be, * * I will suffer with pleasure until a court-martial can have an opportunity of doing me justice, by acquitting me of these charges a second time."[2]

He wrote at once to Washington, advising him of the

1. Trial of Gen. Arnold, pp. 136-137.
2. Letter of Arnold to Congress, April 14, 1779—Trial p. 152.

proceedings, complaining of the injustice done to him, and begging that an early day might be fixed for his trial. Washington ordered a court to meet on the first of May. The executive committee of Pennsylvania applied for further time, and made such representations as induced General Washington to postpone the trial to June 1st, 1779.

Arnold, impatient and chafing at this delay, wrote to Washington, May 5th, saying:

"Delay is worse than death, and when it is considered that the President and council have had three months to produce the evidence, I cannot suppose the ordering a court-martial to determine the matter immediately, is the least precipitating it. I entreat that the court may be ordered to sit as soon as possible."[1]

In a letter to Washington, written on the fourteenth of May, in which he expresses his happiness to hear that the court had been fixed for the the first of June, he calls attention to the "cruel situation he was in, as his character was suffering," and he was prevented by it from joining the army, "which I wish to do," says he, "as soon as my wounds will permit."[2]

Washington writes to Reed on the fifteenth of May, saying he had received another letter from Arnold, "pressing for a speedy trial," and adding that "that gentleman has a right to expect from me, as a piece of justice, that his fate may be decided, as soon as it can be done consistently with a full and fair investigation."[3]

On the same day he wrote to Arnold:

"I feel my situation truly delicate and embarrassing." "Your anxiety —natural under the circumstances—strongly urges me to bring the affair to a speedy conclusion: on the other side, the pointed representations of the State, on the subject of witnesses, seem to leave me no choice."[4]

1. Sparks' Writings of Washington, Vol. VI, p. 522.
2. Sparks' Writings of Washington, Vol. VI, p. 523.
3. Sparks' Writings of Washington, Vol. VI, p. 524.
4. Sparks' Writings of Washington, Vol, VI, p. 524.

To this letter Arnold promptly replied on the 18th, saying:

"I have not the least doubt of your excellency's wishing to bring my affair to a speedy conclusion, and of doing me ample justice. I am extremely sorry my cruel situation should cause your excellency the least embarrassment."[1]

He then calls attention to the fact that his prosecutors had had nearly four months to procure their testimony, etc.

The movements of the enemy prevented the meeting of the court in June, and on the 13th of July, Arnold again addressed Washington, asking whether the situation of the army would not admit the court-martial to proceed with the trial, and again begging him to appoint as early a day as possible.[2]

At length, and not until the 19th of December, 1779, the court was convened at Morristown, New Jersey, and continued in session until its final judgment was rendered on the 26th of January, 1780, after nearly a year of most irritating and vexatious delay, during every period of which Arnold had begged and implored prompt action; he had now the satisfaction of meeting before a court of brother officers his accusers face to face. The position of Washington had been "delicate and embarrassing," but with his usual discretion, he so conducted as to satisfy both parties of his impartiality. The court was composed of Major General Robert Howe, of North Carolina, President, and Brigadier Generals Knox, Maxwell and Gest, and eight Colonels.[3]

The evidence is published in full in the trial, to which I have already referred, and occupies nearly one hundred pages.

1. Sparks' Writings of Washington, Vol. VI, p. 526.
2. Sparks' Writings of Washington, Vol. VI, p. 527.
3. Trial of Arnold, p. 2.

CHAPTER XIV.

ARNOLD'S TRIAL—WASHINGTON'S REPRIMAND.

"Exhibit anew those noble qualities which have placed you on the list of our most valued commanders. I will, myself, furnish you as far as it may be in my power, with the opportunities of regaining the esteem of your country."—Washington to Arnold.

ARNOLD'S TRIAL CONTINUED—HIS DEFENSE—JUDGEMENT OF THE COURT—WASHINGTON'S REPRIMAND AND EULOGY.

GENERAL ARNOLD appeared before the court without counsel. He conducted his own defense, examining his own witnesses, and cross-examining those produced by the prosecution.

The spectacle of this trial was not without a certain element of pathos. The accused was in the full buff and blue uniform of his rank. He walked with difficulty, leaning upon his cane, for the leg broken above the knee at Saratoga, and below the knee at Quebec, still disabled him, making it impossible for him to ride on horseback, and he could not, therefore, mount the horse which Congress had presented to him for his gallantry at Ridgefield; but he wore the epauletts and sword-knots which Washington had presented to him as among "the bravest of the brave" of his generals, and which he had received as a testimony of Washington's "sincere regard and approbation of his conduct."

Though still young, not having reached the meridian of life, his face bronzed and darkened by fatigue and exposure, indicated that he had seen the severest hardships of a soldier's life. No one could look upon his weather-beaten features and his still crippled condition without thinking of Ticonderoga, St. Johns, the Wilderness, the Plains of Abraham, the forlorn hope in the assault on Quebec, Montreal, the naval conflict off Valcour Island, Ridgefield and Compo, the valley of the Mohawk, the relief of Fort Schuyler, the battle of the 19th of September, near Saratoga, and the last desperate and bloody charge at Bemis' Heights.

He, who had never failed to share with his soldiers the extreme of every danger, and had shed his blood very freely for his country, was now to struggle for his laurels, for his honor, for everything which makes life valuable, against the overwhelming official power and influence of Pennsylvania.

He can scarcely be blamed for wishing to crush his enemies, and he certainly had a right to present the record of his past life, and to have the benefit of all the presumptions justly arising from previous good conduct.

A man accused of crime is never blamed for proving his previous good character, to raise a presumption of innocence, and yet General Arnold has been censured and sneered at because he spread before the court his record as a soldier, and the commendations which Congress and Washington had bestowed upon him.

At the close of the evidence he addressed the court at great length. He did not confine himself to the four charges upon which he was being tried, but took up each of the eight which had been presented to Congress, and attempted to make a full answer to every one of them. He began:

"*Mr. President, and gentlemen of this honourable court:*

"I appear before you, to answer charges brought against me by the late supreme executive council of the commonwealth of Pennsylvania. It is disagreeable to be accused; but when an accusation is made, I feel it a great source of consolation, to have an opportunity of being tried by gentlemen whose delicate and refined sensations of honour will lead them to entertain similar sentiments concerning those who accuse unjustly, and those who are justly accused. In the former case, your feelings revolt against the conduct of the prosecutors; in the latter, against those who are deserved objects of a prosecution. Whether those feelings will be directed against me, or against those, whose charges have brought me before you, will be known by your just and impartial determination of this cause.

"When the present necessary war against Great Britain commenced, I was in easy circumstances, and enjoyed a fair prospect of improving them. I was happy in domestic connections, and blessed with a rising family, who claimed my care and attention. The liberties of my country were in danger. The voice of my country called upon all her faithful sons to join in her defence. With cheerfulness I obeyed the call. I sacrificed domestic ease and happiness to the service of my country, and in her service have I sacrificed a great part of a handsome fortune. I was one of the first that appeared in the field, and from that time, to the present hour, have not abandoned her service.

"When one is charged with practices which his soul abhors, and which conscious innocence tells him he has never committed, an honest indignation will draw from him expressions in his own favour, which, on other occasions, might be ascribed to an ostentatious turn of mind. The part which I have acted in the American cause, has been acknowledged by our friends, and by our enemies, to have been far from an indifferent one. My time, my fortune, and my person have been devoted to my country, in this war; and if the sentiments of those who are supreme in the United States, in civil and military affairs, are allowed to have any weight, my time, my fortune, and my person have not been devoted in vain. You will indulge me, gentlemen, while I lay before you some honorable testimonies, which congress, and the commander in chief of the armies of the United States, have been pleased to give of my conduct. The place where I now stand justifies me in producing them."

He then read to the court some of the complimentary letters of Washington, and among others, the one presenting him with epaulets and sword-knots "as a testimony of his sincere regard and approbation;" also Washington's letters to Congress, requesting that body to send him to the Northern Department to repel Burgoyne, because he was "active, judicious and brave," and an "officer in whom the militia had great confidence."

He also read the proceedings of Congress, directing that he be presented with "a horse properly caparisoned," etc., for "his gallant conduct at Ridgefield;" also the resolution of thanks passed by Congress for his brave and successful efforts in the capture of Burgoyne. After this review of his military career, he asked whether it was probable, after having gained these favorable opinions, he should all at once sink into a course of conduct "equally unworthy of a patriot and a soldier?" After alluding to the long and cruel delays in obtaining a trial, caused by his persecutors, he expressed his sanguine hopes of being able to satisfy the court, and through its judgment, the world, that the charges against him were "false, malicious and scandalous."

He then took up and examined the charges, one by one. The first, in regard to granting protection for a vessel to sail into the ports of the United States, it is stated, as a part of the charge, that it was given "without the knowledge of the Commander-in-Chief."

After justifying the giving the pass, adverting to that part of the charge relative to Washington, he says:

"I think it peculiarly unfortunate that the armies of the United States have a gentleman at their head who knows so little about his own honour, or regards it so little, as to lay the president and council of Pennsylvania under the necessity of stepping forth in its defence, perhaps it may be of use to hint,

"*Non tali auxilio eget, nec defensoribus istis.*

"The general is invested with power, and he possesses spirit to check and to punish every instance of disrespect shewn to his authority; but he will not prostitute his power by exerting it upon a trifling occasion; far less will he pervert it when no occasion is given at all."

In regard to that part of the second charge, which alleges that while he prohibited others from purchasing goods, he himself privately made purchases for his own benefit, "as is alleged and believed," he says :

"If this is true, I stand confessed in the presence of this Honorable Court the vilest of men; I stand stigmatized with indelible disgrace, the disgrace of having abused an appointment of high trust and importance, to accomplish the meanest and most unworthy purposes: the blood I have spent in defence of my country, will be insufficient to obliterate the stain.

"But if this part of the case is void of truth; if it has not even the semblance of truth, what shall I say of my accusers? what epithets will characterize their conduct, the sentence of this honourable court will soon determine.

"* * Who 'alledge and believe' this accusation? None, I trust, but the president and council of Pennsylvania; because, I trust, none else would alledge and believe anything tending to ruin a character, without sufficient evidence. Where is the evidence of this accusation? I call upon my accusers to produce it: I call upon them to produce it, under the pain of being held forth to the world, and to posterity, upon the proceedings of this court, as public defamers and murderers of reputation."

After examining the proof against him on this charge, he says:

"On the honor of a gentleman and a soldier, I declare to gentlemen and soldiers, it is false."

He adds:

"If I made considerable purchases, considerable sales must have been made to me by some person in Philadelphia. Why are not these persons produced? Have my prosecutors so little power and influence in that city, as to be unable to furnish evidence of the truth?"

* * * * "I flatter myself the time is not far off, when, by the glorious establishment of our independence, I shall again return into the mass of citizens: 'tis a period I look forward to with anxiety; I shall then cheerfully submit as a citizen, to be governed by the same principle of subordination, which has been tortured into a wanton exertion of arbitrary power.

"This insinuation comes, in my opinion, with an ill grace from the state of Pennsylvania, in whose more immediate defence I sacrificed my feelings as a soldier, when I conceived them incompatible with the duties of a citizen, and the welfare of that state.

"By a resolution of congress, I found myself superseded (in consequence of a new mode of appointment of general officers) by several who were my juniors in service; those who know the feelings of an officer, (whose utmost ambition is the good opinion of his country) must judge what my sensations were at this apparent mark of neglect. I repaired to the city of Philadelphia in the month of May, 1777, in order either to attain a restoration of my rank, or a permission to resign my commission; during this interval, the van of General Howe's army advanced, by a rapid march, to Somerset court house, with a view (as was then generally supposed) to penetrate to the city of Philadelphia.

"Notwithstanding I had been superseded, and my feelings as an officer wounded, yet, on finding the state was in imminent danger from the designs of the enemy, I sacrificed those feelings, and with alacrity put myself at the head of the militia, who were collected to oppose the enemy, determined to exert myself for the benefit of the public, although I conceived myself injured by their representatives. How far the good countenance of the militia under my command operated, in deterring General Howe from marching to the city of Philadelphia, I will not pretend to say; certain it is, he altered his route.

"What returns I have met with from the state of Pennsylvania, I leave to themselves to judge, in the cool hour of reflection, which (notwithstanding the phrenzy of party, and the pains so industriously taken to support a clamour against me) must sooner or later arise."

Thus, he went through each charge in detail, and in replying to the eighth and last, which charged him with neglecting the friends of his country and bestowing his attentions and courtesies on its enemies, he says:

"I am not sensible, Mr. President, of having neglected any gentlemen, either in the civil or military line, who have adhered to the cause of their country, and who have put it into my power to take notice of them; with respect to gentlemen in the civil line and army, I can appeal to the candour of congress and to the army, as scarcely a day passed but many of both were entertained by me; they are the best judges of my company and conduct.

"With respect to attention to those of an opposite character, I have paid none but such, as in my situation, was justifiable on the principles of common humanity and politeness. The president and council of Pennsylvania will pardon me, if I cannot divest myself of humanity, merely out of complaisance to them.

"It is enough for me, Mr. President, to contend with men in the field; I have not yet learned to carry on a warfare against *women*, or to consider every man as disaffected to our glorious cause, who, from an opposition in sentiment to those in power in the state of Pennsylvania, may, by the *clamour of party, be stiled a tory;* it is well known, that this odious appellation has, in that state been applied by some, indiscriminately, to several of illustrious character, both in the civil and military line.

"On this occasion I think I may be allowed to say, without vanity, that my conduct, from the earliest period of the war to the present time, has been steady and uniform. I have ever obeyed the calls of my country, and stepped forth in her defence in every hour of danger, when many were deserting her cause, which appeared desperate: I have often bled in it; the marks that I bear, are sufficient evidence of my conduct. The impartial public will judge of my services, and whether the returns that I have met with are not tinctured with the basest ingratitude. Conscious of my own innocence, and the unworthy methods taken to injure me, I can with boldness say to my persecutors in general, and to the *chief* of them in particular, that in the hour of *danger,* when the affairs of America wore a *gloomy aspect,* when our illustrious general was retreating through New-Jersey, with a handful of men, I did not propose to my associates, basely to quit the general, and sacrifice the cause of my country to my personal safety, by going over to the enemy, and making my peace. I can say I never basked in the sunshine of my general's favour, and courted him to his face, when I was at the same time treating him with the greatest disrespect, and villifying his character when absent. This is more than a ruling member of the council of the state of Pennsylvania can say, '*as it is alleged and believed.*'"[1]

He concluded as follows:

"I have now gone through all the charges exhibited against me; and have given to each such an answer as I thought it deserved. Are they all, or any of them supported by truth and evidence? or rather, does not each of them appear to this honourable court to be totally destitute of

---

[1] The above allusion to President Reed is explained by the statement of Gen. John Cadwalader, in his reply to Reed, published in Philadelphia in 1783.

He says: "Arnold having received his information (about Gen. Reed), from me, when he (Arnold) apologised to me for inserting it in his defence without my permission, I remarked that an apology was unnecessary, from the public manner in which he mentioned it. Arnold was commanding in this city; very generally visited by the officers of the army, citizens and strangers. I received the usual civilities from him and returned them, and often met him at the tables of gentlemen of this city. To my civilities, at that time, I thought him entitled, from the signal services he had rendered the country; services infinitely superior to those you boast of. He stood high as a military character, even in France, and even after your persecution he was continued in command by Congress; appointed first by the Commander-in-Chief, to the left wing of the army, and afterwards to the important post of West Point, where his treacherous conduct exceeded, I fancy, even your ideas of his baseness."—*Cadwalader's Reply to Reed,* p. 143.

every semblance of a foundation in fact? and yet baseless as they themselves are, they were intended to support a fabric with the weight of which attempts were made to crush my reputation and fortunes: I allude to the preliminary resolution of the council, containing severe but general strictures upon my character and conduct; strictures of such a serious and important nature, that they themselves were sensible the public would not think them justified in making them, unless upon the most unquestionable grounds. Let them now be measured by their own standard. Had they unquestionable grounds to go upon? Why then, in opposition to every principle of candour and justice, in opposition to their own ideas of candour and justice, did they make and publish resolutions, containing censures of such a high import against me?

"An artful appearance of tenderness, and regard for my services, by which the council are pleased to say, I *formerly* distinguished myself, is held forth in the introduction to their charges. Did they mean by this to pour balsam, or to pour poison into my wounds? I leave it to this court, and to the world to judge, whether they intended it to balance the demerits they then urged against me, by my former good conduct, as far as it would go; or whether they designed it as a sting to their charges, by persuading the public, that my demerits were so enormous, that even the greatest and most unaffected tenderness for my character, would not excuse them in continuing silent any longer.

"If, in the course of my defence, I have taken up the time of the court longer than they expected, they will, I trust, impute it to the nature of the accusations against me; many of which, though not immediately before you as charges, were alledged as facts, and were of such a complexion as to render it necessary to make some observations upon them; because they were evidently calculated to raise a prejudice against me, not only among the people at large, but in the minds of those who were to be my judges.

"I have looked forward with pleasing anxiety to the present day, when, by the judgment of my fellow soldiers, I shall (I doubt not) stand honourably acquitted of all the charges brought against me, and again share with them the glory and danger of this just war."

On the 22nd of January, 1798, the Judge Advocate, in reply to General Arnold's address, stated the evidence in relation to every charge, and submitted the case. On the 26th the court met and announced their final judgment. After stating that they had carefully considered the several charges, the evidence, and the defense, they decided, first:

that the permission Arnold had given for a vessel to leave a port in the possession of the enemy, to enter a port in the United States, was illegal. In regard to the second charge, that of the order closing the shops and stores of Philadelphia, the court decided that he was justified in doing so by the resolution of Congress and by the instructions of General Washington; and in regard to the latter part of the same charge, that of making purchases for his own benefit, they say they "are clearly of opinion *that it is unsupported, and they do fully acquit General Arnold.*"

They also acquit of the third charge (that of imposing menial offices on the military). Respecting the fourth charge (relating to the use of the wagons) the court say, "It appears that General Arnold made application to the Quartermaster-General, to supply him with wagons to remove property in imminent danger from the enemy; that the wagons were supplied on this application, which had been drawn from the State of Pennsylvania for the public service, and that General Arnold intended this application as a private request, and had no design of employing the wagons otherwise than at his own private expense, nor of defrauding the public, nor of injuring or impeding the public service: but considering the delicacy attending the high station in which he acted, and that requests from him might operate as commands, the court were of opinion the request was imprudent and improper, and therefore ought not to have been made." The court sentenced him to receive a reprimand from the Commander-in-Chief.[1]

It will be observed that the court exonerate and acquit General Arnold of all intentional wrong, expressly declaring that the charge of making purchases for his own benefit was entirely unsupported, and they therefore "fully acquit him;" and that, in the use of the wagons, that it was done

1. See judgment in full, Arnold's Trial, pp. 144-5.

"without any design of defrauding the public or impeding the public service."

The charge of making purchases for his own benefit, notwithstanding the declaration of the court that it was "clearly their opinion that it was entirely unsupported, and their full acquittal," has been repeated and reiterated in most of the histories of the war of the Revolution. I submit that the judgment of the court after a month's most thorough investigation, with a prosecution zealous, active, and bitter, and with the whole power and influence of the State authorities to aid, that the judgment of the court, after an investigation so searching and exhaustive, ought to be regarded as final and conclusive.

In regard to the fourth charge, relating to the prize of the sloop "Active," it seems to me the answer of General Arnold is complete. By a statement of his found among the "Shippen Papers," it appears that the original captors were from Connecticut, his native State, and that they applied to him for aid in securing their rights, and that he did aid them by his purse and advice, and that in the Court of Appeals they succeeded by a unanimous vote as against Pennsylvania. These claimants were poor, and to secure himself for necessary advances, Arnold purchased an interest in their claim. He may have done this from motives of kindness to the claimants, or as a speculation. If he took advantage of their necessities to obtain the interest for less than its value, he certainly did wrong; but occupying the high and delicate official position he did in the State of Pennsylvania, he ought to have declined having anything to do with the controversy. But there was nothing necessarily involving his integrity in the transaction, and so upon the whole I think the judgment of Washington Irving will be concurred in by all candid and fair judges who attentively consider the question. "No turpitude had been proved against him, —his brilliant exploits shed a splendor around his name, and he appeared before the public a soldier crippled in their service. All these should have pleaded in his favor — should have produced indulgence of his errors, and mitigated that animosity which he always contended had been the cause of his ruin." [1]

The result of this trial may be summed up in a few words. Arnold was fully exonerated and acquitted of all intentional wrong; of all private speculation; the court finding he had no design of defrauding or injuring the public; but the pass he had issued was "irregular" and "illegal;" and idle public wagons, without impeding the public service, had been used to remove property in imminent danger from the enemy, which they say, in their opinion, "was imprudent and improper." These errors Irving justly characterises as "venial." The finding of the court was approved by Congress. The sentence, implying to a sensitive soldier the idea of guilt and public disgrace, must have been yielded as a concession to the State of Pennsylvania, for certainly it was a *non-sequitor* to the verdict of the court expressly exonerating him from all intentional wrong, and such finding would not demand a punishment so severe.

He had confidently expected a full acquittal. He had closed his defense by saying, with deep feeling: "I have looked forward with pleasing anxiety to the present day, when, by the judgment of my fellow soldiers I shall (I doubt not) stand honorably acquitted of all the charges brought against me, and again share with them the glory and the danger of this just war." When, therefore, he was so severely sentenced, he was astounded. It was an unexpected, a terrible, a fatal blow. I cannot resist the conclu-

---

1. Irving's Life of Washington, Vol. IV, p. 23.

sion that, if he had been honorably discharged, as he had a right to expect when the court acquitted him of all intentional wrong, and found that he had "no design of defrauding the public," he would gladly and eagerly have joined General Washington; have accepted the position of second in command, soon to be offered him, and shared with his great chief in the "danger and the glory of the war." I say this, not unmindful that he had probably before this time listened to secret overtures from the enemy—perhaps held secret correspondence with him; but while he was already guilty of having listened to and encouraged their overtures, he was not yet irretrievably lost.[1]

No alternative on the part of Washington was left but publicly to reprimand and disgrace a favorite officer. Nothing can be conceived more honorable to the generous feelings of Washington, more delicate towards the wounded pride of Arnold, than the reprimand.

"Our profession is the chastest of all; even the shadow of a fault tarnishes the lustre of our finest achievements. The least inadvertence may rob us of the public favor, so hard to be acquired. I reprimand you for having forgotten that in proportion as you have rendered yourself formidable to our enemies, you should have been guarded and temperate in your deportment towards your fellow-citizens. Exhibit anew those noble qualities which have placed you on the list of our most valued commanders. I will myself furnish you, as far as it may be in my power, with opportunities of regaining the esteem of your country."[2]

[1] In the manuscript copy of General Clinton's report to Lord Geo. Germain, dated Oct. 11, 1780, he says: "About eighteen months since, I had some reason to conclude that the American Major-General Arnold was desirous of quitting the rebel service and joining the cause of Great Britain."

This is, so far as I know, the most direct evidence, tending to show the date of the begining of the criminal negotiations.

[2] "Nor is there an opportunity of acquiring honor, which I can shape for you, to which as it occurs I will not gladly prefer you.—*Scott's Count Robert, of Paris, to Hereward, p. 391.*

This reprimand has been much admired in Europe, as well as in America. Certainly nothing in the writings of Washington is more beautiful in language, more generous and noble in sentiment. His words are those of one brother-soldier to another, compelled to inflict pain which he obviously thinks undeserved.

In reading it, it is somewhat difficult to say for what offence Washington reprimands Arnold. Was it for "the shadow of a fault?" or "an inadvertence?" Literally because, "as you have rendered yourself formidable to our enemies, you should have been guarded and temperate in your deportment towards your fellow-citizens." But it is not difficult to see for what virtues Washington honored the object upon whom he was compelled to inflict disgrace. He hastens to say "exhibit anew those noble qualities which have placed you on the list of our most valued commanders; I will myself furnish you the opportunities." If Washington could have sent him at once into some terrible battle, to lead some "forlorn hope," or on any desperate enterprise, where death or victory could have been sought, Arnold might have been saved; might have again shared with his comrades "the glory and the danger of a just war."

What the public opinion of the people and of the army was in regard to this sentence of the court, may be inferred from the proceedings of the Executive Council of Pennsylvania. On the 3d of February, 1780, the following action seems to have been extorted from his prosecutors by the indignation of the army and the people at the sentence. "We do not" say they "think it proper to affect ignorance of what is the subject of public conversation, and the sentence of the court-martial tending to impose a mark of reprehension upon General Arnold. We find his sufferings for, and services to, his country so deeply impressed upon our minds as to obliterate every opposing sentiment, and therefore beg leave to request that Congress will be pleased to dispense with the part of the sentence which imposes a public censure, and may most affect the feelings of a brave and gallant officer."[1]

But Congress did not modify the sentence, and Arnold was publicly disgraced. The feelings of Washington towards him are described in a letter from Schuyler to Arnold, dated June 2nd, 1780. "He (Washington) says Schuyler, "expressed a desire to do whatever was agreeable to you; dwelt on your abilities, your merits, your sufferings, and on the well earned claims you have on your country. * * * He expressed himself with regard to you in terms such as the friends who love you could wish."[2]

---

1. Trial of Arnold p. 168.
2. The following is the letter in full:

"MORRISTOWN, June 2, 1780.
"MY DEAR SIR:

"The letter which I did myself the pleasure to write you on the 11th of May, you had not received when yours of the 25th was written. In that I advised you that I had conversed with the General on the subject which passed between us before I left Philadelphia; that he appeared undecided on the occasion, I believe because no arrangement was made, for he expressed himself with regard to you in terms such as the friends who love you could wish. When I received yours of the 25th May, I read it to him; he was much ingaged; next day he requested to know the contents again. I put it into his hands; he expressed a desire to do whatever was agreable to you, dwelt on your abilities, your merits, your sufferings, and on the well earned claims you have on your country, and intimated that as soon as his arrangements for the campaign should take place, that he would properly consider you. I believe you will have an alternative proposed, either to take charge of an important post, with an honorable command, or your station in the field. Your reputation, my dear sir, so established, your honorable scars, put it decidedly in your power to take either. A State which has full confidence in you will wish to see its banner entrusted to you. If the command at West Point is offered, it will be honorable; if a division in the field, you must judge whether you can support the fatigues, circumstanced as you are.

"Mrs. Schuyler proposes a jaunt to Philadelphia; if she goes I shall accompany her, and have the pleasure of seeing you. She joins me in every friendly wish; please to make my respects to your lady and her amiable sisters.

"Believe me, with the most affectionate regard and esteem,
"Yours, most sincerely, etc., etc.,
"PHILIP SCHUYLER."

—*Schuyler to Arnold, June 2, 1780. See Life of Reed, Vol. II, pp. 276-7.*

I am aware that after Arnold's treason, Washington, as was natural, used very different language in regard to him, and makes some qualifications of the language

But this public disgrace left a wound which no kind words, no sympathy from Washington or Schuyler, or other friends, could ever heal. Proud, high spirited, a sense of injustice and wrong rankled and irritated, until it poisoned and prepared the way for the consummation of his crime.

attributed to him by Schuyler. But in the same letter, Washington says the conversation detailed by Schuyler made very little impression upon him, and Schuyler's letter was written very soon after the conversation took place, and Washington did, a few days after this interview with Schuyler, offer to General Arnold the command of the left wing of his own army.

CHAPTER XV.

ARNOLD'S TREASON.

<blockquote>"He falls like Lucifer,
Never to hope again."</blockquote>

THE MOTIVES WHICH LED TO ARNOLD'S TREASON—HIS WRONGS—INDUCEMENTS HELD OUT TO HIM BY BRITISH EMISSARIES—THEY TRY TO CONVINCE HIM THE CONTEST HOPELESS, AND THAT ENGLAND OFFERS ALL FOR WHICH HE DREW HIS SWORD—SUPPOSED MEETING BETWEEN HIM AND BEVERLY ROBINSON—LETTER TO ARNOLD, ATTRIBUTED TO ROBINSON BY MARBOIS—ARNOLD YIELDS TO THE TEMPTATIONS OFFERED AND SEEKS THE COMMAND OF WEST POINT—MEETS WASHINGTON AT KING'S FERRY, WHO OFFERS HIM THE COMMAND OF THE LEFT WING OF HIS ARMY—TRADITION THAT ARNOLD SAID HIS DEFECTION WAS TO PREVENT MORE BLOODSHED—MEETING OF ARNOLD AND ANDRE—SUPPOSED CONVERSATION BETWEEN THEM—ANDRE'S CAPTURE—HIS LETTER TO WASHINGTON.

THE rising sun is bright, warm and genial: the eclipse, dark, cold, dreary and repulsive.

We have followed the rising glory of Arnold's fame, and now approach its eclipse; an eclipse from which he never emerged. Let us try and analyze the causes which led to his fall, a melancholy fall, a fall which Irving said will make his name "sadly conspicuous to the end of time." Let us try to ascertain, if possible, what motives controlled, what temptations seduced him.

The reader of the previous pages will not need to have recalled the strange, mysterious, almost inexplicable acts of cruel injustice with which Congress had treated him:

acts which no remonstrance of Washington could prevent, no expostulation or entreaty of his could induce them to correct; acts which indicated a hostility which no service of Arnold could entirely overcome or conciliate. Beginning early in his military life and continuing down to their approval of the severe sentence by the court-martial, of a "reprimand"—a public disgrace which even his bitter enemies of the Pennsylvania Council asked Congress to dispense with. Either from magnanimity or a less worthy motive, they sent a letter to Congress, in which they "beg leave to request that Congress will be pleased to dispense with that part of the sentence which imposes a public censure, and may most affect the feelings of a brave and gallant officer."[1] Neither his crippled condition, the blood he had shed in the service of his country, the finding of the court exonerating him from all intentional wrong, nor even the request of his prosecutors, could overcome the hostility of his enemies in Congress, and that body approved the sentence, and left him to be disgraced by a "public censure."

The numerous letters of General Washington, quoted on these pages, the letter of General Schuyler, mentioned in the last chapter, and the so-called reprimand, clearly indicate the opinion of Washington as between Arnold and his enemies. Indeed, it is very probable that a portion of the hostility on the part of some members of Congress towards Arnold, may be attributed to Washington's known friendship for him. It was safer to strike one of Washington's favorite officers, who had faults, and was often indiscreet, than to strike the Commander-in-Chief. The action of Congress, and the public disgrace of a reprimand, drove him to desperation; and from that time he inclined to the temptations which, since his residence in Philadelphia, had been constantly addressed to him; and he now heard, day

[1] Reed to Congress. Arnold's Trial, p. 168.

after day, without rebuke, if not with satisfaction, the loyalists of that city denounce Congress and expatiate upon his wrongs and sufferings. His connection with the Shippen family brought him into social relations with the old tory families of that city, and he lived largely in an atmosphere of loyalty to the crown. It is difficult to overestimate the influence of such a social circle upon opinions and conduct. I am unable, by any positive or clear evidence, to fix upon the exact date when Arnold's correspondence with the enemy began. It is stated by Mr. Sparks, " that he had already made secret advances to the enemy, under a feigned name, intending to square his conduct according to circumstances; and prepared, if the court decided against him, to seek revenge at any hazard." I have good reason to believe the advances were made from the other side.[1] That the idea of leaving the service of his country had occurred to him, or had been suggested to him some time before his trial, but only to be spurned with indignation, appears from a letter of his to General Gates as early as August, 1777, in which he says "a few days since I was informed that Congress had accepted my resignation.[2] I have had no advice of it from the President. No public or private injury or insult shall prevail on me *to forsake the cause of my injured and oppressed country* until I see peace and liberty restored, or nobly die in the attempt."[3] At a still earlier period, when, although Washington had said to Congress there was not in his army " a more active, a more spirited, a more sensible officer" than Arnold, then the senior Brigadier General,

---

1. See letter ascribed to Beverly Robinson, quoted hereafter.

2. This resignation he had tendered after Congress had refused him his proper rank: he withdrew it and joined Schuyler at the approach of Burgoyne, as stated in a former chapter.

3. From Gates' papers, Vol. IX, p. 42, in New York Historical Society.

yet in the promotions he was passed, and in writing to Gates, he said:

"By heavens, I am a villain, if I seek not a brave revenge for injured honor." In the light of his subsequent conduct, by "*a brave revenge*," he may fairly be understood to have meant a still more efficient service of his country, and a still more hazardous exposure of his life in her defense. How deplorable that this sentiment, this kind of "revenge" did not control him to the end! Does he not exhibit another illustration of the truth, that

> "Vice is a monster of so frightful mien,
> As, to be hated, needs but to be seen.
> Yet seen too oft, familiar with her face,
> We first endure, then pity, then embrace."

Did Arnold, when the idea of desertion was first suggested to him, spurn it; then, when other wrongs and injuries brought it back, first "endure," then encourage, and finally "embrace" it? When he was fighting the battles of his country, and his known wrongs caused the friends of the crown to suggest desertion, he replied with all the indignation of Hazael to the prophet, "Is thy servant a dog that he should do this great thing?"

I return to the question, what were his controlling motives? I dismiss as unworthy of a moment's consideration the idea that a money bribe had any controlling influence upon him. He received a compensation for his losses, as the English General, Charles Lee, who resigned and sought and received a commission from Congress, received thirty thousand dollars from the United States to cover his losses.[1] Arnold sought money, and sometimes

---

[1] Charles Lee demanded and received from Congress $30,000 as an indemnity for his losses in quitting the British and joining the Americans.—*Bancroft, Vol. IX, p. 168.*

When captured by the British and threatened with punishment as a deserter, he betrayed the United States, and was, therefore, unfaithful by turns to both governments.—*See Treason of Charles Lee by Geo. H. Moore; Bancroft, Vol. IX, pp. 330, 331.*

by means unworthy of a distinguished soldier, but when acquired, few scattered it more freely. He squandered it upon himself and family; he shared it generously with his friends. His purse, when there was anything in it, was always open to Mansfield and Lamb and Frank and others. He was no miserly hoarder; he did not care for money for itself, but his lavish expenditures induced him to seek to supply his wants by commerce, and by buying interests in privateers preying upon English merchantmen. The controlling influences which prepared the way for the tempter and led to his crime, were a deep and bitter sense of long continued wrong, and personal resentment, and revenge. He was a proud, strong hater, constant to his friends, and unyielding to his enemies, though placable when they made the first advances. To a burning sense of public injustice was added the humiliation of the personal triumph over him of bitter, cruel, and persistent enemies. His defense before the court-martial shows how deeply his passions were stirred against his foes, in and out of Congress. "Such a vile prostitution of power, and such instances of glaring tyranny and injustice, I believe," says he, "are unparalleled in the history of a free people." He characterizes the charges against him "as false, malicious, and scandalous." His accusers were "the murderers of his reputation." How keenly he felt the delay caused by the prosecution, appears from his earnest, sometimes pathetic, appeals to Washington for a speedy trial. "Delay to him, he said, was worse than death." I seek not to extenuate, much less to justify Arnold's crime. Indeed, for his treason there can be no plea but the one plea of "guilty." No provocation can extenuate, no ingratitude or injustice excuse it. There are circumstances of aggravation, if anything can aggravate treachery and treason. Among these circumstances were his obligations as a soldier, Washington's enduring friendship, and the personal devotion to him of some of his subordinates and comrades, such as Varick, Livingston, Frank, Lamb, Schuyler and others. Most of them had fought with him, and some of them had fought for him, in defense of his reputation. Nothing but his desertion could alienate their devoted attachment. Therefore, I repeat, I can neither extenuate nor excuse his crime. I do not qualify my abhorrence and detestation of that crime, but I am trying to lift the veil, and see the working of the motives, the struggles of the proud heart, by which this once earnest, sincere, zealous patriot was converted into a traitor. Let us then try to imagine his feelings after his disgrace. His enemies were exulting in their triumph. The wounds inflicted upon his person by the enemies of his country he could bear, but not those upon his character, by his personal enemies in the name of his country. While thus humiliated and desperate, he allowed himself to speak intemperately, unguardedly of Congress, and especially of the authorities of Pennsylvania. The loyalists of Philadelphia hearing these remarks, and eager for the defection and acquisition of a soldier so distinguished, deliberately set about to seduce him. Men and women of high personal character, of reputation, culture and ability, flattered him, filled his ears with sympathy for his wrongs, exaggerated the injustice of his country, kept alive his indignation towards his enemies, insisted that the contest for independence was hopeless, and endeavored to convince him that he might redress all his wrongs, triumph over his enemies, and that, too, as they perhaps honestly believed, without injury, but with advantage to his country. "Britain now offers," said they, "all and more than all which the colonies asked when you drew your sword, and the war began. She now offers everything, independence only excepted. She now declares there shall be no taxation without representation. The colonies shall impose what taxes they please, and make their own laws. Every grievance shall be redressed, and paternal and filial relations restored." The loyalists appealed to Arnold to become the reconciler between contending brothers.

"Stop, we pray you," said they, "the fast flowing blood of kindred and countrymen." "Stop this cruel war, and the wives and mothers of the starving, naked, bare-footed, unpaid soldiers of the Continental army will rise up and bless you as the peace-maker."

"Why," said the British emissary, "why shed more blood when we are willing to grant all you are fighting for? Save the people from the factions of Congress. Save them from anarchy. Save these Protestant colonies from becoming the vassals of Roman Catholic France. Act the part of General Monk in English history. United by a just and cordial union, England and her American colonies can defy the world. We have the same language, the same laws and literature; the same great Magna Charta which secures the rights and liberties of Englishmen at home, shall protect the Americans here. As Clive saved the British Empire in India, we implore you to save it in America." Such, we may believe, were the appeals addressed to him by British agents, and especially by Colonel Beverly Robinson, and the loyalists of Philadelphia.[1]

And then these emissaries, disguising, or perhaps not fully realizing the baseness of the treachery they were tempting

---

1. See letter found among Arnold's papers at West Point, attributed to Robinson by Marbois, quoted hereafter. See, also, Life of Andre by Sargent, Appendix, p. 447; also Marbois' Conspiracy of Arnold. Colonel Beverly Robinson, the son of President Robinson, born in Virginia, and until separated by political events, the friend of Washington. He died in England after the war, and his large estate in New York was confiscated. He was a correspondent of Arnold before Arnold went to West Point. He accompanied Andre up the Hudson, on the Vulture. It is stated in a note by the translator of Chastellux' Travels, published in London, 1787, that a Lieutenant Hele was an active spy in Philadelphia, in 1778, and it has been suggested that he was the first to make treasonable suggestions to Arnold.

him to practice, pointed out to him the glory he would achieve. "You," said they, "can end the war. You can secure the liberties of your country. You can be her benefactor. You will receive the gratitude of both Britain and America by re-uniting both in one great commonwealth; and this accomplished, what title among England's proud nobility will be too high a reward for such a service? "We appeal to you to restore the union between your native land and the land of your forefathers. Great Britain is not like France, a foreign country. Your ancestors for many generations sleep in the soil of Old England, and now with an offer to redress every grievance for which you drew your sword, she asks you to give both countries, Old England, your fatherland, and New England, your native land, peace and harmony." And then pointing to the disordered finances, the feeble and starving army of Washington, the factions and corruptions so generally prevailing, they tried to show him that to fight longer was hopeless as well as unnecessary. The careful student of the history of those days will find much to justify grave doubts of final success. These depressing facts, some of which I will enumerate, only make the constancy and fortitude of Washington and his faithful associates more conspicuous. In a letter to Schuyler, Washington says, "I hardly thought it possible at one period to keep the army together."[1] "At one time the soldiers eat every kind of horse food but hay." "Unless," says he, "Congress and the States act with more energy than they have hitherto done, our cause is lost."[2]

Lafayette writing to Washington, says, "There are open dissensions in Congress—parties who hate one another as much as the common enemy."[3]

1. Marshall's Life of Washington, Vol. IV, p. 196.
2. Marshall's Life of Washington, p. 214.
3. Sparks' Writings of Washington, Vol. V, p. 488.

While the army was nearly starving, ragged and almost naked, the treasury without money, the States and Congress rent by factions, and affairs generally in the most gloomy condition, Washington's effective force was reduced to little more than 3,000 men, and Sir Henry Clinton returned from the conquest of South Carolina with 4,000 troops.[1] And the British force in and about New York was 12,000. Washington, writing to Congress at this crisis, says: "There is no time to be lost; the danger is imminent and pressing; the obstacles to be overcome are great and numerous, and our efforts must be instant, unreserved, and universal." Hamilton, writing to George Clinton, says: "They (Congress) have disgusted the army by repeated instances of the most whimsical favoritism."[2]

Many of the best patriots were in despair. Washington himself says in a letter dated May 28, 1780, "Unless a system very different from that which has long prevailed be immediately adopted throughout the States, our affairs must soon become desperate, beyond the possibility of recovery. * * *Indeed, I have almost ceased to hope.*"[3] It was when everything looked so dark and discouraging that the emissaries of Britain and the tories made their most determined efforts to win over Arnold to the royal cause. I have endeavored to recall some of the arguments and sophistries they breathed into his ears at a moment when he was desperate and chafing with real injuries. The English view of his conduct appears by the press of that day. His desertion is compared to that of Churchill (Marlborough) who deserted James, Lord Cornbury at Honiton, the great Montrose and others.[4] There is a

[1.] Marshall's Life of Washington, Vol. IV, pp. 32-3.
[2.] Sparks' Writings of Washington, Vol. V, p. 506.
[3.] Sparks' Writings of Washington, Vol. VII, p. 58.
[4.] The following letter, quoted from the *London Chronicle*, of Dec. 14th, 1780, p. 572, will verify the text:
"CHARACTER OF BENEDICT ARNOLD.
"SIR: We in the country have been looking up to your town writers, to see whether

tradition among some of Arnold's descendants, of a meeting between him and Beverly Robinson. I do not vouch for its truth, but I have more reason to believe it than to

any one would speak of Arnold as he ought to be spoken of. His joining the King's troops is a matter of importance. He is not only a heaven-born soldier, as Clive was called, and a proof how soon a man of spirit may become an excellent officer, and may step from a shop and a counting-house into the first military ranks, and there distinguish himself; but he seems to have acted throughout from a spirit which would have adorned nobility. When he imagined his country was wronged, he rushed forth into arms; and his Canada expedition, so well wrote in the Annual Register of 1776, shows him not second to the brave Montgomery.

"Wherever you find Arnold mentioned in action during this war, he shines above all his compeers. We have looked upon him only as a soldier, but in his last action we find him a true American citizen, who having resisted what he thought to be British tyranny as briskly and determinedly as any man, would no longer uphold the *tyranny of the usurpers in America, who criminally protract the war from sinister views at the ex ense of the public interest, by artifices after Britain, with the open arms of an indulgent parent offered to embrace them as children, and grant the wished for redress of greviances which had made him a soldier. 'The welfare of his country once attained, he thought all strife should have ceased. He lamented the impolicy, tyranny and injustice which with a sovereign contempt of the people of America studiously neglected to take their collective sentiments of the British proposals of peace which exceeded all the general wishes and expectations.* The same usurpation had the insolence without the authority of the people, to conclude a *treaty which to this very hour the people have not ratified, with France, the proud, ancient and crafty foe, whose business and whose aim it is to destroy both the mother Country and the provinces.* When he saw no man in the American lines dared to speak, or write his sentiments on the tyranny of a desperate party in Congress who were ruining and enslaving America, and rendering her a vassal of France (an abject appendage to the crown of that kingdom), what could a brave mind like that of Arnold do but resist the evil of his former party, refuse to be the tool to set up ruin, tyranny and vassalage to France, forsake himself, and cause as many as he could to forsake the destroyers of his country, and make that event of service to America! I honour him for it, as I did Churchill who left James II. Every Whig will honor Lord Cornbury, who, under pretence of beating up the Prince of Orange's quarters at Honiton, carried off to the Prince four regiments of horse. There are public moments which oblige men thus to act, and for which, if there be no private emolument in the case, no bargain and sale to vitiate the principle, but high regard only for the general welfare, men of really just minds must honour them. I remember the great Montrose, when before his judges at Edinburgh, who upbraided him with having broken the covenant, answered: '*He had done nothing of which he was ashamed, or had cause to repent: that the first covenant he had taken, and complied with it, and with them who took it, as long as the ends for which it was ordained were observed; but when he discovered, which was now evident to all the world, that private and particular men designed to satisfy their own ambition and interest, instead of considering the public benefit, etc., he had withdrawn himself from that engagement.*" *

It is not necessary to say that the foregoing is quoted simply to show how Englishmen regarded Arnold's treason.

* In Clarendon's History.

credit the accuracy of the speeches put into the mouths of Luzerne and Arnold by Marbois.

A manuscript letter, without signature, found at West Point after Arnold's flight, and which has been attributed to Beverly Robinson, contains a statement of many of the considerations supposed to have been addressed to him, urging his defection.[1]

1. In Sargent's Life of Andre, p. 447, it is said: "It is probable that the letter which Marbois says was found among his papers, was written by Robinson." Count Barbe Marbois, Secretary of the French Legation at the time of the conspiracy, in his "*Complot D'Arnold et De Sir Henry Clinton, contre Les Etats-Unis D'Amerique*" published in Paris in 1816, declares the letter was found at West Point, and says: "*Il étoit conçu en ces termes*," and he then inserts the letter in quotation marks. It is not probable that Marbois forged the letter. It tends to show that Arnold may have been influenced in part by less selfish and less criminal motives than those usually attributed to him; but Marbois shows no disposition to extenuate his guilt.

Sabine in his *Loyalists*, declares it certain that Robinson was in communication with Arnold, and this is corroborated by Joshua H. Smith.

The following is the text of the letter, as translated from Marbois by Sargent:

"Among the Americans who have joined the rebel standard, there are very many good citizens whose only object has been the happiness of their country. Such men will not be influenced by motives of private interest to abandon the cause they have espoused. They are now offered everything which can render the colonies really happy; and this is the only compensation worthy of their virtue.

"*The American colonies shall have their Parliament, composed of two chambers, with all its members of American birth.* Those of the upper house shall have titles and rank similar to those of the house of peers in England. All their laws, and particularly such as relate to money matters, shall be the production of this assembly, with the concurrence of a viceroy. Commerce, in every part of the globe subject to British sway, shall be as free to the people of the thirteen colonies as to the English of Europe. They will enjoy, in every sense of the phrase, the blessings of good government. They shall be sustained, in time of need, by all the power necessary to uphold them, without being themselves exposed to the dangers or subjected to the expenses that are always inseparable from the condition of a state.

"Such are the terms proffered by England at the very moment when she is displaying extraordinary efforts to conquer the obedience of her colonies.

"Shall America remain, without limitation of time, a scene of desolation,—or are you desirous of enjoying Peace and all the blessings of her train? Shall your Provinces, as in former days, flourish under the protection of the most puissant nation of the world? Or will you forever pursue that shadow of liberty which still escapes from your hand, even when in the act of grasping it? And how soon would that very liberty, once obtained, turn into licentiousness, if it be not under the safeguard of a great European power? Will you rely upon the guaranty of France? They among you whom she has seduced may assure you that her assistance will be generous and disinterested, and that she will never exact from you a servile obedience. They are frantic with joy at the alliance already estab-

Sabine is authority, as before stated, that Robinson and Arnold were in communication before Arnold went to West Point. Smith declares that while Arnold occupied the Robinson House, in 1780, he often dined with him, and

lished, and promise you that Spain will immediately follow the example of France. Are they ignorant that each of these States has an equal interest in keeping you under, and will combine to accomplish their end? Thousands of men have perished; immense resources have been exhausted; and yet, since that fatal alliance the dispute has become more embittered than ever. Everything urges us to put a conclusion to dissensions not less detrimental to the victors than to the vanquished: but desirable as peace is, it cannot be negotiated and agreed upon between us as between two independent powers; it is necessary that a decisive advantage should put Britain in a condition to dictate the terms of reconciliation. It is her interest as well as her policy to make these as advantageous to one side as the other; but it is at the same time advisable to arrive at it without any unnecessary waste of that blood of which we are already as sparing as though it were again our own.

"There is no one but Gen. Arnold who can surmount obstacles so great as these. A man of so much courage will never despair of the republic, even when every door to a reconciliation seems sealed.

" Render then, brave General, this important service to your country. The colonies cannot sustain much longer the unequal strife. Your troops are perishing in misery. They are badly armed, half naked, and crying for bread. The efforts of Congress are futile against the languor of the people. Your fields are untilled, trade languishes, learning dies. The neglected education of a whole generation is an irreparable loss to society. Your youth, torn by thousands from their rustic pursuits or useful employments, are mown down by war. Such as survive have lost the vigor of their prime, or are maimed in battle; the greater part bring back to their families the idleness and the corrupt manners of the camp. Let us put an end to so many calamities; you and ourselves have the same origin, the same language, the same laws. We are inaccessible in our island; and you, the masters of a vast and fertile territory, have no other neighbors than the people of our loyal colonies. We possess rich establishments in every quarter of the globe, and reign over the fairest portions of Hindostan. The ocean is our home, and we pass across it as a monarch traversing his dominions. From the northern to the southern pole, from the east to the west, our vessels find everywhere a neighboring harbor belonging to Great Britain. So many islands, so many countries acknowledging our sway, are all ruled by a uniform system that bears on every feature the stamp of liberty, yet is as well adapted to the genius of different nations and of various climes.

" While the Continental powers ruin themselves by war, and are exhausted in erecting the ramparts that separate them from each other, our bulwarks are our ships. They enrich us; they protect us; they provide us as readily with the means of invading our enemies as of succoring our friends.

" Beware, then, of breaking forever the links and ties of a friendship whose benefits are proven by the experience of a hundred and fifty years. Time gives to human institutions a strength which what is new can only attain, in its turn, by the lapse of ages. Royalty itself experiences the need of this useful prestige, and the race that has reigned over us for sixty years has been illustrious for ten centuries.

that he told him that Robinson anxiously sought an interview to explain propositions which, if acceded to, would terminate the war.'

It is not improbable that an interview between Arnold and Robinson had been had, at Smith's or elsewhere, before Robinson came up in the Vulture. The tradition before mentioned is that at at such meeting Robinson pressed and urged upon Arnold the considerations contained in the West Point letter. If this interview really took place— and it is probable — aided by the letter, the disclosures of Smith, and Arnold's address to his countrymen, giving the reasons for his desertion, we can readily imagine the topics discussed between them. Arnold, recalling the former friendly relations between Washington and Robinson, may have said:

"Col. Robinson, how can you urge me to abandon your old schoolmate, Washington; surely you have not forgotten your old friend and the friend of your father?"

"United in equality we will rule the universe we will hold it bound, not by arms and violence, but by the ties of commerce—the lightest and most gentle bonds that human kind can wear."—*Sargent's Life of Andre*, pp. 447, 8-9.

Joshua H. Smith, in his narrative, corroborates to some extent the statement of Marbois. He speaks of Arnold's often dining at his house, and at dinner expressing sentiments similar to those contained in the letter attributed to Robinson. (See narrative of Smith London edition, pp 21, 22, 31.) Among other things he says: "Gen. Arnold then said he had received another flag of truce, and that Col. Beverly Robinson had anxiously solicited an interview to be more explanatory of the propositions that were to produce, if acceded to by Congress, a general peace, and happily terminate the expense of blood and treasure, that were ruinous to both countries in the prosecution of a war without an object. He (Arnold) said he conceived the overtures * * made by Great Britain were founded in all sincerity and good faith, and they fully met the ultimatum which the generality of Americans desired, *but by what he could learn from Col. Robinson, the present terms held out went much farther than the propositions of* 1788, *and he made no doubt they would be the basis of an honorable peace.* This event he said he most cordially wished, being heartily tired of the war." "And he then complained of his personal wrongs." (See this Curious narrative.) I am aware, of course, that anything said by Joshua Hett Smith must be taken with great caution and needs corroboration. But I think it not improbable that Robinson, either by letters or personal interview, and perhaps both, held out these inducements to Arnold.

1. Smith's narrative of the death of Andre (London Ed.), pp. 21 to 37.

"No," replied Robinson; "I have not forgotten my old schoolmate; I love and honor Washington, and I regret he is not now, as he was in early life, fighting for the Crown."

"But," continued he, "General Arnold, why do *you* still hesitate? You admit that the attainment of absolute independence by the colonies is very doubtful, and even if successful they will become the wards of France, in place of being the sons of England. Why hesitate when we now offer all that the colonies can justly demand? You admit that even Washington almost despairs of success. To-day Great Britain is ready to grant everything except independence. Is it wise to delay until she may impose upon our country the terms of a conqueror?"

"Robinson," was the reply, "I know the terrible sufferings of my country, and I deeply feel my own wrongs, but you know my name is to-day honored by soldiers in both armies, and is not unknown among the people. You urge me to betray a sacred trust—to be treacherous to my comrades, to abandon the cause for which I have often bled, to break faith with my comrades and my noble chief; in a word, to become a *traitor*."

"If I yield to your views, and Britain finally fails, I shall be doomed to everlasting infamy, and my own *children* will hate me for leaving them a name besmirched with foul dishonor!"

"But," said Robinson, "with your aid we shall not, cannot fail. Look at your feeble, exhausted colonies, and then at the vast power of Great Britain. With your aid, I repeat, failure is impossible, and remember how generously Britain rewards those who render her great and signal service. You have been in England; were you ever at Blenheim Palace? Did you see there towering high above the old oaks of the park, the majestic column which England reared to the memory of John Churchill, Duke of

Marlborough? Contrast the honors and the treasure which she lavished upon that heroic traitor, with the ingratitude, the injustice, the meanness, with which Congress has treated you and others of your fellow-soldiers."

"Churchill was, if you please to call him so, doubly a traitor. He betrayed his benefactor James, deserted him, and went over to the Prince of Orange; and then, pretending the deepest remorse, broke faith with William; acted as a spy in his court and camp, and offered to corrupt the troops and lead them over to James; and yet all this was forgotten in the real service he rendered his country, and his name has gone into history among the proudest on her records. Here you have a precedent and an example; trample your scruples under foot. In great national affairs the end must sometimes justify the means. Do this great deed; end the war, and history will write your justification, and England will reward you as generously in titles and in honors, and in wealth, as she did Churchill." [1]

Such were the appeals to which Arnold finally yielded.

Whether the letter which Marbois alleges was found in Arnold's quarters after his flight, and which has been attributed to Beverly Robinson, is genuine, is a question

---

[1] If these appeals seem extravagant, let the reader remember that Arnold was vain, and intensely ambitious. Let him recollect for what purpose they were used, and that they were successful. Lord Macaulay, speaking of Churchill's desertion of James, says: "He was bound to James not only by the common obligation of allegiance, but by military honor, by personal gratitude."

"There was no guilt, no disgrace he was not ready to incur."

See Macaulay's History of England. Vol. III, p. 82. Again: Churchill, when holding King James' commission, writing treacherously to the Prince of Orange, says: "He puts his honor absolutely into his hands." Macaulay says: "William read those words with one of his bitter and cynical sneers." "It was not his business to take care of the honor of other men, nor had the most rigid casuist pronounced it unlawful in a General to invite, use and reward the services of deserters, whom he could not but despise. History of England, Vol. III, p. 250.

And when Marlborough subsequently deserted and betrayed William, Macaulay calls him "the Arch Traitor." Vol. VI, p. 178. Those who wish to compare or contrast this great English with the American traitor, may consult Macaulay.

which perhaps cannot be determined with absolute certainty. That inducements and arguments similar to those in the letter, and which Robinson pressed upon Arnold in their supposed interview, were addressed to him by British agents, there can be no reasonable doubt. The British authorities were advised by the loyalists of Philadelphia that Arnold was dissatisfied, and that he felt deeply wronged. To secure his defection, and through him bring about peace, was deemed a matter of the highest importance. Such temptations were presented to him personally, and such considerations in regard to his country as it was supposed would be most likely to influence him. If the letter is not genuine, it was ingeniously and ably written, and presents just the considerations to which Arnold would be most likely to yield, and to which he himself declares in his address to his countrymen, and to his old comrades, he did yield.[1]

Now, let us suppose André had not been taken prisoner, and that the plot had succeeded: that West Point had been captured without bloodshed, and then, Arnold clothed by Great Britain with full credentials, had offered to the United States everything but independence, and that through his instrumentality the war had been closed, and liberty secured, an American parliament to make the laws for the confederated colonies, with a nominal recognition of the British crown—what would have been the judgment of the world upon his conduct? Thousands who have cried, and justly, "crucify him! crucify him!" would have said with equal zeal, "crown him with honor." Such is the influence

---

[1]. Dining at the table of Smith, a short time before Andre's visit, Arnold said : "By what he could learn from Colonel Robinson, the present terms held out went much further than the propositions of 1780, and he made no doubt they would be the basis of an honorable peace. This event he most cordially wished."—*Smith's Narrative*, p. 21. *See General Arnold's Address to His Countrymen.*

of success or failure.¹ But success would not have changed the character of his acts. Is it incredible that a desperate man, trodden upon by his enemies,

> "Within whose heated bosom throngs
> The memory of a thousand wrongs,"

as he regarded them, may perhaps, for some brief moments, carried away by the violence of his passions, have deceived himself, or permitted himself to be deceived by these sophistries, and for one moment excused himself to himself for his crime?

If he did, it was a fatal error, and terribly and justly did he suffer for it. Repentance, however, after the first overt act was too late; the fault was fatal, irrevocable, without remedy, and for which nothing could condone. For conceding all, admitting that his passions so misled his judgment as to make him believe that he could by betraying his post really benefit his country, this is no excuse for his treachery; if honestly satisfied that the war should be no further prosecuted, he should have resigned and left his comrades—not sought to betray them.

In March, 1780, while not yet fully committed to the English emissaries, and it may be, hesitating on the brink of the precipice of his crime, his restless spirit devised an enterprise against the enemy upon the sea, which in its execution would require several ships of war, and three or four hundred troops, of which expedition he offered to take command; his wound still rendering him unfit for active duty in the field. Washington favored the project, but the exigencies of the service rendered it impossible to spare the troops, and it was finally abandoned. At another time he seems to have

---

1. "Treason doth never prosper. What's the reason?
Why, if it prosper, none dare call it treason."

It is conceivable that if Washington had failed, the English would have called him the traitor.

entertained the idea of resigning his post in the army and retiring into the forests, and putting himself like the Johnsons, on the Mohawk, at the head of an Indian tribe.

His conduct and plans, after his disgrace in the spring and summer of 1780, are involved in an obscurity which will probably never be dispelled; yet it is evident that he had no fixed purpose, and was undetermined what to do; now he was brooding over the past, and then pondering the future, and sometimes almost in despair; various and wild schemes were presented, considered and rejected. He had listened to the tempter, and to hesitate and deliberate over a crime so desperate, was to fall. Like a rudderless ship in the violence of a wild ocean tempest, uncontrolled by principle, he was drifting hither and thither, wherever the storm of passion might carry him.

At about this time, while pecuniarily embarrassed, and tossing on the surges of passion, it is alledged by Marbois, he sought with corrupt motives, a loan from the envoy of France, the Chevalier de LaLuzerne.[1]

The account of the interview between Arnold and Luzerne, given by Marbois, is evidently embellished, and no one can draw the line between fact and fancy. Marbois wrote history with poetic license, taking the liberty of putting such speeches into the mouths of the persons he introduced as he imagined they might have made, and such as would make his narrative lively and picturesque.[2] The speeches between Arnold and Luzerne, as given by him, are to be taken, therefore, not as literal truth, but simply as what he imagined might have passed. He does not claim to have been present, or even to give the language as

---

[1]. The conspiracy of Arnold and Sir Henry Clinton by Marbois.—*American Register, Vol II, p. 26.*

[2]. Sargent, in his *Life* of Andre, cautions the reader against Marbois, even comparing him with Joshua Hett Smith, saying, "Smith, like *Marbois*, must always be received *distrustfully*."—p. 337.

reported by Luzerne. He says that the chevalier "had been charmed with the talents and bravery of Arnold, and took pleasure in testifying a particular predilection for him. He thought that if it were wished to reclaim this man, it would be indispensable to recollect only the glorious circumstances of his life." "He continued the same deportment towards him as before his disgrace, and this generosity won the respect and confidence of the general."[1] Having thus won Arnold's confidence, the latter in his distress opened his heart to Luzerne, detailed his misfortunes and embarrassments and sought a loan from the French Envoy. Luzerne declined the loan, but gave him some very good advice instead, but this not being what Arnold sought, he received with a very ill grace. Washington Irving expressed the opinion that "the first idea of proving recreant to the cause he had so bravely vindicated, appears to have entered his mind when the charges preferred against him by the Council of Pennsylvania were referred by Congress to a court-martial."[2]

It will be remembered that his accounts for back pay, and disbursements in Canada, and elsewhere, were still unsettled. Mr. Sparks, speaking on this subject, says: "Whether entire justice was rendered him amidst so many obstacles to a perfect knowledge of the merits of the case, it would be difficult to determine."[3] Mr. Sparks also says that up to the time of his disgrace, "his intercourse with the enemy, though of several months' continuance, had been without a definite aim—clothed in such a shape that it might be consummated or dropped, according to the complexion of future events."[4]

At length, won by the specious arguments and allure-

1. Marbois. American Register, p. 27.
2. Life of Washington. Vol. IV, p. 111.
3. Sparks' Writings of Washington, Vol. VI, p. 530.
4. Life of Arnold, p. 151.

ments of his tempters, and urged to desperation by despair, he seems now to have adopted the fatal resolution of betraying his country, and of making his desertion as useful and effective to the enemy as possible. On the 28th of March, 1780, Washington gave him leave of absence from the army to regain his health, but expressed the hope that he might soon be in a condition for "active service," and for himself and Lady Washington, congratulates him on the birth of his son, Edward Shippen, born March 19th, at Philadelphia.

It is not my purpose to go minutely into the details of the treasonable correspondence and conspiracy of Arnold and Sir Henry Clinton. The life of Arnold, by Sparks, goes over this ground very fully, and little could be said in addition to the narrative there given. The correspondence began under assumed names, the letters of Arnold being signed "*Gustavus*," and those of Major André, who carried on the correspondence on the part of the British, were signed "*Anderson.*" Through the influence of his friends, General Schuyler and Robert R. Livingston,[1] Arnold sought and obtained the command of West Point, regarded as the most important military position in the colonies; and here were stored, as in the safest place on the continent, a large quantity of supplies and material of war. On the last day of July, 1780, Arnold, who had been on a visit to Connecticut, now on his way back to Philadelphia, reached the camp of Washington while the army was crossing the Hudson at King's Ferry. He met Washington, on horseback, riding to see the last division cross the river, and asked if any place had been assigned to him? Washington replied, "Yes, you are to command the left

---

[1] Livingston to Washington, June 22, 1780, speaking of Arnold, says: "His courage is undoubted. He is the favorite of the Militia, and who will agree perfectly with our Governor."—*Sparks' Writings of Washington, Vol. VII, p. 95.*

wing, the post of honor." At these words his countenance changed, but he made no reply.[1] Washington invited him to go to headquarters, where in a short time the Commander-in-Chief arrived, and learned with some surprise that Arnold still complained of his wound, and of his inability in consequence, of doing "proper service" in the field, and that he still desired the command of West Point. Washington had hoped to have had his services in the field in the stirring campaign now at hand, and had given him command of the left wing because of its importance, and because he wished it led by an able and efficient officer, as there was a prospect of fighting, and for such work no one could fill the place better, for as a fighting General, "Arnold stood pre-eminent for courage, skill, and good conduct." [2]

When, therefore, Arnold changed countenance, as Washington, notwithstanding Arnold's public disgrace, announced to him his selection to command the left wing, thus carrying out the generous words in the so-called reprimand, in which Washington had exhorted him to "exhibit anew those noble qualities which had placed him in the list of our most valued commanders," and said, "I will furnish you with opportunities of regaining the esteem of your countrymen,"—was not Arnold's change of countenance because he now saw his fatal error—saw it, alas, when too late ? It must ever add a still darker shade to his treason, that he could thus deceive his old and ever faithful friend.

Seeing that Arnold really wished the command at West Point, Washington on the third of August gave him his instructions, and he immediately repaired to that post, and fixed his quarters at Beverly, formerly the beautiful country seat of Col. Beverly Robinson. This gentleman was in

[1] Hamilton's Letters to Laurens.—*Sparks' Life of Arnold*, p. 159.
[2] Sparks' Life of Arnold, p. 159.

the full confidence of Sir Henry Clinton. His picturesque mansion stood a short distance below West Point, on the eastern side of the Hudson, in a lonely part of the far-famed Highlands, high up from the river, and yet at the foot of a mountain covered with woods.[1]

From this seclusion Arnold carried on his secret correspondence with André. Here, somewhat secluded from the officers of the post, he lived, and was often seen walking alone on the banks of the Hudson, his face stern and sorrowful, brooding over his fancied wrongs.

Here, in September, came Mrs. Arnold, bringing with her their infant son, Edward Shippen; and to her while here, was addressed the touching letter of Miss Hannah Arnold, set forth on a preceding page. Here, on the 14th of September, he wrote a long letter to General Washington, replying to questions which the Commander-in-Chief had propounded to the council of general officers, as to the conduct of the campaign. Here, on the 12th of September, he addressed a letter to General Greene, "with sentiments of the most sincere regard and affection," criticising his early friend and later enemy, General Gates, who had lately been terribly defeated in South Carolina, and among other things, saying: "It is a most unfortunate piece of business for that *hero*, and may possibly blot his escutcheon with indelible infamy."[2]

It was his own "escutcheon" that he was now blotting with "indelible infamy."

In a letter to Washington, September 5th, he says: "I had the pleasure of General Schuyler's company last night."

It was thus, while in daily intercourse and correspondence with his fellow soldiers, in the full enjoyment of their friendship and sympathy, and in the unshaken confidence

[1] Irving's Washington, Vol. IV, p. 112.
[2] Manuscript letter in the State Department at Washington.

of his chief, his home hallowed by the devoted affection of his young and beautiful wife, and brightened by the playfulness of his child, the idol of his sister, the pride of his elder boys at school, he was conspiring with the enemy to betray the cause for which he and his comrades had so often fought.

I have heard from a descendant of Arnold the existence of a tradition that he often said, and repeated over and over again, to his dying day. "I believed our cause was hopeless; I thought we never could succeed, and I did it to save the shedding of blood." If this language expressed his real sentiments and opinions, how infinitely more noble would it have been to stand or fall, live or die with his comrades. How inexcusable to betray them!

The importance of West Point with its military stores, was fully realized by Sir Henry Clinton. Its possession would secure the Hudson, cut off New England, facilitate intercourse with Canada by the lakes, and, in fact, accomplish nearly all which Burgoyne and St. Leger's expeditions, with their ten thousand men, had sought to effect.

The conspiracy had been carried forward by correspondence under fictitious names, by Arnold and André, and its consummation now required a personal meeting; and at Arnold's request, André, then holding the position of Adjutant-General in the British Army, was detailed to meet the American general and settle all details. On the 20th of September André went on board the British sloop of war, Vulture, with Colonel Beverly Robinson,[1] and proceeded up the Hudson, with a view of holding an interview with Arnold. On the night of the 21st, a boat was sent by Arnold to the Vulture, which brought André to the shore about six miles below Stoney Point; and there

---

1. I think the circumstantial evidence is very strong, that Robinson had been one of the agents to seduce Arnold.

under the shadow of the mountains, after midnight, the conspirators met. As the dawn of day drew near, the conference not being concluded, André was induced to accompany Arnold to the house of Joshua Hett Smith, about two miles below Stoney Point. Soon after they reached the house the booming of cannon was heard, and directly they saw the Vulture weigh anchor and proceed down the river. Colonel Livingston, of the American army, thought she was too near the American outposts, and brought cannon to bear, and compelled her to descend the river. Arnold and André breakfasted together at Smith's, and then completed the arrangements for the surrender of West Point. Plans of the works, their armament, the number of troops, etc., were furnished by Arnold to André, and concealed by the latter in his boots, between his stockings and his feet. Arnold then, in case André should not be able to reach the Vulture by water, furnished him with a horse, and a pass in these words:

"Permit *Mr. John Anderson* to pass the guards to the White Plains, or below if he chooses, he being on public business by my direction.
"B. ARNOLD, *M. General.*"

Also a pass for Smith by water, and another by land.

After breakfast, before Arnold and André separated, they walked out towards the river, and pausing on the banks of the Hudson, Arnold said:

"André, you have strangely won my confidence. I cannot part without opening my heart to you. I have cherished the hope of associating my name with that of Washington in achieving the independence of my country. Look out upon this magnificent river," extending his arm towards the Hudson; "is it not fit to bear the commerce of an empire to the ocean?" Musing a moment, he added:

"I thought it time this vast continent was independent and free; how long, I used to ask myself, must the territory drained by this great outlet be subordinate to your petty Thames; our continent to your little island?" "Do you appreciate," he continued, "all I hazard by the scheme we have agreed upon?" "My name is now associated in history forever with the Hudson and the Mohawk Valley; few will recall Saratoga without thinking of the bloody charge I made." "*I* certainly shall not forget it," said he, smiling bitterly, "so long as I drag about this crippled leg."

"But," broke in André, interrupting him, "what cares Congress for your services, your wounds, and your losses? Your enemies in Congress do not thank you. I have even been told that in your last fight with Burgoyne, when you so crippled him as to compel his surrender, you fought as a volunteer, and without a command; and that while *you* were leading the troops Gates was in his tent, not even going upon the field at all: yet *he* received Burgoyne's sword, a medal from Congress, all the honors of the victory, and *he*, forsooth, is the *hero* of Saratoga, while you were tried by court-martial and disgraced."

"Yes," replied Arnold, "all this and more, is true; and this, in part, has driven me to my present conduct. Independence must be postponed. Half a century hence it will come, and without war."

"Yes, General Arnold," said André, "we will restore peace and reconciliation; and for you there shall be honor, appreciation, and an English peerage, in place of ingratitude, neglect, disgrace, and a public 'reprimand.'"

"And for my country," said Arnold, "peace and reconciliation will, I hope, be better than blood and suffering, and a French vassalage; but, André, this treachery to Washington, my best and most faithful friend—this is what I hate. Ah, André, you do not know him; there is a simple dignity about him, a sense of justice, a patience, a sympathy, a generosity which makes me both love and reverence him, and besides, I am bound to him by gratitude for a thousand acts of kindness, and I sometimes feel that I would rather die than deceive him. If I could buy this peace with my own blood, if by giving the other leg I could obtain a triumph over my enemies and peace for my country; nay, were it not for my wife (you know her André, and what I have to live for), were it not for her and the boys, my life might freely go; yes, as freely as I periled it at Quebec, at Valcour Island, at Ridgefield, at Bemis Heights. * * * * "They have driven me to this," exclaimed he, bitterly, "they have made me the *villain*, all the world will call me, if we fail!"

"But we must not, will not fail! Go, André, hasten back to Sir Henry Clinton, bring up your troops, and West Point is yours!"[1]

Thus ended the interview, and Arnold returned to his quarters.

André passed the day at Smith's house, expecting to be put on board the Vulture at night. As evening approached, Smith refused to put him on board, fearing for his own safety; but proposed to cross the river with him, and put him in the way of returning to New York by land. André was disappointed, but was finally induced to put Smith's overcoat on over his uniform, and about sunset they started, crossing at King's Ferry. After proceeding about eight miles they were stopped by an American patrol. Arnold's pass satisfied the officer in command, but he warned them against proceeding further at night. They stopped and passed the night.

The next morning at day-break they started again, and now approached what was called the "neutral ground," a

---

1. I need scarcely say I have no authority for the above dialogue, but every reader may judge for himself what degree of probability there is that it occurred. I mention this because for every fact, stated without qualification, I have given the authority, or have had authority which I believed sufficient.

HIS PATRIOTISM AND HIS TREASON. 291

part of the the country some thirty miles in extent, and lying between the lines of the two armies; after going two or three miles further towards New York, André and Smith breakfasted at a farm house and then parted; Smith returning home and André going on towards New York, cheerful, and with the conviction that the dangerous part of his journey was over.

As he was proceeding, he was arrested in a wooded glen by three men, the foremost of which wore a uniform indicating that he belonged to the British army. André, losing all caution, imprudently exclaimed, "Gentlemen I hope you belong to our party."[1] "What party?" was the reply. "The lower party," said André. "We do," replied the leader.

André, thrown entirely off his guard, immediately declared himself to be a British officer; that he had been up the country on important business, and must not be detained; drawing out his gold watch, as evidence of the truth of his statement, whereupon his captors avowed themselves Americans, and that André was their prisoner. They were yeomanry of the neighborhood, and their names were John Paulding, Isaac Van Wort and David Williams. It seems that the coat of Paulding, which had misled André, was one received by him from the enemy who had lately held him a prisoner, and stripping him of his better farmer's clothes, had given him this coat in exchange.

André, now too late, exhibited his pass, which if exhibited when he was first halted, would have been sufficient; but now he having avowed himself a British officer, they seized the bridle of his horse, ordered him to dismount, searched him, and in his boots found the concealed papers, when Paulding exclaimed, "My God! he is a spy."[1]

André now offered his captors any sum of money, goods,

1. Irving's Washington.

anything, if they would let him go. These offers they refused, and conducted their prisoner to Lieut. Colonel Jameson, who commanded the post at New Castle. He immediately sent the papers found in André's boots, by express to General Washington, who was returning from a visit to the French at Hartford. André begged Colonel Jameson to inform his commander at West Point, that *John Anderson*, though bearing his pass, was detained as a prisoner. Jameson wrote a statement of the facts to General Arnold, and thoughtlessly sent it forward with the prisoner. Major Tallmadge, soon after, coming in, and learning the facts, and suspecting something was wrong, induced Jameson to send an express after the officer who had André in charge, with orders to bring him back to New Castle, but the letter to Arnold was permitted to go forward to its destination.

André was then conducted to Colonel Sheldon, and there being informed that the papers found on his person had been forwarded to Washington, he wrote to him a letter, frankly declaring his real character, and stating the circumstances of his expedition and capture, as follows:

"MAJOR ANDRE TO GENERAL WASHINGTON.
"SALEM, 24 September, 1780.

"SIR:—What I have as yet said concerning myself was in the justifiable attempt to be extricated; I am too little accustomed to duplicity to have succeeded.

"I beg your Excellency will be persuaded that no alteration in the temper of my mind, or apprehension for my safety, induces me to take the step of addressing you, but that it is to rescue myself from an imputation of having assumed a mean character for treacherous purposes or self-interest; a conduct incompatible with the principles that actuate me, as well as with my condition in life.

"It is to vindicate my fame that I speak, and not to solicit security.

"The person in your possession is Major John Andre, adjutant-general to the British army.

"The influence of one commander in the army of his adversary is an advantage taken in war. A correspondence for this purpose I held as confidential (in the present instance) with his Excellency, Sir Henry Clinton.

"To favor it, I agreed to meet upon ground not within the posts of either party, a person who was to give me intelligence; I came up in the Vulture man-of-war for this effect, and was fetched by a boat from the ship to the beach. Being there, I was told that the approach of day would prevent my return, and that I must be concealed until the next night. I was in my regimentals, and had fairly risked my person.

"Against my stipulation, my intention, and without my knowledge beforehand, I was conducted within one of your posts. Your Excellency may conceive my sensation on this occasion, and will imagine how much more must I have been affected by a refusal to re-conduct me back the next night as I had been brought. Thus become a prisoner, I had to concert my escape. I quitted my uniform, and was passed another way in the night, without the American posts to neutral ground, and informed I was beyond all armed parties, and left to press for New York. I was taken at Tarrytown by some volunteers.

"Thus, as I have had the honor to relate, was I betrayed (being adjutant-general of the British army) into the vile condition of an enemy in disguise within your posts.

"Having avowed myself a British officer, I have nothing to reveal but what relates to myself, which is true on the honor of an officer and a gentleman.

"The request I have to make to your Excellency, and I am conscious I address myself well, is, that in any rigor policy may dictate, a decency of conduct towards me may mark, that though unfortunate I am branded with nothing dishonorable, as no motive could be mine but the service of my King, and as I was involuntarily an impostor.

"Another request is, that I may be permitted to write an open letter to Sir Henry Clinton, and another to a friend for clothes and linen.

"I take the liberty to mention the condition of some gentlemen at Charleston, who, being either on parole or under protection, were engaged in a conspiracy against us. Though their situation is not similar, they are objects who may be set in exchange for me, or are persons whom the treatment I receive might affect.

"It is no less, sir, in a confidence of the generosity of your mind, than on account of your superior station, that I have chosen to importune you with this letter. I have the honor to be, with great respect, Sir, your Excellency's most obedient humble servant,

"JOHN ANDRE, Adjutant-General."[1]

---

1. Sparks' Writings of Washington, Vol. VII, p. 531.

CHAPTER XVI.

ARNOLD'S ESCAPE—ANDRE'S EXECUTION.

> "Is there not some chosen curse,
> Some hidden thunder in the stores of Heaven,
> Red with uncommon wrath to blast the man,
> Who seeks his greatness by his country's ruin?"

ARNOLD HEARS OF ANDRE'S CAPTURE—FLIES TO THE VULTURE—WASHINGTON ARRIVES AT WEST POINT—MRS. ARNOLD'S DISTRESS—ARNOLD'S LETTER TO WASHINGTON DECLARING HER INNOCENCE, AND BEGGING WASHINGTON TO PROTECT HER—DECLARES HIS MILITARY FAMILY INNOCENT—HANNAH ARNOLD'S LETTER BEGGING THE PITY OF ALL HER FRIENDS, AND PRAYING THEM NOT TO FORSAKE HER—ANDRE'S TRIAL AS A SPY—EFFORTS TO SAVE HIS LIFE—HIS EXECUTION—ARNOLD'S ALLEGED OFFER TO GIVE HIMSELF UP, TO SAVE THE LIFE OF ANDRE.

ON the day of the treasonable conference between Arnold and André, on the banks of the Hudson, Washington met the French officers at Hartford. With him, besides his own military family, were LaFayette and his suite, and General Knox and his staff. On the morning of the 25th September, having sent on their baggage, and a message to General Arnold that the party would breakfast with him on that day, Washington's party were very early in the saddle, riding towards Arnold's headquarters at the Robinson House. As they approached that place, Washington turned off from the direct route, to visit the defenses on the east side of the Hudson. Lafayette, with the politeness of his nation and the gallantry of a young soldier, suggested to the general that Mrs. Arnold would be waiting breakfast for them. "Ah, Marquis," replied Washington, "you young men are all in love with Mrs. Arnold. I see you are eager to be with her as soon as possible. Go and breakfast with her, and tell her not to wait for me. I must ride down and examine the redoubts on this side the river, but will be with you shortly." Lafayette and Knox, however, accompanied Washington, but Col. Hamilton and others of the staff went directly to Arnold's headquarters, bearing Washington's message to Mrs. Arnold.

In accordance with his request, they all sat down to breakfast. Mrs. Arnold with her child had arrived from Philadelphia a few days previous. She, it is said, received her guests cordially, and was as usual, bright, happy, gay and fascinating. Arnold was grave and thoughtful. Well he might be.

Washington had arrived two days sooner than he had been expected, and this was the eventful day on which the treason was to be consummated. He had arranged with André that the garrison should be scattered through the passes and defiles of the highlands, and the enemy's ships, with the British troops on board, were on this very day to ascend the river and take possession of the post; and now came Washington unexpectedly to disconcert everything.

In the midst of the breakfast a horseman galloped to the door. It was Lieutenant Allen, with Jameson's letter to Arnold, containing the startling statement that André is a prisoner, and the papers found in his boots have been forwarded to Washington. It was a terrible crisis in the life of Arnold. "Yet," says Irving, "in this awful moment he gave evidence of that quickness of mind which had won laurels for him when in the path of duty."[1]

With a self-control that was amazing, he excused himself to his guests, retired, ordered a horse, and then going

1. Irving's Washington, Vol. IV, p. 133.

to Mrs. Arnold's room, sent for her, and disclosed his perilous position, saying: "I must fly instantly! My life depends on my reaching the British lines without detection."

Startled, bewildered, and completely overcome, she fell senseless at his feet;[1] he laid her upon the bed, calling a servant to her assistance, and then returning again to the breakfast-room, he asked his guests to excuse him; he said he must hasten to West Point to prepare for the reception of the General; and then springing upon his horse, ready saddled at the door, he galloped down a steep, along what is still called "Arnold's path," towards the landing place, where his six-oared barge was moored. How terrible must have been his feelings as he dashed down the hill, leaving behind him his wife and child, country, friends, honor and faith! Not now could he exclaim, as in other days: "I am in the discharge of duty, and know no fear!" Like guilty Macbeth, he could not respond: "Amen" to "God bless our patriot cause."

"Never had shaken his nerves in fight."

But as his horse's hoofs struck fire from the rocks in his headlong speed, the very echo seemed the voice of the avenger. Danger and death were behind him, and what was infinitely worse, dishonor was before him and around him. From death he might escape by flight, but from dishonor—this man who so loved glory—from dishonor for him there was from henceforth forever no escape!

Seizing his pistols from his holsters, he sprang into the barge and directed the oarsmen to pull into the middle of

---

[1]. "Dr. Eustis, who had charge of the hospital in the vicinity, was called to the assistance of Mrs. Arnold, whose situation was alarming. He found her at the head of the staircase, in great dishabille, her hair disheveled, knowing no one, and frantic, in the arms of her maid and Arnold's two aids, struggling to liberate herself from them. She was carried back to her chamber, and fell into convulsions, which lasted several hours."—*Thatcher's American Revolution*, pp. 471-2.

the river, and then row with speed for Teller's Point, saying he must hasten, as he wished to return and meet General Washington. As the boat passed Verplank's Point, Arnold raised a white handkerchief and ordered the boatmen to row directly to the Vulture, which was in sight. All the way he sat in the prow, his pistols either in his hand or within his reach. He would not have been captured alive. The boat reached the schooner, and the fugitive springing on deck, was safe from pursuit.

After Arnold had had an interview with the commander of the Vulture, he came on deck, and is reported to have said to the bargemen, who had taken him to the schooner: "My lads, I have quitted the *rebel army* and joined the standard of his Brittanic Majesty. If you will join me I will make sergeants and corporals of you all, and for you, Larvey, (who was coxswain), I will do something more." Larvey indignantly replied, "No, sir, one coat is enough for me to wear at a time."[1] General Heath, in his memoirs, gives the following account of the incident:

"When Arnold had got under the guns of the Vulture, he told Corporal Larvey, who was cockswain of the barge, that he was going on board the ship, not to return, and that if he, Larvey, would stay with him, he should have a commission in the British service. To this Larvey, who was a smart fellow, replied, that he would be d—d if he fought on both sides. The General replied that he would send him on shore. Arnold then told the barge crew that if any of them would stay with him they should be treated well, but if they declined staying, they should be sent on shore. One or two stayed, the rest with the cockswain, were sent on shore in the ships' boat; the barge was kept. Larvey, for his fidelity, was made a sargeant. He thought he merited more, and that he ought to have had as much as Arnold promised him. He continued uneasy until, at his repeated request, he was allowed to leave the army."[2]

These are, probably, the facts in relation to the crew.

1. Thatcher, p. 472.
2. Heath's Memoirs, 1798, p. 255.
This account is confirmed by Larvey himself, as given by Eustis, in Mass. Hist. Soc. Col., Vol. XIV, p. 52.

An hour after Arnold's flight, Washington arrived at the Robinson House, and being informed that Mrs. Arnold was in her room ill, and that Arnold had gone to West Point to prepare to receive him, he hastily took his breakfast, and he and party, with the exception of Hamilton, started for the fortress, leaving word that he would return to dinner.

As the party were crossing the Hudson, between the overhanging cliffs, Washington, looking up at the grand scenery around him, said: "Gentlemen, I am glad General Arnold has gone before us, for we shall now have a salute, and the roaring of the cannon will have a fine effect among these mountains."

> "The castled crag of Drachenfels
> Frowns o'er the wide and winding Rhine"

with no more wild and picturesque beauty than the fortress of West Point rose above the waters of the majestic Hudson.

But no salute greeted the ears of Washington, and as his boat approached the western shore, an officer was seen winding his way down the side of the rocky cliff. It was Colonel Lamb, who seemed very much surprised, and apologized for not receiving the Commander-in-Chief with the honors due to his rank. "Is not General Arnold here?" inquired Washington.

"No, sir; he has not been here for two days past, nor have I heard from him in that time."

Washington remained during the morning, ascending to Fort Putnam, and inspecting the fortifications. Meanwhile, the messenger from Jameson, with the papers found upon the person of André, having missed Washington on his way from Hartford, and hearing that the General had passed him by a different road, had returned and followed him to the Robinson House, and on his way had taken and brought the letter from André to Washington, disclosing the conspiracy. These letters and papers being presented to Colonel Hamilton, Washington's confidential aid, were opened and read by him. Hastening to find Washington, he met the General and party coming up from the river. Hamilton addressed a few words to him in a low tone, and they retired into the house. The papers told their own too sad story—the leader of the daring expedition through the wilderness, wounded at Quebec, the hero of Saratoga, he who, with the militia had driven Tryon from his native State, was a traitor, and had fled to the enemy! Hamilton was ordered to mount and ride with speed to try to overtake and capture the fugitive. In vain; Arnold had had four or five hours the start.

Washington was calm; calling to Lafayette and Knox, he told them the story, and said, sadly, "Whom can we trust now?"

James Fenimore Cooper, in giving an account of this incident, derived, as is supposed, from Lafayette, says: "When Washington and Lafayette met, the former put the report of Jameson into the hands of the latter, and said with tears in his eyes, 'Arnold is a traitor, and has fled to the British.' General Knox was present at this scene." [1]

Hamilton returned and reported Arnold's escape, and brought with him the following letter from the fugitive, which had been sent ashore by a flag from the Vulture:

"ON BOARD THE VULTURE, 25 September, 1780.

"SIR,—The heart which is conscious of its own rectitude, cannot attempt to palliate a step which the world may censure as wrong, I have ever acted from a principle of love to my country since the commencement of the present unhappy contest between Great Britain and the Colonies. The same principle of love to my country actuates my present conduct, however it may appear inconsistent to the world, who very seldom judge right of any man's actions.

[1] Cooper's Notions of the Americans, picked up by a Traveling Bachelor, p. 214.

"I have no favor to ask for myself. I have too often experienced the ingratitude of my country to attempt it; but, from the known humanity of your Excellency, I am induced to ask your protection for Mrs. Arnold from every insult and injury that a mistaken vengeance of my country may expose her to. It ought to fall only on me; she is as good and as innocent as an angel, and is incapable of doing wrong. I beg she may be permitted to return to her friends in Philadelphia, or to come to me, as she may choose. From your Excellency I have no fears on her account, but she may suffer from the mistaken fury of the country.

"I have to request that the enclosed letter may be delivered to Mrs. Arnold, and she be permitted to write to me.

"I have also to ask that my clothes and baggage, which are of little consequence, may be sent to me; if required, their value shall be paid in money.

"I have the honor to be, with great regard and esteem, your Excellency's most obedient, humble servant.   B. ARNOLD.

"N. B.—In justice to the gentlemen of my family, Colonel Varick and Major Franks, I think myself in honor bound to declare that they, as well as Joshua Smith, Esq. (who I know is suspected), are totally ignorant of any transactions of mine, that they had reason to believe were injurious to the public.   B. A."

The paragraph in Arnold's letter in relation to his wife, declaring that "she is as good and as innocent as an angel, and as incapable of doing wrong," shows his devotion to her in this hour of supreme peril and desolation, and his efforts to prevent unjust suspicion falling upon his military family, Colonel Varick and Major Franks, are honorable to him. Let us not overlook any bright spot in the character now blackened with treachery. In the meantime, Washington took every precaution against an attack by the enemy, and it is worthy of remark that no one of Arnold's military family, nor any among his personal friends, was to any extent implicated in his treachery. Washington did not betray any unusual excitement or anxiety. When dinner was announced, he said: "Come gentlemen; since Mrs. Arnold is ill, and the General is absent, let us sit down without ceremony."

Mrs. Arnold remained in her room, crushed with sorrow

and anxiety, and in a state bordering on phrensy. Arnold did not overestimate the generosity and chivalry of Washington when he begged his protection for her. Washington regarded her with the deepest sympathy and commiseration, believing her ignorant of all previous knowledge of her husband's guilt. When he delivered to her the letter which her husband had enclosed in the one to himself, he told her that he had, in accordance with his duty, done all in his power to have her husband arrested, but not having succeeded, it gave him pleasure to assure her of his safety.[1]

The following letter from Hamilton to Miss Schuyler, the daughter of General Schuyler, to whom he was then engaged, gives a touching picture of the interview between Washington and Mrs. Arnold, and shows how vivid the impression her distress and beauty made upon this young soldier:[2]

"September 25, 1780.

"Arnold, hearing of the plot being detected, immediately fled to the enemy. I went in pursuit of him, but was much too late, and could hardly regret the disappointment, when, on my return, I saw an amiable woman, frantic with distress for the loss of a husband she tenderly loved, a traitor to his country and to his fame; a disgrace to his connections; it was the most affecting scene I ever was witness to. She, for a considerable time, entirely lost herself. The General went up to see her and she upbraided him with being in a plot to murder her child. One moment she raved; another she melted into tears. Sometimes she pressed her infant to her bosom and lamented its fate, occasioned by the imprudence of its father, in a manner that would have pierced insensibility itself. All the sweetness of beauty, all the loveliness of innocence, all the tenderness of a wife, and all the fondness of a mother showed themselves in her appearance and conduct. We have every reason to believe that she was entirely unacquainted with the plan, and that the first knowledge of it was when Arnold went to tell her he must banish himself from his country and from her forever. She instantly fell into a convulsion, and he left her in that situation.

"This morning she is more composed. I paid her a visit, and endeav-

1. Irving's Washington, Vol. IV, p. 145.
2. Hamilton papers, Vol. I, p. 478.

ored to soothe her by every method in my power; though you may imagine she is not easily to be consoled. Added to her other distresses, she is very apprehensive the resentment of her country will fall upon her (who is only unfortunate) for the guilt of her husband.

"I have tried to persuade her that her fears are ill founded; but she will not be convinced. She received us in bed, with every circumstance that would interest our sympathy, and her sufferings were so eloquent that I wished myself her brother, to have a right to become her defender. As it is, I have entreated her to enable me to give her proofs of my friendship. Could I forgive Arnold for sacrificing his honor, reputation, and duty, I could not forgive him for acting a part that must have forfeited the esteem of so fine a woman. At present she almost forgets his crime in his misfortunes, and her horror at the guilt of the traitor, is lost in her love of the man. But a virtuous mind cannot long esteem a base one; and time will make her despise, if it cannot make her hate.

"A. HAMILTON."

On the evening of the 25th the Vulture sailed to New York, carrying General Arnold, who reached that city the next morning, and communicated to Sir Henry Clinton the first intelligence he received of the capture of André.

It would be difficult to conceive a more painful position than that which Arnold now occupied. Going into the British headquarters with the *éclat* of a great, though guilty exploit, by which it was expected the war might be brought to an early close, was one thing; to fly to these quarters for refuge, a detected traitor, and a powerless, valueless fugitive, having accomplished nothing but the exposure of his own treachery, and the hazard of André's life, was another.[1]

Without anticipating the narration of future events, I pause to say that Arnold's life from that day forward, though he received many gracious favors from the King and the tory party in England, yet his life was a sad one, and adds another, and one of the most striking and conspicuous in history, to the verification of the truth that "the way of the transgressor is hard."

1. "He stood alone—a renegade
   Against the country he betrayed."

The news of Arnold's treason created a popular *furore* against him, the violence of which is indescribable. None felt the disgrace more keenly than his devoted sister. She had been proud of her brother, and had rejoiced with all a sister's fondness in his glory, and she deeply sympathized in his wrongs. But now the message from Edith to Morton in Old Mortality, would have aptly expressed her feelings: "Tell him that Edith Bellenden has wept more over his fallen character, blighted prospects, and disgraced name, than over all her own sufferings." No more could she proudly write, as she had done in his hour of victory, "'Ben' is eager to hear everything in relation to his father."[1] Yet she stood by him faithfully and heroically, and no popular hatred could ever alienate her attachment. She could and did always say, "Your health and prosperity are dear to me as my own." It will be rememberd that she addressed a letter from Philadelphia to Mrs. Arnold, at West Point, about the middle of September. This letter, full of hope and affection, speaks fondly, as a tender maiden sister would, of the sons of General Arnold, the two elder of which, Ben and Richard, were at school in Maryland, and the younger, Henry, was with her in Philadelphia. When the tidings of her brother's flight to the enemy reached her, she wrote to an old friend in New Haven as follows:

"DEAR SIR:— My unfortunate brother wrote me some time since that he had desired you to send for my bed from Maj. Atwater, and to forward it to him If it was not done before the distressful step he has taken, I beg you would desire Maj. Atwater to keep it until I send for it, as 'tis most probable, if my wretched life is continued, that I shall one day quit this land of strangers, and return to that of my birth. Be so good as to desire Mr. Shipman to keep the money for the china, unless he has paid it to you; if he has, you will be so good as to reserve it in your hands.

---

1. "Worse than absence, worse than death,
   She wept her brother's sullied fame,
   And fired with all the pride of birth,
   She wept a soldier's injured name."

Let me ask the pity of all my friends; there never was a more proper object of it. Do write. Forsake me not in my distress, I conjure you, but let me hear by all opportunities. I am glad Captain Sloan is fortunate. May you all be so, prays the miserable   HANNAH ARNOLD.

"The little unfortunate boys in Maryland are well, as is Harry, who desires his love. I was so swallowed up in my own distress, I had forgot yours, in the loss of your little son! But mourn not for him, my friends, he has escaped the snares and miseries of a wretched, deceitful and sorrowing vale of tears.   H. A." [1]

The above most pathetic letter was written from Philadelphia, and while popular fury was raging with the greatest violence against Arnold. I anticipate the narration so far as to say that she made her home during life with Richard and Henry, sons of her brother by his first wife, and that her sisterly devotion was never forgotten by him. When an exile from his country, and amid all changes of fortune, he never forgot to remit to her a pension, and this was religiously continued after General Arnold's death, by his widow.

On the the 26th September, Major Tallmadge, having in custody, André, arrived at the Robinson House. Washington declined seeing the prisoner, but gave orders that he should be treated with every courtesy and civility consistent with his absolute security.

Major Tallmadge, and indeed every one who was brought into personal intercourse with André, was fascinated by his engaging qualities. He says:

"It often drew tears from my eyes to find him so agreeable in conversation on different subjects, when I reflected on his future fate, and that, too, as I feared, so near at hand."

While Tallmadge was on the way with André to the American head-quarters, their conversation became very cordial and frank, and finally André asked Tallmadge in what light he would be regarded by General Washington and a

---

[1] From a copy in possession of Chicago His. Society.

military tribunal. Tallmadge evaded an answer, but being pressed, he finally said : [1]

"I had a much-loved class-mate in Yale College, by the name of Nathan Hale, who entered the army in 1775. Immediately after the battle of Long Island, General Washington wanted information respecting the strength, position and probable movements of the ennemy. Captain Hale tendered his services, went over to Brooklyn, and was taken just as he was passing the outposts of the enemy on his return Said I, with emphasis : '*Do you remember the sequel of the story?* '~ 'Yes,' said Andre, 'he was hanged as a spy! But you surely do not consider his case and mine alike?' 'Yes, precisely similar; and similar will be your fate!'"

The arrival of Arnold in New York, and the news of André's capture, caused a great sensation in the British army. André was very popular, and an especial favorite with the Commander-in-Chief. Clinton and Arnold and Robinson, conferred together as to the means of obtaining the release of André. Arnold wrote a letter to Clinton assuming the responsibility for André's conduct, declaring that he came to him under the protection of a flag of truce, and that he gave him passports to go to White Plains, on his return to New York.[2] This letter, enclosed in one from

1. Irving's Washington, Vol. IV, pp. 149-150.

2. The following is Arnold's letter, copied from Sparks' Writings of Washington, Vol. VII, p.p 534-2.

"NEW YORK, 26th September, 1780.

"SIR: In answer to your Excellency's message, respecting your Adjutant-General, Major Andre, and desiring my idea of the reasons why he is detained, being under my passports, I have the honor to inform you, Sir, that I apprehend a few hours must return Major Andre to your Excellency's Orders, as that officer is assuredly under the protection of a flag of truce sent by me to him for the purpose of a conversation, which I requested to hold with him relating to myself, and which I wished to communicate, through that officer, to your Excellency.

"I commanded at the time at West Point, and had an undoubted right to send my flag of truce for Major Andre, who came to me under that protection, and, having held my conversation with him, I delivered him confidential papers in my own hand-writing, to deliver to your Excellency; thinking it much properer he should return by land, I directed him to make use of the feigned name of John Anderson, under which he had, by my direction, come on shore, and gave him my passports to go to the White Plains on his way to New York. This officer cannot, therefore, fail of being immediately sent to New York, as he was invited to a conversation with me, for which I sent him a flag of truce, and finally gave him passports

himself, Clinton forwarded to Washington, claiming that André should be permitted to return to New York."[1]

These papers had no influence upon the action of Washington, except possibly to render him still more careful and circumspect in regard to the prisoner. He referred the case of Major André to a board of general officers, which he ordered to meet on the 29th, and directed that after a careful examination, this board should report their opinion "of the light in which he ought to be considered, and the punishment that ought to be inflicted." This Board consisted of six major-generals and eight brigadier-generals.[2] Hamilton, in a letter to Col. Laurens has given many very interesting particulars concerning the conduct, trial and execution of André.

"'When brought before the Board of officers, he met with every indulgence, and was requested to answer no interrogatory which would even embarrass his feelings.' 'He frankly confessed all the facts relating to himself.' Indeed, the facts were not controverted, and the Board reported that Andre ought to be considered as a spy, and agreeably to the law and usages of nations, must suffer death. 'Andre met the result with manly firmness.' 'I foresee my fate,' said he; 'and though I pre-

for his safe return to your Excellency, all which I had then a right to do, being in the actual service of America, under the orders of General Washington and commanding general at West Point and its dependencies.

"I have the honor to be, &c.
"B. ARNOLD."

1. The letter from Clinton is as follows, copied from Sparks' Writings of Washington, Vol. VII., p. 534.

"NEW YORK, 26th September, 1780.

"SIR: Being informed that the King's Adjutant-general in America has been stopped under Major-General Arnold's passports, and is detained a prisoner by your Excellency's Army, I have the honor to inform you, sir, that I permitted Major Andre to go to Major-General Arnold at the particular request of that general officer. You will preceive, Sir, by the inclosed paper, that a flag of truce was sent to receive Major Andre, and passports granted for his return. I therefore can have no doubt but your Excellency will immediately direct that this officer have permission to return to my orders at New York.

"I have the honor to be, &c."

2. Their names were, Major-Generals Greene, Stirling, St. Clair, Lafayette, Howe and Steuben. Brigadier-Generals Parsons, James Clinton, Knox, Glover, Paterson, Hand, Huntington and Stark.

tend not to play the hero, or to be indifferent about life, yet I am reconciled to whatever may happen, conscious that misfortune, not guilt, has brought it upon me.' "

On the 30th of September General Washington sent to Sir Henry Clinton the following statement in regard to André:

"HEAD-QUARTERS, 30 September, 1780.

"SIR: — In answer to your Excellency's letter of the 26th instant, which I had the honor to receive, I have to inform you that Major Andre was taken under such circumstances as would have justified the most summary proceeding against him. I determined, however, to refer his case to the examination and decision of a board of general officers, who have reported, on his free and voluntary confession and letters: 'First, That he came on shore from the Vulture Sloop-of-War in the night of the 21st of September instant, on an interview with General Arnold, in a private and secret manner.

"'Secondly, That he changed his dress within our lines; and, under a feigned name, and in a disguised habit, passed our works at Stony & Verplank's Points, the evening of the 22nd of September instant, and was taken the morning of the 23d of September instant, at Tarry Town, in a disguised habit, being then on his way to New York; and when taken, he had in his possession several papers which contained intelligence for the enemy.'

"'From these proceedings it is evident that Major Andre was employed in the execution of measures very foreign to the objects of flags of truce, and such as they were never meant to authorize or countenance in the most distant degree; and this gentleman confessed, with the greatest candor, in the course of his examination, 'that it was impossible for him to suppose that he came on shore under the sanction of a flag.' I have the honor to be, &c.

"GEORGE WASHINGTON."

—*Sparks' Writings of Washington, Vol. VII*, p. 538.

The closing part of the report of the Board of Officers was not quoted in the letter to Sir Henry Clinton. It was in the following words:

"The Board, having maturely considered these facts, do also report to his Excellency, General Washington, that Major Andre, adjutant-general to the British army, ought to be considered as a spy from the enemy, and that agreeably to the law and usage of nations, it is their opinion he ought to suffer death."

The execution was to have taken place on the first of October, at 5 P. M., but Washington received a second letter from Clinton, expressing the opinion that the Board had not been 'rightly informed of all the circumstances on which a judgment ought to be formed,' and adding: 'I think it of the highest moment to humanity that your Excellency should be perfectly apprised of the state of this matter before you proceed to put that judgment in execution:' and he sent Lieut.-General Robertson, Lieut.-General Andrew Elliot, and the Hon. Wm. Smith, Chief Justice, 'to give Washington a true state of the facts,' as he wrote, and "to declare to you my sentiments and resolutions."

These gentlemen came up, accompanied by Col. Beverly Robinson. General Greene, on the part of Washington, met Gen. Robertson on behalf of this party, and a long conference was held. Greene left to report to Washington all that had been urged in behalf of André, and said he would inform Robertson of the result. A letter from Arnold was also delivered to Greene for Washington, expressing his gratitude and thanks for kindness to Mrs. Arnold in her distress, and then making an argument attempting to prove that André ought not to be considered as a spy; and he closed by making a most earnest appeal to Washington for the life of André. "Suffer me to entreat your excellency for your own and the honor of humanity, and the love you have of justice, that you suffer not an unjust sentence to touch the life of Major André." "But," he unwisely added, "if this warning should be disregarded, and he suffer, I call heaven and earth to witness, that your excellency will be justly answerable for the torrent of blood that may be spilt in consequence.[1]

Greene sent a note to General Robertson, informing him

[1] Writings of Washington, Vol. VII, p. 541.

that he had made as full a report of their conference as his memory would enable him to do, but that it made no alteration in the opinion and determination of Washington. Robertson then dispatched a letter to Washington, going over the subject and arguing it again, and then the party returned to New York.

André, on the morning of October the first, the day he expected to suffer, sent the following note to Washington:

"TAPPAN, 1 October, 1780.

"SIR:— Buoyed above the terror of death by the consciousness of a life devoted to honorable pursuits, and stained with no action that can give me remorse, I trust that the request I make to your Excellency at this serious period, and which is to soften my last moments, will not be rejected.

"Sympathy towards a soldier will surely induce your Excellency and a military tribunal to adapt the mode of my death to the feelings of a man of honor.

"Let me hope, Sir, that if aught in my character impresses you with esteem towards me; if aught in my misfortunes marks me as the victim of policy and not of resentment, I shall experience the operation of those feelings in your breast, by being informed that I am not to die on a gibbet.

"I have the honor to be your Excellency's most obedient and most humble servant,[1] JOHN ANDRE."

This touching request Washington felt that he could not grant, and therefore did not reply to the note. The following letter, from Hamilton to Miss Schuyler, narrates the end of this most melancholy tragedy.[2]

"TAPPAN, Oct. 2, 1780.

"Poor Andre suffers to-day. Everything that is amiable in virtue, in fortitude, in delicate sentiment and accomplished manners, pleads for him, but hard-hearted policy calls for a sacrifice. He must die. I send you my account of Arnold's affair: and to justify myself to your sentiments, I must inform you that I urged a compliance with Andre's request to be shot; and I do not think it would have had an ill-effect, but some people are only sensible to motives of policy, and sometimes, from a narrow disposition, mistake it.

1. Writings of Washington, Vol. VII, p. 543.
2. Hamilton's Papers, Vol. I, p. 408.

"When Andre's tale comes to be told, and present resentment is over, the refusing him the privilege of choosing the manner of his death will be branded with too much obstinacy.

"It was proposed to me to suggest to him the idea of an exchange for Arnold, but I knew I should have forfeited his esteem by doing it, and therefore declined it. As a man of honor, he could not but reject it, and I would not for the world have proposed to him a thing which must have placed me in the unamiable light of supposing him capable of meanness, or of not feeling myself the impropriety of the measure. I confess to you, I had the weakness to value the esteem of a dying man, because I reverenced his merit.   A. HAMILTON."

There are indications that neither Arnold nor André, nor Sir Henry Clinton, at first fully realized the danger of André's position. All of them seemed to have assumed that Arnold's safe conduct would protect him. Colonel Robinson, Washington's old Virginia friend, in a letter to him, after stating that André went up the Hudson at request of Arnold, with a flag of truce, and held that officer's pass to return, seems to have taken it for granted that André would be set at liberty, for he closes by saying: "Under these circumstances, André cannot be detained by you." [1] Clinton concludes his first letter to Washington on the subject by saying: "I can have no doubt your Excellency will immediately direct that this officer have permission to return." [2]

André's conversation with Colonel Tallmadge, before quoted, seems to have been the first occasion on which there was brought to his knowledge the gravity of his danger.

When Arnold was made to appreciate André's extreme peril, his anxiety and deep solicitude are manifested in his impassioned letter to Washington above quoted, in which he implored and "entreated" his old commander not to "suffer an unjust sentence to touch the life of André."

[1] Writings of Washington, Vol. VII, p. 533.
[2] Writings of Washington, Vol. VII, p. 534.

It was proposed to Hamilton that he should suggest to André his exchange for Arnold. That chivalric young officer at once declined. He says:

"As a man of honor he (Andre) could not but reject the proposition. And I would not for the world have proposed anything which must have placed me in the unamiable light of supposing him capable of meanness."[1]

An intimation was sent to Sir Henry Clinton, that the only way to save André was to surrender Arnold to die in his place, and this fact was brought to the knowledge of General Arnold.

It has been stated, on authority which I will give, that Arnold thereupon proposed to go back and give himself up to save the life of André. The facts are thus stated in Sargent's life of André.[2]

In 1782 a personal controversy in regard to Arnold arose in London, between one Robert Morris and Capt. James Battersby, of the British army. Morris published in a newspaper[3] a violent attack upon Arnold, charging among other things, "that he made no offer of his own person to save that of André."

Captain Battersby, who (Sargent says) "enjoyed the friendship of military men of the highest social rank, came forward declaring he verily believed Arnold did offer to surrender himself, and with the statement,[4] for the truth of which he appealed to the gentlemen who were, in the fall of 1780, members of Clinton's family." "He declared he was with the English army when André was captured and Arnold came in, and that it was currently reported and believed in the lines, that Arnold himself proposed to Sir

---

1. Life of Andre, p. 364.
2. Life of Andre, pp. 375, 456.
3. Letter of Feb'y 9, 1782, in the "General Advertiser," quoted from Sargent's Life of Andre. p. 456.
4. In the *Morning Herald*.

Henry that he might be permitted to go out and surrender himself in exchange for André, and that the reply was, 'Your proposal, sir, does you great honor, but if André was my own brother I could not agree to it." [1]

No denial of the truth of this statement and that Arnold made such an offer appears, although the appeal was publicly made to the gentlemen of Clinton's staff to make such denial if it was untrue. When it is remembered how André was beloved by his comrades in the family of Clinton and by his fellow soldiers of the army, and the position of Arnold is recalled, it appears to me that if the statement of Captain Battersby was untrue, it would have been promptly contradicted. Sargent adds that "the anecdote is not devoid of support from what we know of the man's (Arnold's) nature."

No one who has read Sargent's indignant denunciation of Arnold, will suspect him of any disposition to lighten the shades of Arnold's infamy, and yet this careful writer says, " Such an overture would have been perfectly in keeping with his reckless intrepidity of character." [2] The biographer of André would not be too credulous in believing on insufficient evidence such a statement.

I regret that I have no additional proof of its truth. I think those who have studied Arnold's character most closely, will agree with Sargent, that such an act "would have been perfectly in keeping with the intrepidity," and I add, the impulsiveness "of his nature." Besides what was there now left for Arnold to live for after his disgrace and the failure of the conspiracy? That he realized his unhappy fate, I do not doubt. Such a sensational death, a voluntary sacrifice of his life to save the life of André, exhibiting alike his courage and his generosity, would not, in his despair, have been altogether repulsive. It would unquestion-

1. Life of Andre, p. 375.
2. Life of Andre, p. 375.

ably have been better for his fame if Sir Henry Clinton had assented to his offer.

If the suggestion proposed to Hamilton had been made to André, there cannot be a doubt he would have looked upon it as Hamilton did; he would have rejected it with indignation. He would have said, "We took our chances and our hazards. General Arnold, by good fortune and by his wonderful coolness and prompt decision, escaped. I have been less fortunate, but it would be unmanly in me not to abide the issue." There can scarcely be a doubt that if André, when halted by the militia men, had promptly presented his pass, he would not have been detained. Paulding, the leader of the party, said: "Had he pulled out General Arnold's pass first, I should have let him go." [1]

André was an elegant and accomplished gentleman, and died possessing the sympathy of his judges, and the friendship of all the American officers with whom he had been brought into familiar intercourse. Both Tallmadge and Hamilton expressed for him an attachment almost passionate. He died in the full uniform of his rank in the British army.

A letter from André to Sir Henry Clinton, dated the 29th of September, expressing gratitude for his kindness, and commending to his consideration his mother and sisters, and exonerating his Commander from all responsibility for his fate, is very touching, and shows the delicacy of his feelings.[2] The following is the letter:

"TAPPAN, 29 September, 1780.

"SIR: — Your Excellency is doubtless already apprized of the manner in which I was taken, and possibly of the serious light in which my conduct is considered, and the rigorous determination that is impending. Under the circumstances, I have obtained General Washington's permission to send you this letter, the object of which is to remove from

[1] Life of André, p. 314.
[2] Sparks' Writings of Washington, Vol. VII, p. 537.

your breast any suspicion that I could imagine I was bound by your Excellency's orders to expose myself to what has happened. The events of coming within an enemy's posts and of changing my dress, which led me to my present situation, were contrary to my own intentions, as they were to your orders; and the circuitous route which I took to return was imposed (perhaps unavoidably) without alternative upon me.

"I am perfectly tranquil in mind, and prepared for any fate to which an honest zeal for my King's service may have devoted me.

"In addressing myself to your Excellency, on this occasion, the force of all my obligations to you, and of the attachment and gratitude I bear you, recurs to me. With all the warmth of my heart, I give you thanks for your Excellency's profuse kindness to me; and I send you the most earnest wishes for your welfare, which a faithful, affectionate, and respectful attendant can frame.

"I have a mother and three sisters, to whom the value of my commission would be an object, as the loss of Grenada has much affected their income. It is needless to be more explicit on this subject. I am persuaded of your Excellency's goodness.

"I receive the greatest attention from his Excellency, General Washington, and from every person under whose charge I happen to be placed.

"I have the honor to be, with the most respectful attachment, your Excellency's most obedient, humble servant, JOHN ANDRE,

"*Adjutant-General.*"

The circumstances under which this letter was written, are thus detailed by Hamilton:

"In one of the visits I made to him," said Hamilton "(and I saw him several times during his confinement), he begged me to be the bearer of a request to the General for permission to send an open letter to Sir Henry Clinton. 'There is only one thing,' said he, 'that disturbs my tranquility. Sir Henry Clinton has been too good to me; he has been lavish of his kindness; I am bound to him by too many obligations, and love him too well, to bear the thought that he should reproach himself or others should reproach him, on the supposition of my having conceived myself obliged, by his instructions, to run the risk I did. I would not, for the world, leave a sting in his mind that should embitter his future days.' He could scarce finish the sentence, bursting into tears in spite of his efforts to suppress them, and with difficulty collected himself enough afterward to add, 'I wish to be permitted to assure him I did not act under this impression, but submitted to a necessity imposed upon me, as contrary to my own inclination as to his orders.'"

On the 10th of August, 1821, the remains of André were removed from the banks of the Hudson to Westminster Abbey, and interred there, near the monument which had been long before erected to his memory.

In the south aisle, near the window, and surrounded by the greatest names in English history, is André's monument:[1]

"Sacred to the memory of Major John André, who, raised by his merits at an early period of life, to the rank of Adjutant-General of the British forces in America, and, employed in an important but hazardous enterprise, fell a sacrifice to his zeal for his King and Country, on the 2nd of October, 1780, aged twenty-nine, universally beloved and esteemed by the army in which he served, and lamented even by his foes. His gracious sovereign, King George III, has caused this monument to be erected."

On the plinth these words have since been added : "The remains of Major John André were, on the 10th of August, 1821, removed from Tappan by James Buchanan, Esq., his Majesty's Consul, at New York, under instructions from his Royal Highness, the Duke of York, and with permission of the Dean and Chapter, finally deposited in a grave contiguous to this monument, on the 28th of November, 1821."

Although few can regard with approval the enterprise in which André lost his life, none will regret the honors conferred upon him in the venerable old Abbey which enshrines so many of England's worthies.

[1] Sargent's Life of Andre, p. 411.

CHAPTER XVII.

MRS. ARNOLD'S INNOCENCE—WAS ANDRE A SPY?

"She" (Mrs. Arnold) "is as good and as innocent as an angel, and is incapable of doing wrong.—*Arnold to Washington.*

WAS MRS. ARNOLD GUILTY OF COMPLICITY WITH HER HUSBAND'S TREASON?—WAS ANDRE A SPY, AND EXECUTED IN ACCORDANCE WITH THE LAWS OF WAR?

WHEN the attention of the reader was last called to Mrs. Arnold, she "was overwhelmed with grief," and made frantic by fear and apprehension for her husband's life. She was somewhat relieved by Washington's assurance of his escape and safety.

General Arnold had entreated that she might "be permitted to return to her friends in Philadelphia, or come to him in New York, as she might choose." She was treated by Washington and his officers, while she remained at the Robinson House, with the utmost courtesy and attention, and when she started to go to her father in Philadelphia, Major Franks, late the aide and devoted friend of her husband, and who had been intimate with her family, was kindly detailed by Washington to escort her on her journey.

Aaron Burr, the third Vice-President of the United States, in the biography of Burr, by Mathew L. Davis, is made to allege that Mrs. Arnold was not only privy to her husband's treachery, but that she "induced him to do what he had done." In other words, like Eve, she had tempted and allured him to his fall.

This charge, made by Burr to Davis, rests upon his statement alone, and is entirely without corroboration. After describing the arrival of Mrs. Arnold at the house of Mrs. Provost, on her journey to Philadelphia, Mr. Davis says:

"As soon as they (Mrs. Arnold and Mrs. Provost) were left alone, Mrs. Arnold became tranquilized, and assured Mrs. Provost that she was heartily tired of the theatricals she was exhibiting. * * Stated that she had corresponded with the British commander, and that she was disgusted with the American cause, and those who had the management of public affairs, and that through great persuasion and unceasing perseverance, she had ultimately brought the General into an arrangement to surrender West Point." Mrs. Provost afterwards became the wife of Col. Burr, and repeated to him, as Davis states, these confessions of Mrs. Arnold.[1] Col. Burr and Mrs. Provost were married in July, 1782.

The case, then, is this: Mr. Davis says that Colonel Burr told him that Mrs. Provost said that Mrs. Arnold declared she had seduced General Arnold from fidelity to his country and his flag.

Some time after their marriage—how long we are not told—Mrs. Burr repeated the conversation to her husband, and Burr, some time within the half-century following, repeated the conversation to Davis. It is hearsay evidence, three times removed, and repeated with years of interval between the repetitions. As such, it is worthless, independent of the notorious character of Burr.

Mrs. Provost may have misunderstood Mrs. Arnold; when detailing the conversation to Colonel Burr she may have given her own impressions, instead of the facts. Burr may

[1] Life of Burr, by Mathew L. Davis, Vol. I, page, 219.

have done the same when repeating it to Davis. Every one at all familiar with judicial investigations, knows by experience how utterly unreliable this sort of evidence is. Parton, in re-stating the story, does not claim to have any additional evidence, but repeats the tale of Davis with embellishments.

This story is extremely improbable. Her youth, being then only twenty years of age, renders such complicity very unlikely. Arnold himself entirely exonerates her. "The mistaken vengeance of my countrymen," says he, in his letter to Washington, "ought to fall only on me. She is as good and innocent as an angel." This testimony must be taken cautiously, for whatever it is worth. But it seems rather the passionate and impulsive declaration of her innocence than an artful attempt to screen her. Besides, Hamilton and Washington both believed her innocent, and their opportunities for judging were better than those of any others, except Major Franks. The following is his very important, and, under the circumstances, conclusive testimony on the subject:

"Major Franks, of the Revolutionary army, was a well-known acquaintance of my parents," says Mrs. Gibson.[1] "He was respected and welcomed wherever he went, for his social good humor and manly candor. In one of his visits to Philadelphia, where his near relations resided, he was often at my father's, and one day, when dining with other gentlemen at our home, and my father and the others had retired to the parlor, my mother detained Major Franks to converse with him respecting Mrs. Arnold, whom she had recently heard very unjustly spoken of. He entered upon the subject with alacrity. Mamma said to him: 'Tell me, Major Franks, what is your opinion and belief concerning her knowledge of her husband's plans.' He quickly replied: 'Madam, she knew nothing of them—nothing; she was ignorant of them as a babe.' His manner was solemn and earnest, and I began to think it might be proper for me to withdraw, but he said, 'don't let Betsy go—I have nothing to say that she may not hear.' Of course I

[1] The statement is made by Mrs. James Gibson, daughter of Jno. Beal Bordly, Washington's correspondent, and is extracted from the Shippen Papers.

gladly resumed my seat at table, and he went on:—'Madam, I am glad you have mentioned this subject. I have much to say. I am much distressed by it. Within a few days I have heard for the first time things said of her that are contrary to truth—false! utterly false! You know I was one of General Arnold's aides. He paid me the compliment to assign me the particular duty of protecting Mrs. Arnold; of attending to her safety, her general welfare, and her health. I was, in the General's family, laughingly called 'the nurse!' Her health was then delicate, and while Gen. Arnold was in command at West Point he frequently sent her to different, and sometimes distant parts of the country, on that side of the river. He always sent a guard with her, besides her female attendant, and gave me very particular charge over her welfare. He spoke of her suffering in the bustle of the camp, and wished her to be relieved from it during the summer. I obeyed, nothing doubting, but considering him a pattern for a husband. * * But, madam, she knew nothing of his projects. In truth, she was subject to occasional paroxysms of physical indisposition, attended by nervous debility, during which she would give utterance to anything and everything on her mind. This was a fact well known amongst us of the General's family; so much so as to cause us to be scrupulous of what we told her, or said in her hearing. General Arnold was guarded and impenetrable towards all around him, and I should believe her to have been ignorant of his plans, even without my knowledge of this peculiar feature in her constitution; but *with it*, such a strong corroborative proof, I am most solemnly and firmly convinced that General Arnold never confided his detestable scheme to her. *He could not have ventured to do it.* He was, moreover, too well aware of her *warm patriotic feelings. You know, Madam, how completely she was American at that important period.* Madam, I can aver solemnly *she was totally ignorant of his schemes.*'"

The following facts are vouched for as known in the Shippen family at the time of the Revolution; they have been often privately repeated, but never mentioned beyond its most intimate circle, till the publication of what they style the base calumny contained in the memoirs of Aaron Burr:

"Mrs. Arnold having determined to go to her father, in Philadelphia, set out with her young child and nurse in her carriage, to travel there by easy stages. On her way she stopped to spend the night at Mrs. Provost's, an old acquaintance, and afterwards the wife of Col. Burr, and at that time on terms of tender friendship, if not indeed engaged to him.

"These facts are told by Burr's biographer, who no doubt, follows Burr's narrative accurately, but he omits the fact that Burr himself met Mrs. Arnold at Mrs. Provosts, and when she left the house in the morning, offered his escort, which he pretended might be useful to her in the then excited state of the public mind on the subject of her husband's treason. Still less does he disclose what his friends would not have ventured to repeat, that on the way he basely made love to this afflicted lady, thinking to take advantage of her just feelings of indignation towards her husband and her helpless condition, to help him in his infamous design. Yet this is the fact if the family tradition is true. And being indignantly repelled, he treasured up his revenge, and left a story behind him worthy of his false and malignant heart, to blast this amiable lady's fame, when there might be no one to disprove or deny it.[1]"

Besides, the conduct of Mrs. Arnold, on the discovery of her husband's treason, is utterly inconsistent with guilt. That a young woman of her years, still almost a child, should have been capable of imposing upon Washington and his aids, is incredible. If guilty, when Arnold announced to her his flight, all papers indicating guilt would have been destroyed; and when Washington gave her permission to join her husband in New York, or go to her father in Philadelphia, if conscious of guilt, what would she have done? Guilt is ever fearful; it flies when none pursue. If guilty, her punishment would have been death. In the intense excitement then existing, neither her youth and beauty, nor all her domestic virtues, could have saved her from the fury of her enraged country. If conscious of guilt, she would have seized the opportunity to have found safety by the side of her husband, whom "she dearly loved," within the British lines, in New York. Instead of this, she fearlessly goes to Philadelphia, where Congress was in session, and where an outraged people were clamoring for a victim! Nothing but a consciousness of innocence could have induced her to remain within the power of the American government, when Washington offered her an

[1] Shippen Papers.

HIS PATRIOTISM AND HIS TREASON. 321

escort to her husband and a place of safety. It is incredible, if she were guilty, that she would have voluntarily confronted Congress at a moment of such exasperation, and when the people were eager for a victim. No one who reads her letters contained in this volume, will believe her capable of acting the double part with which she has been charged. On the contrary, if Arnold had disclosed his plans to her, she would have been much more likely, prompted alike by her love and her clear perception of right, to have tried to save him from the commission of a fearful crime and a terrible blunder.

Whatever might have been Mrs. Arnold's final decision, as to whether she should remain with her father and friends in Philadelphia, or join her husband in New York, the choice was not left her by the Council of Pennsylvania. On the 29th of October the Council of that State adopted a resolution compelling her to leave the State, and forbidding her return during the war.[1]

Mrs. Arnold followed her husband to New York, and shared his fate in evil, as in good report. Her letters to her father's family, full of respect and tenderness, bear abundant testimony that whatever may have been her husband's faults, he was ever a most devoted, faithful and affectionate husband. In a letter to her father, dated July 13th, 1785, she says: "General Arnold's affection for me is unbounded;" and in another, she says, "he is the best of hus-

---

1. The following is a copy, from the minutes in Council:

PHILADELPHIA, Friday, Oct. 27, 1780.

"The Counsel, taking into consideration the case of Mrs. Margaret Arnold (the wife of Benedict Arnold, an attainted traitor, with the enemy at New York), whose residence in this city has become dangerous to the public safety; and this board being desirous, as much as possible, to prevent any correspondence and intercourse being carried on with persons of disaffected character in this State and the enemy at New York, and especially with the said Benedict Arnold, therefore, Resolved, That the said Margaret Arnold depart this State within fourteen days from the date hereof, and that she do not return again during the continuance of the present war."

bands;" and all her letters indicate that there never existed a family more kind and affectionate, tender and unselfish towards each other.

The sad tragedy of André, the romance of his life, and early death, the treason of Arnold, closing in disgrace a brilliant military career, and Mrs. Arnold's great beauty and fascination, have all contributed to make the events I have been describing among the most interesting in American history.

Washington's action in ordering the execution of Andre, was, in the excited feelings of that day, severely criticised and unqualifiedly denounced by the English, but his conduct has since been sanctioned by the deliberate judgment of the candid and enlightened world. An exception to this judgment is found in Lord Mahon's history of England,[1] in which he says :

"Unless I greatly deceive myself, the intelligent classes of his (Washton's) countrymen, will ere long join others in condemning the death-warrant of Andre, certainly by far the greatest, perhaps the only, blot in his noble career."

This declaration by an English historian so distinguished, re-opened the question of André's execution, and of Washington's conduct, and brought again before the world the question, "Was André a spy, and was his death in accordance with the laws of war, as practiced and settled by the civilized nations of the earth?"

There has never been any serious dispute about the facts of the case.

André, at the instance of Arnold, came ashore and went within the American lines, to further a treacherous conspiracy between the commander at West Point and Sir Henry Clinton, for the surrender of that post to the British army. He came at midnight, under an assumed name,

1. Vol. VII. London, 1854.

met Arnold in secret, and finding the objects of the interview could not be concluded without longer time, went to the house of Smith, and there concluded the corrupt agreement, received from Arnold the papers which it was supposed would enable Clinton to take the post, and concealed these papers in his boots. While André was concealed at Smith's, an American officer, bringing his guns to bear upon the Vulture, which had brought André ashore, compelled her to move down the river, and rendered it difficult and dangerous for him to go back to her, and compelled him to return to New York with his concealed papers by land. Disguised in clothes loaned him by Smith, with Smith as a guide, and with Arnold's pass or safe conduct, under an assumed name, in his pocket, he crossed the river and proceeded towards New York, the pass of Arnold proving his sufficient protection until he arrived at a place called Crompond, where he and his guide stayed all night. At daylight André again started, accompanied by Smith. and they passed on beyond the American lines into what was called the "Neutral Ground," between the two armies. Smith them left him, and it was supposed all danger was passed, when, as has been before described, André was arrested, searched, the secret and treasonable papers found upon him, and Paulding, one of his captors, exclaimed: "My God, he is a spy!"

Was this true?

Washington convened a court, consisting of all the general officers in the neighborhood, to investigate the case, report the facts, and in what light André should be considered, and the punishment that ought to be inflicted. The board reported the facts, their conclusion, that "he ought to be considered a spy from the enemy, and that agreeably to the law and usage of nations, it is their opinion he ought to suffer death."

Washington considered the question carefully, heard everything which Arnold, Clinton, Robinson, and indeed every one else, could offer in his behalf, but his judgment concurring in the report of the court, he reluctantly but firmly ordered his execution. Was this decision legal?

What is a spy? Vattel's definition is: "Spies are those who introduce themselves among the enemy to discover the condition of his affairs, penetrate his designs, and communicate them to his employers."

Professor Martin's summary of the Law of Nations, a work commended by Chancellor Kent, gives this definition: "Those who, under a false name and disguised character, enter the camp of the enemy to serve as spies, and to empoison, assassinate or *corrupt*, are punished with death;" and in the foot-note is added, "See the instance of Major André."[1]

This principle has been adopted by the British Parliament in legislation. That body in 1749 enacted "that all spies, and persons whatsoever who shall come, or be found in the nature of spies, to bring any seducing letter, or message from any enemy or rebel, or endeavor to *corrupt* any captain, *officer* or mariner * * to betray his trust, on being convicted by a court-martial, shall suffer death, &c."[2] "Those seeking to surprise a town, and if they were in disguise, or had employed treachery, would be treated as spies."[3]

But Lord Mahon attempts to shield André from responsibility, and argues that he ought not to have suffered the penalty of a detected spy because he bore the pass of General Arnold.

Should the pass of Arnold, a co-conspirator, protect André?

What was the extent of the power of the commander of

[1]. The case of Major Andre, by Charles J. Biddle.
[2]. The case of Major Andre, by Charles J Biddle.
[3]. Vattel. Note to page 373—quoting Grotius' History of the disturbance in the Netherlands.

West Point! He could bind the authorities of the United States only when acting in good faith, and within the scope of the authority conferred upon him. When he went outside of that, his acts were a legal nullity, especially when acting in collusion with one who knew that he was violating his trust, and who had fraudulently conspired with him to betray his principal.

The idea that a conspirator's pass will protect a co-conspirator, is a position which is scarcely debatable. An officer, when acting clearly beyond the scope of his authority, does not bind his principal any more than an ordinary agent. When an officer acts in collusion with the enemy, to betray his trust, the act has no color of validity, legal or moral, as against the principal who is to be injured.

"The treacherous betrayal of his trust was beyond the scope of Arnold's authority; it was known to be so by André, and a pass or agreement in furtherance of the conspiracy, would be absolutely void."

The pass was given to André, to enable him to carry to his commander, Sir Henry Clinton, papers and intelligence which it was supposed would enable that officer to capture West Point. That such a paper should be set up as a protection, is as absurd as it would have been for Clinton to have called upon General Washington to surrender West Point, because Arnold, while in command, had agreed to surrender it!

Again, the pass was a sham on the face of it. It was given to *John Anderson*, not to Major André. It is perfectly well settled that a pass is not transferable, and a pass to a man under a false or fictitious name, is void. "The person named in the *safe conduct* cannot transfer his privilege to another."[1]

Washington expresses with accuracy the condition of

1. Vattel, p. 414.

André, with reference to the flag of truce, in his letter to Clinton. "It is evident that André was employed in the execution of measures very foreign to the objects of a flag of truce, and such as they were never meant to authorize or countenance in the most remote degree; and this gentleman confessed, with the greatest candor, in the course of his examination, "that it was impossible for him to suppose he came under the sanction of a flag." Perhaps it may seem harsh in this connection to say, a detected impostor has never been and should never be permitted to claim the immunities of the sacred emblem he has abused. To use a flag of truce under which to concert treachery and treason, is certainly as great an abuse of that emblem of faith as can be conceived. The sacred character of such flag—sacred and respected among all nations—makes its prostitution and abuse the more criminal. He who so abuses it can hardly expect, nor did André claim, when detected, its immunity against punishment.

The opinion of Romilly, afterwards the great English jurist and law-reformer, shows the fallacy of those who sought to save André from responsibility as a spy. He says:

"What do you think of Arnold's conduct? You may well suppose he does not want advocates here. I cannot join with them. The arguments used by Clinton and Arnold, in their letters to Washington, to prove that Andre could not be considered a spy, are: First, that he had with him, when he was taken, a protection of Arnold's, who was at that time acting under a commission of the Congress, and therefore competent to give protection. Certainly, he was, to all strangers to his negotiations with Clinton, but not to Andre, who knew him to be at that time a traitor to the Congress; nay more, whose protection was granted for no other purpose but to promote and give effect to his treachery. In the second place, they say that at the time he was taken he was upon neutral ground; but then they do not deny that he had been within the American lines in disguise. . . . Panegyrics on the gallant Andre are unbounded; they call him the English Mutius, and talk of erecting monuments to his memory. Certainly no man in his situation could have acted with more determined courage, but his situation was by no means such as to admit of these exaggerated praises."[1]

But, conceding André's guilt, and that by the laws of war, he was liable to suffer death, might not Washington have spared his life without prejudice to the cause of his country?

In answering this question, we must remember that the United States were then struggling for existence and recognition as an independent nation, and that the result was yet in doubt. To take human life for a violation of law is an act of the highest sovereignty. Here was a conspicuous case: the Adjutant-General of the British army, caught and condemned as a spy, with unmistakeable evidence of his guilt upon his person. The drama was being enacted in the face of the British, American and French armies, and with all the world as observers. Had there been hesitation or vacillation, or failure on the part of Washington to exercise in this clear case the high act of sovereignty, it would have been attributed to a want of confidence in the success of his cause; and it would have been ascribed to weakness, perhaps to cowardice.

Lookers on might have said: "Washington fears the result of the war; he himself may be tried as a rebel, and he dare not execute André because he fears that, in the event of failure, it might add to his own personal danger! It was therefore necessary that André should die. It was felt by Washington to be necessary to show the world that "no greater impunity would attend the acts of him who, as a spy, sought the destruction of this young republic, than would have attended the act if committed against

[1] Contributions to Am. Hist., Pa. Hist. Society, 1858, p. 386, quoted from Life of Sir Samuel Romilly, Vol. I, 104.

For a full, able, and exhaustive discussion of this question, see "The Case of Major Andre," by Charles J. Biddle, in Publications of Pa. Hist. Society, 1858.

the oldest and strongest government in the world." [1] This act of national sovereignty was executed with a dignity, a humanity, yet with an inflexible firmness, that showed how strong was the hand of Washington at the helm.

[1] The British had then lately hung as a spy a young American, Captain Nathan Hale, an officer as accomplished and engaging as Andre. Should the Royal army exercise exclusively the right of executing spies? Would it not be just and expedient for Washington to follow the example of the enemy?

CHAPTER XVIII.

ARNOLD VAINLY ATTEMPTS TO JUSTIFY HIS TREASON.

"I fought for much less than Great Britain is willing to grant."—*Arnold the Traitor.*[1]

ARNOLD IN NEW YORK CITY—HIS ADDRESS TO THE AMERICAN PEOPLE—HIS PROCLAMATION TO THE OFFICERS AND SOLDIERS OF THE AMERICAN ARMY—ATTEMPT TO KIDNAP HIM—HIS WIFE JOINS HIM IN NEW YORK.

NOTWITHSTANDING the discovery and consequent utter failure of the conspiracy between General Arnold and Sir Henry Clinton, by the arrest of André, Arnold, always sanguine in every enterprise he undertook, still entertained hopes of the final success of the Royal cause, and felt confident that he could contribute largely to that success.

He lost no time in preparing and issuing an address "To the Inhabitants of America," in which he undertook to explain and justify his conduct. This address, the original of which, in the handwriting of General Arnold, furnished by his grandson,[2] is now before me, and I insert it here in full, on the principle that all persons, not excepting the worst criminals, are entitled to be heard in their own defense before sentence is passed upon them:

---

1. "The American colonies shall have their Parliament, composed of two chambers, all its members of American birth. Those of the Upper House, with titles, similar to the House of Peers. All their laws, and particularly such as relate to money matters, shall be the production of this Assembly, with the concurrence of a Viceroy."—*The Letter to Arnold attributed to Robinson.*

2. Rev. Edward Gladwin Arnold. I find no printed copy of this paper entirely accurate.

"To the Inhabitants of America.

"I should forfeit even in my own Opinion, the place I have so long held in yours, if I could be indifferent to your Approbation, and silent on the Motives which have induced me to join the King's Arms.

"A very few words, however, shall suffice upon a Subject so personal, for to the thousands who suffer under the tyranny of the Usurpers in the revolted Provinces, as well as to the great multitude who have long wished for its Subversion, this instance of my Conduct can want no Vindication, as to that class of Men who are Criminally protracting the War from Sinister Views, at the expense of the Public Interest, I prefer their Enmity to their applause. I am only, therefore, Concerned in this address to explain myself to such of my Countrymen as want Abilities or Opportunities to detect the Artifices by which they are duped.

"Having fought by your side when the love of our Country animated our Arms, I shall expect from your Justice and Candor, what your deceivers, with more Art and less honesty, will find it inconsistent with their own Views to admit.

"When I quitted Domestick happiness for the Perils of the Field, I conceived the rights of my Country in Danger, and that Duty and Honor called me to her Defence—a Redress of Grievances was my only Object and aim; however, I acquiesced in a step which I thought precipitate the Declaration of Independence; to Justify the measure many plausible reasons were urged, which could no longer exist, when Great Britain with the open arms of a Parent offered to embrace us as Children, and grant the wished for redress.

"And now that her worst Enemies are in her own bosom, I should change my Principles, If I conspired with their Designs. Yourselves being Judges, was the war the less Just, because Fellow Subjects were considered as our Foes? You have felt the torture in which we raised our arms against a Brother—God Incline the Guilty protractors of these unnatural Dissentions, to resign their Ambition, and Cease from their Delusions, in Compassion to kindred blood.

"I anticipate your question: was not the War a defensive one until the French Joined in the Combination? I answer, that I thought so. You will add, was it not afterwards necessary till the Separation of the British Empire was compleat? By no means; in Contending for the Welfare of my Country, I am free to declare my Opinion, that this End attained, all strife should have ceased.

"I lamented therefore the Impolicy, tyranny, and Injustice, which with a Sovereign Contempt of the People of America, studiously neglected to take their Collective Sentiments of the British proposals of Peace, and to negotiate under a suspension of Arms, for an adjustment of differences, as a dangerous Sacrifice of the great Interest of this Country to the Partial Views of a Proud, Antient, and Crafty Foe. I had my suspicions of some imperfections in Our Councils, on Proposals prior to the Parliamentary Commission of 1778; but having then less to do in the Cabinet than the Field (I will not pronounce peremptorily as some may, and perhaps Justly, that Congress have veiled them from the Publick Eye), I continued to be guided in the negligent Confidence of a soldier. But the whole world saw, and all America confessed, the Overtures of the Second Commission exceeded our wishes and expectations. If there was any Suspicion of the National liberality, it arose from its excess.

"Do any believe we were at that time really entangled by an Alliance with France? Unfortunate deception! and thus they have been duped by a virtuous Credulity, in the incautious moments of intemperate passion, to give up their fidelity to serve a Nation counting both the will and the power to protect us, and aiming at the Destruction both of the Mother Country and the Provinces. In the Plainess of Common Sense, for I pretend to no Casuistry, did the pretended Treaty with the Court of Versailles amount to more than an Overture to America? Certainly not, because no Authority had been given by the People to conclude it, nor to this very hour have they authorized its ratification—the Articles of Confederation remain still unsigned.

"In the firm persuasion, therefore, that the private Judgment of any Individual Citizen of this Country is as free from all Conventional Restraints since, as before the Insidious offers of France, I preferred those from Great Britain, thinking it infinitely wiser and safer to cast my Confidence upon her Justice and Generosity, than to trust a Monarchy too feeble to establish your Independency, so Perilous to her distant Dominions, the Enemy of the Protestant Faith, and fraudulently avowing an affection for the liberties of mankind, while she holds her Native Sons in Vassalage and Chains.

"I affect no disguise, and therefore Frankly declare that in these Principles, I had determined to retain my arms and Command for an opportunity to surrender them to Great Britain, and in concerting the Measures for a purpose, in my Opinion, as grateful as it would have been beneficial to my Country; I was only solicitous to accomplish an event of decisive Importance, and to prevent, as much as possible in the Execution of it, the Effusion of blood.

"With the highest satisfaction I bear testimony to my old Fellow Soldiers and Citizens, that I find solid Ground to rely upon the Clemency of our Sovereign, and abundant Conviction that it is the generous Intention of Great Britain, not only to have the Rights and privileges of the Colonies unimpaired, together with their perpetual exemption from taxation, but to superadd such further benefits as may consist with the Common prosperity of the Empire. In short, I fought for much less than the Parent Country is as willing to grant to her Colonies, as they can be to receive or enjoy.

"Some may think I continued in the struggle of those unhappy days too long, and others that I quitted it too soon. To the first I reply, that I did not see with their Eyes, nor perhaps had so favorable a situation to look from, and that to one Common Master I am willing to stand or fall. In behalf of the Candid among the latter, some of whom I believe serve blindly but honestly in the Ranks I have left, I pray God to give them all the lights requisite to their Own Safety before it is too late; and with respect to that kind of Censurers whose Enmity to me Originates in their hatred to the Principles, by which I am now led to devote my life to the Reunion of the British Empire, as the best and only means to dry up the streams of misery that have deluged this country, they may be assured that, Conscious of the Rectitude of my Intentions, I shall treat their Malice and Calumnies with Contempt and neglect.

"B. ARNOLD.

"NEW YORK, Oct. 7th, 1780."

A few days thereafter he issued a proclamation "To the officers and soldiers of the Continental Army who have the real interests of their Country at heart and who are determined to be no longer the dupes of Congress or of France."[1]

---

[1] The following is the Proclamation in full, copied from the original draft among the *Force papers*, in the Congressional Library at Washington:

"BY
"BRIGADIER GENERAL ARNOLD.
"A PROCLAMATION.

"To the Officers and Soldiers of the Continental Army who have the real Interest of their Country at Heart, and who are determined to be no longer the Tools and Dupes of Congress, or of France.

"Having Reason to believe that the Principles I have avowed, in my Address to y° Public of the 7th instant, animated y° greatest part of this Continent, I rejoice in the Opportunity I have of inviting you to join his Majesty's Arms.

"His Excellency, Sir Henry Clinton, has authorized me to raise a Corps of Cavalry and Infantry, who are to be clothed, subsisted and paid as the other Corps are in the british Service, and those who bring in Horses, Arms, or Accoutrements, are to be paid their value, or have liberty to sell them. To every non-Commissioned Officer and Private a Bounty of three Guineas will be given, and as the Commander-in-Chief is pleased to allow me to nominate the officers, I shall with infinite Satisfaction embrace this Opportunity of advancing men whose valor I have witnessed, and whose Principles are favorable to an union with Britain and true American Liberty.

He announces to his former fellow-soldiers that Sir Henry Clinton had authorized him to raise a corps of cavalry and infantry, and he then goes on to state the inducements offered to those who will join him. He says:

"As the Commander-in-Chief is pleased to allow me to nominate the Officers, I shall with infinite satisfaction embrace this opportunity of advancing men whose valor I have witnessed, and whose principles are favorable to an union with Britain and true American liberty."

After alluding to the liberal pay and other inducements

"The Rank they obtain in the King's service will bear a Proportion to their former Rank and ye Number of Men they bring with them.

"It is expected that a Lieutenant-Colonel of Cavalry will bring with him or recruit in a reasonable time—"75 men. Major of Horse, 50 Men; Lieut. Col. of Infantry, 75 Men; Captain of Horse, 30 Men; Major of Infantry, 50 Men; Lieut. of Horse, 15 Men; Captain of Infantry, 30 Men; Cornet of Horse, 12 Men; Lieutenant of Infantry, 15 Men; Sergeant of Horse 6 Men; Ensign of Infantry, 12 Men; Sergeant of Infantry, 6 Men.

"N. B. Each Field Officer will have a Company. Great as this Encouragement must appear to such as have suffered every Distress, of Want, of Pain, Hunger and Nakedness, from the Neglect, Contempt and Corruption of Congress, they are nothing to the Motives which I expect will influence the brave and generous Minds I hope to have the Honor to command, and I wish to have a Chosen Band of Americans to ye Attainment of Peace, Liberty, and Safety (that first object in taking the Field) and with them to share in the glory of rescuing our native Country from the grasping Hand of France as well as from the ambitious and interested Views of a desperate Party among ourselves, who, in listening to French Overtures, and rejecting those from Great Britain, have brought ye Colonies to ye very Brink of Destruction.

"Friends, fellow Soldiers, and Citizens, arouse and judge for yourselves—reflect on what you have lost—consider to what you are reduced, and by your Courage repel the Ruin that still threatens you.

"Your Country once was happy, and had the proffered Peace been embraced, your last two years of Misery had been spent in Peace and Plenty, and repairing the Desolations of a Quarrel that would have set ye Interest of Great Britain and America in its true Light, and cemented their Friendship; whereas, you are now the Prey of Avarice, the scorn of your Enemies, and ye Pity of your Friends.

"You were promised Liberty by ye Leaders of your affairs, but is there an individual in ye Enjoyment of it, saving your Oppressors? Who among you dare speak or write what he thinks, against the Tyranny which has robbed you of your Property, imprisons your Persons, drags you to ye Field of Battle, and is daily deluging your Country with your Blood.

"You were flattered with Independence as preferable to a Redress of Grievances, and for that Shadow, instead of real Felicity, are sunk into all ye Wretchedness of Poverty by the Rapacity of your own Rulers. Already are you disqualified to support ye Pride of Character they taught you to aim at, and must inevitably shortly belong to one or other of the great Powers, their folly and wickedness have drawn offered "to such as have suffered every distress of want, pain, hunger and nakedness, from the neglect and corruption of Congress," he says, speaking of these considerations:

"They are nothing to the motives which I expect will influence the brave and generous minds I hope to have the honor to Command. I wish to have a chosen band of Americans to yͤ attainment of peace, liberty and safety, that first object in taking yͤ field, and with them to share in the glory of rescuing our native Country from the grasping hand of France, as well as from the ambitious and interested Views of a desperate party among ourselves, who in listening to French Overtures, and rejecting those from Great Britain, have brought yͤ Colonies to the very brink of destruction. I, therefore, only add my promise of the most affectionate welcome and attention to all who are disposed to join me, in the measures necessary to close the scene of our afflictions. With yͤ restoration of our ancient priviledges, civil and sacred, and a perpetual exemption from all taxes but such as we shall see fit to impose upon ourselves."

into Conflict. Happy for you that you may still become the fellow subjects of Great Britain, if you nobly disdain to be Vasals of France.

"What is America but a Land of Widows, Beggars, and Orphans?—and should the Parent Nation cease her Exertion to deliver you, what security remains to you for the enjoyment of yͤ Consolations of that Religion for which your Fathers braved the Ocean, yͤ Heathen, and yͤ Wilderness? Do you know that the Eye which guides this pen lately saw your mean and profligate Congress at Mass for the soul of a Roman Catholic in purgatory, and participating in the rights of a Church against whose Anti-christian Corruptions your pious Ancestors would have witnessed with their Blood.

"As to you who have been Soldiers in the Continental Army, can you at this Day want Evidence that the Funds of your Country are exhausted, or that the Managers have applyed them to their own private Uses? In either case you surely can continue no longer in their Service with Honor or Advantage; yet you have hitherto been their Supporters of that Cruelty, which, with an equal Indifference to your, as well as to the Labor and Blood of others, is devouring a Country, which yͤ moment you quit their Colours, will be redeemed from their Tyranny.

"But what Need of Arguments to such as feel infinitely more Misery than Language can express? I therefore only add my Promise of yͤ most affectionate Welcome and Attention to all who are disposed to joyn me in the Measures necessary to close the scene of our afflictions, which intolerable as they are, must continue to increase untill We have the Wisdom (shewn of late by Ireland) in being contented with yͤ Liberality of the Parent Country, who still offers her Protection, with yͤ immediate Restoration of our ancient Privileges, civil and Sacred, and a perpetual Exemption from all Taxes, but such as we shall think fit to impose on ourselves.

"B. ARNOLD.

"NEW YORK, October 20, 1780."

Such was Arnold's anxious but disingenuous defense, and such his impassioned appeal to his late fellow soldiers to join him.

"I fought for much less," says he, "than the Parent Country is willing to grant."

Most of his countrymen read his address with scorn and derision, and all that can be said now, when prejudice and feeling are beginning to pass away, and when candid men are disposed by his wrongs and his heroism to consider favorably every circumstance, the most they can say is, that while his conduct was in the highest degree culpable, and his guilt clear, yet giving him the benefit of a doubt, it is possible that, led astray by his wrongs and his passions, he may at times have tried to deceive himself into the belief that he was justifiable.

His efforts to induce the soldiers of the Continental army to desert, met with no considerable success. However severe their sufferings, and however hard their treatment, no consideration could induce them to desert their flag. There were indeed a considerable number of loyal Americans, tories and refugees, and from these Arnold succeeded in organizing his corps. The American reader of Sabine's Loyalists is often surprised by his representations of the number and respectability of those who adhered to the Crown.[1]

Lord George Germain, the British minister for the Colonies, wrote to Arnold, confirming the rank of brigadier-general, conferred upon him by Sir Henry Clinton, and giv-

---

[1]. Sabine says, Vol. I, p. 48: "The examination * * * leads to the conclusion that the number of our Countrymen who wished to continue their connection with the mother country was very large." The Loyalists in nearly every colony claimed a majority, but that they were mistaken, he thinks, is certain. A considerable portion of the learned professions adhered to the crown. He estimates that the number of Loyalists who took up arms for the King, "were 25,000 at the lowest computation." (Sabine Vol. I, p. 70.) This estimate surprises me, and is far more than I had supposed, but Sabine's judgment on the subject is entitled to great respect.

ing the sanction of the government to the authority which had been conferred upon him to raise a corps of loyal Americans. He also said:

"His Majesty was graciously pleased to express his satisfaction in the demonstration you have given of the sincerity of your allegiance, and of your earnest desire to atone for past errors, by a zealous attachment to his royal person and government in future."

Meanwhile, such was the indignation towards Arnold in the American army and among the people, that rewards were offered for his capture, and a project was devised to kidnap and bring him within the American lines for execution. On the 16th of October, Major Lee wrote to Washington saying: "I have engaged two persons to undertake the accomplishment of your Excellency's wishes"[1]

"The outlines of the scheme which I have recommended, are, that the sergeant (Champe) should join General Arnold as a deserter from us, should engage in his corps now raising; should contrive to insinuate himself into some menial or military birth about the General's person; that a correspondence should be kept up with the man in Newark (a confederate), by the latter's visiting the former every two days, and that when the favorable moment arrives, they should seize the prize in the night, gag him, and bring him across to Bergen Woods.

"If your Excellency approves, the sergeant will desert to-morrow—a few guineas will be necessary, &c."[2]

To which Washington replied, approving the scheme, and furnishing the guineas, with the express stipulation that Arnold should be brought to him alive.

"No circumstance whatever shall obtain my consent to his being put to death. The idea that would accompany such an act would be that ruffi-

[1] Sparks' Writings of Washington, Vol. VII, p. 545.
[2] Lee to Washington. Sparks' Writings of Washington, Vol. VII, p. 546.

ans had been hired to assassinate him. My aim is to make a public example of him."[1]

On the 21st of October, the sergeant, John Champe, deserted Lee's command, reached the British lines, treacherously enlisted into the corps Arnold was raising. He had the cunning and address to "insinuate himself" into a berth or employment about that officer's person, and every arrangement was made to kidnap Arnold at night, in a garden in the rear of the house he occupied, to gag him, carry him to a boat, and across the Hudson, and deliver him to Lee to be made "a public example of." Lee, on the night appointed, repaired with three of his dragoons, and led horses to the woods of Hoboken, in New Jersey, opposite New York, and waited some hours to receive the captive.

But on the night in which the conspiracy was to be executed, Arnold removed his quarters, and the project failed.

Had Arnold been captured in battle his execution would have been summary and prompt, and by his own treacher-

---

[1]. The following is the text of Washington's letter—(Writings of Washington, Vol. VII, 546-7):

"HEAD QUARTERS, 20 October, 1780.

"DEAR SIR:—The plan proposed for taking A——, the outlines of which are communicated in your letter, which was this moment put into my hands without a date, has every mark of a good one. I therefore agree to the promised rewards, and have such entire confidence in your management of the business, as to give it my fullest approbation; and leave the whole to the guidance of your own judgment, with this express stipulation and pointed injunction, that he (Ar—d) is brought to me alive. No circumstance whatever shall obtain my consent to his being put to death. The idea which would accompany such an event would be that ruffians had been hired to assassinate him. My aim is to make a public example of him; & this should be strongly impressed upon those who are employed to bring him off. The sergeant must be very circumspect; too much zeal may create suspicion, and too much precipitancy may defeat the project. The most inviolable secrecy must be observed on all hands. I send you five guineas, but I am not satisfied of the propriety of the Sergeant's appearing with much specie. This circumstance may also lead to suspicion, as it is but too well known to the enemy, that we do not abound in this article. The interviews between the party in & out of the city should be managed with much caution & seeming indifference or else the frequency of their meetings may betray the design and involve bad consequences; but I am persuaded you will place every matter in a proper point of view to the conductors of this interesting business, and therefore I shall only add that

"I am, dear sir, &c."

ous conduct at West Point he was estopped from complaining of any falsehood or treachery practiced upon him. But would it not have been more in accordance with our highest ideal of Washington—an ideal of almost immaculate nobility and excellence—if this kidnapping and gagging business, a scheme to be accomplished by treachery and breach of trust, had been left entirely to the provost-marshal?[1]

In Washington's instructions to LaFayette, when the latter was sent to Virginia to act against Arnold, he was told, "You are to do no act whatever with Arnold that directly or by implication may screen him from the punishment due to his treason and desertion, which if he should fall into your hands, you will execute in the most summary way."[2]

On the 27th of October, as before stated, the authorities of Pennsylvania passed a resolution requiring Mrs. Arnold to leave that State within fourteen days, and forbidding her return during the war, and soon after she joined her husband in the city of New York. She would have remained longer with her father and friends in Philadelphia but for this resolution.

Judging from the tone and character of all her letters,

---

1. Perhaps from an American stand-point, even this criticism may be thought over-nice. Arnold was, to the army he had deserted, *an outlaw;* and a sanction of the proposed abduction of higher authority than that of Sir Walter Scott might be found, when he says:

"The beast of game,
The privilege of chase may claim.
 *   *   *   *   *
Though space, and law the stag we lend,
E'er hound we slip, or bow we bend,
Who ever recked, where, how, or when
The prowling fox was trapped or slain?"

But Arnold, however execrable his conduct at West Point, had not acted like the "prowling Fox" at Ridgefield or at Saratoga. Arnold's conduct would justify the most summary punishment from his comrades, had he been captured. But the question is, whether we would not rather have given him "the privilege of chase;" and if he was to be treacherously kidnapped, whether we would not rather the plan should have been devised and executed by the Provost Marshal?

2. Washington to LaFayette, Feb. 20th, 1781. 'Writings of Washington,' Vol. VII. p. 419.

and her devoted affection for General Arnold, I do not doubt that she would have joined him at an early period without such resolution. She was not one to abandon a friend or relation, much less a husband in misfortune, even although that misfortune was the result of guilt.

Hamilton, writing to Miss Schuyler, speaking of Mrs. Arnold, says: "Her horror at the guilt of the traitor is lost in her love of the man." Indeed, it is clear from her conduct, and her letters to her father, hereafter to be quoted, that her husband never ceased to be the hero of her young imagination. On her way to New York, as well as in Philadelphia, she had abundant and painful evidence of the popular indignation against him. The populace of Philadelphia had burned his effigy with every possible indignity, and on her journey to New York with her young child, night overtook her, and she stopped at a village where preparations had been made to repeat the indignity, but when she appeared with her infant, her sad face, her sorrowful air, her gentleness, her beauty, so touched the hearts of the people, that with a delicacy and consideration honorable to the American character, they postponed the exhibition until after her departure. On her arrival in New York she was welcomed by many old friends among the British officers and their families, who had been the guests of her father in Philadelphia while that city was held by the Royal army, yet her sadness and melancholy was the subject of remark and sympathy. Gradually, however, in the society of her husband, and the company of her child, and the kind and affectionate attentions of her friends, she recovered her spirits, and her beauty and her grace made her there, as she had been in her native town, the favorite among the best and most cultured circles of that city.

Arnold's explanation of his conduct and motives, as expressed in his address to his countrymen and proclamation to the soldiers of the army in which he had lately served, while they were received and read, as has been stated, with indignation and scorn by the American people and his old comrades, was generally accepted as satisfactory by the British officers, and by the large number of loyalists then congregated in the city of New York. They looked upon the act as a return to his allegiance.

To understand this, one must go back and try to realize the views of the officers and adherents of the Crown.

The Colonies took up arms to obtain a redress of grievances, disavowing at first, with indignation, that their purpose was separation and independence.

Even John Adams said, after the war was over, "there was not a moment during the Revolution when I would not have given everything I possessed for a restoration to the state of things before the contest began, provided we could have had a sufficient security for its continuation."[1] The leaders of the Revolution have been canonized, and they merited all the honors they have received, for they were among the noblest patriots that ever lived, but like other men they were mortal and subject to like frailties. The American Loyalists were not all of them deserving of damnation. The student of history will find some names of men of high personal character and of culture; and many who, but for political differences, would have been considered ornaments to any State. Such were some of the Wentworths of New Hampshire; the Fairfaxes and Robinsons of Virginia; Dana and Coffin and Prescott, of Massachusetts; Ogden and Governor Franklin, of New Jersey (son of Dr. Franklin); The Crugars, some of the DeLanceys, and DePeysters, Van Schaacks, Clintons and Jays, of New York; and it was among men of this class that Arnold was now thrown, some of whom were much more likely to condemn

[1] Sabine's Loyalists, Vol. I, p. 64.

him for his delay in joining the British army than for joining it when he did. Still few, if any, honorable British soldier or upright loyalist could, even from their standpoint, justify his desertion, and especially the manner of his change from the American to the British side.

It is not impossible, had the conspiracy been successful, that independence might have been postponed. In the light of to-day, and with the wonderful advance, and the brilliant record our country has made, all will rejoice in the failure of the conspiracy; and all can realize how greatly our country has been benefited by the success of the Revolution:—as colonies that advance would have been greatly retarded.

Had Great Britain succeeded re-establishing her supremacy, taught by experience, she probably would have been wisely moderate, and permitted to the Colonies substantial self-government. The men of culture and wealth, the men of the learned professions, who, Sabine says, to a considerable extent adhered to the Crown, uniting with the more conservative part of the revolutionary party, of whom Washington, Hamilton, Jay, and many of the old Federal party were representatives, as against those represented by Thomas Paine and Jefferson, and the more radical and extreme democrats, might for a time at least have influenced, probably controlled, affairs, and the blessings and evils of extreme democracy and universal suffrage might have been delayed.

It is not impossible that institutions modeled more upon the views of Hamilton might have been finally adopted.

The first century of our existence as a nation, in the happiness and prosperity of the people, will compare favorably with that of any other, and thus far we have good reason to be well satisfied with our institutions, and profoundly grateful to those who achieved our independence and established our national government.

CHAPTER XIX.

ARNOLD LEADS BRITISH SOLDIERS AGAINST HIS NATIVE COUNTRY.

> "He felt how faint and feebly dim
> The fame that could accrue to him
> Who cheered the band and waved the sword—
> A *Traitor* in a turbaned horde."

ARNOLD LEADS AN EXPEDITION AGAINST VIRGINIA AND CONNECTICUT—MASSACRE AT FORT GRISWOLD—ARNOLD'S NARROW ESCAPE FROM DEATH BY THE HANDS OF A WOMAN AT NEW LONDON.

WHEN General Arnold accepted the commission of King George in 1780, he was thirty-nine and his wife twenty-one years of age.

He had four sons then living. Benedict about twelve, Richard about eleven, and Henry, eight years of age—children by his first wife, and an infant, Edward Shippen, by his second wife.

Two months after his arrival in New York, restless and eager to take the field, he sought and obtained the command of an expedition composed of about 1,600 men, against Virginia. He sailed from New York about the 20th of December, 1780. A violent gale separated the fleet on which the troops were embarked, but the scattered vessels gathered near the Capes of the Chesapeake, and on the 30th of December, he, with the fleet, entered Hampton Roads, except one armed ship and three transports, with upwards of four hundred troops, which did not arrive until several days after. Without waiting for the arrival of the missing transports, with his usual activity, Arnold pushed up the James River, and on the 3d of January he anchored near Jamestown, and the next day proceeded to Westover, where he landed, and with about eight hundred troops marched into Richmond, destroying all public property, and all such private property as might be useful in carrying on the war; making his headquarters at the old City Tavern on Main street. Before setting fire to the warehouses, he sent a proposition to Jefferson, Governor of the State, offering to spare the town and warehouses on condition the British ships should be permitted to come up unmolested and carry away the tobacco and stores. The Governor promptly rejected the proposition, and the torch was applied, and it is said there never was such a smell of tobacco in Richmond, before nor since, down to the time of the burning of that city in 1865, on its evacuation by Jefferson Davis.

This accomplished, and the foundries and magazines at Westham having been also destroyed, he retired down the river, landed, and marched to Portsmouth, where he threw up entrenchments for his winter camp.[1]

During the winter, Washington, in conjunction with the French, sent a powerful force under LaFayette to attempt his capture, and very strong hopes were entertained by the American commander that he would succeed in seizing him before reinforcements could arrive from New York. On the 26th of March he was strengthened by the arrival of General Phillips with additional troops, and General Phillips out-ranking him, took command. The following is the report of General Arnold to Sir Henry Clinton, giving the detail of his further operations in Virginia:

1. Expedition of LaFayette against Arnold, by J. Austin Stephens.

[1]"PETERSBURGH, May 16, 1781.

"I am extremely sorry to inform your Excellency that Major-General Phillips is reduced so low by a fever, which seized him on the 2nd instant, that he is incapable of business, and the physicians are not without fears for his safety. In this situation I think it my duty to transmit to your Excellency, by express, a detail of the proceedings of the army under the Orders of Major-General Phillips since they left Portsmouth (which his indisposition prevented him from doing as he intended).

"On the 18th of April the light infantry, part of the 76th and 80th regiments, the Queen's Rangers, Yagers, and American Legion, embarked at Portsmouth, and fell down to Hampton Roads; on the 19th proceeded up James River to Burwell's Ferry; on the 20th Lieut. Col. Abercrombie with the light infantry, proceeded up the Chickahominy in boats; Lieut. Col. Simcoe, with a detachment to York; Lieut. Col. Dundas, with another detachment landed at the mouth of the Chickahominy; and Major-General Phillips and myself landed with part of the army at Williamsburgh, where about 500 militia were posted, who retired upon our approach. The militia at York crossed the river before the arrival of Lieut. Col. Simcoe, who made a few prisoners, spiked and destroyed some cannon, and next day returned to Williamsburgh.

"On the 22nd the troops marched to Chickahominy. We were met on the road, five miles from the mouth of the river, by Lieut. Col. Dundas, with his detachment. This evening the troops, cavalry, artillery, &c., were reimbarked. The next morning we were joined by Lieut. Col. Abercrombie, with the light infantry, who had been ten or twelve miles up the Chickahominy, and destroyed several armed ships, the State ship yards, warehouses, &c.

"At ten o'clock the fleet weighed, and proceeded up the James river, within four miles of Westover.

"The 24th, weighed anchor at eleven, and ran up to City Point, where the troops, &c., were all landed at six in the evening.

"The 25th, marched at ten o'clock for Petersburgh, where we arrived about five P. M. We were opposed about one mile from town by a body of militia under the orders of Brigadier General Muhlenberg, supposed to be about one thousand men, who were soon obliged to retire over the bridge with the loss of near one hundred men killed and wounded, as we have since been informed: our loss only one man killed and ten wounded. The enemy took up the bridge, which prevented our pursuing them.

"26th. Destroyed at Petersburgh four thousand hogsheads of tobacco,

1. Extract of Brigadier General Arnold's letter to Sir Henry Clinton, copied from *The London Chronicle*, June 23, 26, 1781; Vol. XLIX, p. 601.

one ship and a number of small vessels on the stocks and in the river.

"27th. Major General Phillips, with the light infantry, part of the cavalry of the Queen's Rangers, and a part of the Yagers, marched to Chesterfield Court House, where they burnt a range of barracks for two thousand men, and three hundred barrels of flour, &c.

"The same day I marched to Osborn's with the 76th and 80th regiments, Queen's Rangers, part of the Yagers, and American Legion, where we arrived about noon. Finding the enemy had a very considerable force of ships four miles above Osborn's, drawn up in a line to oppose us, I sent a flag to the Commodore, proposing to treat with him for the surrender of his fleet, which he refused, with this answer, "that he was determined to defend it to the last extremity." I immediately ordered down two six and two three-pounders, brass field pieces, to a bank of the river, nearly level with the water, and within one hundred yards of the Tempest, a twenty gun State ship, which began immediately to fire upon us, as did the Renown, of twenty-six guns, the Jefferson, a State brigantine of fourteen guns, and several other armed ships and brigantines. About two or three hundred militia on the opposite shore, at the same time kept up a heavy fire of musquetry upon us: notwithstanding which, the fire of the artillery, under the direction of Captain Fage and Lieut. Rogers, took such effect, that the ships were soon obliged to strike their colours, and the militia drove from the opposite shore. Want of boats, and the wind blowing hard, prevented our capturing many of the seamen, who took to their boats, and escaped on shore; but not without first scuttling and setting fire to some of their ships, which could not be saved.

"Two ships, three brigantines, five sloops, and two schooners, loaded with tobacco, cordage, flour, &c., fell into our hands.

"Four ships, five brigantines, and a number of small vessels were sunk and burnt. On board the whole fleet (none of which escaped) were taken and destroyed about two thousand hogsheads of tobacco, &c., &c., &c., and very fortunately we had not a man killed or wounded this day: but have reason to believe the enemy suffered considerably. About five o'clock P. M. we were joined by Major-General Phillips, with the light infan ry.

"28th. The troops remained at Osborn's, waiting for boats from the fleet; part of them were employed in securing the prizes, and carrying them to Osborn's as a place of safety.

"29th. The boats having arrived, the troops were put in motion. Major-General Phillips marched with the main body; at the same time I proceeded up the river with a detachment in boats, and met him between Cary's Mills and Warwick.

"30th. The troops marched to Manchester, and destroyed twelve hundred hogsheads of tobacco. The Marquis de La Fayette having arrived with his army at Richmond, opposite to Manchester, the day before, and being joined by the militia, driven from Petersburgh and Williamsburgh, they were spectators of the conflagration, without attempting to molest us. The same evening we returned to Warwick, where we destroyed a magazine of 500 barrels of flour, and Colonel Cary's fine mills were destroyed in burning the magazine of flour. We also burnt several warehouses, with one hundred and fifty hogsheads of tobacco, a large ship and a brigantine afloat, and three vessels on the stocks, a large range of public ropewalks and store houses, and some tan and bark houses full of hides and bark.

"May 1st. Marched to Osborn's and despatched our prizes and boats down the river; and in the evening marched to Bermuda Hundreds, opposite City Point.

"May 2nd. Embarked the troops, &c., &c.

"May 3rd. Fell down the river to Westover.

"May 4th. Proceeded down to Tappahannock.

"5th and 6th. Part of the fleet fell down to Hog Island.

"7th. Major-General Phillips having received a letter from Lord Cornwallis, orders were given for the fleet to return up the river again. We arrived at Brandon about 5 o'clock, and most of the troops, cavalry, &c., were landed this evening, though it blew a gale of wind.

"May 8th. Remained at Brandon; Major-General Phillips being very ill, and unable to travel on horseback, a post chaise was procured for him.

"May 9th. The light infantry and part of the Queen's Rangers, in boats, were ordered, with the Formidable and Spitfire, to proceed to City Point, and land there. The rest of the Army was put in motion for Petersburgh, where they arrived late in the night, having marched near thirty miles this day.

"On our leaving Bermuda Hundreds, and going down the river, the Marquis de LaFayette with his army moved towards Williamsburgh, and by forced marches had crossed the Chickahominy at Long Bridge, when our fleet returned to Brandon; which retrograde motion of ours occasioned him to return as rapidly by forced marches to Osborn's, where he arrived the 8th, and was preparing to cross the river to Petersburg, when we arrived there, which was so unexpected, that we surprised and took two Majors (one of them Aid-de-Camp to Baron Steuben, the other to General Smallwood), one Captain, and three lieutenants of dragoons; two lieutenants of foot; a commissary and a surgeon; some of these gentlemen arrived only two hours before us, with an intention of collecting the boats for the Marquis to cross his Army.

"On the 10th the Marquis made his appearance on the opposite side of the river with a strong escort, and having staid some time to reconnoitre our army, returned to his camp at Osborn's, and we are this day informed he is marched to Richmond, where it is said Wayne with the Pennsylvania line has arrived; this is, however, uncertain; but he is certainly expected there.

"An express passed through this place the day before our arrival here, who left Halifax on the 7th, and informed that the advance of Lord Cornwallis's army arrived there that morning; this report we have from several quarters, and I am inclined to believe it is true. Several expresses have been sent to his Lordship, informing him of our being here ready to co-operate with his Lordship. We are in anxious expectation of having particular intelligence from him every minute.

"As soon as it is reduced to a certainty that Lord Cornwallis has crossed the Roanoke, and is on his march for this place, the army will advance one or two days' march from hence to meet his Lordship, and carry a supply of provisions for his army.

"A considerable number of magazines of flour and bread have fallen into our hands near this place, and the country abounds with cattle.

"Major-General Phillips is so weak and low that it will be some considerable time before he can go through the fatigue of business. In this critical situation I am happy to have the assistance of so many good and experienced officers with me commanding corps. If joined by Cornwallis, or the reinforcement said to be coming from New York, we shall be in force to operate as we please in Virginia or Maryland.

"I have the honor to be, &c.,
"(Signed,) B. ARNOLD."

General Phillips was one of the officers captured with Burgoyne at Saratoga, and died very soon after the date of Arnold's report.

It was during this expedition that General Arnold inquired of a captain of the patriot army who had been taken prisoner: "What would be my fate, if *I* should be taken prisoner?"

"They will cut off," replied the captain, "that shortened leg of yours wounded at Quebec and at Saratoga, and bury it with all the honors of war, and then hang the rest of you on a gibbet."

While in Virginia Governor Jefferson offered a reward

of 5,000 guineas to any one who would capture Arnold. In June, 1781, he returned to the city of New York, where Mrs. Arnold had remained during his absence, and where, on the 27th of August, she gave birth to their second son, named James Robertson, and who lived to attain the rank of Lieutenant-General in the British army, and to serve as military aid of the King. Arnold's return to New York removed him from the impending conflict between Washington and Cornwallis.

Early in September, notwithstanding the delicate condition of his wife, among strangers and with an infant but a few days old, he was compelled to leave her, and lead an expedition against his native State. At New London, in Connecticut, was deposited a large quantity of public stores, feebly defended by Forts Trumbull and Griswold. Arnold was selected to command because of his familiarity with the localities, but it was a severe trial of his fidelity to his new friends, to send him at such a time at the head of this expedition. The massacre, so-called, at Fort Griswold, was one of the most tragic incidents of the war, and is a sad chapter of this gloomy period in Arnold's history.

To what extent he was responsible for the burning of the town, and the destruction of life in the Fort, is a controverted question. That he did not prevent these acts is at least clear, and he certainly ought, if possible, to have taken such measures as would have prevented them.

I give his own report, and the testimony in his favor of the British Commander, and then the statement of the transaction by General Heath, of the American army.[1]

"SOUND, OFF PLUMB ISLAND, Sept. 3, 1781.

"Sir: I have the honor to inform your Excellency that the transports with the detachment of troops under my orders, anchored on the Long Island shore, on the 5th instant, at two o'clock P. M., about ten leagues from

[1]. Copy of a letter from Brigadier General Arnold to his Excellency, the Commander in-Chief, extracted from 'The *London Chronicle*,' Nov. 3-6, 1781, p. 437.

New London; and having made some necessary arrangements, weighed anchor at 7 o'clock P. M., and stood for New London with a fair wind. At one o'clock the next morning, we arrived off the harbour, when the wind suddenly shifted to the northward, and it was nine o'clock before the transports could beat in. At ten o'clock, the troops in two divisions, and in four debarkations, were landed: one on each side the harbour, about three miles from New London; that on the Groton side, consisting of the 40th and 54th regiments, and the 3rd battalion of New Jersey Volunteers, with a detachment of Yagers and artillery, were under the command of Lieut. Col. Eyre. The division on the New London side consisted of the 38th regiment, the Loyal Americans, the American Legion, Refugees, and a detachment of sixty Yagers, who were immediately on landing put in motion: and at eleven o'clock, being within half a mile of Fort Trumbull, which commands New London harbour, I detached Captain Millet with four companies of the 38th regiment to attack the fort, who was joined on his march by Captain Frink with one company of the American Legion. At the same time I advanced with the remainder of the division, west of Fort Trumbull, on the road to the town, to attack a redoubt which had kept up a brisk fire upon us for some time, but which the enemy evacuated upon our approach. In this work we found six pieces of cannon mounted, and two dismounted: soon after I had the pleasure to see Captain Millet march into Fort Trumbull under a shower of grape shot from a number of cannon, which the enemy had turned upon him; and I have the pleasure to inform your Excellency, that, by the sudden attack and determined bravery of the troops, the fort was carried with the loss of only four or five men killed and wounded. Captain Millet had orders to leave one company in Fort Trumbull, to detach one to the redoubt we had taken, and to join me with the other two companies. No time on my part was lost in gaining the town of New London. We were opposed by a small body of the enemy with one field piece, which being iron, was spiked and left.

"As soon as the enemy were alarmed in the morning, we could perceive they were busily employed in bending sails, and endeavouring to get their privateers and other ships at Norwich river, out of our reach; but the wind being small, and the tide against them, they were obliged to anchor again. From information I received before and after my landing, I had reason to believe that Fort Griswold, on Groton side, was very incomplete; and I was assured (by friends to government) after my landing, that there were only twenty or thirty men in the fort, the inhabitants in general being on board their ships, and busy in saving their property. On taking possession of Fort Trumbull, I found the enemy's ships would escape, unless we could possess ourselves of Fort Griswold; I therefore dispatched an Officer to Lieutenat Colonel Eyre, with the intelligence I had received, and requested him to make an attack upon the fort as soon as possible; at which time I expected the howitzer was up, and would have been made use of.

"On my gaining a height of ground in the rear of New London, from which I had a good prospect of Fort Griswold, I found it much more formidable than I expected, or than I had formed an idea of from the information I had before received; I observed at the same time, that the men who had escaped from Fort Trumbull had crossed in boats and thrown themselves into Fort Griswold, and a favorable wind springing up about this time, the enemy's ships were escaping up the river, notwithstanding the fire from Fort Trumbull, and a six pounder which I had with me. I immediately dispatched a boat with an officer to Lieut. Col. Eyre, to countermand my first orders to attack the fort, but the officer arrived a few minutes too late.

"Lieutenant Col. Eyre had sent Captain Beckwith with a flag to demand a surrender of the fort, which was peremptorily refused, and the attack had commenced. After a most obstinate defense of near forty minutes, the fort was carried by the superior bravery and perseverance of the assailants. The attack was judicious and spirited, and reflects the highest honor on the officers and troops engaged, who seemed to vie with each other in being first in danger. The troops approached on three sides of the work, which was a square with flanks, made a lodgement in the ditch, and under a heavy fire, which they kept up on the works, effected a second lodgment on the friezing, which was attended with great difficulty, as only a few pickets could be forced out or broken in a place, and was so high that the soldiers could not ascend without assisting each other. Here the coolness and bravery of the troops were very conspicuous—as the first who ascended the frieze were obliged to silence a nine-pounder, which infladed the place on which they stood, until a sufficient body had collected to enter the works, which was done with fixed bayonets through the embrazures, where they were opposed with great obstinacy by the garrison with long spears. On this occasion I have to regret the loss of Major Montgomery, who was killed by a spear in entering the enemy's works; also of Ensign Whillock, of the 40th regiment, who was killed in the attack. Three other officers of the same regiment were wounded. Lieutenant Colonel Eyre and three other officers of the 54th regiment were also wounded, but I have the satisfaction to inform your Excellency that they are all in a fair way of recovery.

"Lieutenant Colonel Eyre, who behaved with great gallantry, having received his wound near the works, and Major Montgomery being killed immediately after, the command devolved upon Major Bromfield, whose behaviour on this occasion does him great honour.

"Lieutenant Colonel Buskirk, with the New Jersey Volunteers and artillery, being the second debarkation, came up soon after the work was carried, having been retarded by the roughness of the country. I am much obliged to this gentleman for his exertions, although the Artillery did not arrive in time.

"I have enclosed a return of the killed and wounded, by which your Excellency will observe that our loss, though very considerable, is very short of the enemy's, who lost most of their officers, among whom was their commander, Col. Ledyard. Eighty-five men were found dead in Fort Griswold, and 60 wounded, most of them mortally; their loss on the opposite side must have been considerable, but cannot be ascertained. I believe we have about 70 prisoners, besides the wounded, who were left paroled.

"Ten or twelve of the enemy's ships were burned; among them were three or four armed vessels, and one loaded with naval stores; an immense quantity of European and West India goods were found in the stores; among the former, the cargo of the Hannah, Captain Watson, from London, lately captured by the enemy: The whole of which was burnt with the stores, which proved to contain a large quantity of powder, unknown to us; the explosion of the powder, and change of wind, soon after the stores were fired, communicated the flames to a part of the town, which was, notwithstanding every effort to prevent it, unfortunately destroyed.

"Upwards of 50 pieces of iron cannon were destroyed in the different works (exclusive of the guns of the ships), a particular return of which I cannot do myself the honor to transmit to your Excellency at this time.

"A very considerable magazine of powder, and barracks to contain 300 men were found in Fort Griswold, which Captain Lemoine, of the Royal Artillery, had my positive directions to destroy. An attempt was made by him, but unfortunately failed. He had my orders to make a second attempt; the reasons why it was not done, Captain Lemoine will have the honour to explain to your Excellency.

"I should be wanting in justice to the gentlemen of the navy did I omit to acknowledge that upon this expedition I have received every possible aid from them; Captain Beasley has made every exertion to assist our operations, and not only gave up his cabin to the sick and wounded officers, but furnished them with every assistance and refreshment that his ship afforded.

"Lord Dalrymple will have the honour to deliver my dispatches. I beg leave to refer your Excellency to his Lordship for the particulars of our operations on the New London side. I feel myself under great obligations to him for his exertions upon the occasion.

"Captain Beckwith, who was extremely serviceable to me, returns with his Lordship. His spirited conduct in the attack of Fort Griswold, does him great honor, being one of the first officers who entered the works. I beg leave to refer your Excellency to him for the particulars of our operations on that side, and to say I have the highest opinion of his abilities as an officer.

"I am greatly indebted to Captain Stapleton (who acted as Major of Brigade), for his spirited conduct and assistance: in particular on the attack upon Fort Trumbull, and his endeavours to prevent plundering (when the public stores were burnt), and the destruction of private buildings.

"The officers and troops in general behaved with the greatest intrepidity and firmness.

"I have the honor to be, &c.,

"B. ARNOLD."

It seems quite clear—and indeed such is the statement of General Heath—that Arnold did not cross the river, and that during the attack upon Fort Griswold he was on the opposite side; and this being true, he must be acquitted of any direct personal responsibility for what occurred at the Fort. His conduct in leading this expedition against his native State is bad enough, without darkening the picture with the cruelties which occurred on the opposite side of the stream.

General Clinton, in general orders expresses his obligations to General Arnold "for his very spirited conduct," and assures him that he is convinced that "he" (General Arnold) "took every precaution in his power to prevent the destruction of the Town, which is a misfortune which gives him much concern."[1]

---

[1] From *London Chronicle*, Nov. 3–6, 1781, p. 438, *Vol. L.*

"GENERAL ORDERS, HEAD-QUARTERS,
"NEW YORK, Sept. 17.

"Brigadier General Arnold having reported to the Commander-in-Chief the success of the expedition under his direction against New London, on the 6th instant, his Excellency has the pleasure of signifying to the army the high sense he entertains of the very distinguished merit of the Corps employed upon that service; but while he draws the greatest satisfaction from the ardour of the troops, which enabled them to carry by assault a work of such strength as Fort Griswold is represented to be, he cannot but lament, with the deepest concern, the heavy loss in offi-

At the time of this expedition, General Heath was in command of a part of the American army in the State of New York, and in his Diary and Memoirs, under date of Sept. 10, 1781, after giving an account of the expedition against New London, he says:

"In Govr. Trumbull's letter, the Enemy were charged with behaving in a wanton and barbarous manner, and that between seventy and eighty were killed, three only before the Enemy entered the Fort and the garrison had submitted; that on Colonel Ledyard's delivering his sword, reversed, to the commanding officer, who entered the fort, the officer immediately plunged it in the Colonel's body, on which several soldiers bayoneted him. It is also asserted, that upon the foregoing taking place, an American officer who stood near to Colonel Ledyard, instantly stabbed the British officer who had stabbed the Colonel, on which the British indiscriminately bayoneted a great number of Americans.

"This expedition was commanded by Arnold. The British loss was very considerable in killed and wounded; among the former was Major Montgomery. *Arnold himself continued on the New London side*, and while his troops were plundering and burning, was said to have been at a house where he was treated very politely; that while he was sitting with the gentleman regaling himself, the latter observed that he hoped his house and property would be safe; he was answered that while he (Arnold) was there, it would not be touched; but the house, except the room in which they were, was soon plundered, and found to be on fire. During the plunder of the town, the British (as is always the case in a plunder), were in great confusion, setting their arms against trees and fences, while they were collecting and carrying off their plunder; in this situation they might have been easily defeated; nor would it have been the first time an army in possession of victory, lost it in this way: hence by the articles of war, "If any officer or soldier shall leave his post or colors, to go in search of plunder, he is liable to suffer death for the offence."

"It is not meant to exculpate or to aggravate the conduct of the cers and men sustained by the 40th and 54th Regiments, who had the honor of that attack; and as no words can do proper justice to the discipline and spirit which they showed on that occasion, his Excellency can only request they will accept his thanks, with assurances that he will not fail to represent their conduct to their sovereign in the most honorable terms.

"The Commander-in-Chief begs leave to express his obligations to Brigadier General Arnold, for his very spirited conduct on the occasion; and he assures that general officer that he is convinced he took every precaution in his power to prevent the destruction of the town, which is a misfortune that gives him much concern. * * *"

enemy on this occasion—but two things are to be remembered; first, that in almost all cases the slaughter does but begin when the vanquished give way; and it has been said, that if this was fully considered, troops would never turn their backs, if it were possible to face their enemy; secondly, in all attacks by assault, the assailants, between the feelings of danger on the one hand, and resolution to overcome it on the other, have their minds worked up almost to a point of fury and madness, which those who are assailed, from a confidence in their works, do not feel; and that consequently when a place is carried, and the assailed submit, the assailants cannot instantaneously curb their fury to reason, and in this interval, many are slain in a way which a cool bystander would call wanton and barbarous, and even the perpetrators themselves, when their rage subsided, would condemn; *but while the human passions* remain as they now are, there is scarcely a remedy."

It is said that during the attack Arnold had a very narrow escape from death by the hands of a Mrs. Hinman, a resident of New London. She had known Arnold in earlier years, he having often been the guest of her husband. Seeing him riding up the street, she addressed him, and he immediately recognized her, and offered her his protection. He told her to point out her property, and he would take care that it should not be injured. She pointed out not only her own, but the houses of several of her friends, as her own, and all were spared.

At length, seeing the cruel destruction going on around her, the attack upon and capture of Fort Griswold, she became so incensed against Arnold that she seized a gun, and aiming it at him as he sat on his horse in front of the house, she pulled the trigger, but the piece missed fire, and the traitor escaped. The Lord did not on that day deliver *Sisera* into the hands of this modern *Jael*.[1]

[1] *New York Daily Times*, January, 1873.

CHAPTER XX.

ARNOLD AT THE COURT OF GEORGE THE III.

"On foreign shores a man exiled
Disowned, deserted, and distressed."

ARNOLD'S DEPARTURE WITH LORD CORNWALLIS FOR ENGLAND—HIS RECEPTION BY THE KING AND CABINET—HIS PAPER ON A RE-UNION BETWEEN THE COLONIES AND THE CROWN—GENERAL AND MRS. ARNOLD AT ANDRE'S MONUMENT IN WESTMINSTER ABBEY.

ON the 19th of October, 1781, Lord Cornwallis, with his entire army of near 10,000 men, surrendered to General Washington. When intelligence of this event reached the British Cabinet, the firmness of Lord North, the Minister, gave way, and he exclaimed, "All is lost!"[1] This success caused most men to conclude that the subjugation of the Colonies was impossible, and led to the acknowledgment of the independence of our country.

In the December following, Arnold, with his family, sailed for England. In the expeditions which he commanded against Virginia and into Connecticut, he had accomplished all that was expected of him, had displayed energy and executive ability, had received the thanks of Sir Henry Clinton, but no opportunity had occurred for the exhibition of those brilliant exploits and feats of personal heroism, for which his career in the patriot army had been so distinguished. Independently of the reproach brought upon him

---

1. Wraxall's Memoirs.

by the affair at New London, he had not added anything to his military reputation. Indeed, he was so heavily handicapped while in the service of the king, as to make it very difficult for him to achieve anything great. It is not unlikely some distrust may have been felt towards him in some quarters among his new friends, though I discover no indication of it in the treatment of him by the British commander. Even if there had been no blot upon his record as an officer, as a colonist he would have labored under great disadvantage.

Besides, it was well known at the British Headquarters, that he was constantly exposed to dangers far greater and of a different character from those of any other officer. Hundreds of riflemen and sharp-shooters were on the watch to take his life. Heavy rewards for his capture, for his abduction had been offered, and if taken his execution would have been summary. He was therefore sent to England to confer with the Ministers upon the conduct of the war; and he prepared to leave with little or no probability of ever returning. He was now to become an exile from his native land, probably forever.

How painful this exile, with what shattered hopes, nay, almost despair, he left his home, the land of his glory, and of his disgrace, it is difficult to conceive. One must remember his ambition, his passionate nature; how he had struggled for fame; how, when ill-treated, and deeply injured, carried away by his passions, he had listened to British emissaries, and yielding to their specious arguments and persuasions, had at last staked everything on the success of his treason, to appreciate the bitter feelings of self-reproach with which he sailed away from his home. It has been said, that the hardships he had endured and his exposure and wounds in battle, were the result, not of patriotism, but of ambition only; but "Greater love hath no man than this: that a man lay down his life for his friend;" and it would be difficult to find stronger evidence of love of country than he had exhibited up to the time of his treason.

Yet few, if any, among those he left behind would now remember,

"That this poor victim of self-will
Patriot no more, had once been patriot all."

It was impossible for him not to recall the day, when brought home from Saratoga, still weak and a cripple from unhealed wounds so honorably received, his native State went out to meet, welcome and honor him. He could not fail to remember when, returning to Philadelphia after having, by a heroism never surpassed, driven Tryon back to his ships, Congress replaced the horse riddled with bullets under him, with another completely caparisoned, and gave him the promotion so long and so unjustly withheld. Nor did he fail to recall how often he had been honored by Washington, and that the Commander-in-Chief had offered him the second place in his own army, and had he been true to that chief, it might have been into his hands that the sword of Lord Cornwallis would have been surrendered. Musing upon all these recollections and all his old campaigns, from Ticonderoga and the Wilderness of Maine to the assault upon Quebec and the long Canadian winter, when "in the path of duty" he "knew no fear," he paced the deck of the packet and saw his native land disappear forever in the distance. He might now be compared to a melancholy *flotsom*, thrown up by the waves of a stormy sea, the wreck of a once noble career, now the wretched relic of an abortive and guilty enterprise.

He had staked all—and lost all. Execrated and cursed by his own countrymen and their army, and regarded coldly by the other side, he must have felt uncertain of his reception by the government to which he was fleeing. He could not fail to speculate on what might have been his position, as the brilliant second of Washington, in establishing the independence of his country. He was now going empty-handed of success, to meet strangers, without a country or a home. Truly, his treason was not only a crime, but a sad and terrible blunder. No wonder that he struggled against despair!

But his devoted wife, in this hour of deep depression was ever at his side to soothe and sustain him. To her Arnold was still a hero. It was hard for her to leave father, family, home and friends, but with all of woman's devotion, she clung to her husband, and made his life endurable.

Sir Henry Clinton gave to Arnold letters to Lord George Germain and others, bearing generous testimony "to his spirited and meritorious conduct since he had joined the British army," and "earnestly commending him to his Lordship's countenance and protection."

Lord Cornwallis was a fellow passenger with Arnold and his family across the ocean to England. His lordship, after his surrender at Yorktown, had been exchanged for Henry Laurens, late president of Congress, who had been captured at sea, and confined in the Tower of London. The kindness of Cornwallis towards the family of Arnold, manifested on various occasions, and especially some years afterwards, in aiding to place his sons at the military school, may be attributed, in part at least, to the friendly relations created by this voyage together.[1] In the protracted passage across the Atlantic, then made by sail, these two gentlemen had abundant time to discuss the probabilities of future success of the war. Cornwallis had nearly given up all hope, while Arnold professed to be still sanguine.

"Arnold," it is said in a private letter from a gentleman

[1] Cornwallis and Arnold "were brother passengers to England." Drake's Historic Fields and Mansions of Middlesex, p. 257.

who was in Europe when he arrived there, and whose acquaintance in diplomatic circles placed him in a position to be well informed, "was received with open arms by the King, caressed by the ministers, and all imaginable attention shown him by all people on that side of the question."[1]

Leaning on the arm of Sir Guy Carleton, he was presented at Court by Sir Walter Stirling.[2]

He was much consulted by Lord Germain and the Cabinet, and regarded as a very sensible man, familiar with American affairs. "He had many private conferences with the King, and was seen walking with the Prince of Wales and the King's brother in the public gardens."[3]

It must have been a suggestive spectacle to have seen General Arnold in the parks of London, leaning on the arm of the Prince of Wales, seeking his aid under a lameness arising from wounds received in fighting against the crown.

From the letter above quoted and other sources, I learn that the King, who had a passionate desire to retain the Colonies, regarded him as a man whose opinions were entitled to great consideration. All of Arnold's future after his treason, for obvious reasons, depended upon a reconciliation between the Colonies and the Crown, and he was as reluctant as King George himself to see their independence established; hence, notwithstanding the surrender of Lord Cornwallis, his hopeful temperament at times still cherished the belief that a re-union was possible. Not long after his presentation at court, at the personal request of the King, he prepared a paper, dated 1782, entitled, "Thoughts on the American War."

---
1. Drake's Historic Fields and Mansions of Middlesex, p. 258.
2. Sargent's 'Life of Andre,' Appendix, p. 453.
3. Drake—private letter quoted by Drake, as above stated, p. 258.
"We hear much of audiences given to Arnold, and his being present at councils."
—*Benjamin Franklin's Letter to R. R. Livingston; Bigelow's Life of Franklin, Vo . III*, p. 48.

It contains a carefully considered plan for a reconciliation and re-union between the Crown and the Colonies. The grandson of General Arnold[1] has placed the original draft of the paper, which is in the handwriting of General Arnold, in my hands. So far as I know, it has never before been printed.[2] It is a curious and interesting document, and seems to me to exhibit some political sagacity. Arnold had already in his address to his countrymen declared that he had devoted his life to the "re-union of the British Empire, as the best and only means to dry up the streams of misery that have deluged the country."

He had expressed the conviction that it was the intention of Great Britain to leave the rights and privileges of the Colonies unimpaired, including "their perpetual exemption from taxation."

On his arrival in London, Arnold learned, that while the King had no thought of yielding, the British people were getting tired of the war, and hopeless of success.

In the paper referred to, he enters into an elaborate argument to show that a majority of the Americans were opposed to a separation; he earnestly recommends a change in the conduct of the war, commenting cautiously on the delicate subject of "the inactivity and misdirection of the King's arms in the past."

He calls attention to the great mistake, as he regarded it, that no attempt had been made to set up "the civil authority in any part of America," and asserts that until this was done, "the loyalists will not, nor indeed can they, give any special assistance to the royal cause."

The reason for this he explains at some length, saying:

"I have said they *will not*. Because they are *Englishmen*. Nay, an American Husbandman will no sooner quit his farm and Family, to be-

1. The Rev. Edward Gladwin Arnold.
2. See paper in full in the Appendix.

come a common Soldier at six Pence a day Wages, with rations, than an English Gentleman of £500 a year in the Funds. He will not lend his hand to erect a military Misrule over himself and his Friends, and put all his Property at the Discretion of an Arbitrary Police, that has cut the Throat of the King's Interest wherever it has been set up.

"He has, however, no Objection to serve in the Militia *within* his own Colony, under officers who are *of it*, and to assist in supporting its Government and defending himself *in it*, and may perhaps pursue the Rebel out of it, or meet him on a menaced Invasion near the Borders.

"But for this Purpose the Civil Authority of the Crown must first be set up; and without it, Great Britain (the American being what he is) can neither be benefitted by his Councils, his Purse, nor his arms. He will be passive while under the Power of the Usurpers, and when they are flying before the King's Troops, continue if he can at home, giving aid to neither Party, and certainly not oppose the royal army, if he finds it possible to avoid it; and, in short, behave in the manner Lord Cornwallis experienced; distrusting both the strength of his Army to give protection, and what is worse, to afford the Protection of the *Laws of the Land*."

After speaking of the feeble and exhausted condition of the Colonies, the great depreciation of their paper currency, and the small number of Continental soldiers in the field, he alludes to the discontented condition of Vermont, and suggests measures for detaching her from the Union; and he concludes this topic by saying:

"By the complete Detachment of Vermont from the Rebel Interest, and the Reduction of the Highland Forts *early in the spring*, much may be expected in the next Campaign, especially since the New Yorkers in general, and a very great proportion of the Country between them and Connecticut River are known to be very favourably inclined to the Reunion."

He then recommended "a new peace commission to the Colonies," saying, "a new peace Commission is indispensably necessary."

"Perplexed as the Congress must be under the growing uneasiness of the People, neither affection to the French, nor a republican Attachment, nor even the Aims of Ambition, would prevent them from listening to Overtures *that were decisive and irreversible*, if themselves could be secured from the vindictive rage of the Multitude they have misled, oppressed and ruined, as well as from the resentment of the Crown. * *

"It can scarcely be necessary to add, that the new Peace Commissioners should have every Power of the Crown, for the appointment to offices—from Governors downwards, that when they return to England, they may have the Government established upon such a Plan, as all things considered, may appear to be expedient, nor that the success of the Commission will depend much upon their being persons of Rank, *and rather Statesmen than Soldiers*, and of Characters in such estimation for the Fulness of their powers as to influence the Executive Instruments, both of the army and navy, to a *faithful, spirited*, and harmonious Conduct."

"All these things," says he, "are suggested on the supposition that Great Britain has such an interest in her Colonies as is worth fostering for the common good."

He expresses the conviction that "the war was now nearly at an end," unless Britain despairs of success.

Had the policy towards the Colonies, both civil and military, pointed out in this paper been pursued by the British government early in the war, independence would have been a far more difficult achievement.

It is apparent that Arnold hoped to have been appointed one of the New Peace Commissioners in the plan of settlement proposed by him, and it is probable that he anticipated that by contributing towards peace, and securing for the Colonies substantial self-government, he might mitigate to some extent the hatred felt towards him in America. Although the paper was read with great satisfaction by the King, and added to Arnold's influence at Court, it came too late; the British nation was tired of the war, the paper led to no action, and it soon became very clear that American independence was a fact accomplished, and nothing was left to England but to accept the inevitable.

The fascination which Mrs. Arnold by her beauty, her goodness and her grace exercised over all, was not less marked in England than in America. Tarlteon and other officers who had met her in Philadelphia and New York, were enthusiastic in their expressions of admiration, and, as has been stated, declared her the most "beautiful woman in England." However this may have been, the letter before quoted says, "the queen was so interested in favor of Mrs. Arnold as to desire the ladies of the court to pay much attention to her."

At the same time Arnold was most severely assailed by the Whig newspapers, and received many mortifying indignities from persons in the opposition. He received for his alleged losses, in consequence of his joining the British, the sum of £6315; £5000 of which he invested in four per cent. consols, realizing therefrom £7000 in stocks.

Mrs. Arnold, some time after her arrival in England, received a pension of £500 per annum, and each of her children £100 per annum, from the British government.[1]

In Rhode Island, upon an old gravestone, erected to the memory of Oliver Arnold, who died in 1770, are carved the arms of the family.[2] The crest was a demi-lyon-rampant, etc., and the motto, "*Gloria mihi sursum.*"

---

1. Manuscript letter of Rev. Edward Gladwin Arnold.
The following is a copy of the Royal warrant for Mrs. Arnold's pension:
"GEORGE R. Our will & pleasure is, and we do hereby direct, authorize & command, that an annuity or Yearly pension of Five hundred pounds be established & paid by You unto Margaret Arnold, wife of our trusty & well beloved Brigadier General, Benedict Arnold, to commence from the day of the date hereof, & continue during our pleasure, in such & like manner as other our established pensions, payable by You are, &c., and this shall be therefor a sufficient Warrant. Given at our court at St. James, the 19th day of March, 1782, In the 22d year of our Reign. By his Majesty's command.
"NORTH.
"PALMENTON.
"R. SUTTON.
"To our right Trusty & well beloved
WILLIAM HALL, VICOUNT GAGE,
Paymaster of our Pensions, &c."

2. "They (the arms) are identical with those engraved on the Tomb-Stone of Oliver Arnold, of Rhode Island, who died in 1770, and those of Sir Nicholas Arnold, of Higham Court, county of Gloucester, whose family came from Monmouth, Wales. The motto, '*Mihi gloria sursum*,' is traditional. * * we translate it '*Through glory yielded to me.*'" C. H. ARNOLD."
Others have translated it: "My glory is on high," and "All I seek is glory."

These arms, or something very similar, had been sometimes used on his seal by Benedict Arnold, in America.

It is a significant fact that after his arrival in England, General Arnold changed the motto to "*Nil desperandum.*" It seems to me this change is full of pathos, and it is not the least expressive among the very few indications his proud spirit ever gave, of the suffering against which he struggled. In all the correspondence of his future life and that of his family, I find hardly an allusion to his career in America; no complaint; whatever his regrets and feelings, he gave no sign, but this change in the motto on his seal—from "*Mihi gloria sursum,*" to "*Nil desperandum*" ("Never despair")—tells the story of his sufferings, and how he struggled against despair.

The kindness shown to the exile and his family by the King and Queen was honorable to them, especially to King George, who, whatever Arnold's faults, seems to have been touched by his reverses of fortune, caused by what was treason to his country, but which the King regarded as a return to his allegiance. However Arnold's conduct might look to others, and however justly and severely it might be condemned by his countrymen and the world, perhaps it was not unnatural for the King to see in it a sincere and honest change of opinion, and a return of personal loyalty to himself. He took Arnold at his word, and always treated him and his family as though he believed he had sincerely and honestly and from good motives returned to his allegiance. Hence the favor with which he was received at court; hence the pension to Mrs. Arnold and her children, and the King's active aid in placing Arnold's sons in the way of obtaining a military education preparatory to commissions in the British army, as will be hereafter more fully detailed.

The sad fate of Major André had created a profound sensation in England, and when, soon after Arnold's arrival there, it was suggested to the King to erect a monument to his memory in Westminster Abbey, Arnold took a warm interest in the movement, and both he and his wife watched its progress to completion with the deepest sympathy.

An American loyalist, an exile in England for his opinions, mentions in his diary the incident of seeing General Arnold and his wife in Westminster Abbey, reading the inscription on André's monument and conversing together.[1]

"Many a citizen of the great Western Republic," as Dean Stanley says,[2] "has paused before the sight of this sad story," but never any with hearts more deeply touched than were those of Arnold and his wife.

Had the loyalist who recorded the above incident been behind some contiguous monument he would probably have heard a sad dialogue between these exiles, lamenting the pitiable fate of poor André. He would have heard Mrs. Arnold recall the bright days of her girlhood, when André, the gayest of the gay, was the frequent guest of her father, and the brilliant favorite of the social circle in which she moved.

He would have heard Arnold recall his parting from André, on the banks of the Hudson, and he might have heard the exiled general, when looking back upon the terrible fate of André and his own still more unhappy life, exclaim:

"Would that I had died in battle at Quebec, or on the bloody deck of my ship on Lake Champlain, or at Saratoga, rather than this terrible drama! Then André might have been alive to-day, and you happy at your father's fireside."

"Do not reproach yourself," interrupted his wife. "My own life can never be unhappy while you and our children are with me."

[1] Life of Peter Van Schaack, p. 147.
[2] Stanley's Westminster Abbey, p. 282.

After a pause Arnold continued:

"Yonder," pointing towards the chapel of Henry VII, "yonder, among England's kings, lie the remains of General Monk, Duke of Albemarle,[1] whose part in England's history I was to re-enact in America, *as they told me*," said Arnold, with a smile of bitter irony upon himself.

"If I had succeeded, as I hoped," said he, "in re-uniting the Empire, I too might have found a place and a monument here—as they promised me."[2]

As he lingered, sadly leaning on André's monument, among the graves of so many who have made the greatness and the glory of England, he realized that,

> "No nation's eyes would on *his* tomb be bent,
> No hero envy him *his* monument,
> However boldly his warm blood was spilt,
> His life was shame, his epitaph was guilt."

---

1. "They (Monk and Montague and Ormond), were all buried among the Kings, in the chapel of Henry VII."—*Stanley's Westminster Abbey*, p. 249.

2. "Had the scheme succeeded," wrote an officer of the Coldstream Guards, "no rank would have overpaid so important a service" as Arnold's.—*Life of André*, p. 450.

CHAPTER XXI.

GENERAL ARNOLD ENGAGES IN BUSINESS.

"I am one whom the world loves not."

ARNOLD SETTLES IN PORTMAN SQUARE, LONDON—LIVES BEYOND HIS MEANS—ENGAGES IN TRADE—REMOVES TO ST. JOHN'S, NEW BRUNSWICK—FAMILY CORRESPONDENCE—MRS. ARNOLD VISITS HER FAMILY AT PHILADELPHIA.

THE definitive treaty of peace between the United States and Great Britain was signed September 3d, 1783. The feeling among the people of England against a further prosecution of the war, had been constantly increasing since the surrender of Cornwallis, and no hostile movements of very great importance occurred after that event. Arnold does not appear to have seen any active service as a soldier after his arrival in England. There seem to have been great difficulties in regard to his employment, and it is not hard to understand what they were, and they must have been most galling to one with a spirit so haughty and proud. None doubted either his bravery or his great ability as a soldier, and the King was his friend, and would have gladly given him positions where he might have distinguished himself. That he passionately sought such positions, and especially in the wars with France, eagerly seeking an opportunity to wash off with his blood the blot upon his fame, was well known, and was made manifest by his appeal to the Duke of York and Earl Spencer, which will appear hereafter. But the officers of the British army were made up largely of the sons of the nobility, and how they regarded a Colonist appears in the treatment of Washington in the old French war by Braddock and the English government; besides, and of much greater importance, Arnold's conduct at West Point was condemned almost as severely by the liberal party in England as by his own countrymen, and there were very few who approved it. With this strong feeling against him pervading one party, and existing extensively in the other, it was difficult to give him employment as a soldier. He chafed and struggled against this exclusion as an imprisoned eagle struggles for liberty, but in vain.

During this period his social life involved much larger expenditure than his means supplied. It was a fault of his character to be lavish and extravagant, and his expenses were never measured by his income. Being without military employment, he had no source of revenue except his small investment in the funds, his pay as an officer, and the pension of his wife.

He seems finally to have resolved to devote his attention to the education and advancement of his family, and the acquisition of a fortune adequate to their wants. He resumed the employments of his early years, and again became a merchant. In these efforts to mend his fortune Arnold was seconded by his wife, with an executive ability and good sense which it would have been well for him if he had implicitly followed.

The family correspondence shows that both General and Mrs. Arnold were persons of unusually strong family attachments. His correspondence with his sister Hannah, and with his sons by his first wife, who remained during their childhood and youth under his sister's care, was frequent and affectionate. The letters of Mrs. Arnold to her father and sisters in Philadelphia, are models of filial and sisterly affection; and her attentions to her husband's sister, and his elder sons, Ben, Richard and Henry, were constant and devoted.

In January, 1783, there was born to them their first daughter, named for her mother, Margaret, but she lived only to the next August.

George, their third son and fourth child, was born in March, 1784, and died very soon thereafter.

Sophia Matilda, their second daughter and fifth child, was born in London, July 28th, 1785.

On the 13th of July, in the same year, Mrs. Arnold writes to her father in relation to Mount Pleasant, the country-seat which General Arnold had settled upon her and her children at the time of their marriage, saying:

"General Arnold desires you will be so good as to sell Mount Pleasant for as much as you can, and if it should fall short of the sum which you gave (besides paying off the mortgage), he desires you will be so good as to draw on him for that ballance, as he thinks it better to put up with the first loss than to advance any more money on Mount Pleasant.[1] *

"I must request my dearest Papa to present my tender love to the family. General Arnold begs to be remembered to you all in the most affectionate manner."

Meanwhile, General Arnold had fitted out a ship for a trading voyage to the West Indies, in which he sailed. In his absence, and living among strangers, Mrs. Arnold struggled to maintain her fortitude. In a letter to her father, dated April 11th, 1786, she details her embarrassments and sorrows in a letter full of pathos.

She says:

"MY DEAR AND EVER HONORED PAPA:

" * * * I am still in the most unhappy state of suspense respecting the General, not having heard from him since the account of his ship's being lost. * * *

[1] Autograph letter, July 13, 1785.

"I assure you, my dear Papa, I find it necessary to summon all my philosophy to my aid to support myself under my present situation.

"Separated from, and anxious for the fate of the best of husbands, torn from almost every body that is dear to me, harrassed with a troublesome and expensive law-suit,[1] having all the General's business to transact, and feeling that I am in a strange country, without a creature near me that is really interested in my fate, you will not wonder if I am unhappy.

"But I will not distress you, my beloved Papa, with my unavailing complaints, which I seldom suffer to engross either my pen or my tongue; but deprived of all domestic society, I have too much time to indulge them."

Like a devoted mother, she turns to her children for consolation, and adds:

"My children are perfectly well—my little girl the picture of health, and has never had an hour's illness. I still continue to nurse her. I beg, my dearest Papa, you will present my tender love to all the family. With unceasing prayers for your and their health and happiness, believe me, Yours affectionately."[2]

She was soon relieved by news of her husband's safety.

In 1787, General Arnold removed to St. Johns, New Brunswick, and entered largely into mercantile business, engaging principally in the West India trade. Mr. Sparks suggests that the English Government granted him facilities in the way of contracts for supplying the troops there with provisions.[3] He carried on an extensive business, building ships, and sending cargoes to the West Indies. His two sons, Richard and Henry, joined him, and aided him in his extensive operations. At St. Johns were a large number of loyalists, refugees from the United States, who had fled, or been exiled from their native country, and at the close of the war had settled on this island.

Arnold is said to have exhibited here some of his characteristic faults, living in a style of ostentation and display,

---

1. An old claim against General Arnold, which was decided by the court in his favor.
2. Autograph letter, September 11, 1786.
3. Sparks' Life of Arnold, p. 332.

and to have been haughty and reserved in his intercourse, so that he became personally obnoxious.

While the family were residing at St. Johns, George Arnold, their sixth child, was born.

An incident occurred while he was a resident on the island, which has been told in such a way as to throw discredit upon General Arnold, and to exhibit the injustice with which he has often been treated. In his absence on a visit to England, a warehouse in which his goods were stored, took fire on the 11th of July, 1788, at night, and with its contents was entirely consumed. His son, Henry Arnold, sleeping in the store, was severely burned, barely escaping with his life. The goods, amounting to several thousand pounds, were insured. His enemies circulated reports that he himself had caused the fire, to defraud the underwriters, and they made such representations that the insurance officers refused payment of the insurance money. Arnold brought suit, and after a full investigation and trial, he recovered the full amount.

Yet, notwithstanding the judicial investigation and judgment of the court, Arnold's absence in England at the time of the fire, and the fact that his son came near being burned to death in the conflagration, the cruel charge has been made, and repeated time and time again, that he burned his warehouse in St. Johns to defraud the underwriters.

This is one of the thousand slanders which have been eagerly seized, and without investigation put in circulation, and often repeated without care, whether true or false; yet this is one of the penalties for his great crime. His virtues all ignored, his faults exaggerated, and a thousand falsehoods heaped upon his memory. "Verily, the way of the transgressor is hard!"

In 1788 General Arnold and family returned to London, and in August of that year Chief Justice Shippen writes to his daughter, addressing her at No. 18 Gloucester Place, Portman Square, London, in which he says:

"I write from my country-place, about four miles from the city, which is again visited by a malignant fever, and therefore unsafe to reside in. This dreadful sickness, added to the apprehensions of a war with our former friends, the French, has damped our spirits, and threatens to check the progress of our once prosperous country. * * *

"By way of domestic news, I must tell you that our nabob, Mr. Bingham, has just married his oldest daughter to Alexander Baring, son of Sir Francis Baring, of your country."[1]

Mrs. Arnold, after an absence of seven years, yearned to see her father and her family once more, and on the 14th of August, 1778, writes to her sister, Mrs. Burd, as follows:

"As the time draws near when I hope to be blessed with the society of my beloved sister, I find my impatience increases,—I sometimes fear that it is impossible I shall ever be so happy as to behold my dearest, tenderly beloved parents and sisters; yet as I have got the better of almost every obstacle to my paying you a visit, I ought to anticipate nothing but pleasure—I feel great regret at the idea of leaving the General alone, and much perplexed with business, but as he strongly urges a measure that will be productive of so much happiness to me, I think there can be no impropriety in taking the step. * * There is an excellent vessel that sails between this place and New York, entirely fitted out for the accommodation of passengers—It is generally much crowded, but to avoid that inconvenience, the General proposes taking the whole cabin for me, if it can be procured upon tolerably reasonable terms, in which case it will be optional with me to admit any other persons. I hope to leave this some time in October—I hope, my dear Sister, that I shall not put Mamma to the least additional trouble on my account; it would distress me extremely if I did, in the present state of her health. I cannot *conveniently* go without one maid and child; yet if that would enlarge the family too much, I would make my arrangements differently, and leave only for a couple of months—I am sure when I am with you, that Mamma will find that it is my wish rather to lessen, than to add to the cares of her family. Pray let me hear from you soon; I am extremely anxious about Mamma, the account you gave me of her situation has almost broken my heart—she must suffer extremely from the loss of her limbs, as she has been accustomed to so much exercise."

1. Of the family of the great bankers, and whose son negotiated with Daniel Webster the Ashburton Treaty.

* * * * * * * * *

"A thousand loves to Mr. B. and the family; I wrote to my Mamma and sister some days ago but was disappointed in sending my letters."

Mrs. Arnold made the journey and visited her family in Philadelphia, in accordance with the plans mentioned in the above letter, but her reception by nearly all her old friends, outside of her immediate family, was so cold and repelling, that her warm and affectionate heart was chilled, and she was deeply grieved.

Perhaps this was not surprising, but she was not prepared for it. The feeling against her husband, and to some extent against herself, made her visit to America very uncomfortable. She returned to London, and the family went back to St. Johns, where they remained until 1791.

In a letter to Mr. Burd, her sister's husband, dated April 13th, 1791, Mrs. Arnold says:

"We are in pleasing expectation of returning this summer to England, a country less hostile to our interests, and much better calculated to promote our happiness than this. The escheating lands and some other arbitrary acts of the government here, are causing this country to depopulate very fast. The poor flee to their native places in the States for refuge. Their reception there, I fear, is very doubtful; at least if I may judge from my own."

In the same letter she says:

"Accept, my dear Mr. Burd, the tribute of a grateful heart, animated by the most sincere and lively affection. Your conduct towards me has ever marked the real friend and brother."

A letter from her father to Mrs. Arnold, written in July, 1788, is interesting, as showing the kind and generous consideration and affection he ever manifested for her. Her brother had become indebted to General Arnold in the sum of £750 pounds sterling, and the General had expressed a desire that it should be settled upon Mrs. Arnold and her children, for their sole and separate use. Mr. Shippen writes to his daughter, that

"If he (the son) does not discharge the debt in my lifetime, you may rest assured I will make such a provision in my will, that it shall be paid out of such parts of my estate as I shall allot for the use of him or his family."[1]

In the summer of 1791, General Arnold and his family returned to England, and settled permanently in London.

---

[1] Manuscript letter.

CHAPTER XXII.

ARNOLD'S DUEL WITH THE EARL OF LAUDERDALE.

"Through the perils of chance and the scowl of disdain
May thy front be unaltered, thy courage elate!"

ARNOLD AND TALLEYRAND—ARNOLD'S DUEL WITH THE EARL OF LAUDERDALE—STATEMENT OF LORD HAWKE—MRS. ARNOLD'S LETTERS TO HER FATHER AND TO RICHARD ARNOLD, GIVING AN ACCOUNT OF THE DUEL.

THOSE who have supposed that Arnold was not keenly sensitive to the opinions of his countrymen and the world, because he was too proud to complain and generally reticent, never seeking to excuse or palliate his conduct, did not comprehend the man. An anecdote, which I believe to be substantially true, has been published of an interview between him and Talleyrand, which is significant on this phase of his character. Arnold and the distinguished French diplomat happened to meet at an English country inn. They were strangers, neither knowing the name of the other; but there being no other guests, they dined together, and were mutually pleased with each other. The subject of the United States and American affairs was introduced and discussed, and after dinner, they lingered some time over their wine. Talleyrand, impressed with the intelligence of the stranger, and his familiar knowledge of the public men of America, at length said to him: "From your knowledge of all that relates to the United States, I am sure you must be an American; my name is Talleyrand," handing to the General his card, "and I am about to visit that country; perhaps you will be so kind as to give me some letters of introduction to your friends there."

Arnold replied: "You are right in supposing I am an American. I was born and have spent nearly all my life there, yet I am probably the only American living who can say, 'I have not one friend in America! No, not one!' I am Benedict Arnold."

The duel between General Arnold and the Earl of Lauderdale has been the subject of much misrepresentation. I have the means of stating the exact truth in regard to it, and of adding that this was the only duel in which he was ever engaged while in England.

The meeting grew out of what was said by Lord Lauderdale in the House of Lords, on the 31st of May, 1792, in a very warm, excited and personal debate on the King's proclamation against seditious meetings. After the Marquis of Abercorn, the Earl of Harrington, Lord Hawke, His Royal Highness the Prince of Wales, and others, had addressed their Lordships, the Earl of Lauderdale followed, and with great vehemence charged the Ministers with gross inconsistency. He compared their conduct to that of Mr. Pitt and the Duke of Richmond at the close of the American war.

"How the noble Duke and Mr. Pitt would vindicate such a change of conduct he knew not, but would leave it to them," etc.

"The Earl at length took notice of the camp at Bagshot, which he said the noble Duke (of Richmond), who had been so strenuous for reform, was appointed to command, to overawe the people, and destroy their endeavors to obtain a reform. He declared he was glad the Duke was to command the camp. If *apostacy* could justify promotion, he was the most fit person for that command, *General Arnold alone excepted*." [1]

1. Cobbett's Parliamentary Debates, Vol. XXIX, p. 1518-19.
"To these remarks the Duke of Richmond replied in language which called

When these remarks appeared in the report of the debate, General Arnold instantly saw his opportunity. A soldier with a blot upon his name, he had been an exile for ten years, bearing in silence every mortification and indignity which bitter enemies could inflict.

These indignities and mortifications had generally been in a form and from sources he could neither notice nor resent, and he had borne them in haughty silence. Now the Earl of Lauderdale, a nobleman as high in character as in rank, the hereditary standard-bearer of Scotland,[1] in the House of Lords, in the face of the peers of all England, and in the knowledge of all the world, had assailed him in a manner which no soldier could endure. Arnold knew that the words of the Earl would be seized by his enraged countrymen as the judgment of England upon his conduct.

Such an attack was not a manly thing on the part of the Earl of Lauderdale. Whatever Arnold's guilt, he was a stranger, with not too many friends, struggling unequally against a torrent of troubles. True, he had brought these troubles upon himself, but it is not a manly or a generous act to taunt even the guilty when on the scaffold. Besides, it was hardly fair for a high official of the government which had seduced him, now in his exile to scoff at his treason. The Earl, however, had no personal hostility to Arnold; in the heat of debate he had used his name "to point a moral," if not "to adorn a tale."

He had capped his brilliant rhetorical climax of apostacy with the name of Benedict Arnold. However amusing this

from the Earl of Lauderdale, through Mr. Grey, a demand for an explanation or a meeting. After discussion, the Earl of Lauderdale declared the expression used by him, applied solely to the Duke of Richmond's public conduct, and that he meant nothing in any respect to his Grace's private character. The Duke of Richmond, on his part, declared he did not persist in the terms he used to Lord Lauderdale, those expressions having been suggested solely by the idea of his private character's having been attacked."—*Cobbett's Parliamentary Debates*, Vol. XXIX, p. 1519, *note*.

1. Lodge's British Peerage.

may have been to the Earl, it was terribly severe, not to say cruel, to Arnold. He felt that his hour had come, both "the hour and the man."

He had waited for such an opportunity to seek such poor vindication of himself as "the field of honor," so-called, would afford, and none better suited to his purpose could have been devised—the place of the assault, one of the most dignified deliberative assemblies in the world; the assailant, in position, rank and character, among the highest in England.

Arnold gladly seized the opportunity to show that he was yet willing to die, if need be, in vindication of his name, and in teaching such assailants forbearance. His warm personal friend, Lord Hawke, volunteered to carry his message to the Earl, demanding an apology or a hostile meeting. The Earl declined to apologize, and a meeting was arranged, Lord Hawke acting for General Arnold, and Charles James Fox, the great parliamentary orator, acting for Lord Lauderdale.[1]

The meeting was appointed for 7 o'clock on Sunday morning, a short distance out of London, near Kilburn Wells.

Mrs. Arnold, in a letter to her father, set forth hereafter, says: "A variety of circumstances combined to make me acquainted with the whole transaction. What I suffered for nearly a week is not to be described; the suppression of my feelings, lest I should unman the General, almost at last proved too much for me, and for some hours my reason was despaired of, and I was confined to my bed for some days after."

The picture of Mrs. Arnold, separated from every rela-

---

[1] Fox, Pitt and Burke—Fox, of whom Byron said,

"The first of the wondrous three,
Whose words were sparks of immortality."

tion in the world, "feeling," as she said to her father in a letter before mentioned, "feeling that she was in a strange country, without a creature near her really interested in her fate," with her young children around her, struggling to suppress her feelings lest she should "unman" her husband, is an exhibition of heroism, fortitude and devotion rarely surpassed.

On the Sunday morning appointed, General Arnold arose very early, and Mrs. Arnold awake, conscious that her husband was going to a hostile meeting, which might result in his death, yet feigned sleep, lest the parting should unnerve him. He kissed her tenderly, but careful not to awaken her, spoke no parting words, and accompanied Lord Hawke to the place of meeting. There they were met by the Earl and Mr. Fox.[1]

It was arranged that the principals were to fire on the word, to be given by Mr. Fox. Lord Lauderdale received General Arnold's fire, which was without effect, but did not return the fire. Lord Hawke, supposing Lord Lauderdale's pistol had missed fire, desired him to fire. General Arnold, calmly and firmly keeping his ground, to receive the Earl's shot, called out to him to "fire." His Lordship declined, saying he had no enmity to General Arnold. Lord Hawke then said he supposed Lord Lauderdale would not object to say that he did not mean to asperse General Arnold's character. His Lordship declined, saying he had formerly said he did not mean to wound General Arnold's feelings; he should not explain what he had said; General Arnold might fire again if he chose. This Lord Hawke and General Arnold said was impossible. Then Lord Lauderdale said he could not retract his words, but was sorry if any man felt hurt by them. On which General Arnold said, "that is not a proper apology—such as I would make myself in a

[1] For this incident I am indebted to Rev. Edward G. Arnold.

similar situation," and he again insisted on his Lordship's firing. Lord Lauderdale did not fire, but after a few words with General Arnold, and with Lord Hawke, *and Mr. Fox*, he came forward, and said: "I have no enmity against General Arnold; I did *not mean to asperse his character*,' or wound his feelings, and I am sorry that General Arnold or any other person should be hurt at what I have said."

To which General Arnold replied: "Lord Lauderdale, I am perfectly satisfied with your apology, provided our seconds as men of honor will say that I ought to be."

Both Lord Hawke and Mr. Fox agreed that the apology ought to be deemed perfectly satisfactory.

Before the parties left the ground, the Earl, on learning from a messenger which Mrs. Arnold, in her extreme anxiety had sent to the place of meeting, that she was ill from anxiety and apprehension, with true chivalry expressed great concern and regret, and begged permission to wait upon her to express his sorrow and make his apology.

The following statement was drawn up July 7, 1792, by General Arnold at his residence in Portland Place, and endorsed and verified by Lord Hawke, as "a moderate and unexaggerated statement of the dispute between General Arnold and Lord Lauderdale:"[2]

"A STATE OF THE AFFAIR OF HONOR DECIDED BETWEEN LORD LAUDERDALE AND GENERAL ARNOLD, ON SUNDAY MORNING, THE 1ST OF JULY, NEAR KILBURN WELLS.

"The parties met at about 8 o'clock—Lord Lauderdale with his friend, Mr. Fox, and Lord Hawke, as the friend of General Arnold. The parties agreed to fire together. on a word given by Mr. Fox. Lord Lauderdale received General Arnold's fire (which was without effect), and

1. I believe it was the suggestion of Fox, whose generous feelings were touched by Arnold's misfortunes, that induced the Earl to withdraw the aspersions upon Arnold's character.

2. The original paper, in the handwriting of General Arnold, and the endorsement, in the handwriting of Lord Hawke, furnished by a grandson of General Arnold, is now before me.

reserved his own. Lord Hawke told Lord Lauderdale that he believed his pistol had missed fire, and desired him to fire. He was also called upon by General Arnold to fire (who kept his ground for that purpose), which his Lordship declined, saying that he had no enmity to General Arnold. Lord Hawke then observed that he supposed Lord Lauderdale would not object to say that he did not mean to asperse General Arnold's character, which his Lordship declined, saying that he had formerly said he did not mean to wound General Arnold's feelings; he should not explain what he had said, and that General Arnold might fire again if he chose. This Lord Hawke and General Arnold said was impossible. Then Lord Lauderdale said he could not retract his words, but was sorry if any man felt hurt by them; on which General Arnold said that was not a proper apology—such as he should make himself in a similar situation—and again insisted on his Lordship's firing.

"Lord Lauderdale, after having some short conversation with General Arnold and the seconds, came forward very handsomely, like a man of honor, and declared "that he had no enmity against General Arnold, that he did not mean to asperse General Arnold's character, or wound his feelings, and was sorry that General Arnold, or any other person should be hurt at what he had said."

"General Arnold told Lord Lauderdale that he was perfectly satisfied with his apology, provided their seconds, as men of honor, would say that he ought to be so, which they both did.

"PORTLAND PLACE,
"July 7th, 1792,

"This is a moderate and unexaggerated statement of the dispute between General Arnold and Lord Lauderdale, to the best of my knowledge and belief, on the part of General Arnold.

"HAWKE."

On the sixth of July Mrs. Arnold wrote to her father, giving the details of the duel. If she speaks with some pride of the conduct of her husband, and colors some circumstances in his favor, it will be forgiven to the partiality of a devoted wife.

"MY BELOVED AND RESPECTED PARENT:

"The anxiety which my last letter must have occasioned, as I then mentioned the probability of a Duel's taking place between the Earl of Lauderdale and General Arnold, I am happy now to have it in my power to relieve; as the affair is settled most honorably for the General, and his conduct upon the occasion has gained him great applause. The circumstances that gave rise to it you may wish to hear: Lord Lauderdale (who is violent in the opposition, and who was the only man in the House of Lords who voted against an address of thanks to the King, upon a late Proclamation), in an attack upon the Duke of Richmond, respecting the reform in Parliament, is said to have used the following expressions: 'That he did not know any instance of Political Apostacy equal to the Duke of Richmond's, except General Arnold's,' and that 'the intended Encampment was designed to overawe the inhabitants of the Kingdom, and the Metropolis in particular; and prevent a Reform in Parliament, that the Duke of Richmond was the most proper person he knew of to command it, General Arnold first struck off the list.' Upon the General's demanding an apology for this unprovoked attack upon his character, his Lordship positively denied having made use of the last expression, or any similar to it; the first he acknowledged, and made a kind of apology for it; but, it not satisfying the General, he drew up such a one as he would accept, which his Lordship refused to sign.

Lord Hawke (who is a most respectable Peer, and our particular friend) voluntarily offered his services upon the occasion; and as the matter could not be amicably settled, his Lordship waited upon Lord Lauderdale, and a place was named for a meeting. The time appointed was seven o'clock on Sunday morning last—Mr. Charles Fox, as second to Lord Lauderdale; Lord Hawke, the General's. It was agreed that they should fire at the same time, upon a word given, which the General did, without effect. Lord L. refused to fire, saying he had no enmity to General Arnold. He at the same time refused making an apology, and said the General might fire again, if he chose. This was impossible, but the General desired Lord Hawke to tell Mr. Fox, that he would not leave the field without satisfaction; and that if Lord Lauderdale persisted in his refusal of giving it to him, either by an apology or firing again, that he should be under the necessity of using such expressions to him, as would oblige him to do the latter. Upon this, the seconds had a conference, during which time Lord Lauderdale and the General met; when he told his Lordship that he did not come there to convince the world that he dare fight, but for satisfaction for the injury done his character; and that he certainly would not quit the field without it. After a consultation between Lord L. & Mr. Fox, his Lordship came forward, and said that he had no enmity to General Arnold—that he did not mean to asperse his character or wound his feelings, and was sorry for what he had said. General A. said he was perfectly satisfied with this apology, provided the seconds, as men of honor, declared he ought to be so, which they, without hesitation, did. Before they left the ground, Lord Lauderdale expressed great concern at finding that I had been made unhappy, and begged leave to wait upon me, to make an apology. A variety of circumstances combined to make me acquainted with the whole transaction; what I suffered for near a week is not to be described; the suppression of my feelings, lest I should unman the General, almost at last proved too much for me; and for some hours, my reason was dispaired of. I was confined to my bed for some days after, but am now so much better that I shall go out an airing this afternoon. It has been highly gratifying to find the General's conduct so much applauded, which it has been universally, and particularly by a number of the first characters in the Kingdom, who have called upon him in consequence of it. Nor am I displeased at the great commendations bestowed on my own conduct upon this trying occasion. I wrote you a long letter about ten days ago, upon the subject of the little money that has been received as a provision for my children, which letter I hope you will receive safe. I intended sending a duplicate, but am not at present equal to copying it. I mentioned that we could not, in the Funds, get above 4 per cent. for money, and by annuities, insured, not more than 6 per cent.; Expressed the great anxiety I should feel until something was secured to my children, as the greatest part of our Income depended upon our lives: (Ah! how lately has one of them been endangered) and entreated your advice and assistance in the disposal of it to advantage. I suggested a wish that Mr. Lea would employ a small sum in business for the advantage of my children, but left the matter entirely to your discretion, and begged that if you were of opinion that it would be better to place the money in Philadelphia, and that it would there produce a good Interest, and be safe, that you would have the goodness to undertake the business for me,—and authorized you to draw upon me, if Bills were at or above Par, on Messrs. Dorset & Co., Bankers, New Bond street, for £2,000 sterling. I shall impatiently wait your answer, my beloved Papa, as we shall not think of disposing of the money otherways till then. The honorable and advantageous Peace made by Lord Cornwallis in the East Indies, has afforded great pleasure to all *loyal subjects* here. Many people look forward with dread to the 14th of July, as they are fearful of Riots on that day, but I sincerely hope it is without cause.—I beg to be most affectionately remembered to all the family, in which the General begs leave to join.

"Believe me, my dearly beloved Parent,

"Most truly Yours,

"M. ARNOLD."[1]

In a letter to Richard, the second son of General Arnold by his first wife, written in August, 1792, Mrs. Arnold says:

[1] The foregoing is copied from the original, in the possession of Edward Shippen, Esq., of Philadelphia.

"I was greatly distressed about six weeks ago by your Father's being concerned in a duel, but it has ended so safely and honorably to him, I am happy it has taken place. The Earl of Lauderdale cast some reflections upon his political character in the House of Lords, for which your Father demanded an apology, which his Lordship refused to make. On Sunday morning, the 1st of July, they went out a few miles from town, with their Seconds and Surgeons—Lord Hawke, your Father's, and Mr. Charles Fox, Lord Lauderdale's.

"Lord Lauderdale received your Father's fire, but refused to return it, saying he had no enmity to him. After a little deliberation, and your Father's declaring that he would not quit the field without an apology, his Lordship made a very satisfactory one. Your Father has gained very great credit in this business, and I fancy it will deter others from taking liberties with him. * *"

I extract the following paragraphs from a letter from Mrs. Arnold to Richard, dated July 28, 1793, showing her deep interest in his welfare, and how kindly and discreetly she discharged the duties of a mother towards him:

"I shall always be happy," says she, "to consider you as a son, whose welfare is dear to me."

"You request, my dear Richard, my influence with your father to induce him to consent to your marrying. With respect to him, I must beg not to interfere;—but give me leave, as a friend interested for your happiness, to offer you my advice. I should by no means wish you to give up a young lady to whom your love and honor are engaged, and who, from everything I can hear, is worthy of your affection. But by the love you bear her, let me admonish you not to marry her till you are enabled to support her in a comfortable style. How many people are there who are for years engaged, while prudence forbids an union, who afterwards come together, and are happier for their self-denial, till fortune smiled upon them. You are particularly fortunate in not b ing severed from the object of your affections; you can enjoy her society, and your desire to unite yourself to her will stimulate your Industry.

"By precipitating yourself into matrimony till you are established in business, you would probably render yourself and the object of your regards miserable;—but by your exertions, a short time may make a material change in your affairs, and you will then be enabled to marry her. with a prospect of happiness, and with the approbation of your friends.

* * * * * * * * *

"Your affectionate, &c."

CHAPTER XXIII.

ARNOLD'S SERVICES IN THE WEST INDIES—HIS DEATH.

*"Seek out—less often sought than found—
A soldier's grave, for thee the best."*

GENERAL ARNOLD IN 1794 FITS OUT A SHIP FOR THE WEST INDIES—SHIP LOST—AT GAUDALOUPE—HIS DANGER—ESCAPES TO THE ENGLISH FLEET—HIS SERVICES TO THE GOVERNMENT IN THE WEST INDIES—RECEIVES THE THANKS OF THE PLANTERS—THE KING GRANTS TO HIM 13,500 ACRES OF CANADA LANDS FOR HIS "GALLANTRY," &c.—HE BEGS THE DUKE OF YORK FOR MILITARY SERVICE AGAINST THE FRENCH—HIS DEATH.

IN the spring of 1794, General Arnold purchased a ship for the purpose of going to the West Indies, and engaging in trade and commerce.

To avoid the dangers of the British Channel, he went by land to Falmouth, and after waiting some two weeks for the arrival of his ship, just as she was about coming into port, he fortunately concluded not to sail in her, but stepped on board the packet, ready to put to sea. A few days there after, his ship with a va'uable cargo, was captured by the French, but he arrived in safety at St. Kitto.[1] In a letter to Richard, Mrs. Arnold says:

"I am now in a state of most extreme misery, from the report of your Father's being a prisoner to the French at Point-a-Peter, Gaudaloupe. It is contradicted by some gentlemen lately from St. Kitto, but your Father's last letter to me, being of the first of June, wherein he says he shall set-off the next day for Point-a-Peter, makes it but too probable,

---

1. Manuscript letter from Mrs. Arnold to Richard Arnold, dated Aug. 1794.

as the French took possession of that Place the 4th of June. We are in hourly expectation of its re-capture, till I hear of which I shall not know a moment's peace of mind."[1]

It seems that early in June, he arrived at Point-a-Peter, with about five thousand pounds in cash, with which to buy sugar; not knowing that the Island had fallen into the hands of the French. When he learned that the French were already in possession, assuming the name of *Anderson*, he passed for an American, come there to buy a cargo. He knew of course, that if his rank and person were discovered, he would be taken prisoner, and held as a British General. Not daring to be seen in the town, he concealed himself near the shore, and set to work to construct a raft for his escape. The French fleet lay near the fortifications, guarding the island, and outside of the French lay the British fleet. Waiting for a favorable juncture of wind and tide— as darkness closed over the island and the sea, he put himself afloat on his frail raft, to take the hazards of passing undiscovered through the French to the English fleet.[2] Without a single attendant, aided by the tide and the wind, he rowed silently through the hostile fleet, and although hailed by the French guard-boat, he at length reached the deck of a British man-of-war, and was taken on board. His usual boldness and readiness in extricating himself from danger, had not deserted him, and he was able to render the English great service.

It was not long before he was able to send to Mrs. Arnold intelligence of his escape and safe arrival on board the British flag-ship.

On the 25th of June, 1794, was born William Fitch, the fifth son of General Arnold.

In the same letter to Richard, from which I have already quoted, Mrs. Arnold, alluding to the capture of the ship

[1] Manuscript letter, Aug., 1794.
[2] The Gentleman's Magazine. Aug., 1794. Vol. LXIV, p. 685.

and cargo before referred to, and other losses, says : "I am extremely distressed to find that your father is likely to be so ill-rewarded for all the risks he has run. * * * * There seems to be a cruel fatality attending all his exertions."

Speaking of Henry, the younger brother of Richard, she says :

"I suppose my dear Henry is long ere this in the West Indies; I scarcely know whether or not to wish it, as, though I think his prospects in going very good, yet the fever that rages there proves so fatal to young people, that I dread his falling a victim to it. * * * "

She recommends Richard, then at New Haven, Connecticut, "not to meddle with the politics of the country, and to avoid writing to any one on the subject." She adds :

"We have not heard from poor Ben (General Arnold's oldest son by his first wife) for a long time past, and have reason to fear he is a prisoner, as about 6,000 English are now in that situation in France, and those who previous to the war resided there; have been told they are very well treated, but I think I have now got things in a train to get certain information of him, and to furnish him with money.

"Should you wish to forward me your certificate and draw for your half-pay, I will attend to your business.[1]

"Edward, James and George are all at school, and coming on very well; they and Sophia send their tender love to you. The latter is remarkably handsome, and promises to make a very fine woman."

While in the West Indies at another time, engaged in commerce, General Arnold was himself taken prisoner by the French, and although not known as a British officer, he was put on board a French prison-ship. He learned from a sentinel that he was suspected of being other than he appeared, and in great danger. At night he let himself down from the side of the ship, and by the aid of some planks, used as a raft, reached a small boat, in which he escaped to the English.

[1.] Both Richard and Henry were commissioned by Sir Henry Clinton as lieutenants of cavalry in the American Legion, raised by General Arnold, and were now receiving half-pay, as retired officers.

He rendered great service to Sir Charles Grey, commanding on that station,[1] in consideration whereof, and of other services to the government, he received in August, 1795, from Gilbert Franklin, Chairman of the Committee of West India planters and merchants, resolutions of the Standing Committee, expressing their high appreciation and approbation of his conduct in the West Indies, and the wish that he might be further employed in the public service.[2]

In December, 1796, General Arnold conceived a plan for the capture by the British of the Spanish possessions in the West Indies. This plan, through the kindness of his friend, Lord Cornwallis, was laid before Mr. Pitt, then Prime Minister. I have now before me the draft of a letter to Cornwallis, in which General Arnold says:

---

1. See Gentleman's Magazine, Vol. XC, p. 670.

2. The following is a copy of the resolution, and Gen. Arnold's reply to the Chairman of the Committee:

"*Resolved*, That the standing committee of the West India planters and merchants, beg leave to return him (Gen. A.) their thanks; that they are fully sensible of his services in the West Indies, and feel themselves particularly obliged by his exertions, at the request of the commander in-chief, which were attended, with such beneficial effects, in covering the retreat of the troops at Gaudaloupe, and they cannot refrain from expressing their concern at his having quitted the Islands at a time when their safety is in the utmost hazard, and they beg leave to assure him it would give them the most entire satisfaction to find he was again in a situation to render further service to his Majesty in that part of the world."

"QUEEN ANN ST. E., AUG. 1st, 1795.

"SIR.—I have had the honor of receiving your very obliging letter of this day, enclosing a copy of a resolution of the standing committee of the West India planters and merchants, expressive of their appreciation of my conduct in the West Indies, and a wish for my being further employed. The approbation of so very respectable a body of gentlemen cannot fail of being highly gratifying to me, and I beg you will do me the favor of returning them my sincere thanks for the honor they have done me, and assure them that nothing would afford me greater pleasure than having an opportunity of rendering them essential service in the West Indies.

"I have the honor to be,
"With great respect and esteem,
"Sir, your most obedient
"And humble Servant,
"B. ARNOLD.

"To GILBERT FRANKLIN,
"Chairman of the Standing Committee
"Of the West India Planters and Merchants."

HIS PATRIOTISM AND HIS TREASON. 389

"I beg you will accept my thanks for your friendly attention in speaking to Mr. Pitt on the subject of my plan, which the more I consider it the more important it appears to me in its consequences. * * * "I will pledge myself, with such a covering fleet as I have mentioned, and 5,000 effective men, to begin operations; I will raise so formidable an army of the natives, creoles, and people of colour, that no force that Spain has there, or can send to that country, will be able to resist or prevent their freeing the country from the Spanish Government. Permit me to request the favor, my Lord, should there appear a favorable opertunity to carry such plan into effect, that you will have the goodness to remind Mr. Pitt of it, & my wishes to be employed in it."[1]

In the following year, 1797, Arnold addressed a letter to Earl Spencer, of the British cabinet, in which he says:

"Having had some experience in conducting naval as well as military affairs, I think it my duty at this alarming crisis, to tender my services to your Lordship, to be employed as you may think proper."[2]

In 1798, the King of Great Britain granted to General Arnold and to his family 13,400 acres of land, to be selected from the Waste Lands of the Crown in Upper Canada. It is recited in the letter of the Duke of Portland, Secretary of State, to President Russell, of Canada, that "his (Arnold's) very gallant and meritorious service at Guadaloupe, in the present war," has induced his majesty to dispense with the condition requiring his residence in Canada.[3]

While General Arnold was in the West Indies, the war between Great Britain and France was waged with great

1. Manuscript Letter of Dec 29, 1796.
2. Manuscript Letter of June 1, 1797.
3. Manuscript letter from the Duke of Portland, Secretary of State for the Home Department, to President Russell, Canada, dated—
"Whitehall," June 12, 1798, in which he says:
"His (Arnold's) very gallant and meritorious conduct at Gaudeloupe, in the present war, has induced his Majesty, in consequence of the General's situation and that of his family here, to dispense in this instance, with that part of the Royal instructions, which would require the residence of the General and that of his family in the Province.
"You will therefore make out the grants to the General and his family, on the usual terms and conditions—that of residence alone excepted.
"I am, &c.,
"PORTLAND."

vigor, and party spirit raged in England with extreme violence. Great excitement prevailed, and when, in 1798, all England was arming against the French, the martial spirit of Arnold was once more thoroughly roused, and he made a last, most earnest and pressing appeal, through the Duke of York, for active service. Like an old war-horse when he hears the sound of the bugle, he was again fired with military ardor.

He addressed the following letter to his Royal Highness, the Duke of York, then commanding the British armies:

"GLOUCESTER PLACE,
"April 22, 1798.
"SIR:
"At this important crisis, I feel it a duty that I owe both to the public and to myself, to offer my services to your Royal Highness in any way that I can be most useful to the country.
"I have the honor to be most Respectfully, Sir,
"Your Royal Highness' most Obedient
"And most devoted Humble Servant,
"B. ARNOLD.[1]

"HIS ROYAL HIGHNESS,
"THE DUKE OF YORK,
"&c., &c., &c."

This appeal was in vain. For reasons already given, he was apprised that his offer of service could not be accepted, and he sadly and bitterly realized that he could no longer hope for active service in the British army.

If there had been any desperate duty involving the most hazardous personal exposure, any "forlorn hope" to have been led, he was the man, and in the mood, to have led it to victory or death. He begged for service in the West Indies, where unacclimated officers were dying in great numbers from disease. He would have gladly welcomed death on any field of battle. He was now made to feel more keenly

---

1. The original draft of the letter is before me, furnished by Rev. Edward Gladwin Arnold.

than ever, the full extent of his sacrifice, his blunder and his crime. Returning from an unsuccessful personal application at the war-office, he said to his wife, "They will not give me a chance to seek a soldier's death."

With a crushed heart, he felt the utter ruin of all his ambitious hopes.

"Oh, now, forever,
  *   *   *   *   *
Farewell, the plumed troop, and the big wars,
That make ambition virtue! O, farewell!
Farewell, the neighing steed, and the shrill trump,
The spirit-stirring drum, the ear piercing fife,
The royal banner, and all quality,
Pride, pomp and circumstance of glorious war.
  *   *   *   *   *
Othello's occupation 's gone!"

From this time on to his death, he was a changed man. He lingered after this blow for about two years, but during the remainder of his life he was subject to periods of moody melancholy and deep dejection. He sought excitement in desperate adventures, to restore his shattered fortunes.

Against the advice and entreaties of his wife, he was active in fitting out privateers against France, involving large expenditures and great hazards. The little that is known of the details of these, his last years, is gathered from the letters of his wife and children. Whatever indignities he received abroad, whatever of regret, or remorse he suffered, his wife and children did all that was possible to soothe and comfort a bitterly disappointed and unhappy man; and in their perfect union and affection, and in their devotion to him, he found his best consolation for his many troubles. His elder sons were being educated at the government military school. Earl Cornwallis had already manifested his kind interest in their behalf.

In December, 1799, Arnold's extreme solicitude to secure for his son George, then a lad of twelve, a place in the India service, induced him to write to Lord Cornwallis begging his further aid.[1]

This appeal was not in vain. Mrs. Arnold, writing to her step-sons in Canada, says: "George has lately been admitted into the Royal Academy, through the interest of the Marquis Cornwallis, and is educating for India."

In one of his northern campaigns in America, between 1775 and 1777, General Arnold became the father of an illegitimate son. The circumstances of his association with the mother—how much of romance and sentiment and what of wrong—are all involved in obscurity. I can only state that in all the vicissitudes of his life, and amidst all his changing fortunes, in adversity as well as in prosperity, this son was never forgotten. Provision was made for his maintenance and education, and he was remembered in General Arnold's will. After his marriage, the conduct of General Arnold in his domestic relations was without reproach, and for more than twenty years of married life, his devotion and fidelity were such as to secure from Mrs. Arnold the utmost confidence and affection. She always spoke of him as the best of husbands, and it was an incident of her life, which illustrates her noble character, that she herself took care

---

1. The following is the letter of General Arnold:

"LONDON, Dec. 10, 1799.

"MY LORD:

"Nothing but my very great confidence in your Lordship's goodness, which I have experienced on so many occasions, and my extreme solicitude to make provision for my son, would induce me to again take the liberty of troubling your Lordship.

"He is extremely anxious to go to India, and having failed in my endeavours to procure him a writership, he has for some time past been qualifying himself as an engineer, in which he has made great proficiency, and proposes spending the winter in studying with the master of the Academy at Woolwich, and has no doubt, in a few months, of procuring their testimonials of his being perfectly qualified for the situation. Your Lordship was once kind enough to offer him a Cadetship to India, and the offer has lately been repeated by a friend here, which he will accept provided he can be assured of the respect with which I have the honor to be

"Your Lordship's

"Most obedient and humble Servant,

"B. ARNOLD.

"LORD CORNWALLIS."

—'Historical Magazine,' Aug., 1870, Vol. VIII, No. 2, p. 110.

that the provision made by her husband in his will, for this son, was scrupulously carried into effect, even at the expense of her own more happy and fortunate children.

In May, 1796, writing to her father, Mrs. Arnold says:

"I am extremely impatient for the arrival of your picture, which I hope is on its way; you could not have bestowed upon me so valuable a gift.[1]

"Repining is useless, but it is surely a hard lot, to be separated from all my relations: do not suffer absence to weaken your affection for me, and believe, that though fate has deprived me of the happiness of contributing to the comfort of your later days, I would sacrifice almost my life to render them easy and free from care and pain."[2]

As time passed on, the bitter disappointments, cares and embarrassments of General Arnold pressed heavily upon him, and his strong physique and hardy frame began to show signs of breaking up. He became more and more the subject of nervous disease—sleep fled from him, and on the 14th of June, 1801, he died at his residence in London, aged sixty years. A letter of a friend of the family to Chief Justice Shippen, gives some details of the event:

"It is the request of my tenderly beloved friend, your deeply afflicted daughter, that I should inform you of the melancholy change which has taken place in her situation by the death of her ever dear and honored husband. General Arnold died on the 14th inst. (June), at half-past six in the morning. His health has been in a declining state for several months, but the danger which awaited him his poor wife was not fully aware of, from the flattering assurances constantly given her by the Physician who attended. * * *

"My sister and myself were with Mrs. Arnold when her husband expired, and we shall not be separated from her for some time, and there is not any attention which friendship and affection can suggest to soothe and soften her sorrows, which shall be omitted.

"She evinces upon this occasion, as you know she has done upon many trying ones before, that fortitude and resignation, which a superior and well-regulated mind only is capable of exerting."[3]

1. A portrait of Chief Justice Shippen, by Stuart.
2. Manuscript letter from Mrs. A. to her father.
3. Manuscript letter of Mrs. Ann Fitch, to Chief Justice Shippen.

394   LIFE OF BENEDICT ARNOLD.

On the first of July thereafter, Mrs. Arnold wrote to Richard and Henry, announcing their father's death. She says:

"Your dear Father, whose long declining state of health you have been acquainted with, is no more. In him his family have lost an affectionate husband, Father and friend: and to his exertions to make a provision for them may be attributed the loss of his life. His last unsuccessful speculation, with the mortification and distress attending it, pressed heavily upon him, and for many months before his death, he never lay two hours of a night in his bed, and he had every dreadful nervous symptom, attended with great difficulty of breathing, that can possibly be imagined. I had flattered myself that a favorable change in his circumstances, which would restore peace to his mind, and enable him to get a horse, and go into the country, and resume his favorite exercise of horse-back riding, would renovate his health, but the wished-for change never took place, but on the contrary he had heavy demands upon him from different quarters.

"On the 8th of June he became much worse, and suffered greatly for several days, and on Sunday, the 14th, at halfpast six o'clock in the morning, expired without a groan. For same days previous to his death he had but short intervals of reason, when the distressed situation of his family preyed greatly on his mind, and he was constantly imploring blessings upon them."[1]

At the same time, Mrs. Arnold wrote to General Arnold's sister, Hannah, giving an account of her husband's last sickness and death, and saying that in his last hours, she (the sister) was not forgotten; and she adds:

"His last moments were embittered by apprehensions of the distress which you might suffer, if, as he feared, his Estate might be left in a condition to render the continuance of your pension impossible; but I assure you that so long as my own pension from the government is paid, or so long as I have the means from any source, your pension shall be continued."

It is said that in those varying moments of consciousness and delirium which often immediately precede death, the mind is more apt to recall the earlier rather than the later scenes and incidents of life. This I have reason to believe

---

[1] Manuscript letter of Mrs. Arnold, to Richard and Henry, dated July 1, 1801.

was true in the case of General Arnold. It will be remembered that when at West Point, on the morning of his flight, on hearing of André's capture, Arnold was at breakfast at his head-quarters, on the Hudson. He had expected Washington to breakfast with him, and Colonel Hamilton, the aid of Washington, and others were at his table. He was in the full uniform of a Major-General of the Continental army. It was in this uniform that he escaped to the Vulture; it was in this dress (for he had no other clothes with him) that he arrived in New York.[1]

This uniform, associated with his military life before his desertion, he carefully preserved, and took with him to England. Tradition says, that as death drew near, after one of those short intervals of reason, "when the distressed condition of his family preyed greatly on his mind," and he was, as Mrs. Arnold writes, "imploring blessings upon his children," his mind wandered again, and in imagination he seemed to be fighting his battles over, he called for his old uniform, and desired to put it on, saying, "Bring me, I beg you, the epaulettes and sword-knots which Washington gave me; let me die in my old American uniform, the uniform in which I fought my battles."

"God forgive me," he muttered, "for ever putting on any other."

Thus, in bitter distress, in self-reproach, in poverty, died Benedict Arnold.

His example will never produce another traitor! There is no character in history, nor is there any in poetry or fiction, better calculated to teach and illustrate the beauty and the wisdom of fidelity, and the infamy and the folly of treachery, than his. Oh, chief among the virtues, is fidelity based on integrity. "Faithful to his trust!" "Faithful

---

[1] See his letter to Washington, asking that his clothes might be sent to him, and offering to pay for them, heretofore quoted.

unto death!" "Faithful and true!" These are the noblest words in all the legends of chivalry.[1] General Arnold did well, after betraying his trust and deceiving Washington, to erase from his family arms the word "Glory," and write in place of it "*Despair*."

In doing this, he indicated how gladly he would have washed out his guilt with his own blood.

All Americans have been taught to think of him only as a *traitor*. I appeal to a just and generous people to remember that he was a *patriot* also ; that no one ever shed his blood more freely for the liberties of his country, and that it was Washington who declared no more brave, active, spirited, no more sensible officer "filled any place" in the Revolutionary army.

In regard to his character, I have little to add to what has been said in the progress of this work. As a soldier he exhibited a superb courage, that was never surpassed, and which made him the idol of his men. He possessed an endurance, a capacity for leadership, an ability for organization, a power over men, a fertility of invention, a coolness in danger, and a quickness of perception, which marked him as among the best, if not the very best fighting general of the Revolutionary war.[2]

He was a man of violent passions, and impatient of control, but towards his friends, his mother, his sister, his wife, his children, his heart was gentle and most affectionate, and he died, as Mrs. Arnold says, a sacrifice to his efforts in their behalf, and "imploring blessings" upon them. He was extravagant and improvident in his habits, but liberal and generous to his friends. He was proud, and very sensi-

---

[1] "*Fidelete est de Dieu.*"
[2] The following extravagant eulogy is by an English writer:
"Arnold displayed more real military genius and inspiration, than all the generals put together, on both sides, engaged in the war, with the most undaunted personal courage."—*Knight's History of England*, Vol. I, N. S. p. 430.

tive to personal wrongs, and I repeat what I said early in this work, if Washington had been invested with the uncontrolled power of appointments and promotion in his army, history would never have recorded "*traitor*" opposite the name of Benedict Arnold.

The following extract from a letter of Mrs. Arnold to Richard and Henry, her step-sons, in Canada, written not long after their father's death, shows the affection which pervaded the family, and their reverence for his memory. Speaking of her management of his affairs, she says:

"My conduct has been dictated by regard to you, respect to your dear Father's memory, and an earnest desire to act with uprightness, feeling and tenderness. Although I had much to be thankful for during your Father's lifetime, I had much to struggle with; the solicitude he felt to make a handsome provision for all his family, often involved him in difficulties, and eventually proved the cause of his death.   *   *   *

"But the solicitude was in itself so praiseworthy, and so disinterested, and never induced him *to deviate from rectitude*, that his children should ever reverence his memory; and for myself, I am determined in my conduct to them, to do everything which I think would be pleasing to him, could he view the actions of those he has left behind."

It seems that his sons in Canada, in ignorance of their father's embarrassments, had without much consideration, uttered some complaints against him, which, when they came to understand all the facts, pained them, and for which they bitterly reproached themselves.

Mrs. Arnold's reply to their self-reproaches is so beautiful, and the sentiments expressed so noble, that although in a private family letter, I cannot forbear quoting a few paragraphs. She says:

"It is certainly greatly to be regretted, that you so little know your dear Father's heart, his motives, and embarrassed circumstances, as to be induced to write to him in a style to wound and distress him, and now to cause bitter self-reproach to yourselves—but as the evil is now irremediable I beg you will not suffer it to corrode your future happiness. We are all frail mortals, and sincere repentance is the first step to amendment.

"Your dear Father forgave and blessed you. God will accept your contrition, and I will not only destroy the proofs in my possession, of your misguided judgment, but will endeavor to attribute it to the distress of your minds at the time, and as much as possible lose all recollections of it. It will afford me sincere pleasure to be of service to you, not only as the children of him whom I loved, but I trust from your future conduct; at present my means of befriending anybody are but slender, but if I live, my Father and my sons may enable me better to gratify the feelings of my heart.

"I am sorry you have had so much to encounter in settling your farms, and that you are still struggling with many hardships."

She recommends "perseverance, and in a little while," she says, "you will enjoy the fruits of your hard labor."

She closes this part of her letter by saying, "Should fortune smile upon the exertions of my excellent sons, you will find in them *Brothers.*"[1]

This assurance was, as we shall see hereafter, abundantly verified.

1. Manuscript letter of Mrs. Arnold to Richard and Henry Arnold.

CHAPTER XXIV.

THE FAMILY OF GENERAL ARNOLD.

"I have rescued your Father's memory from disrespect by paying all his just debts."—Mrs. Arnold to her children.

MRS ARNOLD'S EXECUTIVE ABILITY—SHE SETTLES GENERAL ARNOLD'S ESTATE, AND PAYS HIS DEBTS—EDUCATES HER CHILDREN, AND PROCURES FOR HER SONS COMMISSIONS IN THE ARMY—HER DEATH—THE ARNOLD FAMILY IN CANADA—" POOR BEN'S" DEATH FROM A WOUND RECEIVED IN BATTLE—THE FAMILY IN ENGLAND—ALL THE SONS IN THE PUBLIC SERVICE—JAMES APPOINTED MILITARY AID TO THE KING—ATTAINS THE RANK OF LIEUT. GENERAL—A GRANDSON KILLED AT SEBASTOPOL.

THE extracts from the letters of Mrs. Arnold already given, and her conduct already detailed, show that with her affectionate heart, her clear good sense, and almost unerring judgment, she united great executive ability. General Arnold left his affairs in a very embarrassed and complicated condition: heavy debts had been pressing upon him, rude creditors and unscrupulous claimants had been annoying him, and his means were very limited.

In delicate health, with young children demanding her care, Mrs. Arnold was now to assume the heavy burden of settling his estate. In her letter to Richard and Henry, announcing their father's death, she says,[1]

"I shall send you a copy of your Father's will, if I can possibly copy it, by this opportunity; if not, in a few days; I have not yet proved it, but shall as soon as I am able to return to town."

1. Manuscript letter of Mrs. Arnold, July 1, 1801.

He had made her his executrix, and left his estate in her hands. She says:

"Your Father was obliged to sell the lease of the house before his death, to make provisions for the payment of his accepted bills, not having it in his power to raise the money in any other way. * *

"I have not yet heard from Edward: James is in Egypt (in the army), exposed to the greatest danger, but he writes in good spirits: your sister is in great affliction and ill-health. In short, we are a wretched family, and in addition to our severe loss, we shall have pecuniary distress to contend with."

I cannot describe the difficulties with which this heroic woman struggled so well, as by quoting from her own letters. She had proved the will, and assumed the responsibility of executrix, and in November, 1802, she writes to Richard and Henry, saying:

"I have just received your affectionate letters of June 28th, and am much obliged for the kind concern you express for me and my children. * * *

"I very early informed you, that in undertaking the settlement of the most troublesome business that ever devolved upon a female, I had not been actuated in the smallest degree by the hope of benefiting myself or my children; that I was induced to do it only from respect to your Father's memory—the certainty that I could do more justice to others than any other person could, and the wish to prevent all private letters from falling into the hands of strangers."

After describing the dangerous effects of her exertions upon her health, she says:

"But thanks to the goodness of God, I am restored to serenity and the power of exertion, and I shall perseveringly go on in the arduous task I have undertaken; the only recompense will be the consciousness that I have done my duty.

"I have been under the necessity of parting with my furniture, wine, and many other comforts provided for me by the indulgent hand of affection; and have by these sacrifices paid all the *ascertained* debts, within a few hundred pounds, and hope to be enabled to discharge the remainder, and to pay a part of the legacies, provided a demand to a large amount, made by a *Swede* for the detention of his Vessel, is not substantiated. I have a hint that this has been decided against us; if so, I have the mortification of knowing that neither myself nor my children will ever have the value of a guinea from their dear Father's property, and that even the uncommon liberality of my Sons in giving up their pensions for the use of the family, has been of no avail. But these things are wisely ordained by the Almighty for some good purpose, and His justice and mercy we cannot doubt. A few months will bring things near to a close, when I will give you every particular.

"While I have the means of preventing it, I will never suffer the sister of my husband to want, and shall supply her from my own little income with what is necessary for her. I approve highly of her residing with you in future. * *

"My dear Edward is one of the most noble of youths; he writes sanguinely of his prospects in India; from his pay he insists upon taking upon himself the entire expense of little William's education; he had before made over his pension irrevocably to his sister. Dear James is equally generous and disinterested, and is now living with great difficulty upon his pay, that his pension may be appropriated to the use of the family. My dear girl is all that is amiable and excellent, and George and William promise fair to emulate the example of their elder brothers. Such children compensate for a thousand ills."

In the same letter she writes in regard to the lands in Canada, which had been granted to General Arnold and his family. He had authorized his sons, Richard and Henry, to locate these lands, an authority confirmed by Mrs. Arnold after her husband's death. She now asks them "to do everything in their power to get them located in the best situations and on the best terms possible. "All necessary expenses I will thankfully repay."

"Your poor Father thought these lands an object, and expended a great deal of interest and trouble in procuring them. Everything depends on their judicious location. * * *

"I am now living in a very small house in Bryanston Street, using furniture purchased from Carlow (a servant), who is now a more independant woman than her mistress. * * * My Father is very good to me; but for his aid, I should have suffered still more wretchedness. He and my Sisters are very desirous of my going to reside with them, but my anxiety to get your little brothers on in life, will deprive me of this gratification. I have placed George at the New Royal Military College, to which he was appointed (through the interest of the

Marquis Cornwallis) by the India Company, who will pay half the expenses of his education, he being designed for their Service. It is a most excellent Seminary, and embraces every part of education necessary to to form the soldier and the gentleman.

"I shall write to your aunt by this packet."[1]

In another letter she says:

"I have been so fortunate, through the interest of the Marquis Cornwallis, to get George into the Royal Military College, nominated by the East India Company, who defray half the expense, which is ninety guineas per annum. They (the boys) are taught everything that can form the soldier and the gentleman, riding, fencing, and every other accomplishment, with the Oriental languages, which is very important, and brings them into much notice.

"George's character stands very high."

In July, 1803, this admirable mother writes to her "Dear Sons" in Canada, saying: "I have written you very fully respecting the Canada lands, and sent you a power of attorney to act in the business." She speaks of her greatly impaired health, and says she was to "have a consultation of Physicians two days hence. * * *"

"God knows how it (her disease) will terminate; I am endeavouring to prepare my mind for the worst, but when I reflect upon the unprotected state of my children, whose welfare so greatly depends upon my exertions for them, I am almost deprived of that fortitude so essential to my own support. * * *

"I have from time to time given you an account of your dear Father's affairs. I have nearly accomplished what I am convinced no other person could have done—the payment of all the just debts.

"I have lately had several demands made upon me on account of the *Vile Privateers*, which I know not whether I can resist, or even if they are just.

"The claim of the Swede for the detention of his vessel and total loss of his cargo, is in the Court of Admiralty.

"You can form not the smallest idea of the trouble and perplexity in which I have been involved. The only reward is, the having saved you from distress, and the gratification of having paid all your dear Father's just debts, so that no reflection on that score can ever be cast upon his memory.

1. Manuscript letter of Mrs. Arnold, Nov. 5, 1802.

"I am uneasy at not hearing from your aunt for a long time; I am fearful she may be in distress for money. I have written repeatedly to her, and requested her to draw on me for twenty-four pounds, which I will endeavor to allow her annually.

"I have heard lately from Edward, who had just had a severe action with the army of one of the native chiefs. James is now on his passage to the West Indies; George is at the Royal Military school, and if I live, will go to the East Indies next year. Your sister is with me, and little William goes to the school at which all his brothers were educated."[1]

In a letter written the same year to her sons in Canada, she says:

"I feel gratified by your affectionate anxiety for me, and am happy to have it in my power to relieve it, by assuring you that I am infinitely better, and thank God, restored to a good degree of comfort. * * A variety of the most agonizing scenes, followed by a press of the most harrassing business, had nearly subdued that fortitude which never before forsook me.

"The excellence of my children is a never-failing source of delight to me, and the kindness I experience from my friends, tends to make me much less sensible of the material change in my situation.

"The situation of your dear Father's affairs has made it necessary for me to have the most trifling article disposed of, or valued and paid for by myself—this has extended even to his clothing."

"The *Swede* has not withdrawn his claim—but does not press it with much vigor."

After speaking in detail of all her children, she says, "No mother was ever more blessed in good children than I am."

"I shall send you by Mr. Morley some of your dear Father's hair, his seal with *his Arms*, and sleeve-buttons, knee and stock-buckles, &c., &c., which as having been long worn by him, will I doubt not be valued by you."

In August, 1803, Mrs. Arnold writes, "I have the greatest satisfaction in informing you that the long pending Admiralty cause of the Swedish ship is decided, and in our favor. Their claim was for the loss of the ship, cargo, and two years' detention. Had they succeeded, ten times the property I have would not have satisfied their demand."

She adds, "Upon this decision everything depended, and until it was given, it was impossible to bring the business to a close."

After speaking in detail of her difficulties, she adds:

[1] Manuscript letter of Mrs. Arnold, July 27, 1803.

"Although I have suffered, in my choice of evils, almost beyond human endurance, I now repent not at having made it.

"To you I have rendered an essential service; I have rescued your Father's memory from disrespect, by paying all his just debts; and his Children will now never have the mortification of being reproached with his speculations having injured anybody beyond his own family; and his motives, not the unfortunate termination, will be considered by them, and his memory will be doubly dear to them.

"It has been a dreadful business, and minute as I have been in my detail, it is quite impossible for you to form an idea of what I have had to encounter, besides the sacrifice of all my accustomed comforts. I have not even a tea-spoon, a towel, or a bottle of wine, that I have not paid for. But having nearly completed my great work, I was beginning to enjoy some degree of comfort, to which however my ill health is a great interruption.

"And now to the important business of the Canada lands. I am very glad to hear that the difficulty of the grant is overcome—more particularly as I understand, that if they are judiciously located they will certainly be of considerable value."[1]

The letters above quoted, from Mrs. Arnold to Richard and Henry, speak more eloquently than any words I could use, of her most estimable character.

In some earlier letters she referred most affectionately on several occasions to "Poor Ben," General Arnold's oldest son. On his father's defection, he, as well as Richard and Henry, although so young, received commissions from the British government. Benedict saw active service as an officer in the artillery. He died October 24th, 1795, at Iron Shore, on the north side of the island of Jamaica, in the West Indies, aged twenty-seven years. He had been severely wounded in the leg, in a recent action, and refusing to have the leg amputated, the wound resulted in his death.

In a letter of Mrs. Arnold to Richard, written after the General's death, she says: "I shall send, when a good opportunity occurs, some few things belonging to your Father;

[1]. Manuscript letter of Mrs. Arnold, dated Clay-Hall, Old Windsor, Aug. 1803.

HIS PATRIOTISM AND HIS TREASON. 405

also your poor brother Ben's sword, which Sir Grenville Temple brought from the West Indies, and gave to your Father."[1]

Both Richard and Henry were commissioned as lieutenants of cavalry in the American Legion, raised by their father in 1780, as before stated, and afterwards received from the British government half-pay as retired officers.

Richard married Margaret Weatherhead, daughter of Samuel Weatherhead, Esq., of Augusta, Upper Canada, December 30th, 1804, and left a large and highly respectable family of sons and daughters.

Henry, the third son of General Arnold by his first wife, married Hannah Ten Eyck, daughter of Richard Ten Eyck, of New York, December 4th, 1796. He died in the city of New York, Dec. 8th, 1826, and left a respectabie family.

Hannah, their aunt, and the only sister of General Arnold, as has been stated, spent the later years of her life with her nephews Henry and Richard, and died at the house of Henry, at Montigue, Canada, August 31st, 1803.[2]

She was unusually tall, of a very graceful figure, blonde hair, with bluish gray eyes. She was a woman of much more than ordinary ability, high-spirited, warm-hearted and sincere, faithful to her friends, and devotedly attached to her brother and his children;[3] she was a staunch Presbyterian, and that was the religion of the family, until the

[1] Manuscript letter of Mrs. Arnold, 1802.
As an illustration of the injustice done to Arnold and his family, and visiting "the sins of the father upon the children," Sabine, in his "Loyalists of the American Revolution," speaking of the eldest son, says: "Benedict was an officer of artillery in the British army, who, *it is believed*, was compelled to quit the service."—Vol. I, p. 182.
And even Mr. Sparks says, "He was a violent, headstrong youth, and *it is supposed* came to an untimely end."—*Sparks' Life of Arnold*, p. 10.
"Poor Ben," as Mrs. Arnold calls him, was *not* compelled to quit the service; he may have come to an "untimely end," but it was from a wound received in battle.
[2] Records of Family of Henry Arnold.
[3] Manuscript Letter of Rev. J. L. Leake.

marriage of General Arnold with Miss Shippen, who belonged to the Anglican Church; after this marriage, he and all his family by his second wife, became members of the English Episcopal Church.

Mrs. Arnold, who after the death of her husband, seemed to cling to life only that she might serve her children, had the pleasure of seeing her son George fitted out for the India service; so that all her children, except her daughter and the lad William, were provided for and settled in life. She died in London, August 24, 1804, aged forty-four years.

There is a portrait of her, and of her oldest son when a child, by Sir Thomas Lawrence, showing that the traditions of her extraordinary beauty, did her no more than justice.

This admirable woman was, it seems to me, an almost perfect wife and mother, and I cannot discover that she ever did an act, or wrote a word, that would bring a blush to the cheek of the most sensitive American. On the contrary, in the circles in which she moved, and in the difficult position she occupied as the wife of General Arnold, she bore herself with a dignity and grace, and with a modesty, sincerity and truth, of which any people might be justly proud.

Those who have read her letters will have learned something of her character, and I hazard nothing in saying that the reader will agree with me that the charge made by Aaron Burr, that Mrs. Arnold seduced her husband to his fall, is untrue.

General Arnold left surviving him by his second wife four sons and one daughter. The three older sons, Edward Shippen, James Robertson, and George, were at the time of Mrs. Arnold's death, in the public service; and the youngest, William, was at school preparing himself for the life of a soldier, so that Mrs. Arnold left a family of soldiers.

A brief sketch of their lives and the life of their sister, Sophia Matilda, and some extracts from family letters, illustrative of their characters, will, I think, be interesting.

The eldest, Edward Shippen, born in Philadelphia, 19th of March, 1780, and on the birth of whom General and Mrs. Arnold received the congratulations of General and Lady Washington,[1] commenced his military life as Lieutenant in the 6th Bengal cavalry. He was promoted to the position of paymaster, and disbursed, with the utmost fidelity and scrupulous care, immense sums of money. He died at Dinapoor, Bengal, Dec. 17, 1813.

His moral character was without a stain: he was unwearied in acts of beneficence. In the fearful famine, which prevailed in the Northern India provinces, while he was in India, the wealth which his industry, capacity, and providence had accumulated, his generous liberality induced him to dispense freely among the suffering people of Muttra, on whom he bestowed secretly large sums, in food, through the agency of a native: and so unostentatiously was this done, that it was not known to his friends and family until after his death.[2]

The beauty of his domestic character, and his devotion to his mother, his brothers and sister, fully appears in the family correspondence.

James Robertson, born in New York, August 28th 1781, married March 21st 1807, Virginia Goodrich, fourth daughter of Bartlett Goodrich, Esq., of Saling Grove, Isle of Wight. He entered the Corps of Royal Engineers in 1798, and served as an officer for more than half a century, rising by merit to the rank of Lieutenant-General. He served through all the wars of England against France, at the close of the last and early part of the present century. In 1800 he was

---
1. Letter of Washington to Arnold, March 28th, 1780.
2. Rev. Edward Gladwin Arnold—Manuscript letter.

present and in active service at the blockade and surrender of Malta. In 1801 he participated in the campaign in Egypt.[1]

He was engaged in the capture of Aboukir Castle, in the battle of Alexandria, and the expulsion of the French from Grand Cairo. Afterwards he served in the West Indies, and took part in the conquest of the colonies of Demerara, Essequibo, Berbice, and Surinam. At Surinam he successfully led the storming party against the redoubt Frederic and Fort Leyden. An incident connected with the storming of this redoubt has been told by a connection of Lieutenant General Arnold, the truth of which, although I cannot vouch for, I have no reason to doubt.

When the British commander determined to storm the redoubt, knowing the extreme danger which would be encountered by the attacking party, and unwilling to order his officers to almost certain death, he called for volunteers to lead the assault. Several young officers volunteered, and among them Arnold; and before the selection was made, he said to the commander: "I claim the privilege of leading this assault. No braver man than my father ever lived, but you know how bitterly he has been condemned for his conduct at West Point; permit me, I beg you, to do what I can to redeem the same."

The command was given to him; he led it gallantly and successfully, displaying all that impetuous courage which had so distinguished his father. He received a very severe wound in the leg—but the redoubt and fort were taken.[2]

For his gallantry he was honorably mentioned in the dispatches, and was presented by the committee of the patriotic fund with a sword of the value of £100 pounds. He served several years in Bermuda, and commanded the Engineers in British North America.

[1] Illustrated London News, January, 1855.
[2] See *Illustrated London News*, January, 1855.

On the accession of King William the IV. to the throne, General Arnold was appointed one of his Majesty's aides-de-camp. He was created a knight of the Hanoverian Guelphic Order, and Knight of the Crescent. No soldier was ever more sensitive to anything affecting his honor. He felt most keenly and painfully the stain upon his name. When at St. Johns, in British North America, he visited the house in which his father had lived, and it is said he "wept like a child."[1]

He kept up a most affectionate correspondence with his mother's family in America, and expressed a desire to visit them, but was prevented by his knowledge of the intense feeling against his father. To one of his mother's family in Philadelphia, writing from Malta, in 1806, he says:

"Although a stranger, my heart is with you. Much of the unbounded attachment of my lamented Mother for her family was instilled into her children, and there is nothing to which I look forward with more pleasure than to being with you once again. I do propose to visit America a very few years hence, if after the long period that has elapsed, former circumstances are sufficiently obliterated to render it proper."[2]

He died without issue, on the 27th of December, 1854, at his residence, in Onslow Square, London.[3] He is said to have resembled his father in personal appearance.

George, born at St. Johns, New Brunswick, September 5th, 1787, married Anne Martinez Brown, and died in India, November 1st, 1828, holding at the time of his death the rank of Lieutenant-Colonel in the 2nd Bengal cavalry. It is said that he was named by his father, George, after George Washington, his early, and George the Third, his later friend.

William Fitch, born in London, June 25th, 1794. Mar-

---

1. Sabine's Loyalists, Vol. I, p. 180.
2. It will be recollected he was born in New York.
3. Manuscript Letter from his nephew, Rev. Edward Gladwin Arnold.

ried May 19th, 1819, Elizabeth Cecilia, only daughter of Alexander Ruddock, Esq., of Tobago, and captain in the Royal navy. William was a captain in the 19th Royal Lancers, and justice of the peace for the county of Buckinghamshire. His residence and country seat was Little Messenden Abbey, in Bucks. He left six children, two sons and four daughters. One of his sons, the Rev. Edward Gladwin Arnold, married April 27th, 1852, Lady Charlotte, daughter of the Marquis of Cholmondelay. William Trail, the second son, was a captain in the 4th (King's Own) regiment of foot, in the British army. He served with great distinction in the war in the Crimea, in 1854-5. He was in the battles of the Alma, Inkerman, and served with his regiment before Sebastopol during the severe and terrible winter of 1854-5.

"He met his death in the following manner: He was in command of his regiment in the advanced trenches on the night of May 5th, 1855, when his duty was to post double sentinels in advance of the advanced trenches, and this was not done until it was nearly dark. He had posted all but six men, and was advancing with them and a sergeant, when a picket of Russians, some thirty or forty, it was said, which had been lying in wait for him under a hillock, rose up and fired a volley at him, when he was but a few yards from them. He cried out to his men, 'Fire and retire,' and fell to the earth, saying, 'O, God! I am killed.' The men made the best of the way back to the Trenches, when the next officer in command advanced the regiment in the hope of recovering his body, but though they found the exact spot where he fell, he had been carried into Sebastopol.

"Lord Raglan sent in a flag of truce, but all that could be learned was, 'Captain Arnold died the same night he was wounded, in Sebastopol.'"

Lord Raglan, the Commander-in-chief, in his dispatches, May 8th, 1855, speaks as follows: "On the same night Captain Arnold, of the 4th Foot, was wounded and taken prisoner while posting the advance sentries on the left. The loss of the services of this officer is greatly to be lamented. *He has done his duty* unremittingly, and in the most spirited *manner throughout the operations of the siege.*"

"He was a fine fellow, in every way, and had all the energy and spirit of his grandfather." [1]

Sophia Matilda, daughter of General Arnold, was born in London, July 28th, 1785; she was married April 17th, 1813, at Muttra, in Bengal, to Captain, afterwards Lieutenant Colonel, Pownall Phipps, of the Mulgrave family, Knight of the Crescent, &c.

She was distinguished for her beauty, her culture, and her marked religious character. She died in Sunbury, England, June 10th, 1828.[2]

I will now give a few extracts from the correspondence of the family, illustrative of the characters of its members. These extracts might be very largely increased, as the correspondence is voluminous, and runs through many years.

On the 23d of May, 1806, James Robertson, writing from Barbadoes to his grandfather, Chief Justice Shippen, speaks of having been in the West Indies "nearly three years, during which time," he says, "I have been tolerably well employed. The fortunes of war, will, I trust, shortly permit me to return to England, for which I am more particularly anxious on my darling sister's account." He laments having been prevented "from embracing these dear relations, whose love and affection," he says, "would have cheered the dreary hours of my life."

"I never cease to pray God to bless and protect them. Assure them all, my dear Sir, of these sentiments, the extent of which I am ill able

---

1. Rev. Edward Gladwin Arnold.

The following notice, taken from the Leicester *Advertiser*, England, of July 21, 1855, shows how he was regarded by his comrades:

"Amongst the fearful list of losses and casualties to which our army in the Crimea is exposed, I lately read, with feelings of mingled sorrow and regret, the name of Captain William Trail Arnold, of the 4th King's Own Regiment, who was, whilst commanding a skirmishing party before Sebastopol, severely wounded, and taken prisoner on the 5th of May last, and died of his wounds a few hours after."

* * * * * * *

2. For the dates and facts in relation to the descendants of General Arnold, in England, I am indebted to his grandson, the Rev. Edward Gladwin Arnold.

to express, and entreat them sometimes to think of me, who often, very often thinks of, and prays for them.

"My sister will probably remain in Devonshire Place, * * till my return, when I hope to form some scheme for our living together, and for making her as happy and comfortable as my fondest wishes have desired.

"Poor girl! she has felt and still feels most keenly the loss of our best of mothers. But I will try to heal the wound. Whatever fraternal love can devise, shall not be wanting to soothe her, and I trust God will crown my endeavors with success. She is as truly good and amiable as the tenderest love can wish, and my heart swells with gratitude to Almighty God for having given me such a sister.

"My dear Brothers in India, Edward and George, are doing extremely well, and in a fair way of promotion. They are an honor to their name and family. Little William is at School, and Sophia tells me improving fast.

"The establishment in life of that poor little orphan shall be one of my chief cares, and I am determined he shall never feel the want of those advantages which his brothers have enjoyed. He shall have the choice, as we had, of his profession, which I think from all I hear, will be that of a soldier.

"We are very dull here.—No laurels I fear for the West India army."

He speaks enthusiastically of Lord Nelson, and says: "If heroes are entitled to a seat in Heaven he (Nelson) must be there."

Of Napoleon he says:

"One would imagine that the repeated Naval defeats the usurper has sustained would have checked his ardor; it seems, however, only to have inflamed it. While he exists Europe can expect no tranquility. His ambition knows no bounds. * * I trust the Almighty will not suffer much longer this scourge to desolate the world.

* * * * * * * * *

"I heartily pity the poor old King. His has been an eventful and far from happy reign. It will be long, I fear, before the nation will recover the loss of those three great men—Pitt, Nelson and Cornwallis.

"Pray, my dear Grand-Father, allow me the happiness of hearing from you, and may God forever bless you."[1]

The two older brothers, Edward Shippen, in the East Indies, and James Robertson, in the West Indies, found their strongest motive to action in their orphan sister and little brother in England.

1. Manuscript letter in possession of Edward Shippen, Esq., of Philadelphia.

In 1806, Edward was at Malta, and on receiving intelligence of the death of Chief Justice Shippen, and that his grand-children in England were legatees, writes on the 19th of September to one of the family of his mother, in Philadelphia.

After acknowledging the receipt of the "melancholy intelligence of dear Grand-father's death," etc., he adds:

"The Will, of which you have enclosed a Copy, appears to have been made upon principles of the greatest kindness towards us all. We are all too much attached to our dear Sophia to feel otherwise than highly gratified that she should have been thus handsomely provided for.

"I think it right, both as a guide to your conduct, in a situation which you will perhaps feel as rather delicate, and as a proper mark of respect to my nearest remaining relatives, to give you as much knowledge as possible of our respective views and prospects. Sophia's income, arising from her pension and property, exclusively her own, was about £250 a year, to which was added £100 from my Grand-Father. James, George and myself had relinquished in her favor our pensions, each netting £80, and I had in addition to this, directed my agents to pay to her use £200 a year if she required it, either for herself or for defraying the expenses of William's education. These latter sums, however, she did not seem disposed to appropriate to herself, while we had yet our fortunes to make; but had formed very prudent arrangements for living and educating William without much exceeding the two former. What must now devolve to her will, I should hope, not only compensate for the loss of her allowance from my Grand-Father, but add also so considerably to her income, as to prevent her having occasion for that assistance which she was so delicate in accepting.

"James is now well advanced in an advantageous line of his profession, and with his pension, and a full quarter share of what is to be distributed among us, will be well provided for. George has also been very fortunate in this country. He has a good standing in the service, and every prospect of returning to England after a moderate number of years, with an Independance. I have hitherto been particularly successful, having had the charge for the last ten months of Deputy Field Pay-master to the troops on this establishment, and as my conduct has hitherto been approved by the government, I have every prospect of being confirmed in this situation, and of realizing in a few years enough to satisfy my moderate wishes. William, in short, only remains to be provided for, and he has of his own about £1,300 or £1,400. This it was my intention to have made up by a loan of £3,000—so that a writership to this country (India) might be purchased for him. George and myself greatly wish that from our shares *his* may be made up to a sum sufficient to effect this purpose and to pay his outfit. Should this plan require the whole (of our shares) we willingly relinquish them.   *   *   *

"I cannot close without expressing how much regret I feel in being known by name only to those near relatives with whom other men have an opportunity of forming the most endearing connections of life."

On the 12th of November, 1806, he writes to the same person, saying:

"The Government have now perminently appointed me a Deputy Pay Master to the troops, with a very large district on the frontier. It is a situation of peculiar responsibility and trouble, involving a disbursement of nearly a million sterling a year.   *   *   *   It affords me a certain prospect of a moderate independence at the end of five or six years more.   *   *   It was given me by the Commander-in-chief, after serving three campaigns with him, and confirmed by the Governor-General after a year's trial.

"William is now at the preparatory school to the College, where all the civil servants of the company are educated.

"My brother George is well, and is succeeding beyond most young men of his age in India."

On the 25th of October, 1813, William writes to Richard his half-brother in Canada, saying "Sophia is married to Captain Phipps, of the East India company's service. It is a most desirable match; he is a relation to Lord Mulgrave, and a nephew to Mr. Tierney,[1] a very fine young man, and extremely well-off in pecuniary matters. Edward and George were in good health, and coming on well."

On the 30th of July, 1823, Sophia (Mrs. Phipps) writes to her uncle Burd, saying,

"William has bought a small freehold Estate, Little Messendon Abbey, in Bucks, and is residing quietly there with his wife and three children. We are to pay them a visit, when we leave Bath."

On the 16th of August, 1814, James writes to his brothers Richard and Henry, communicating intelligence of the death of his brother Edward. He says:

"He died on the 17th of December last at Dinapore, on his way to Calcutta.

---

1. Member of Parliament.

"To tell you how miserable this event has made me would be impossible, but you may judge of my feelings, when you reflect that we were brought up together and always loved each other with the most tender affection. * * I am really happy to inform you of poor Edward's affectionate recollection of you both. He has left you each £500 sterling. * * God bless and prosper you, my dear brothers, and may it be long, very long, before we have to deplore the loss of another of our family."

On the 7th of August, 1815, James writes again to his brothers in Canada, saying:

"You will be pleased to learn that I have obtained the important step of Lieutenant Colonel in my Corps. I have more than ever cause to be thankful to our dear Parents and our lamented Brother Edward, by whose advice I came into the Engineers. If they had been spared to witness the result of their exertions for me, my feelings on this occasion would have been delightful indeed. But all is for the best, and we have no right to doubt the goodness and wisdom of that kind Providence who grants or withholds, as He knows to be right. If prosperity and the completion of all our worldly desires make us happier, they do not always make us the better or more deserving; adversity, and those disappointments which mankind call cruel, and which appear so at the time, seldom fail to teach us that it is not here we are to look for happiness; that though we may enjoy it for a time, it cannot last, and that it is only by endeavoring to do our duty that we can expect to attain it in the state to which we are all hastening. This conviction must check unmeasured joy, and must console us in the most trying afflictions.

"As to the Land (the Canada land), a few years may make it of some value, and I shall let it take its chance, as far as I am concerned. I wish we could stick it on to some part of old England, and bring you and your family over with it. It would be of some value with the timber on it. * * *

"I should have liked to have shared in the glory of the late campaign, but having missed that, care very little where I go next. You will have heard before this can reach you, of that noble but bloody affair, the battle of Waterloo. The French are completely humbled, but I doubt the flame being extinguished. I hope the Allies will make them suffer a little more before they leave them. * * *

"You will see what a complete change we have recently had in our administration, and I hope things will now go on better. The Duke of Wellington is a straight-forward, honorable fellow, without any humbug. I have seen a great deal of him since I have been stationed at Dover, and have received much kindness and attention from him. * * "

On the 12th of August, 1836, James was Aide-de-Camp to King William the IV., and was still stationed at Dover, England. His half-brother Richard had written to him, soliciting aid in obtaining some appointment, to which he replies:

"You are mistaken, my dear Richard, as to the influence you seem to imagine the officers on the Kings's staff have with him. The only aide-de-camp constantly about his person is the principal one, Sir Herbert Taylor, and he has much influence. The others, with perhaps few exceptions, have little intercourse with his majesty, excepting on occasions of State, or other duties. There are certain privileges attached to the appointment, but though it brings us all more in the occasional presence of his majesty, more in contact with him through other officers, it gives no *claim* to his confidence, beyond what he may see fit to grant. The ministers of the crown are the heads through whom all chiefly look for the accomplishment of such objects as our friend Jones had in view. * *

"I wish you fully to understand the appointment of King's aid-de-camp though purely military, has always been considered most enviable and desirable, and to be conferred as a mark of Royal approbation of conduct. I value it most highly. You give me the title of 'Sir,' to which I have no right. Remember, I am plain 'Colonel.' I hope you will soon be able to sell some more of our land to advantage.

"God bless you all—Virginia unites with me in kindest love—ever my dear Richard,

"Your affectionate Brother, &c."

On the 23d of June, 1837, James writes from the "United Service Club, London," to his brother Richard, and says, among, other things:

"I have recently been appointed to the command of the Engineer Department in Ireland. * * * * *

"The command is considered the most important we have, and I expect to be placed as a Colonel on the Staff, which will make it much more agreeable. * * * * *

"I understand Phipp's boy is grown a very fine stout fellow. I wonder at his choosing to settle in Ireland, and in such a county, too, as Tipperary! But he tells me they get on well there.

"As to William * * he has a very pretty place in Buckinghamshire, and has been made a Magistrate, which gives him some importance in the County. * * * *

HIS PATRIOTISM AND HIS TREASON. 417

"Pray tell me what prospect there is of selling our land. I wish we could dispose of it to tolerable advantage, and that I believe to be the wish of the family generally. No doubt it *may* be more valuable ten years hence, but then we may not be here to enjoy the benefit of it!

" Pray, do endeavor to sell whenever anything like fair opportunity offer.   *   *   *   *   *

" The death of our excellent King has cast much gloom over London. He will long be deeply and sincerely lamented, and I, for one, feel that in him I have lost an excellent friend. I had the honor of dining with him at Brighton last February, and had an audience the next morning of nearly an hour.   *   *   *   *   *

" The young Queen (Victoria) appears to have given much satisfaction, and to promise all we can expect from her. But it is a serious and heavy charge for a girl of eighteen!   *   *   *

" You shall know how we get on in Ireland.   *

"God bless you and all your family. my dear Richard! I trust you will enjoy many happy years, and that we may yet meet in *this* world, before we are summoned to a better. The next Brevet will most probably make me a Major-General, and I cannot doubt that when *steam* traveling comes more fully into play, I may feel disposed to take another trip across the Atlantic."

These extracts might be continued, but enough have been given to show the character of the family, and the generous affection they all entertained for each other. The letters indicate, what I learn from other sources, that all the sons and the daughter were of marked religious character. An English correspondent, who knew the family, says: "The sons of General Arnold could not but be brave, and the sons of Margaret Shippen could not be other than gentlemen, and her daughter a gentlewoman."

APPENDIX.

THE following paper was drawn up by Gen. Arnold at the request of the King. Its exact date I am unable to give. It is the original draft, with some interlineations, erasures and alterations, and apparently somewhat incomplete, and is all in his hand-writing, and was furnished to me by his grandson, the Rev. Edward Gladwin Arnold:

"THOUGHTS ON THE AMERICAN WAR—BY AN AMERICAN—
(GEN. A.) 1782.

"Great Britain was deceived at the Commencement of the American troubles, when she trusted to what some wrote: that the Discontents were confined to a small faction. Her measures thus became inadequate to her Ends. A great majority of America was at first in the opposition, tho' not all for arming. There are those who now allege that she has few or no Friends in America; and if they are believed, she will be a *second* time and more fatally deluded. Such accounts should be listened to with great jealousy, because they proceed from Ignorance or bad designs, and lead to despair; and the severance of the Empire will be the ruin of it, and of every part of it.

"That a great Majority of the Americans are averse from the Separation, is a Truth supported by every kind of Proof of which the Subject is capable, and nothing is so easy as to detect the Fallacy of the Reasons assigned for doubting it. It appears to be a Parodox to some, how a Minority can maintain the Usurpation in a Government that is democratical. The solution is this: When the Republics were first formed, the Majority were in Favor of them, and disarmed the Rest; they did more—they enacted laws to incapacitate them from holding Offices, or voting for others, for they made it a pre-requisite to both, that the King's Authority should be abjured. *No Loyalist can do that.*

"It is a Demonstration that the Friends of the Restoration are most numerous, if the fact be admitted that the Elections are everywhere attended by a minority; and this has been the case ever since the Overtures of 1778. If it was not believed to be so, how should we account for the resort of so many Thousands to the King's Lines? What induces them to quit their Estates, Families and Friends, and risk their own Lives? It would be the greatest of all Paradoxes to find them staking everything dear to them, upon their preference of the Royal Cause to the Congressional Protection, if they knew the latter to be supported by the general voice. You will hear, indeed, of Diversities in the Proportions of Whig and Tory at different Places, and the accounts would be false if they were not various; but every informer, from whatever District he comes, brings the Intelligence that his Townsmen or Countrymen are in the main for the Restoration, and that their *Numbers daily increase*. Nothing can more strongly confirm this Testimony than the Conduct of the Party in the saddle, and *the conditions of their affairs*.

"It was because the Non-concurrence of the multitude was apprehended, that they were not consulted *on the Propriety of declaring the Independence in* 1776, nor on the *Confederation to authorize foreign alliances* in 1777, nor on the *Rejection of the British Overtures in* 1778. Every one of these Events actually made accessions to the Number of the Loyalists, and frittered down the Independent Party to a proportionable Diminution. The minority increased in Cruelty as they lessened in Numbers, and the Barbarities begot by their fears, disgusting others, and working with general Calamities, the Zealots, at this day for protracting the War, are really become a very small Proportion of the Continent. America is a country of husbandmen, and tho' this class has felt the burthen of Military Service, 'tis but now they find cause to repine under the Load of their Taxes, which are tenfold greater than they were before the War, and are daily increasing, the scarcity of Specie, having reduced the Peace Price of their stinted Productions nearly one-half—Wheat being at 4s. a Bushel.

"If it is thought an Objection that the War would not have been so unsuccessful, if our Friends were so numerous; but that in the several Experiments for penetrating the Country, they would have flocked to the British Standard; and that consequently the truth is, that the Rebels are everywhere an inveterate Majority, and the Loyalists few and timid, as Earl Cornwallis has asserted. I reply that this Timidity should be called Diffidence; and arises from causes easily to be removed by a change in the Conduct of the War, which the American Loyalists have all along disapproved. It would be a tedious and invidious Task to indulge in particular remarks, upon the Inactivity and Misdirection of the King's

Arms; I leave it to others, for a few important Observations to finish with the objection I have started.

"Has any attempt been made to set up the *Civil* Authority in any Part of America, where the usurpation was beaten down? Certainly not—and till this is attended to, the Loyalists in general *will not*, nor indeed *can* give any essential assistance to the Royal Arms. I have said they *will not* because they are *Englishmen*. Nay, an American Husbandman will no sooner quit his farm and family to become a common Soldier at Six Pense a Day Wages with rations, than an English Gentleman of £500 a year in the funds. He will not lend his hand to erect a Military Misrule over himself and his Friends, and put all his Property at the Discretion of an Arbitrary Police, that has cut the throat of the King's Interest whenever it has been set up. He has, however, no objection to serve in the Militia *within* his own colony, under officers who are *of it;* and to assist in supporting its government and defending himself *in it;* and may perhaps pursue the Rebel out of it, or meet him on a Menaced Invasion near the Borders. But for this purpose the Civil Authority of the Crown must first be set up; and without it, Great Britain (the American being what he is) can neither be benefited by his Councils, his Purse, nor his Arms. He will be passive while under the Power of the Usurpers; and when they are flying before the King's troops, continue if he can at home, giving aid to neither Party, and certainly not oppose the Royal Army, if he finds it possible to avoid it; and in short, behave in the manner Lord Cornwallis experienced, distrusting both the strength of his Army, to give Protection, and what is worse, to afford the Protection of the *Laws of the Land.*

"In a war of Posts, therefore, connected with the plan of subjecting the Country to Military Policy, the whole *work must be performed by the King's Troops;* and if this is impracticable, it is a very good reason for adopting a new mode, but no evidence at all of the want of a Disposition in America for the Renewal of the royal Government and the re-union of the Empire. Is there a county in England, that thus circumstanced, would act otherwise, and be easy a month under the Direction of an army?—of an army too, addicted to Plunder, and often willing to suppose a *Friend* to be a Rebel, for the sake of what he has got, or they have seized? I will not admit, though a soldier myself, that the King's Civil Government and the success of the service are incompatable; and have said enough against any further Experiment, that have so long indulged to this Military Partiality. But there is another objection that has weight, and that is, that the new restored Legislature may do injury to the conciliatory Designs of the Crown, by too Vindictive a spirit, and an inordinate Desire to compensate their own Losses, by the Ruin of those who have at any time contributed to the present distractions. Georgia has committed this error. But it might have been prevented by a Governor, disposed to act the part of a mediator between Whig and Tory; and it is certain that the example of Georgia quoted by some, for not restoring the old constitution of South Carolina, furnished the strongest Argument imaginable for its being instantly set up on the Reduction of Charlestown. It was then practicable to have formed an Assembly of Penitents, who being found on their estates, with a moderate Governor and Council, would have given full scope to that Wise Policy, necessary to Ballance between the hatred of Parties, and prevent the Ruin of either, by unconscionable sacrifices inconsistent with the public good.

"Congress took advantage of our Folly in leaving that Province to a Military Police, *bad for a town*, and wholly inadequate to a Province. Left to a state of Nature, the Soldiery began to insult, Robberies sprang up. The injured under the late Usurpation avenged themselves upon their Oppressors. The slaves left their Masters, and the whole Province was prepared to resign all hope of Government for the common Protection, before the Congressional Troops arrived to increase the Confusion; *and if South Carolina is not lost, it is ruined;* so that the only advantage we draw from all our Operations in that Quarter, is the Lesson it teaches to the other Provinces, of consulting their Salvation from Destruction by a timely Reconciliation with the Mother Country. What has been said in part anticipates that Proof of the Number of the King's Friends, which is deducible from the low *Condition* of the Rebel Affairs.

"The Congress is utterly become Bankrupt Not a Bill of theirs now has any Credit, and the only currency is hard money. This must be set down to the distrust began and propagated by the Loyalists; for the Depreciation commenced in 1777. *Old Money, Old Price*, was the vulgar Cantatum of the Friends of Government, from the first moment of the paper Emission in 1775. It is a confirmation of this, that the Bankruptcy has occasioned no such convulsions as the uninformed speculator looked for. No Loyalist *hoarded what he hated as well as despised*. The loss has thus wholly fallen upon the Whigs, who cried up the Paper money; and it is not consistent with their Principles nor Reputation to utter Complaints, and afford Matter of Triumph to their Adversaries. Some of them had treasured up these Bills in Barrels, and are unpitied both by Whig and Tory for profiting by the *public Fraud*. The difficulty of forcing the Militia into the Field; the sanguinary Laws of the Usurpers; the Mutiny and Desertion of their regular Troops; and various other topics, might be mentioned as Proofs of the Declension of the Party, with decisive confessions in the intercepted letters of the Rebels. In a word, but for the late French aid, the Rebellion had sunk under its own weakness. To rid themselves of the burthen of supernumerary officers in the Army (a suspicious but necessary measure), it was, in September, 1780, resolved on to consolidate several Regiments into one, and that it should take place on the 1st of January following, *a Season of the least apprehension.*

"The army then was to consist of:

4 Regiments of Cavalry—in all	1,536
4 Regiments of Artillery	2,340
49 Regiments of Infantry	28,224
1 Regiment of Artificers	480
	32,580

".This was an Establishment on Paper, and doubtless exceeded the Hopes of the Congress, except for the Effect of its appearance *Abroad;* they must, however, have been alarmed to find that their Force in the Field late in June last, in all Parts of the Continent, fell short of 5,000 Men. I speak of *real soldiers*—Continentals and not militia or month's men, who are but Militia, forced out for the short terms of 3, 4, 6 or 9 months, and net always in Congressional, but the still more precarious and slender Pay of the Colony they are sent from. Under Washington there were:

In the Highlands	1,500
At Fort Stanwix and its neighborhood	1,000
With Green, the Debris of the Southern army	800
Under Lafayette, 700, besides the 600 of the Pennsylvania Mutineers re-assembled by Wayne	1,300
	4,600

" It is true the American and French Troops that were convened in West Chester County, from the first of July to the 20th of August for menacing New York, were about 7000. But of these Rochambeau's Force consisted of 2870, and to make up the Ballance of upwards of 4000 in Americans, it must be observed that besides the 1500 from the Highlands, with the 1000 from Fort Stanwix, *then abandoned*, Washington had then so many Militia that when he marched from King's Ferry to Virginia (23d August) with three thousand men, Heath took up to the Highland Forts, about 10 or 12 hundred of the Militia; and that is the number with a small addition of others, that have occupied the Highland Forts ever since, till the appearance of the British from Canada, at Crown Point, in October occasioned a Detachment to the Northward that reduced the Garrison at West Point, as was said lately, to but about 600 men. I say nothing upon the delicate enquiry which the disaster in Virginia will lead to. It is material however to remark, that if the rebels deserve any advantage from it "'twill be as it shall affect the *Councils* of Great Britain this Winter.

" The French Fleet and Army, Rochambeau's Troops excepted, being gone, the Rebels are as unable to undertake any enterprise as before Rochambeau's Troops have laid hold of York in Virginia, and planted the French colours there. And it would seem that the Continentals must Winter in such a Part of the neighboring Country, as to be able to aid them in case of an Insurrection of the numerous British Prisoners and Loyalists, and our visiting the Chesapeak. It is impossible for Washington to have detached to Green, a Force sufficient for the Reduction of Charlestown; tho' he may and doubtless is in strength to ruin *his* friends as well as ours in the Southern Country. The Congress has added vastly to their debt; and cannot avoid increasing the general Discontents, *now the Taxes are commenced in hard money;* so that what they acquire of Reputation by the late victory, which after all is a *French one*, is counterballanced by a growing impatience in all ranks and Classes, under the intollerable and increasing Burthen of the War. The whole Northern quarter is at the same time undefended, and while the Sea Board is every where exposed to our incursions, the Conduct of Vermont fills all the Northern Provinces with apprehension, that may rise to a very formidable fright in the Spring, if Gen'l Haldimand's Compact with the Vermonters is put in a way of being confirmed by Great Britain. On all considerations thinking men among the Rebels see no great change for the better, and exult less than is imagined. And if I can venture a conjecture, it would be that Congress will direct *this Winter* to an accommodation with Great Britain, unless the French promise large succors, both of Land and Sea Forces as well as Money, for the Reduction of New York early in the Spring.

" The Vermonters informed the Congress last August, that the Militia within their *first Bounds* consisted of 7,000. There are 8,000 more in the Towns associated with them between Connecticut River and Mason's Line; and I think nearly 2,000 more in the District they have admitted to a Union with them, out of that part of New York that lays between the Hudson River and the twenty Mile Line East of it; and it is known that large Numbers are flocking to Vermont, and who are interested *in her private* as well as public views out of the Old Colonies of New Hampshire, Massachusetts Bay, Rhode Island, Connecticut and New York; and without Doubt the example of the convention Troops will lead to that country many of the British Soldiers lately made Prisoners in Virginia.

" By the complete Detachment of Vermont from the Rebel Interest, and the Reduction of the Highland Forts *early in the Spring*, much may be expected in the next Campaign; especially since the New Yorkers in general, and a very great proportion of the Country between them and the Connecticut River, are known to be very favorably inclined to the Re-union. If the late loss in Virginia, where the British must be dangerous and unwelcome Guests, is to be made up, it should be early during the Winter, as they can be collected, with a large proportion of them in the Ships of War, setting out with as little Observation as possible in separate and small squadrons of Transports, with a ship or two to carry their Provisions, and not in large Fleets.—And *at all events there must be a Naval Superiority in these Seas in March or April*, Because they will confine French Reinforcements to the Place of their Disembarkation, for the defence of their Ships; As was the Case at Rhode Island, and prevent any Designs against New York.

"I have hinted my Conjecture that Congress will immediately give orders to make offers to negotiate. It appears to me of great importance that these Negotiations should proceed *in this Country*, and not on the other side of the Water, especially if Great Brittain's affairs should wear a good Face for a vigorous and early campaign.

"*But a new Peace Commission is indispensably necessary.* Perplexed as the Congress must be under the growing uneasiness of the People, neither Affection to the French, nor a republican attachment, nor even the Aims of Ambition, would prevent them from listening to Overtures *that were decisive and irreversable*, if themselves could be secured from the vindictive Rage of the Multitude they have misled, oppressed and ruined, as well as from the resentment of the Crown. Hitherto they have been offered pardons and General Privileges, with a Restoration of their old Legislatures. But as much us they once contended for a Plenitude of Power in their *Colony Assemblies*, they have now everything to dread from them; foreseeing as they do, that these Legislatures will be composed of Loyalists, *of injured Loyalists*, who may never be satisfied but by a confiscation of the Fortunes of the Rebels for the Repair of the Waste of their own.

"What is to be done in this case? Pass an act of Parliament for an universal Amnesty and Oblivion? By no means; for it would convert the Loyalists into Rebels. But *another*, to authorize the Crown to appoint Commissioners to come to a final agreement with the Colonies, or either of them, and that every act of the Commissioners shall be as valid as if it was an act of Parliament, non-repealable, without the Consent of the Colony in General Assembly, whether it concern matters *Civil, Commercial, Military or Ecclesiastical*, or the Adjustment of the Affairs of Vermont, or any Disputes among the Provinces respecting their Limits, or any other differences that may or shall subsist between them, or any of them. Such Commissioners will be full handed for the Gratification of the reasonable Desires of all parties, and every Colony in America; and an agreement between them and the Congress, or any partizans of theirs,

426   APPENDIX.

will lay the legislature of the Colony so far under Restraints as to dispel
all their fears; and with this end attained, I have no doubt the Commissioners will find the Tables turned; and more jealously for the Interests
of America in the Loyalists than their Adversaries, and no difficulty at
all in reserving such Points as may really deserve Parliamentary and future discussion and approbation. The Point of Honor in Republics, set
against the Interest of the Leaders, will then avail little; and the French
Court be thus at last dropped by America, an event I always thought
probable, from the difficulty of dissolving antient, strong and natural
Connections and Habits. If there remains any obstinacy, it can extend
to but a few, who must give way to the Torrent of Superior Numbers,
interested more and more, every hour of the hostilities, in the return of
Peace; and a very little activity on our part in the execution of the Plan
which is agreed on, will determine the General Preference of a State of
Tranquility and Prosperity to an unprofitable *Sovereignty*, which the majority already considered as a curse, and many of the Rest as a Phantom.
The exhausted Conditon of the Country, exposing it inevitably to a dependency upon Great Brittain, or upon France, to whom too much is due
not to raise Fears if not Enmity, and *she* will certainly insist upon payment *to the very last Farthing.*

"It can scarcely be necessary to add that the new Peace Commissioners
should have every Power of the crown for the appointment of officers,
from Governors downwards, that when they return to England, they may
leave the Government established upon such a Plan as, all things considered, may appear to be expedient; and that the success of the Commission will depend much upon their being Persons of Rank, *and rather
Statesmen than Soldiers,* and of characters in estimation for the Fulness
of their Powers, as to influence the Executive instruments both of the
Army and Navy, to a faithful, *spirited and harmonious Conduct.* Such
Guardians have been heretofore wanting. If they have a Council, as I
think they should have, to prevent the Indelicacy of Altercation, Regard
should be had to their Tempers, Standing and Friendships in this Country, as well as to their Address and *Knowledge of its Affairs.*

"All these things are suggested, upon the supposition that Great Britain has such an Interest in her Colonies, as is worth fostering for the
Common Good. It will be melancholy if the discovery should be made
too late. It will then bring Home to her Streets and Exchange Evidence
that ought to be known now in her Cabinet, and will pour infinite Disgrace upon those who shall have counselled her to quit her Hold of a
country, which she may make her Instrument against the insular Possessions of France, and the best Interests of Spain, and such Proof, when
too late obtained, *may light up a Civil War in her Native Dominions.*

"Had a measure been adopted which Gen'l Tryon urged upon Sir Henry

Clinton, in August, 1779, Administration would long since have been possessed of the most satisfactory Demonstration of the true and *Real Temper of the Colonies*. It was to set up an Intelligence Office for An Examination in Writing, and upon Oath of Persons of all ranks and ages, and of both sexes, that repaired to the British lines, to be communicated to the General, and another set of copies to the Minister for the American Department, with a weekly digest of the whole, upon the probable Presumption, that the Points in which every ray of Information centered would be the Truth; And when the Concourse is so great and from remote Corners, and the Intelligence so manifold, it is certain that the Complaint of the want of it, must argue great Inattention to the proper means of acquiring it. With due care there are rarely secrets in Civil Wars.

"It cannot be worth the pains of Stating Arguments against the flimsy proposal of some for evacuating New York, the Common center, by means of the Hudson, of the British, Canadian and Indian Interests in America.

"Nor against the wilder scheme of others for yielding Independence to all the Continent, to the Northward and Eastward of a Line of Forts from the Head of Elk River to the Delaware, weakly relying upon a Bargain, for the quick Possession and Retention of the Southern Provinces; for the Produce of the latter, can be no equivalent for the Loss of that Commerce which the former would open to the Disadvantage of the Mother Country, and the Southern Possessions would share in, to say nothing of the insecurity of the Tenure against the Power those districts would acquire very soon after Great Britain's acquiescence in the Impairing of that monopoly by which she has been aggrandized, and for which she had paid down such a price in the Expenses of the present War, *now nearly at an end*, unless she dastardly resigns to Despair, or resolves to continue that strange Conduct which has, by a mixture of Conciliation and Chastisement, been wasting both Countries, as if the Contest was a measuring of Purses; but which, after all, if it ends in the Re-union, can not fail to rivet the future Dependence of the Colonies, on their discovering in the Retrospect, or apprehending that they discern Great Britain's Willingness to carry on the War, as to spare what it was always in her Power to destroy—a credit given by some to the Supreme Direction, who allow nothing to the Generosity of the Subordinate Agents on account of the Speculation and Plunders that have so generally prevailed, and sometimes against the plighted Faith of Solemn Proclamations."

INDEX.

A.

ABERCORN, Marquis of, 376.
ADAMS, JOHN, 104.
ADAMS, SAMUEL, 217.
ADIRONDACKS, 105.
AGNEW, General, 131.
ALLEN, ETHAN, expedition to Lake George, 39; refuses precedence to Arnold, 39; captures Ticonderoga, 40; his dash at Montreal censured by Washington and Schuyler, 46.
ALLEN, Lieutenant, brings letter of Jameson to Arnold, announcing Andre's arrest, 295.
ANDRE, JOHN, Major, a social favorite in Philadelphia, 223; a guest of Chief Justice Shippen, 224; Mischienza, 224; correspondence with Arnold, 287; interview with Arnold, 288; his return to New York, 290; arrested as a spy, 291; conducted to Lieut. Colonel Jameson, at Newcastle, 292; writes to Washington and acknowledges his real character, 292; is brought to the Robinson House—Washington declines to see him, 304; sensation in British army, 305; his trial, 306; efforts to save his life, 308; his letter to Washington, 309; execution, 313; his character, 313; letter to Sir Henry Clinton, 318; Monument in Westminster Abbey—remains removed to, 315; was he a spy? 322; should the pass from Arnold protect him? 324.

ARMS of the Arnold family, 363.
ARNOLD, BENDICT, ancestors of, 16; his father, 17; mother, 17; birth of, 18; his father's death, 19; stories of boyhood, 21; letters of his mother, 23; enlists as a soldier, 24; joins the troops at Albany—deserts, 25; marriage, 27; personal description of, 29; his first duel, 31; in business, 33; indignation at "Boston massacre," 34; Captain of the Governor's Guards, 34; a popular leader, 35; volunteers to Cambridge, 36; proposes expedition to Ticonderoga, 37; commissioned Colonel, 38; joins Allen, 39; Ticonderoga captured, 40; captures St. Johns, 41; Massachusetts thanks him, 43; superseded, 44; resigns and returns to Cambridge, 45; death of his wife, 47; proposes expedi-

(429)

430   INDEX.

tion to Quebec, 50; selected by Washington to command, 50; details of expedition, 53; holds an Indian Council, 73, 74; his address to the Indians, 74; arrives at Point Levi, 75; on the Plains of Abraham, 76; flag fired upon, 78; retires to Pointe-aux-Trembles, 78; assault upon Quebec, 80; is wounded, 83; continues blockade, 87; goes to Montreal, 88; receives the Congressional Commissioners, 90; retreats to St. Johns, 94; letter to Gates, 95; proceeds to Crown Point, 96; integrity attacked, 96; charges against Colonel Hazen, 98; trial of Hazen, 98; protest of Arnold, 100; Gates dissolves the Court, 101; charges against, and inquiry demanded by Brown, 102; refused by Gates, Schuyler and Commissioners of Congress, 103; his conduct approved by Schuyler, 103, 104; appointed to construct fleet on Lake Champlain, 107; his preparations, 108; at Isle Valcour, 109; his letters to and from Gates and Schuyler, 110; battle of Valcour Island, 112; arrives at Crown Point, 117; his report to Schuyler, 118; thanked by Gates, 120; welcomed at Ticonderoga, 121; letter from Chase, 122; visits Washington, 124; sent to Rhode Island, 124; visits his sister and children, 124; friendship and aid for Lamb, 125; letter to Mrs. Knox, 125; superseded by five junior brigadiers, 126; withholds resignation by advice of Washington, 127; other officers equally sensitive, 129; fights battle of Ridgefield, 131; receives promotion, 132; and a horse from Congress, 133; his rank still withheld, 133; charges of Brown declared cruel and groundless, 133; offered command on the Hudson, 134; declines and goes to Philadelphia to ask his proper rank and settlement of his accounts, 134; presents his accounts, 136; appointed to the army gathering to watch General Howe, 137; British General retires to Brunswick and Arnold returns to Philadelphia, 137; again tenders his resignation, 138; Washington requests Congress to send Arnold to join Schuyler against Burgoyne, 139; arrives at Washington's camp, 147; visits a Masonic Lodge with Washington, 148; made second in command, 148; is refused his rank by Congress—withholds resignation at Schuyler's request, 148; volunteers to lead expedition into Tryon county, 154; pushes on to Fort Dayton, 154; calls a council of war, 155; issues proclamation, 156; announces his approach to Gansevoort, 157; by ruse-de-guerre relieves Fort Stanwix, 159; reception at Fort Stanwix, 162; returns to Schuyler's camp, 163; in his letters, *familiar* with Gates, *respectful* to Schuyler, 166; commands left wing, 166; selects Bemis' Heights for camp, 167; a coolness on the part of Gates towards, 168; friendly to Schuyler, 169; leads at Bemis'

Heights, 171; who led the Americans at this battle? 174; testimony showing his conduct in this battle, 175; error of Bancroft, 175; the battle fought by Arnold's divison and under his leadership, 177; letters of Arnold to Gates, 177; Varrick's letters to Schuyler, 168, 179, 184; letter of Schuyler, 180; letters of Livingston, 180, 182; evidence of Neilson, 185; statement of Cochran, 186; Burgoyne's statement, 186; statement of Irving, 187; Lossing, 188; Carrington, 189; statement of Downing, 190; quarrel between Gates and Arnold, 193; deprived of command, 195; in the second battle of Saratoga, 198; directs Morgan to pick off Fraser, 200; wounded, 204; Foster's account of his charge, 204; saves the life of soldier who shot him, 205; Burgoyne's surrender, 209; Arnold receives thanks of Congress, 210; receives from Washington new commission giving him his proper rank, 210; the hero of the campaign of 1777, 211; carried to Albany and there during autumn and winter of 1777-8, 213; goes to Connecticut, 214; Washington presents to him pistols, 214; epaulettes, 215; Washington's letters of approbation, 215; furnishes money for the education and maintenance of the children of General Warren, 216; letters on the subject, 217; arrives at Valley Forge, 221; occupies the Penn House, 226; suitor of Peggy Shippen,—letter to her father, 228; offer, 228; settles upon her Mount Pleasant, 231; his marriage, 231; resides here until his removal to West Point, 232; his domestic life in Philadelphia, 233; visited by his sister, 233; birth of son, 233; letter of Hannah Arnold, 233; Arnold's proclamation to close stores and shops, 238; style of living extravagant, 239; charged with leaning toward loyalists—the Shippen family, 240; his project of settling in Western New York, approved by John Jay, and New York delegation, 241; charges by Executive Council of Pennsylvania, 242; published in newspapers, 242; declares charges cruel and malicious, 242; and demands court of inquiry, 243; list of charges, 243; committee, to investigate, 245; report of committee, 245; sends his resignation, 247; letter to Congress, 247; his trial, 249; his defense, 251; judgment of the court, 257; reprimanded by Washington, 261; letter of Schuyler, 263; his treason, 265; social relations in Philadelphia, 267; date of Arnold's first correspondence with enemy, 267; what his motives, 268; arguments used to seduce him, 271; letter of Beverly Robinson, 275; supposed interview between Arnold and Robinson, 277; proposed enterprise by sea, 281; interview with Luzerne, as given by Marbois, 282; his accounts still unsettled,

283; Washington congratulates him on birth of his son, 284; corresponds with Sir Henry Clinton under name of "Gustavus," 284; given command of West Point—at Robinson House, 285; letters to Washington and Greene, 286; visited by Schuyler, 286; a tradition that Arnold often said: "I did it to save the shedding of blood," 287; requests a personal meeting with Andre, 287; sends a boat for Andre, 287; meeting of Arnold and Andre, 288; gives Andre a pass—supposed conversation between them, 288; Allen arrives with news of Andre's capture, 295; his flight, 296; to the Vulture, 297; the bargemen, 297; letter to Washington, 299; declares his wife and military family innocent, 300; arrives at New York and informs Sir Henry Clinton of Andre's capture, 302; his future, 302; his letter to Sir Henry Clinton in regard to Andre, 305; appeals to Washington for Andre's life, 308; alleged offer to surrender himself for Andre, 311; attempts to justify his conduct—an address: "To the Inhabitants of America," 329; text of address, 330; issues a proclamation: "To the Officers and Soldiers of the Continental Army, &c." 332; his efforts meet with no success, 335; rank of Brigadier-General in British Army confirmed, 335; project to kidnap him, 336; its failure, 337; commands expeditions against Virginia, 343; sails from New York and enters Hampton Roads, 343; takes Richmond, 343; his report to Sir Henry Clinton, 343-4; the American Captain's reply to Arnold's question, 347; 5,000 guineas offered for his capture, 348; returns to New York, 348; expedition against Connecticut, 348; Massacre at Fort Griswold, his report, 348; receives thanks of Sir Henry Clinton, 352; escapes being shot, 354; sails for England, 355; his reflections as he leaves his native land, 357; Lord Cornwallis a fellow passenger, 358; reception by the King, 359; seen walking with the Prince of Wales, 359; prepares "Thoughts on the American War," 359; this paper never before printed, 360; synopsis of this paper, 361; receives £6,315 from the British Government, 363; his family arms, 363; changes motto, 364; the Kings and Queen's kindness, 364; at Andre's monument, 365; refused employment as a soldier in England, 367; reasons for, 368; lives beyond his means, 368; fits out a ship for the West Indies—goes to, 369; removes to St. John's, New Brunswick, and enters into business, 370; his sons Richard and Henry join him, 370; accused of firing his warehouse, 371; returns to London, 371; meets Talleyrand, 375; duel with the Earl of Lauderdale, 378; particulars of duel, 379; again fits out a trading ship and arrives at St. Kitto, 385; his escape from the French, 386; is taken prisoner and again escapes, 387; receives thanks from West India planters, 388; writes to Earl Spencer, desiring to be employed as a soldier, 389; the King grants to him 13,400 acres of land in Canada, 389; appeals to the Duke of York for service, 390; his illegitimate son in Canada, 392; his death, 393; his character, 396.

ARNOLD, EDWARD GLADWIN, Rev., marries, April 27th, 1852, Lady Charlotte, daughter of the Marquis of Cholmondelay, 410.

ARNOLD, EDWARD SHIPPEN, sketch of life; dies at Dinapoor, India, 1813, 407.

ARNOLD, HANNAH, only surviving sister of Benedict, 18; never marries, 27; praised by Sparks, 28; correspondence with Deane, 28; takes charge of her brother's children, 47; letter to her brother, 47, 48; visits her brother at Philadelphia, 233; her letter to Mrs. Arnold, 233; her letter on hearing of her brother's disgrace, 308; her death, 405.

ARNOLD, HENRY, son of Benedict Arnold, by first wife. 27; married Hannah Ten Eyck, 405; commissioned lieutenant in the American Legion, 405: dies in New York, 405.

ARNOLD, GEORGE, a lieutenant colonel; so named by his father after Washington and George IV., 409.

ARNOLD, JAMES ROBERTSON, born in New York, 1781; marries Virginia Goodrich; rises to rank of Lieutenant-General in British army, 407; engaged in capture of Abouker Castle; in battle of Alexandria and in expulsion of the French from Grand Cairo; storms a redoubt, 408; appointed aide-de-camp to George the Fourth, 408; dies in London, 1854, 409.

ARNOLD, Mrs., maiden name Margaret Shippen, daughter of Chief Justice Shippen—marriage of, 231; joins her husband at West Point, 286; her distress when Arnold discloses his position, 295; interview with Washington, 301; kindness of Washington and officers to, 316; was she innocent of her husband's crime? 316; Arnold declares her innocence, 318; Hamilton and Washington believe her innocent, 318; Major Frank's testimony in her favor, 318; conduct incompatible with guilt, 320; compelled to leave by the Council of Pennsylvania—follows her husband to New York, 321; accompanies her husband to England, 355; her fascination and beauty—attention of the Queen, 362; is granted a pension, 363; letter to her father. 369; her father's reply, 372; letter to Mrs. Burd, 372; visits her family in Philadelphia, 373; returns to London, 373 gives details of her husband's duel, 381; letter to Richard, 384; announces to

Richard and Henry their father's death, 394; also to Hannah Arnold, 394; executrix of her husband, 400; her executive ability—letters, 400; death of, 406; character of, 406; her children, from 406–417.

ARNOLD, SOPHIA MATILDA, daughter of Benedict, born in London, July 28th, 1785; marries Lieutenant-Colonel Pownall Phipps—death of, 411.

ARNOLD, RICHARD, birth of, 27; marries, 405; commissioned Lieutenant in the American Legion, 405.

ARNOLD, WILLIAM, an ancestor of Benedict, and a contemporary of Roger Williams, 16.

ARNOLD, WILLIAM FITCH, captain in the 19th Royal Lancers; his residence Little Messenden Abbey, Bucks, 410.

ARNOLD, BEN., his death, note 405.

ARNOLD, WILLIAM TRAIL, brother of the Rev. Edward Gladwin Arnold and grandson of Gen. Arnold, a captain in the British army, 410; in the battles of Inkerman, Alma, and with his regiment before Sebastopol, 410; killed in the trenches—manner of his death, 410.

ATWATER, Major, 308.

B.

BALCARRAS, Earl of, 196.

BANCROFT, comparison of British fleet with Arnold's 111; declares Gates had "no fitness for command," 165; on battle of Bemis' Heights, 175; error in stating that Arnold was not on the field, 175; his description of the death of Fraser, 208.

BARLOW, JOEL, the poet, 21.

BATTLES, Notable on the Lakes, 111.

BAUM, defeat of, near Bennington, 164.

BEDELL, Colonel, under Arnold holds the Cedars—is cashiered, 90.

BEMIS' HEIGHTS, position for camp at selected by Arnold, 169; position of Armies at, 170; battle of, 171.

BETHEL, 130.

BOARD OF OFFICERS to try Andre, 306; reports him a spy and must suffer death, 306.

BOSTON MASSACRE, 33.

BOTTA, the historian, on Arnold's expedition to Quebec, 71.

BREYMAN, Colonel, a British officer killed in 2nd battle of Saratoga, 206.

BRYANT, with Capt. Foster at "the Cedars," 91; with St. Leger, 141.

BROWN, Lieutenant-Col., his difficulties with Arnold, 102; demands a Court of Inquiry, 102; inquiry refused by Generals Wooster, Gates, Schuyler, and Commissioners of Congress, 103; letter of Schuyler criticising Brown, 103.

BRUNSWICK, English retire to, 137.

BUCHANAN, JAMES, British Consul

INDEX. 435

at New York, removes Andre's remains to Westminster Abbey, 315.

BURD, Mrs., sister of Mrs. Arnold, letter to, 372.

BURGOYNE, General, connected by marriage with house of Derby—a soldier in Spain, 143; moves towards Crown Point with his army, 143; reports American army ruined, 145; battle of 19th Sept., 170; speaks of Arnold's bravery in battle of 19th Sept., 186; Battle, Oct. 7th, 195; attempts to retreat, 209; surrenders, 209; describes the burial of Fraser, 208.

BURR, AARON, a volunteer with Arnold, 51; his charge that Mrs. Arnold was privy to her husband's treachery, 316; motives, 320.

C.

CAMBRIDGE, 36, 45, 47, 49.

CARLETON, GUY, Sir, brings reinforcements to Quebec, 78; treats the prisoners with kindness, 86; occupies St. Johns, 106; prepares a fleet for Lake Champlain, 106; at battle of Valcour Island, 102; at court with Arnold, 359.

CARRINGTON, General, statement of Arnold's conduct at Bemis' Heights, 189; at Saratoga, 202.

CARROLL, CHARLES, appointed commissioner to Canada, 90; visits Arnold's headquarters 90; defends Arnold's conduct in removal of goods at Montreal, 102.

CARROLL, JOHN, Rev., first Roman Catholic Archbishop of the United States, accompanies commissioners to Canada, 90.

"CEDARS," The, 90, 91.

CHASE, SAMUEL, Comissioner to Canada, 90; letter to Arnold, 122.

CHAMBLAY, 95.

CHAMPLAIN, LAKE, description of 105; naval battle on, 112-114.

CHAMPE, Sergeant, Agent of Maj. Lee to kidnap Arnold, 336; his attempt, 337.

CHESTER, Major, 183.

CHURCHILL, Duke of Marlborough, 273.

CLINTON, HENRY, Sir, conspiracy with Arnold, 284; realizes importance of West Point, 287; informed by Arnold of Andre's capture, 302; his letter to Washington in regard to Andre, 306; his letter to Lord George Germain on behalf of Arnold, 358.

COCHRAN, Maj., report of, describing Arnold's battle on the 19th Sept., 186.

CONGRESS, OF MASSACHUSETTS, thanks Arnold for his services, 43.

CONGRESS OF UNITED STATES, appoints Commissioners to Canada, 90; elects five Major-Generals, 126; presents a horse to Arnold, 133; passes a resolution of thanks, 133; declares charges of Brown cruel, but refuses his proper rank, 135; action in regard to Warren's children, 220.

CONNECTICUT, Arnold returns from, 284.

COOPER, JAMES FENIMORE, 299.
CORNWALLIS, Lord, surrenders to Washington, 355; a fellow passenger with Arnold to England, 358; letters of Arnold to, 388; uses his interests in behalf of Arnold's sons, 392.
CRAMAHA, Lieutenant Governor, 77.
CROWN POINT. 37; Arnold proceeds to, 96; retreat from, 96.
CROSKIE, Captain, duel with Arnold, 31.
CURTIS, GEORGE WILLIAM, oration on Bemis' Heights, 161.

D.

DAVIS, MATHEW L., biographer, of Burr, 316; charges against Mrs. Arnold, 317.
DANBURY, 130.
DEANE, BARNABAS, 45.
DEANE, SILAS, writes of the bad treatment of Arnold, 45.
DEAD RIVER, the. 53.
DEARBORN, Captain, in the expedition to Quebec, 66; 197.
DEBLOIS, Miss, Arnold in love with, D.
DESCRIPTION, personal, of Arnold, by Downing, 29; by John C. Warren, 221; by Rev. J. L. Leake, 29.
DOWNING, personal description of Arnold, 29; on Arnold's conduct in battle, 190.
DUCONDRAY, a French officer, 129.
DUEL, Arnold's with Captain Croskie, 31; with Earl of Lauderdale, 376.

E.

EDUCATION, Arnold's early, 23.
ELLIOT, ANDREW, Lieutenant General, 308.
ENGLISH, view of Arnold's conduct, 273.
ENOS, ROGER, abandons Arnold's expedition, 65; trial put under arrest by Washington, 69.
EXPEDITIONS, Arnold's, to Ticonderoga, 37; to Quebec, 53; into Virginia, 342; into Connecticut, 348.

F.

FAMILY, of Arnold, 405.
FAIRFIELD, 130.
FORT DAYTON, council held at, 155.
FORT GRISWOLD, so called massacre at, 348.
FORT TRUMBULL, 348.
FOSTER, Senator, relates incidents of Arnold's conduct at Saratoga, 204.
FOX, CHARLES JAMES, the second of the Earl of Lauderdale, in duel with Arnold, 378.
FRANKLIN, BENJAMIN, commissioned by Congress to Canada, 90; at Arnold's Head-Quarters, 90.
FRANKS, Major, declared innocent by Arnold, 300; denial of Mrs. Arnold's knowledge of her husband's treason, 318; accompanies Mrs. Arnold to Philadelphia, 316.
FRAZER, Major-General, 143; at Saratoga mortally wounded, 199; his death—picked off by Mor-

gan's riflemen at Arnold's suggestion, 200; burial, 207.
FREEMASONS, Washington & Arnold at lodge of, 148.
FRENCH WAR, the old, 24.

G.

GANSEVOORT, at Fort Stanwix, in-invested by St. Leger, 149; refuses to surrender, 149; Arnold relieves him, 158.

GATES, General, letter to Arnold, 51; at Crown Point, 96; supports Arnold in affair of Col. Hazen, 101; informs Congress that Arnold has undertaken to command fleet, 107; returns thanks to Arnold after battle of Valcour Island, 120; supersedes Schuyler, 165; concentrates the Northern army on Bemis Heights, 166; thinks of superseding Washington, 168; not on the field at Bemis Heights, 174; in report to Congress makes no mention of Arnold, 177; Pique against Livingston, 183; desires the whole credit against Burgoyne, 193; drives Arnold to demand a pass to Washington, 194; indebted to Arnold for his laurels, 209; Burgoyne surrenders, and Gates is thanked by Congress, 210; Congress votes him a medal, 213.

GENEALOGY, of the Arnold family, 18.

GERMAIN, Lord, Burgoyne reports condition of American army to, 144; letters to, from Sir Henry Clinton, in behalf of Arnold, 358.

GERMAN FLATS, 155.

GIBSON, Mrs. 318.

GREEN, NATHANIEL, requests permission to retire from the service, 129; confers with English officers who came to Washington on behalf of Andre, 308; note to General Robertson, informing him of Washington's decision, 308.

'GREEN MOUNTAIN BOYS,' 45.

H.

HALE, NATHAN, hanged as a spy by the British, 305.

HAMILTON, COL. ALEX., carries Washington's message to Mrs. Arnold, 295; aide to Washington, 299; attempts to capture Arnold —fails, 299; his letter touching Mrs. Arnold—declares her innocent—letter on Andre's death, 309; refuses to propose to Andre his exchange for Arnold, 311.

HAMPTON ROADS, Arnold at, 342.

HARRINGTON, Earl of, 376.

HAWKE, Lord, Arnold's second in duel, 378; endorses Arnold's statement of the duel, 381.

HARTFORD, Washington visits French officers at, 294.

HAZEN, Col., charges made against by Arnold—his trial by Court-Martial, 98.

HEATH, General, Statement of, in regard to Arnold's treatment of crew of his barge, 297; his account of expedition against New London, 353.

HENRY's Journal, 62, 65, 66 to 70.
HENRY, PATRICK, 85.

HERKIMER, General, advances to the relief of Fort Schuyler, 149; caught in an ambush, 151; battle of Oriskany; death of, 152; county and town named for him, 152.

HON YOST, SCHUYLER, sentenced to death as a spy, 159; his ruse to relieve Fort Schuyler, 161.

HONITON, 273.

HORSEMANSHIP, Arnold's, 27.

HOWE, General, threatens Philadelphia, but retires to Brunswick, 137; with a British army takes possession of Philadelphia, 222; he and his officers pass a gay winter in that city, 223.

HUDSON, Arnold offerd command of the, 134.

I.

IRVING, WASHINGTON, the conduct of Arnold in naval affairs on the lakes, 105; battle of Bemis Heights, 187; Arnold's dispute with authorities of Philadelphia, 238; Reed's personal hostility to Arnold, 243; time when Arnold first entertained thoughts of treason, 283.

J.

JAMESON, Lieut. Col., Andre brought prisoner to,—sends to Washington papers found on Andre, 292: sends to Arnold statement of the arrest of John Anderson, 292.

JAY, JOHN, Colonel Livingstone goes to Spain as his secretary, 185; letter in regard to Arnold, 241.

JAMESTOWN, 343.

JAMES RIVER, The, 343.

JEFFERSON, 341; Governor of Virginia, 343; offers reward for Arnold, 347.

JEWETT, Dr., Arnold at school of, 24.

JOHNSON, Sir JOHN, with St. Leger in the valley of the Mohawk, 141.

JOHNSON, Sir WILLIAM, a Tory on the Mohawk, 142.

K.

KENNEBEC, river, 50.

KING GEORGE, the Fourth, Arnold's reception by, 359.

KING's FERRY, 284.

KNOX, Gen., resigns conditionally, 129; with Washington at Hartford, 294.

KNOX, Mrs. Arnold's letter to, 125.

L.

LAFAYETTE, aide to Washington, with Washington at Hartford, 294; at West Point, 294; Washington discloses Arnold's treason to, 299; instructed to execute Arnold, if captured, 338; sent against Arnold, 343.

LAKE GEORGE, 41.

LAMB, Gen'l, in the assault on Quebec, 82; Arnold's friendship for, 125; Arnold procures his exchange, and furnishes £1,000 towards expenses of raising his regiment, 125; his defense of Arnold at Gates' dinner, (note) 206.

LARVEY, Corporal, his reply to Arnold, 297.

LAUDERDALE, Earl of, duel with Arnold, 376.
LAURENS, Col. HENRY, Hamilton's letter to, on Andre's trial, 306 President of Congress — exchanged for Cornwallis, 358.
LEARNED, General, 154.
LEE, Major, undertakes to kidnap Arnold, 336.
LEE, RICHARD HENRY, writes to Jefferson of Arnold's persecution, 135.
LEXINGTON, battle of, 35.
LIVINGSTON, writes to Schuyler, 169; explains cause of quarrel between Arnold and Gates, 169; letters to Schuyler from Bemis' Heights, 180; marries sister of John Jay, 185; becomes justice of the Supreme Court of the United States, 185.
LINCOLN, General, elected Major General, 126; given by Gates' command of right wing at second battle of Saratoga, 195; at Albany, 213.
LONDON CHRONICLE, 273.
LORD, Rev. Dr., restores Arnold to his mother, 24.
LOSSING on General Arnold at Valcour Island, 117; his conduct at Bemis Heights, 188; "officers and soldiers had lost confidence in Gates," 194.
LOYALISTS, during the Revolution, 340.
LUZERNE, 282; his interview with Arnold, as given by Marbois, 282.

M.

MACAULEY, Lord on Churchill's desertion of James, 279.
MAHON, Lord, condemns Washington for ordering the execution of Andre, 322.
MANSFIELD, Margaret, first wife of Arnold, 27; death of, 47.
MARBOIS, states that a letter written by Robinson was found among Arnold's papers, 275; that Arnold tried to obtain 'a loan from Luzerne, 282, 283.
MARRIAGE, Arnold's first, 27; second, 231.
MARTIN, Prof., Law of Nations relating to a spy, 324.
MASSACHUSETTS, commissions Arnold Colonel, 38; commissioners of, sent to Ticonderoga, 44.
MARSHALL, JOHN, on the expedition to Quebec, 89; battle of Valcour Island, 120; distress of troops at time of Arnold's treason, 273.
McLAIN, Colonel, 77.
McCREA, JANE, story of, 145.
McDOUGAL, General, letter of Washington to, in regard to Arnold, 134.
MIDDLETOWN, 213.
MISCHIENZA, the famous, 224.
MIFFLIN, elected major-general, 126.
MOHAWK, valley of the, 141.
MORRISTOWN, Arnold at, 34.
MORGAN, DANIEL, a captain in Arnold's expedition to Quebec, 51; leads his riflemen in the assault

on, 82; taken prisoner, 83; at battle of Saratoga directs riflemen to pick off Fraser, 200.

MONTGOMERY, captures St. Johns and Montreal, 79; joins Arnold, 79; killed in assault upon Quebec, 81; his friendship for Arnold, 80.

MONTRESOR, Colonel, 50.

MONTROSE, 273.

MONTREAL, Allen's unfortunate dash at, 46; Wooster in command at, 83; Arnold takes command of, 88.

N.

NATANIS, an Indian chief, 55.

NELSON, Lord, 164.

NEW CASTLE, Andre prisoner at, 291.

NEW HAVEN, 19; 130; 303.

NEWARK, 336.

NEW LONDON, expedition against, 348.

NEW YORK, Arnold arrives at, 302.

NORTH, Lord, 355.

NORWALK, Tryon at, 132.

NORWICH, 19; occupants of the old Arnold mansion at, 19; Arnold ordered to, 124.

O.

ORISKANY, Battle of, 151.

OSWEGO, 141.

P.

PAINE, THOMAS, 341.

PAPERS, found in Andre's boots, 291; sent on to Washington, 292.

PARSONS, Col. SAMUEL H., letter to Governor Trumbull, about Ticonderoga, 42.

PASS, should Arnold's pass protect Andre? 324.

PAULDING, JOHN, one of the captors of Andre, 291.

PEACE, between United States and Great Britain, 367.

PEACE COMMISSIONERS, New, recommended by Arnold, 361.

PEEKSKILL, 134.

PELLEW, afterwards Viscount Exmouth, at battle of Valcour Island, 112.

PETERS, Rev. SAMUEL, gives anecdote of Arnold, 35.

PETERSBURGH, Arnold at, 361.

PHILLIPS, General, under Burgoyne, 143; sent to Arnold in Virginia, 343; captured with Burgoyne—and death of, 347.

PHILADELPHIA, evacuated by the British, 222; life in that city, 223.

PITT, Mr., 376.

POINT LEVI, Arnold at, 75.

POINT-AUX-TREMBLES, Arnold's camp at, 79.

POINT-A-PETER, Arnold at, 386.

"POOR BEN," General Arnold's oldest son, 404; death of, 405.

PORTLAND, Duke of orders the grant of lands to Arnold, 389.

PORTSMOUTH, Virginia, Arnold marches to, 343.

PROVOST, Mrs., wife of Colonel Burr, 317.

PUTNAM, General, leaves his plough

INDEX. 441

and joins Arnold, 36; at dinner with Lamb, &c., (note) 206.

Q.

QUEBEC, the Gibralter of America, 49; details of Arnold's expedition to 53-73; assault on, 80-83.

R.

RALLE, Father, 59.

REDIESEL, General, 143.

REED, General, persecution of Arnold; makes charges against; letter to Gen. Green, 240; circular with charges widely circulated; his hostility personal, 243.

RICHMOND, Arnold at, 343.

RICHMOND, Duke of, 376.

ROBERTSON, Lieut. General, 308.

ROBINSON, Beverly, Loyalist, tradition of meeting between him and Arnold, 274; their conversation, 277; has the confidence of Sir Henry Clinton, 285; intercedes for Andre, 308.

ROMILLY, the English jurist, considers Andre a spy, 326.

S.

SABINE, says that Robinson was in communication with Arnold before the latter went to West Point, 275; the number of the Loyalists according to, 335. Says "Ben" was driven from the service, 405.

SARATOGA, Battle of, 19th Sept., 171; second battle of, 196.

SARGENT, did Arnold offer to surrender himself for Andre? 311, 312.

SCOTT, Major, 100.

SCOTT, Sir WALTER, 333.

SCHUYLER, PHILIP, General, commanding a provincial company, 25; leads an army into Canada, 50; writes to Washington of the assault on Quebec, 85; with Arnold and Gates at Crown Point, and retreat to Ticonderoga, 96; supports Arnold in difficulty with Colonel Brown, 103; glad to hear Arnold is to command the fleet, 107; is censured for retiring before Burgoyne, 145; retreats to Stillwater, 148; determines to relieve Fort Stanwix, 153; his call for volunteers to conduct the expedition, 154; superseded by Gates, 165; letter to Varick in regard to Arnold, 193; letter to Arnold after his trial, 263.

SCHUYLER, Miss, engaged to Col. Hamilton, 301; letters from Hamilton to, 301, 309.

SENTER, Dr., his journal, 83.

SHIPPEN, EDWARD, Chief Justice, 224; his daughters, 227 portrait of, 393; death of, 413.

SHIPPEN, Miss PEGGY, in the Mischienza, 224; her beauty, 227.

SILLIMAN, General, assists in repelling Tryon, 130.

"SIX NATIONS, The," 150.

SKENE, Major, 41.

SMITH, Chief Justice, 308.

SMITH, JOSHUA HITT, statement of, regarding correspondence between Arnold and Beverly Robinson, 276; Arnold and Andre breakfast at house of, 283; Arnold gives pass to, 288; Andre passes the day at house of, 290; acts as guide to Andre, 290.

SPARKS, on letters of Hannah Arnold, 28; explains Arnold's seizure of goods at Montreal, 101; praises Arnold's bravery at Valcour Island, 117; praises his magnanimity in volunteering against Burgoyne, 139; his account of second battle of Saratoga, 203.

SPY, was Andre a, 322; Vattel's definition of, 324.

STANWIX FORT, where city of Rome, N. Y., now is, 148; siege of, 141; relief of by Arnold, 158.

ST. CLAIR, elected Major-General, 126; occupies Ticonderoga, 143; retreats from, 144; censured for, 145.

STANLEY, DEAN, Americans at Andre's Monument, 365.

STARK, Col., fights battle of Bennington, 165.

STEPHEN, elected Major-General, 126.

STIRLING, commissioned Major-General by Congress, 126.

STIRLING, Sir WALTER, presents Arnold to the King, 359.

STORIES, of Arnold's boyhood, 21.

ST. LEGER, expedition of, into the valley of the Mohawk, 141; demands the surrender of Fort Schuyler, 152; flees at Arnold's approach, 161.

ST. JOHNS, captured by Arnold, 41; occupied by the English, 106.

ST. JOHNS, New Brunswick, Arnold removes to, 370.

SULLIVAN, General, letter on Arnold's retreat from Canada, 95; retreats to Crown Point, 96; sends in resignation, 129.

T.

TALLEYRAND, meeting of, with Arnold, 375.

TALLMADGE, Major, arrives at the Robinson House with Andre, 304; their conversation on the way, 304; his friendship for Andre, 304; advises Andre of his fate, 305.

TAPPAN, Andre hanged as a spy at, 309.

TARLETON, the beauty of Mrs. Arnold, 362.

TARRYTOWN, Andre taken at, 293.

TELLER'S POINT, 297.

TICONDEROGA, Arnold proposes expedition to, 37; captured, 40; accusations made against Arnold at, 96.

TREASON, Arnold's, 265, 287, 293; furore against him on news of, 303.

TRYON, Governor, invasion of Connecticut by, 130; at Norwalk and Compo, 132.

TRUMBULL, Governor, writes of capture of Ticonderoga, 42.

V.

VALCOUR ISLAND, Arnold sails to, 109; naval battle off, 112; Arnold's bravey at, spoken of by

INDEX. 443

Gates, 118, Varick, 119, Lossing, 117, Cooper, 118, Irving, 105, Sparks, 117.

VARICK, RICHARD, letter to Gates after battle of Valcour Island, 119; secretary of Schuyler, 168; a friend of Schuyler and Arnold, 169; his opinion of Gates, 175; his letter, 179; his letter from camp Sept. 25, 1777, to Schuyler, 184, his ignorance of Arnold's treason, 300.

VATTEL, his definition of a spy, 324.

VERPLANK'S POINT, Arnold signals the Vulture at, 297.

VULTURE, The, a British sloop of war, brings Andre and Robinson up the Hudson, 287; takes Arnold on board, 297; takes him to New York, 302.

W.

WARREN, General JOSEPH, his friendship for Arnold, 38; letter to authorities of Conn. about Arnold, 40, 41; his children, aid to, by Arnold, 216, 217.

WARREN, JOHN C. meets Arnold at Margate, 221.

WASHINGTON, GEORGE, under the British flag, 25; censures Allen, 46; a friend of Arnold, 47; selects Arnold to command expedition to Quebec, 48; gives Arnold his instructions, 50; letter to Schuyler about Arnold, 64; his joy at Arnold's safe arrival, letter to Schyler, 70; concern on hearing of Arnold's being wounded, letter to Schuyler, 85; suggests to Gates to appoint Arnold to command fleet on the Lakes, 108; begs Arnold in letter not to resign after he was superseded, 127; asks Lee why Arnold was superseded, 128; letter to Arnold expressing surprise that he did not see his (Arnold's) name among the Major-Generals, 128; writes to President of Congress: "General Arnolds' promotion gives me much pleasure," 134; offers him command of the Hudson, 134; letter to Congress in regard to Arnold's vindication, 134; letter to Congress requesting that Arnold be sent north to repel Burgoyne, 138; repeats this request, 139; sends Arnold to join Schuyler, 147; letter to Schuyler in praise of Arnold, 147; also letter to Heath, 147; sends Arnold commission, giving his proper rank, 210: letter to Arnold presenting epaulettes and sword-knots, 215; gives him command of Philadelphia, 222; his trial, 248; letters to Reed and Arnold about his trial, 248; reprimands Arnold, 261; anxious about final success, 273; gives Arnold command of West Point, 284; visits the French officers at Hartford—at West Point, 294; Hamilton hands to him the papers found on Andre, 299; "whom can we trust now?" 299; refers Andre's case to a board of general officers, 306; his letter to Sir Henry Clinton, 307; receives second letter from Clinton, 308; might not Washington have spared Andre? 327; approves of plan to kidnap Arnold, 336; his letter to Major Lee, 337; Cornwallis surrenders to, 355.

WATERMAN, HANNAH, maiden name of mother of Arnold, 17; her genealogy, 18; her character, 20.

WEBB, Col., 45.

WEST INDIES, Arnold sails to, 83; 369; 385; 389.

WEST POINT, military position, 284; Washington gives command of, to Arnold, 284; the Robinson House, 287.

WESTMINSTER ABBEY, Andre's remains removed to—his monument, 315; Arnold at, 365.

WILKINSON, Adjutant-general to Gates, 175; his statement regarding the battle of 19th September, 175; write his memoirs thirty years after the battle, 177.

WILLIAMS, DAVID, one of the captors of Andre, 291.

WILLIAMS, ROGER, 17.

WILLETT, MARINUS, Col., under Gansevoort at Fort Schuyler, 149.

WOLFE, death of, 76.

WOODRUFF, SAMUEL, 200.

WOOSTER, Gen., wants Arnold to wait for regular orders, 36; in command at Montreal, 83; in command at Quebec, 88; refuses Brown's demand for court of inquiry, 103; mortally wounded at Ridgefield, 130.

WYNCOOP, refuses to obey orders of Arnold, and ordered by Gates to be put under arrest, 110; through Arnold's request, not cashiered, 111.

Y.

YORK, Duke of, Arnold appeals to, for military service, 390.

YORKTOWN, Lord Cornwallis surrenders at, 358.

**PLEASE RETURN TO
ALDERMAN LIBRARY**

DUE	DUE
1-20-86	
1-27-88	
9-7-88	
4-2-91	
1/15/92	

CPSIA information can be obtained
at www.ICGtesting.com
Printed in the USA
BVHW012122100122
625959BV00002B/76